EVOLUTION:
The Grand Experiment

The Quest for an Answer

New Leaf Publishing Group in conjunction with
Audio Visual Consultants Inc.

Third Edition
© Copyright 2007, 2014, Audio Visual Consultants, Inc.

Graphic Design and Production:
Adriana Naylor, Naylor Design Company
aahtst52@yahoo.com
www.portfolios.com/adrianaswork

Copy Editors: Carla Azzara, Alon Prunty, Laura Welch

First Edition, first printing October 2007
First Edition, second printing January 2009
Second Edition, eBook January 2012
Third Edition, first printing April 2014

ISBN-13: 978-0-89221-681-9

Library of Congress Catalog Number: 2007925416

Printed in China

Please visit our websites for other great titles:
www.newleafpress.net
www.TheGrandExperiment.com
www.a-v-consultants.com

New Leaf Press
A Division of New Leaf Publishing Group

*Dedicated to those
who have the courage
to question.*

Dr. Carl Werner

Debbie Werner

About the Author

*Dr. Carl Werner received his undergraduate degree in biology, with distinction, at the University of Missouri, graduating summa cum laude, and his doctoral degree in medicine at the age of 23. He is the author of two more books in the **Evolution: The Grand Experiment** series: **Living Fossils** and the project he is currently working to complete **Human Evolution**. Dr. Werner is also the executive producer of the video series **Evolution: The Grand Experiment**, which has been seen in 70 countries on seven television networks. For more information about the television series visit IMDB.com. You may follow the author on Twitter @DrCarlWerner.*

About the Photographer

*Debbie Werner, principal photographer for **Evolution: The Grand Experiment**, and **Living Fossils**, received her Bachelor of Science degree from Excelsior College in Albany, New York. She is the producer and principal videographer of **Evolution: The Grand Experiment** video series. Debbie is an avid naturalist and the wife of Dr. Carl Werner.*

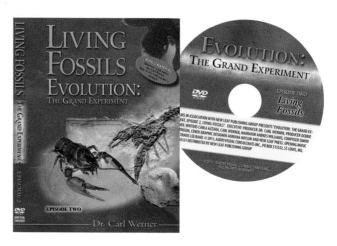

Foreword

When Charles Darwin published *The Origin of Species* in 1859, his ideas were initially met with resistance from the scientific community. Slowly, most scientists came to support his theory. As a result, evolution and its underpinnings and corollaries have been incorporated into the framework of modern scientific thought. Nonetheless, the general public has remained skeptical that evolution is the answer to the origin of life. Additionally, there is a vocal minority of scientists who oppose the theory based on the evidence of the fossil record and concerns in other areas of science, such as physics, genetics, biochemistry, and statistics.

Most people are at least somewhat familiar with the theory of evolution, but few are truly knowledgeable about the theory. Even fewer are aware of new discoveries being made in science which have undermined some of the previously accepted evidence supporting evolution. In this book, the reader will be introduced to the theory of evolution and then afforded the opportunity to view the evidence both for and against it. This book is presented in an easy-to-read style and is intended for the general public.

For those who seek to learn more on this subject, a subsequent volume of this book series is available: Volume II, *Living Fossils*. Volume III, *Human Evolution* is currently under development. Each book focuses on specialty areas, requiring more explanation than could be offered in this text, and presents completely new information in an easy-to-read format. To help you develop a deeper understanding of this topic, an ongoing video series, *Evolution: The Grand Experiment*, is available. This DVD series is not intended to replace the book but serves to supplement the material presented. For each volume, a teacher's manual and an accompanying Presentation CD are also available for use in the classroom and can be used in both public and private schools. Students, teachers and speakers can create PowerPoint lectures using the Presentation CD available through the publisher's or TheGrand-Experiment.com websites.

In closing, the production staff of Audio Visual Consultants, Inc. hopes you enjoy *Evolution: The Grand Experiment*, and even more importantly, that you find your own answer to the question: How did we get here?

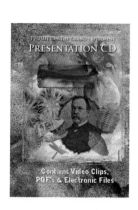

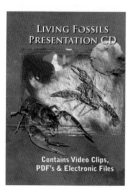
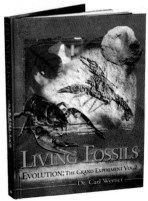

Acknowledgments

Audio Visual Consultants, Inc. would like to thank the scientists who were interviewed for this book, especially: Dr. Andy Knoll, Harvard University; Dr. Clayton Ray, National Museum of Natural History, Smithsonian Institute; Dr. Eugene S. Gaffney, American Museum of Natural History, New York; Dr. Storrs L. Olson, National Museum of Natural History, Smithsonian Institution; Dr. Conrad C. Labandeira, National Museum of Natural History, Smithsonian Institute; Dr. Peter Wellnhofer, Bavarian State Collection of Paleontology, Munich, Germany; Dr. Paul Sereno, University of Chicago; Dr. David Weishampel, Johns Hopkins University; Dr. Angela Milner, Natural History Museum of London; Dr. Gunter Viohl, Jura Museum in Eichstatt, Germany; Dr. John Long, Museum Victoria in Melbourne, Australia; Dr. Lance Grande, Chicago Field Museum; Dr. Joerg Habersetzer, Senckenberg Museum of Natural History, Frankfurt, Germany; Dr. Kevin Padian, University of California-Berkeley; Dr. Phillip Currie, Royal Tyrell Museum of Paleontology, Alberta, Canada; Dr. William Clemens, University of California-Berkeley; Dr. Larry Barnes, Natural History Museum, Los Angeles; Dr. Darryl Domning, Howard University; Dr. James Kirkland, Mygatt Moore Quarry; Dr. James Valentine, University of California-Berkeley; Dr. Gary Morgan, New Mexico Museum of Natural History and Science; Dr. Jim Parham, University of California-Berkeley; Dr. Nicholas Czeplewski, Sam Noble Oklahoma Museum of Science and Natural History; Dr. Irina Koretsky, Howard University; Dr. Annalisa Berta, San Diego State University; Dr. Phil Gingerich, University of Michigan, Ann Arbor; Dr. Taseer Hussain, Howard University; Dr. Timothy Rowe, University of Texas, Austin; Dr. Peter Crane, Royal Botanical Gardens in London; Dr. Monroe Strickberger, University of California-Berkeley; Dr. David Menton, Washington University; Dr. Georgia Purdom, Answers in Genesis, Kentucky; and Dr. Duane Gish, Institute for Creation Research, California.

Thanks to the following institutions for allowing us access to their collections: Harvard Museum of Paleontology, Boston, Massachusetts; Carnegie Museum of Natural History, Pittsburgh, Pennsylvania; California Academy of Sciences, San Francisco; The Down House, England; Chicago Field Museum, Illinois; Museum Victoria, Melbourne, Australia; Messel Museum, Messel, Germany; Fossil Butte National Monument, Kemmerer, Wyoming; Senckenberg Museum of Natural History, Frankfurt, Germany; Dinosaur National Monument, Vernal, Utah; Agate Fossil Beds National Monument, Harrison, Nebraska; Houston Museum of Natural Science, Texas; Alaska Sea Life Center, Seward, Alaska; Seal Bay National Park, Kangaroo Island, Australia; University of California Museum of Paleontology, Berkeley; South Australian Museum, Adelaide, Australia; Museum of Geology - South Dakota School of Mines and Technology, Rapid City, South Dakota; New Mexico Museum of Natural History and Science, Albuquerque; Wyoming Dinosaur Center, Thermopolis, Wyoming; Pink Palace Museum, Memphis, Tennessee; National Aeronautic Space Administration, Washington D.C.; National Oceanic and Atmospheric Administration, Washington, D.C.; University of Michigan Exhibit Museum of Natural History, Ann Arbor; Geological Museum, University of Wisconsin, Madison; Lost World Studios, St. Louis, Missouri; University of Nebraska State Museum, Lincoln; Milwaukee Public Museum, Wisconsin; Utah Field House of Natural History State Park and Museum, Vernal; Jura Museum, Eichstatt, Germany; University of Wyoming Geological Museum, Laramie; Dorr Museum of Natural History, College of the Atlantic, Maine; Mississippi Petrified Forest and Museum, Flora; Sam Noble Oklahoma Museum of Science and Natural History, Norman; CT Lab of the University of Texas, Austin; Florissant Fossil Quarry, Florissant, Colorado; Mesalands Community College's Dinosaur Museum, Tucumari, New Mexico; Ruth Hall Museum of Paleontology, Abiquiu, New Mexico; University of Chicago; and Ulrich's Fossil Quarry, Kemmerer, Wyoming.

Special thanks to Chris Farah, St. Louis University, Mathematics Laboratory, and Ashoka Polpitya, Department of Mathematics at Washington University in St. Louis, for assistance in performing the mathematical calculations in Chapter 4. Thanks to the Solnhofen Tile Quarry, Solnhofen, Germany; Lindenwood University, St. Charles, Missouri; US Geological Survey, Sirenia Project, Gainesville, Florida; Bureau of Land Management, Grand Junction, Colorado; the governments of Australia, Mexico, the United Kingdom, Belgium, U.S. Virgin Islands, Pakistan, Canada, Germany and the United States; Nancy Clare Anderson of the Florissant Fossil Quarry; Ken Ham, Roger Patterson, Dr. Jason Lisle, and Dr. Terry Mortenson of the Creation Museum, Kentucky; Dr. Don Batten of Creation Ministries International; Mark Haville, NPN Videos; Peter Newland; Philip Rayment; Peter Milford; National Geographic; and authors Dougal Dixon, Barry Cox, R.J.G. Savage, Brian Gardiner, Byron Preiss, Robert Silverberg, Dr. Michael Denton, and Matt Reinsch.

We would also like to thank the hundreds of other paleontologists, scientists, curators, museum staff members and fossil preparators who worked to collect and prepare the fossils displayed in this book. The process of displaying a single museum-quality specimen takes up to 10 years. Their efforts and those of others involved in this process, including the museum administrative staffs, are greatly appreciated.

Audio Visual Consultants, Inc. would like to thank the zoological parks, botanical gardens and aquariums for so graciously allowing us to film and photograph at their institutions. The work of the men and women who maintain living examples of plants and animals for all to see is invaluable. Thanks especially to Parndana Wildlife Park, Kangaroo Island, Australia; Taronga Zoo, Sydney, Australia; Mesker Park Zoo and Botanical Gardens, Evansville, Indiana; St. Louis Zoo, Missouri; Milwaukee County Zoo, Wisconsin; Missouri Botanical Gardens, St. Louis; and the St. Louis Children's Aquarium, Missouri.

~~~~~~~~~

The Author, Dr. Carl Werner, would like to add a special thank you to the following people who have worked countless hours on this project:

~To my remarkable and loving wife, Debbie, whose skillful photographic contributions enhance almost every page of this book. Your enduring support and assistance during the many years of research, travel, and production have never gone unnoticed. I am forever grateful. Without your understanding, this book and video series may have only been a dream and not a reality.

~To my board of advisors, friends, and family who have patiently guided this process along for 10 years, thank you for your collective insight, assistance, and moral support. I am deeply indebted to all of you. Special thanks to Mike and Kim Ward, George and Peg Tichacek, the Werner family, the Hubert family, the Welsh family, the McClure family, the Carron family, the Lawson family, the Hubert family, the Deters family, the Puhse family, the Cloud family, Marilyn Dell'Orco, Dr. Quoc Dang, George Thampy, Jr., and the late Chuck Dresner.

~To my friend and assistant, Carla Azzara, whose writing and editorial skills, along with her tenacity and camaraderie, have helped me shape my thoughts into written form. Your array of abilities have been invaluable in guiding this project to completion. I am deeply grateful.

~To my friend and graphic designer, Adriana Naylor, whose creative and artistic skills have made every page of this book come to life. You are deeply appreciated.

~To my friend, Alon Prunty, whose adept editorial skills have been instrumental in preparing this book for presentation by adding the final touch. My sincere thanks to you.

EVOLUTION:
The Grand Experiment

The Quest for an Answer

TABLE OF CONTENTS

CHAPTER 5

Similarities: A Basic Proof of Evolution? 55

CHAPTER 6

The Fossil Record and Darwin's Prediction 73

CHAPTER 15

CHAPTER 16

CHAPTER 17

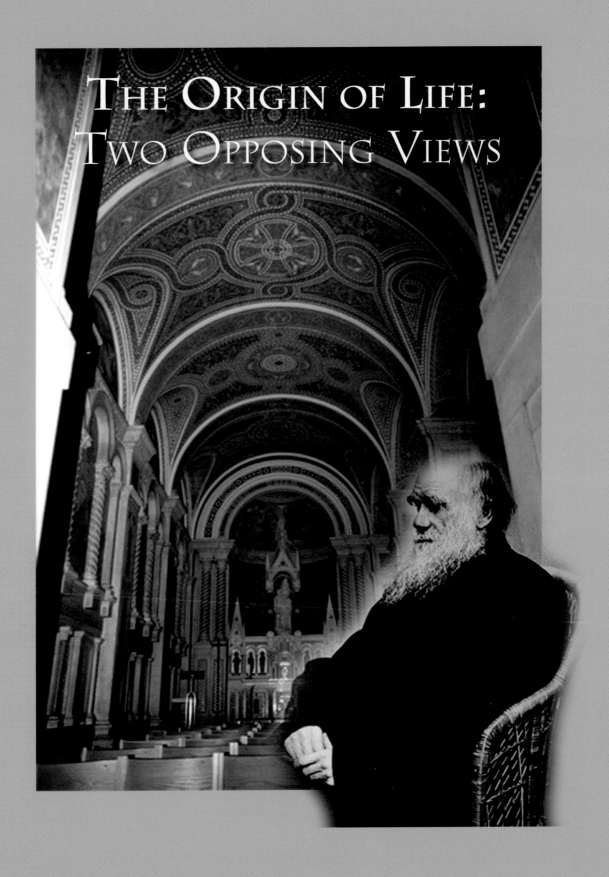

THE ORIGIN OF LIFE: TWO OPPOSING VIEWS

How Did Life Begin?

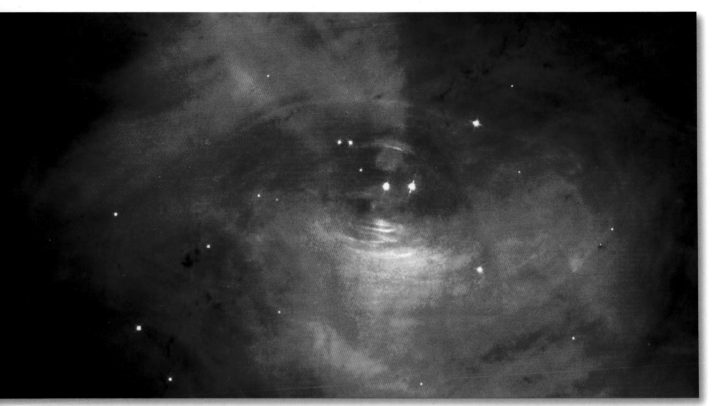

Photo depicting the idea of an explosion in space. Some scientists teach that the universe formed naturally as a result of what they refer to as the "big bang."

What are we to believe?

How did life begin? One view is that an all-powerful God created the entire universe and all forms of life, such as humans and dinosaurs, at the same time (creation).

Another view proposes that the universe began naturally, billions of years ago as a result of an explosion (big bang). Later, a bacterium-like organism arose spontaneously from a mixture of chemicals (abiogenesis) and this single-cell organism evolved into all modern life forms, including humans (evolution).

A third view is that God caused the big bang and then helped the process of evolution along (big bang and evolution with God's aid).

Previous page: *Charles Darwin. St. Louis Basilica Chapel.*

Watch DVD

The Origin of Life

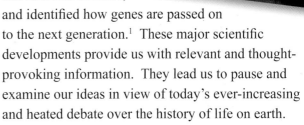

How life came about has been the subject of debate for almost as long as mankind has existed. Did life originate as a result of the intervention by a supernatural deity? Or did life come about as a result of natural laws acting over time? Scientists continue to search for definitive answers to these questions.

The publication of Darwin's theory of evolution in 1859 was a significant catalyst in propelling man's search for a natural understanding of past and present life. Unraveling the mystery of how life began and how life may have changed over time has been the focus of many scientists.

Since Darwin's theory was first made public, scientists have collected nearly one billion fossils, described the structure and function of DNA, and identified how genes are passed on to the next generation.[1] These major scientific developments provide us with relevant and thought-provoking information. They lead us to pause and examine our ideas in view of today's ever-increasing and heated debate over the history of life on earth.

The purpose of this book is to address these and other important scientific discoveries and present the reader with rare and remarkable facts concerning the origin of life — from spontaneous generation, through Darwin's ideas on evolution, to the present-day understanding of mutations and natural selection. The reader is then left to decide what he or she believes.

Michelangelo's painting depicting God creating man (from the ceiling of the Sistine Chapel).

Americans Are Split on Their Beliefs.

According to a Gallup poll taken in 2012, many Americans believe that God created man in the last 10,000 years. This is surprising given the fact that scientists have been teaching evolution for more than a century.

Do most Americans not believe the theory of evolution because it is implausible? Do they not believe evolution because of their religious views? Or, do they not believe in the theory because they are unfamiliar with its concepts?

What Do You Think?

Many Americans Surveyed
Don't Believe Darwin's Theory.

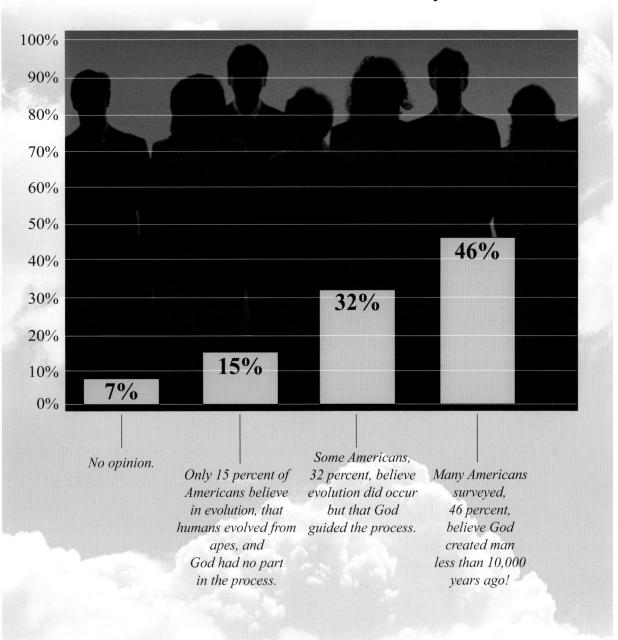

No opinion.

Only 15 percent of Americans believe in evolution, that humans evolved from apes, and God had no part in the process.

Some Americans, 32 percent, believe evolution did occur but that God guided the process.

Many Americans surveyed, 46 percent, believe God created man less than 10,000 years ago!

Source: Gallup poll, May 2012

Do You Believe in Evolution?

Con

"No, I don't believe in evolution at all. I think if you just look at the facts, it's pretty clear; it just can't be."

"Did we come from monkeys? I don't know. There is evidence for it, but there is also some stuff missing, so making that leap with a missing link there, I have some problems with that."

"From what I've seen and heard, we have not evolved from apes for the simple fact that apes are still around. I mean, if we evolved from them, why are they still here?"

Interviews from *Evolution*: *The Grand Experiment* video series

What Do You Think?

Pro

Yes, I do believe in the theory of evolution because I think that we had to come from some place and you know from ape to man to what we are today. I definitely believe in evolution.

I think it's a very sad thing that we're getting religious views mixed up with governmental involvement with education. I think it's a sad comment on how people are trying to fix what they see as social problems in today's world by falling back on religious dogma.

Evolution: Scientists Can't Agree

Ever since Darwin's time there have been scientists who strongly disagree with the theory of evolution. But since the middle of the twentieth century, there have been a growing number of scientists who reject the theory of evolution based on the discovery of processes and structures of which Darwin was unaware. These scientists cite multiple "lines of evidence" that evolution did not occur, including gaps in the fossil record, problems with the big bang theory, the amazing complexity of even the simplest organisms, and the inability of scientists to explain the origin of life using natural laws.

Scientists who support evolution state that the evidence for the theory is clear and overwhelming. They offer observations of natural selection in action, the evolution of birds from dinosaurs, the evolution of whales from a land animal, and the evolution of man from apes, as some of the most convincing proofs for evolution.

From the video series
Evolution: The Grand Experiment

Dr. Duane Gish, Biochemist,
Institute for Creation Research

"Life could not have created itself. Theories on the origin of life, that is the evolutionary origin of life, are modern-day fantasies; they are fairy tales." [2]

— **Dr. Gish**

Con

"You really have to be blind or three days dead not to see the transitions among these. You have to not want to see it." [3]

— **Dr. Padian**

Pro

Dr. Kevin Padian, Paleontologist,
UC Berkeley

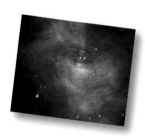

Evolution and Education

Recent Gallup polls reveal that the majority of Americans want both evolution and creationism taught in public schools. This is somewhat surprising given the fact that the majority of scientists believe in evolution and dismiss supernatural creation theories as myths.

There are different reasons parents want both theories taught to their children. Some refer to a sense of fairness. They want their children to learn both sides of the issue and then decide for themselves.

The problem of how to teach students such a controversial topic is challenging for educators. Some fear that teaching two opposing theories would confuse the students, while some believe this approach would encourage students to think critically and openly about the world around them. Others believe that creation is a religious idea and should not be taught in government schools.

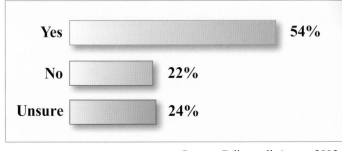

Do you think creationism should be taught in public school science classes?

Yes	54%
No	22%
Unsure	24%

Source: Gallup poll, August 2005

What Should Be Taught?

Interviews from *Evolution: The Grand Experiment* video series

I believe it is good for students to get a balance of both sides so that they can make up their minds for themselves without being forced into one way or another. I know that if I went to school and they taught all evolution, that I would feel somehow a little gypped.

I do feel that everyone is capable of making their own decisions, and I think that students, even at a young age, should be respected enough to be given various kinds of information, various amounts of information, and led to make their own decisions.

I don't really have a problem with evolution being taught in the schools just so long as all the information is given and it is shown that it is not quite fact. And it needs to be very scientific in its presentation as far as listing its faults and its strengths. I think that science that only lists strengths, and not weaknesses, is not science at all.

What Do You Think?

EVOLUTION'S FALSE START: SPONTANEOUS GENERATION
322 B.C.– A.D. 1859

Even Scientists Can Be Wrong!

History teaches us that even scientists can be wrong. In the past, scientists had some rather strange ideas concerning the origin of life. They believed that living organisms could come into being rapidly and "spontaneously" over a period of just a few days or weeks. Remarkably, the theory of spontaneous generation, which originated around the time of Aristotle (fourth century B.C.), was perpetuated for over 2,100 years.[1,2] It was considered an "article of faith"[3] by many biologists until it was finally disproved by Louis Pasteur in 1859. The story of spontaneous generation is one example where scientists, confident in their beliefs, were proven wrong after thousands of years.

First "Proof" of Spontaneous Generation:
Mice from Underwear

In his classic seventeenth century description of spontaneous generation, Dr. Jan Baptista von Helmont, a Flemish physician and chemist, described proof that mice were spontaneously generated from dirty underwear.[4] He wrote:

> *If you press a piece of underwear soiled with sweat, together with some wheat in an open-mouthed jar, after about 21 days the odor changes and the ferment, coming out of the underwear and penetrating through the husks of wheat, changes the wheat into mice...But what is even more remarkable is that the mice which come out of the wheat and underwear are not small mice, not even miniature adults or aborted mice, but adult mice emerge!*[5]
>
> —Dr. Jan Baptista von Helmont

*Dr. Jan Baptista von Helmont
(1580–1644)*

Dr. von Helmont believed mice came from wheat and dirty underwear.

Previous page: *Recreation of Dr. von Helmont's experiment. Dr. von Helmont thought the mice came from the wheat and dirty underwear. He was not aware that the mice crawled into the jar.*

The Experiment

Step 1:
Collect wheat from field.

Step 2:
Put wheat in jar.

Step 3:
Put sweaty, dirty underwear in jar with wheat.

Step 4:
Wait three weeks for spontaneous generation.

The Evidence:
Mice appear in jar. ("They came from the underwear and wheat.")

The First Proof: Bad Science

In retrospect, it seems obvious that Dr. von Helmont's proof was really nothing more than bad science. The mice did not come from the underwear; they simply crawled into the jar to eat the wheat. How is it possible that Dr. von Helmont and other prominent scientists merely accepted the theory of spontaneous generation without adequately testing it to determine the theory's validity? How is it possible that these ideas were believed for over 2,100 years?

During von Helmont's time, questioning spontaneous generation was tantamount to questioning science itself.

Would anyone dare to challenge the prevailing scientific thought of the day? Could the majority of scientists be wrong? Only a courageous scientist would be able to stand up against the proponents, for those who objected to spontaneous generation were thought of as fools. Supporters of spontaneous generation pointed out that it was "obvious" the mice had emerged from the underwear. Besides, there were other lines of evidence to support the theory of spontaneous generation, such as the formation of maggots on rotting meat.

Second "Proof" of Spontaneous Generation:
Maggots from Rotting Meat

A second proof offered by scientists to demonstrate spontaneous generation was the formation of live maggots from a piece of raw meat. Scientists observed that if they put a piece of meat into an open jar, maggots would be found on the meat weeks later. Scientists said this proved that maggots arose from rotting meat spontaneously.

This experiment can still be performed today by placing a piece of meat in a dish and setting it outside in the warm air. Where do the maggots come from? Is this proof that life formed spontaneously? Can you offer a better explanation for why this happens?

The Experiment

Step 1:
Put raw meat in dish.

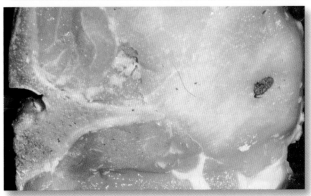

Step 2:
Wait two weeks for spontaneous generation.

The Evidence:
Maggots appear on the meat. ("They came from the rotting meat.")

The Second Proof Is Falsified with Cheesecloth

Although the rotting meat experiment was believed to be evidence for spontaneous generation, it was proved wrong in 1668 by Dr. Francesco Redi, an Italian physician and scientist. He showed that maggots growing on rotting meat did not represent the spontaneous generation of life, but rather the contamination of the meat by flies. Dr. Redi demonstrated that flies had landed on the meat and laid their eggs. Over time, these eggs grew into maggots, the larval stage of flies. When Dr. Redi placed a piece of cheesecloth over the jar, maggots never formed because flies were unable to land on the meat and lay their eggs. [6, 7]

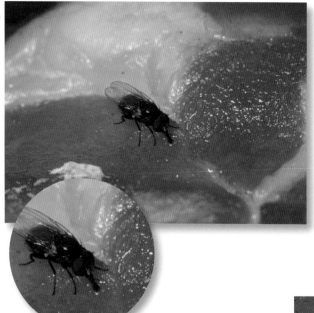

Dr. Francesco Redi disproved the rotting meat experiment with a piece of cheesecloth.

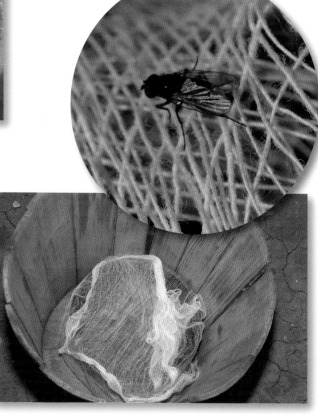

*Dr. Francesco Redi
1626–1697*

Cheesecloth prevented flies from landing on the meat and laying their eggs. Maggots never formed.

Third "Proof" of Spontaneous Generation:
Scum from Clear Pond Water

In the nineteenth century, scientists offered a third proof that life sprang from nonlife. Scientists thought that bacteria (pond scum) were spontaneously generated from water. To demonstrate this, they took clear pond water, boiled it, and poured it into a jar. After a few weeks or so, the pond water became cloudy and scum formed on the water. Where did the scum come from?

Those who believed in spontaneous generation thought that the scum/bacteria (life) had come from the water (nonlife). Scientists were very confident in this proof and scoffed at anyone who dared to question their conclusions.

The Experiment

Step 1:
Boil pond water, pour into jar, and wait for spontaneous generation.

    The water was boiled vigorously before it was poured into the jar. Boiling the water killed off all of the existing bacteria in the pond water.

Step 2:
Wait a few weeks for spontaneous generation.

The Evidence:
The water becomes cloudy and scum appears spontaneously. ("Bacteria formed from water.")

    Even though the pond water was sterilized by boiling, bacteria in the form of scum eventually appeared in the jar. Life came from nonlife.

A similar experiment was performed by John Needham, a British scientist, using broth. He boiled broth to kill the living things that may have been present in the liquid but later the broth turned cloudy. This was considered another proof of the spontaneous generation of life.

The Third Proof Is Falsified with an S-Shaped Flask

Dr. Louis Pasteur
1822–1895

The debate over spontaneous generation finally peaked in the mid-nineteenth century. Based on his previous experiments with fermentation and his familiarity with microorganisms in nature, Louis Pasteur, a French chemist, began a series of experiments in 1859 with the intention of ending the various opinions of his day regarding spontaneous generation. With his experiment, as detailed below, Pasteur "*refuted the theory of spontaneous generation.*"[8]

Dr. Pasteur started with a flask filled with boiled meat broth. He then heated the neck of the flask and stretched it.

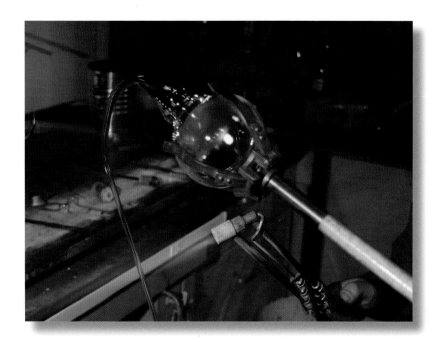

After heating the neck of the flask again, Pasteur then made it s-shaped.

The open end of the s-shaped glass neck pointed upward. Due to gravity, bacteria from the air could only settle in the lowest part of the neck and were prevented from reaching the broth.

*Even after months of waiting,
the liquid in the flask never became cloudy.*

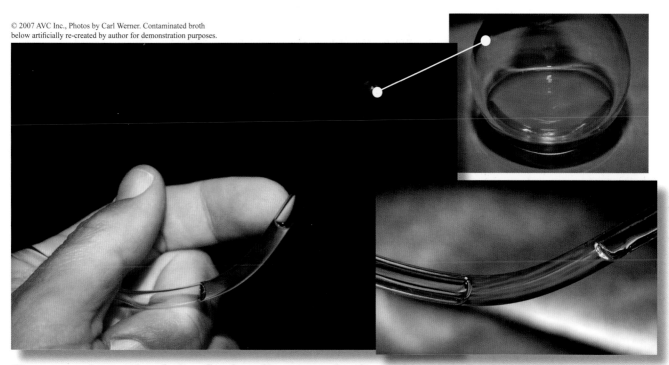

*Pasteur then tilted the flask, allowing the liquid in the flask to come
in contact with the neck. Within a short period of time, the liquid
became cloudy. The microorganisms that had settled in the neck con-
taminated the broth. This proved that bacteria (or in this case scum)
do not form spontaneously from clear water!*

Spontaneous Generation Finally Disproved

When the last pillar of spontaneous generation finally collapsed with Dr. Pasteur's experiments, there was a shift toward accepting the concept that all life must come from pre-existing life. If this was so, how did life originally form? Did God create it? Some scientists did not think it was proper to believe in a god creating life. To them science was a way to explain everything in nature without using any divine or supernatural intervention.

The stage was set for science to offer a new explanation for the origin of life on a purely natural basis. In 1859, Charles Darwin published his theory of evolution, which also supported the idea of life coming from non-living matter. The difference between spontaneous generation and evolution was that Darwin proposed life had formed in the far distant past, in the primordial waters of the early earth, and then changed slowly over millions of years.

A Reflection on Spontaneous Generation. How Were These Scientists Misled?

Only as long as an idea has not been falsified using experimentation, investigation, or observation does it remain a valid idea. Scientific theories and even laws are not permanent but may be challenged, changed, or disproved by new evidence at any time.

At the time of Dr. von Helmont's seventeenth century experiment, spontaneous generation was already accepted by scientists and "known" to be true, just as the theory of evolution is today. With his experiment, von Helmont demonstrated what was already believed. But trying to prove what other scientists already believe is actually bad science. It leads to an artificial body of knowledge, which becomes self-supporting and circular in its proofs. Rather, scientists are obliged to repeat the experiments of others under various conditions to expose any flaws. The scientific process supports ideas that can be repeated independently. Pasteur was able to disprove spontaneous generation because he could test it. Darwin's notion of life arising in the distant past by an unknown biochemical mechanism is not directly testable, making it nearly impossible to falsify.

Today we can learn from the scientific failures of the past. The historical example of spontaneous generation teaches us that scientists can be wrong, even though they may be confident in their convictions. A generous dose of skepticism goes a long way in science. Also, a scientific idea may not be disproved for hundreds, if not thousands, of years. In the case of spontaneous generation, two millennia passed before Dr. Francesco Redi and Dr. Louis Pasteur, once and for all, ended the theory.

In the same way, it is possible that the theory of evolution will also one day be disproved. If the theory of evolution contains assumptions that are ultimately shown to be false, this theory, too, could fall. It is exciting to be living during a time when a major theory is being questioned and tested by many different scientists in many different areas.

DARWIN'S FALSE MECHANISM FOR EVOLUTION: ACQUIRED CHARACTERISTICS
ANTIQUITY– A.D. 1889+

Darwin Never Succeeded in Understanding Inheritance of Traits During His Lifetime.

In 1859, the same year spontaneous generation was disproved, Charles Darwin offered another theory for the origin of life by publishing his book titled *On the Origin of Species by Means of Natural Selection, or the Preservation of Favoured Races in the Struggle for Life*, now simply referred to as *The Origin of Species*.

Darwin proposed that all forms of life evolved from a primordial prototype.[1] The modern theory of evolution suggests that over the course of millions and millions of years, this primordial single-cell organism evolved into a multicellular invertebrate, which evolved into a vertebrate fish, which evolved into a semi-aquatic amphibian, which evolved into a land-based reptile. Then one type of land-based reptile changed into a bird, while another type of land-based reptile changed into a mammal. The mammal then slowly evolved into a primate (ape), which eventually evolved into humans.

Darwin believed evolution occurred through various mechanisms, including acquired characteristics, adaptation, and natural selection. This chapter will define acquired characteristics and explain how this idea was eventually proved wrong.

Acquired characteristics was a theory of great antiquity and had been accepted by many intellectuals for thousands of years.[2] Acquired characteristics was also commonly referred to as the law of use and disuse or "Lamarckianism." (Lamarck was a French naturalist and one of the scientists who promoted the idea of acquired characteristics.) This law proposed that if an animal "acquired" a trait during its lifetime, such as large muscles, this trait would be passed on to the next generation. For example, Darwin and other scientists thought that if a horse was exercised and developed large muscles, its offspring would then have large muscles too. In his book, *The Origin of Species*, Darwin wrote: *"I think that there can be little doubt that use in our domestic animals strengthens and enlarges certain parts, and disuse diminishes them; and that such modifications are inherited."* [3]

Charles Darwin, 1809–1882, father of the theory of evolution.

The law of use and disuse was eventually proved wrong and is no longer believed by modern evolution scientists. The experiment that disproved acquired characteristics was carried out in 1889 and will be discussed at the end of this chapter.

We now know that changes occurring in the body cells of a multicellular animal, such as a horse, cannot be passed on to the next generation. This is because body cells (skin cells or muscle cells for example) have no influence on the DNA in the reproductive cells (eggs and sperm). It is only the genes in the reproductive cells that are passed on to the next generation.

It is interesting to learn about the laws of use and disuse because it is another scientific law that was eventually disproved after thousands of years of support, just as spontaneous generation was. Also, it is important for everyone to learn about acquired characteristics because, even today, some people still incorrectly believe these ideas.

Acquired Characteristics Example #1:
Muscle Building

Even though this man lifts weights every day and develops large muscles, his baby will not be born with large muscles. Darwin did not understand this.

Darwin incorrectly thought that enlarged muscles from exercise would be passed on to the next generation.

Acquired Characteristics Example #2:
Neck Stretching

*Scientists incorrectly thought that
a horse could eventually become a long-necked animal
by stretching its neck to eat food.*

Stretching...

Stretching neck muscles has no effect on the DNA
in the reproductive cells of the horse. A longer neck
cannot be passed on to the next generation.

Acquired Characteristics Example #3:
Sun Tanning

Scientists incorrectly thought that sun tanning would cause children to be born with darker skin.

Jacob, 3 years old

If a woman tans her skin every day, her children will not be born with a suntan. Tanning has no effect on the genes of the reproductive cells; therefore, tanned skin is not passed on to the next generation.

Acquired Characteristics Example #4:
Disuse and Shedding Body Parts

The law of acquired characteristics was also called the law of use and disuse. Disuse was the idea that if an animal did not use a body part, such as a tail or legs, eventually the animal's offspring would be born without these unused, and therefore unnecessary, body parts. But this idea is wrong.

The DNA in the reproductive cells of a multicellular animal cannot sense that another part of the body is not being used. Therefore, an animal's offspring are not affected by the disuse of a body part. For example, if you put your left arm in a sling and did not use it during your entire lifetime, your offspring would still be born with a normal left arm. This is because the arm cells do not communicate with the DNA in the reproductive cells.

How then could an animal, such as a bear, shed its back legs in order to evolve into a whale, as once

proposed by Darwin? If a bear, by virtue of its surroundings, used its legs less and less, would they eventually go away? No, the DNA in the genes of the reproductive cells of the bear cannot sense that the animal is not using its legs. Disuse then cannot be a mechanism for evolution.

Darwin was not aware of the mechanisms of genetics, as these principles were being uncovered in a different country by Austrian priest, Fr. Gregor Mendel, during this same time. As genetics became better understood, the concept of acquired characteristics was eventually disproved.

Darwin's belief that acquired characteristics were partly responsible for evolution increased throughout his lifetime. In fact, in his second book, *The Descent of Man*, he devoted an entire section to the law of use and disuse.

In 1875, sixteen years after writing *The Origin of Species*, Darwin wrote this to his cousin, Francis Galton:

"If this implies that many parts are not modified by **use and disuse** during the life of the individual, I differ widely from you, as every year I come to attribute more and more to such agency." [4]

— *Charles Darwin*

Play Video!

The Experiment That Ended Acquired Characteristics

The law of disuse was dealt a fatal blow in 1889, seven years after Darwin died, with scientist August Weisman's tail cutting experiment.[5] If the law of disuse was correct, body parts not used during life would be absent in future generations. Weisman thought he could prove this by cutting off the tails of mice. He reasoned that if he cut off the tails of mice for 20 generations in a row, the mice would eventually be born without a tail. But no matter how many tails he cut off, the baby mice were always born *with* a tail. With his experiment, Weisman disproved the concept of disuse.

The idea that there is no interaction between the body cells and the reproductive cells in a multicellular animal slowly began to take hold and logical corollaries from this experiment soon followed. If traits are not lost because of disuse, then traits acquired during life (after birth) through use (larger muscles, longer neck, and suntanned skin) cannot be passed to future generations for the same reason. With Weisman's simple experiment, the law of acquired characteristics was invalidated. This story about acquired characteristics demonstrates how scientific laws are often corrected or replaced as new information is gained by studying the world around us.

Once the law of use and disuse was disproved, the theory of evolution did not fall apart, because this was just one of the mechanisms that Darwin proposed to explain how evolution occurred. Darwin's primary mechanism for evolution, natural selection, will be discussed in the next chapter.

NATURAL SELECTION AND CHANCE MUTATIONS

Natural Selection
Darwin's Major Mechanism for Evolution

Charles Darwin observed that *within* a particular animal or plant species, there are various sizes, colors, shapes, and other traits. Along with this observation, he contended that, in nature, the weaker varieties of animals or plants are "killed off" by the stronger varieties due to their better ability to compete for food or withstand environmental changes. This is what he referred to as the survival of the fittest, or natural selection. This process, Darwin thought, would cause the surviving variety of a species to improve over time and evolve into a completely new species. Many scientists today still believe, as Darwin did, that natural selection is one of the major mechanisms by which evolution (theoretically) occurs.

Scientists who oppose evolution disagree with Darwin's idea that natural selection could cause the evolution of all plants and animals living today from a single-cell organism. They argue that natural selection, or the killing off of weaker varieties of animals or plants within a species, only *removes* these weaker animals and plants, but it *does not add completely new body parts* to the population.

To better understand the limits of natural selection, let's examine it in further detail. A particular animal or plant species may have five varieties of color or shape or size coded for in its genes. Using artificial breeding, a horticulturist or a breeder consciously (or artificially) selects which of these traits will be eliminated or preserved in order to create a new variety (or breed) of plant or animal *within* a species. A dog breeder, for example, may take two mutts of average size and hair length and allow only the smaller offspring of these dogs to reproduce. He continues this process generation

Darwin thought natural selection was another mechanism for evolution.

after generation. Later, he allows only the longest-haired varieties to reproduce. Eventually, he would breed a small dog with long hair. This new variety is devoid of certain traits that were present in the original pair, but this new variety is not a new species. It is still a dog, *Canis familiaris*.

By the same token, nature and the environment acting as the selectors may *remove* a particular trait by killing off all of the animals with that trait. For instance, in the snowy environment of the Arctic Circle, if there were two varieties of a particular bear species, one with white fur and one with dark gray fur, the white variety would tend to survive better than the dark gray ones. This is because the snowy background prevents the white bears from being easily spotted when hunting their prey. Since the dark gray bears do not have the advantage of a lighter color, this variety of bear could not as easily sneak up on its prey. By a natural process, the darker bear would eventually be eliminated as it is less able to catch its prey. In this scenario, a new species of bear was not created. Rather, the genes for the gray fur trait were eliminated from the population through the process of natural selection.

Natural selection and artificial breeding may *remove* a trait that is already present; however, these breeding processes never create new information in the DNA and never *create* new genes. They simply select for traits that are already present.

Play Video!

Natural Selection and the Limits of Variability

There is another factor to consider which would further negate the possibility of providing new traits or species through the use of artificial breeding or natural selection alone. This is what is known as the "limits of variability." Modern geneticists recognize that within any particular animal or plant species, there are known limits in the size, limits in the varieties of color, and limits in the shape, as well as limits in other characteristics; hence, the term limits of variability.

For instance, there are tomatoes that range in size from a few ounces to seven pounds. One could not start with an average size tomato and after thousands of years of artificial breeding, or millions of years of natural selection, grow a 900-pound tomato. The size of the tomato is limited (or preset in the genes). Because of the limits of variability, natural selection alone could not cause evolution.

Breeding and natural selection can only remove certain traits.

You cannot grow a 900-pound tomato using artificial breeding or natural selection!

If Natural Selection Does Not Produce New Traits, How Do They Come About?

If natural selection and Darwin's other mechanisms for evolution (the law of use and disuse) cannot create completely new traits, such as a fin or a gill or an eyeball, how then could evolution theoretically occur? What is the mechanism for evolution according to modern scientists who support evolution?

In the early 1900s, Dr. Thomas Hunt Morgan, a scientist at Columbia University, noted that animal and plant species have a variety of traits, just as Darwin had observed. However, in 1910, while studying inheritance through the crossbreeding of

common fruit flies, Dr. Morgan made an incredible discovery — a fruit fly with white (albino) eyes. Dr. Morgan observed that fruit flies were normally born with red eye color and only rarely, once in every 100 generations or more, were they born with white eyes. Since the white eye color was not a normal trait, he correctly deduced that the albino eye occurred through an accident or mutation, though he was not sure how this had happened. It wasn't understood until many years later that albino eyes in fruit flies resulted from a simple, accidental, single-letter change in the DNA. The DNA change occurred in the gene that made the normal red eye pigment.

The Modern Theory of Evolution: New Traits Come from Accidental Mutations

To explain this further, one must understand the simple language of DNA. DNA carries the instruction codes for all of the parts of living organisms and consists of a combination of only four letters (also called nucleotide bases), namely A, C, G, and T. The section of DNA (gene) that determines a fruit fly's normal red eye color is thousands of letters long and looks something like this: ACCGATTTTCACCGC-GAATGCAAGCG, etc. Now, if one of the DNA letters is accidentally changed in this section of DNA (in the eye pigment gene), then the normal eye pigment may be white instead of red and will not function properly.

The mutation of the eye color that Dr. Morgan observed was a pathological variant, a genetic defect or disease of sorts, since the defective eye pigmentation also caused the fruit fly to not see as well as one born with red eye color. Similarly, in humans, genetic diseases, such as sickle-cell anemia, cystic fibrosis, spina bifida, and hemophilia, are also the result of one simple, accidental letter change in a particular section of DNA. In these diseases, one letter of DNA — out of the billions of letters of DNA needed to form a human being — is incorrect.

The next logical question that followed Dr. Morgan's experiment was this: If disease traits come about by accidental or chance mutations in a single letter of DNA, could *new body systems* also form this way? In other words, could new complicated and integrated body systems, such as a fish's gills (and associated structures), or a bird's wing (feathers, bones, and muscles), or a cardiovascular system (heart with blood vessels and lungs), come about through the accumulation of a series of accidental mutations?[1] To form a complicated new body system would require adding or changing *thousands* of letters of DNA in the egg or sperm of the parent organism, not just *one* letter. Moreover, these thousands of letters of DNA would not only have to be accidentally placed in the correct *location*, but also in the correct letter *sequence*.

Let's now look at an analogy of forming a new body system using the proposed modern mechanism for evolution — random mutations combined with natural selection — and see if it is plausible:

You sit down at the computer and type out a list of everything you need to do tomorrow such as "Do the dishes," "Feed the dog," "Take kids to school," "Meet Joe for lunch," or "Go to sales meeting at 7 PM." This "things-to-do list" is analogous to DNA, the genetic code of an animal. This list, like DNA, contains useful planning information, coded for by a series of letters, and is very specific and detailed.

Now imagine putting a blindfold on your three-year-old son and asking him to type on the keyboard of your computer. He can type anything he wants, anywhere he wants, onto your "things-to-do list." He can add or subtract letters as well. Could your

Could Accidental Mutations Eventually Result in New Body Systems?

son's act of randomly adding or deleting letters (similar to random mutations) on your "things-to-do list" (DNA) add a new item to your list (similar to adding a new body system)?

Typing letters randomly over your things-to-do list will change the meaning of the text and much of the original information will be lost. Likewise, when random letter changes occur in DNA, the result is usually an undesirable one — disease. The theory of evolution must reconcile this paradox: Can mistakes in the genetic code (random mutations), which nearly always leads to a loss of information (disease), ultimately result in the improvement of an animal?

Now add natural selection to this analogy and see if it improves your "things-to-do list." You set up ten million computers all over the world (representing a population of ten million animals) and have ten million three-year-old children, blindfolded, typing onto a copy of your "things-to-do list" (representing random mutations in DNA). Since natural selection kills off weaker varieties of animals, then you must delete (kill off) each "things-to-do list" that is

produced, but which is less helpful than your original list, and have the child start over.

Now ask yourself this question: By having ten million blindfolded children typing onto your list and deleting those lists that are less helpful and starting over, could a new item ever be added to your list such as "Pick up Mary after dance lessons"?

Producing a cardiovascular system from blind mutations in the DNA code would be much more complex than typing, "Pick up Mary after dance lessons." Rather it would be equivalent to ten million blindfolded children authoring a short book.

Given this analogy, is it possible that complex body systems could evolve as the result of a series of random mutations and natural selection? Scientists who support evolution say YES, with enough time and chance, nearly anything is possible. Scientists who oppose evolution say the question is ridiculous and answer it with a resounding NO. What do you think?

"Ever since Darwin's day, biologists have debated the mechanisms, but not the fact, of evolution."

—Richard Milner, evolution scientist and author of *The Encyclopedia of Evolution*[2]

Adaptation

Charles Darwin believed adaptation to be one of the mechanisms by which evolution occurred. Adaptation implies that an animal was modified in a beneficial way, making it more capable of surviving the environment or reproducing at a greater rate. In *The Origin of Species,* Darwin wrote: *"...during the process of modification, each has become adapted to the conditions of life of its own region, and has supplanted and exterminated its original parent-form and all the transitional varieties between its past and present states."* [3] He also wrote this: *"We have reason to believe...that a change in the conditions of life* [environment], *by specially acting on the reproductive system, causes or increases variability* [new traits]*...and this would manifestly be favourable to natural selection, by giving a better chance of profitable variations occurring...."* [4] (Words in brackets added by author for clarity.)

Today, some scientists who *support* evolution believe the term adaptation should be eliminated from the scientific vocabulary because it is misleading. One scientist recently wrote this in the *Encyclopedia of Evolution*: *"Adaptation, which at first seems such an easy, common-sense concept, turns out to be slippery, sometimes even circular and paradoxical... Some biologists have even suggested eliminating the concept of adaptation altogether. They find it too vague to be useful and historically abused as a substitute for thoughtful investigation."* [5]

The use of the word "adaptation" has become a matter of semantics and is somewhat confusing to the non-scientist. When a modern evolution scientist says an animal has "adapted," he or she actually means that accidental mutations have occurred, resulting in an animal which is better suited for the environment. These changes *fortuitously* caused the animal to be stronger or better able to withstand the environment in which it lives, and the animal has *accidentally* become "adapted" to the environment.

The public's perception of adaptation is quite different. Many incorrectly believe that when an animal "adapts," the animal changed *in response to* the environment and has done so out of necessity, through purpose. Although the public's perception of adaptation provides a more believable mechanism for evolution, it is incorrect and is very different from how a scientist uses the term. To be more accurate, the word "adaptation" should always be replaced with the words "mutation and natural selection" or "fortuitous adaptation and natural selection."

This polar bear was brought from the Arctic Circle to the St. Louis Zoo where the temperature reaches 100 degrees Fahrenheit. Even in the presence of such warm temperatures, the animal is not capable of adapting to the environment out of necessity. The DNA in the genes of the reproductive cells cannot sense the environment and change accordingly.

Should the Word "Adaptation" Be Removed from Our Vocabulary?

Modern scientists (including those quoted below) *do not* believe that an individual multicellular animal can directly adapt to the environment and pass these changes to the next generation. They know that this kind of adaptation is genetically impossible. Nonetheless, these modern spokesmen for the theory of evolution *occasionally* describe evolution in these terms — as a direct response to the environment. This is not the intent of these scientists, but over the years their occasional poor choice of words has led some of the general public into thinking that this is how evolution works. When described in these terms, evolution — by direct adaptation to the environment — seems very believable, but is not accurate.

Example #1: In 1969, John Pfeiffer, Professor of Anthropology, Fulbright Scholar, National Science Foundation Consultant and former Editor of *Scientific American* wrote: *"The shift* [in hunting] *from small to big game...had an enormous effect on the shaping of man, nearly doubling the size of his brain and transforming one breed of Australopithecus to Homo erectus."* [6] This statement is incorrect. Hunting larger animals, buffaloes instead of rabbits, does not affect the DNA of the reproductive cells, and would not cause an ape to change into a human being. These changes could only theoretically come about by mistaken mutations and natural selection.

Example #2: In 1995, Herbert Thomas, Deputy Director of the Paleoanthropology and Prehistory Laboratory at the College of France, wrote this about humans evolving from apes: *"Around five million years ago bipedalism* [upright walking] *became the primary form of locomotion in the australopithecines, the early primitive hominids. The reason for this major change in behavior was increasing severe drought to the east of the African Rift Valley."* [7] This statement is misleading. An animal cannot change from walking on all fours to upright walking because of a drought or a change in the environment. Environmental changes have no effect on the DNA of the reproductive cells. Again, switching from walking on all fours to upright walking could only theoretically occur through mistaken mutations and natural selection.

Example #3: In 1969, John Pfeiffer, Professor of Anthropology, Fulbright Scholar, National Science Foundation Consultant and former Editor of *Scientific American* wrote: *"*[The ape's] *massive jaw may have evolved as an adaptation to a diet of tough meat, raw or lightly cooked meat."* [8] This statement is incorrect. Eating meat will not cause a change in the jaw size that can be passed to the next generation. Eating specific types of food has no effect on the DNA of the reproductive cells. This change could only occur through mistaken mutations and natural selection.

Example #4: In 1995, Dr. Ian Tattersall, Head of the Anthropology Department at the American Museum of Natural History, wrote this in his book about human evolution: *"...Alan Walker and his colleagues have pointed to a whole suite of characteristics that indicate very specific adaptation to an environment of high radiant heat stress."* [9] This statement is slightly misleading. Again, an individual animal cannot directly change the DNA in its reproductive cells because of a change in the environment.

Example #5: In 1968, Harvard Anthropologist, Dr. David Pilbeam, wrote: *"Tool-using and tool-making have therefore been important catalysts in human evolution."* [10] His statement is genetically impossible. Using a tool or making a tool does not affect the DNA of the reproductive cells.

Example #6: In 1995, Herbert Thomas, Deputy Director of Paleoanthropology and Prehistory Laboratory at the College of France, wrote this in his book, *Human Origins: The Search for Our Beginnings*: *"The diversity of environments that humans have colonized during the last 100,000 years helps to explain their physical differences."* [11] This statement is not true. Racial differences are not brought about by an environmental change, but are simply variations of the DNA in the genes.

The remainder of this chapter takes a look at one sample animal, a whale, and shows how many chance mutations would be needed to cause this animal to come about.

Could a Whale Evolve by Chance?

Whales are members of the order Cetacea, which also includes dolphins and porpoises.[12] There are 84 species in this order of aquatic mammals, ranging in size from the tiny finless porpoise measuring 1.2 meters to the enormous blue whale. The blue whale is possibly the largest animal to ever have lived on earth, weighing 400,000 pounds and measuring 100 feet long.[13] Its tongue is about the weight of a full grown elephant, and its heart the size of a small car.[14] The blood vessels are so large a human could swim through them.[14, 15] Where did these large beasts come from?

Before the theory of evolution, many scientists believed that whales were created by a superior being, but Charles Darwin had other ideas. Because whales are warm-blooded mammals, Darwin reasoned that whales evolved from another warm-blooded mammal, possibly a bear, by means of acquired characteristics and natural selection. In *The Origin of Species*, Darwin wrote:

> *"In North America the black bear was seen by Hearne swimming for hours with widely open mouth, thus catching, like a whale, insects in the water. Even in so extreme a case as this, if the supply of insects were constant, and if better adapted competitors did not already exist in the country, I can see no difficulty in a race of bears being rendered, by natural selection, more and more aquatic in their structure and habits, with larger and larger mouths, till a creature was produced as monstrous as a whale."*[16]
>
> — *Charles Darwin*

Charles Darwin
1809–1882

Darwin's suggestion that bears could have evolved into a whale caused a great uproar in his day. Prominent scientists scoffed. How could a bear evolve into a whale, even if acquired characteristics were inherited? What was Darwin thinking? Some scientists thought that if Darwin did not drop his idea, he would be branded as a teller of tall tales.[17] Zoologists in his day said his story was "preposterous."[17] Darwin sensed that he was beginning to lose a public relations battle. Would scientists reject his whole theory based on this one idea? Professor Richard Owen, Director of the British Museum of Natural History, prevailed on Darwin to leave out the bear-to-whale story or at least tone it down. Darwin acquiesced and cut it from later editions of *The Origin of Species*, although he privately regretted giving in to his critics.[17]

Sir Richard Owen opposed both Darwin's theory of evolution and Darwin's idea that a black bear evolved into a whale. Owen held nearly every scientific honor of his time. As a paleontologist and zoologist, he was instrumental in building the Natural History Museum in London and was its first director. He coined the word "dinosaur" and described the famous bird Archaeopteryx.[18]

Sir Richard Owen
1804–1892

Sir Richard Owen convinced Darwin to tone down his idea that a bear may have evolved into a whale.

Darwin thought that if a bear swam in the water for hours trying to catch insects, eventually it could be changed into a whale by natural selection and acquired characteristics.

Modern evolution scientists do not believe that whales evolved from a black bear by acquired characteristics and natural selection as Charles Darwin once speculated. They now theorize that whales evolved from a land animal through a complicated series of chance mutations in the DNA of the reproductive cells.

Scientists who oppose evolution think the idea of a land animal becoming a whale by a series of accidental mutations in the DNA is even more preposterous than Darwin's idea that a bear could become a whale through acquired characteristics. They argue that the odds of a land animal changing into a whale, by a series of mistakes in the DNA, are statistically impossible.

From *Evolution: The Grand Experiment* video series

*"In trying to understand the evolution of whales and dolphins from four-legged terrestrial carnivores, the first thing you have to keep in mind is that **chance** plays a tremendous role in this."* [19]

— **Dr. Clemens**

Dr. William Clemens, Professor of Integrated Biology, University of California, Berkeley

Whale Progenitors?

Scientists who support evolution suggest whale evolution is one of the best examples to demonstrate evolution from the fossil record, yet they are still not sure what land animal evolved into a whale and keep changing their opinions.

Clockwise from top left:

A: *In 1998, evolution scientists at the California Academy of Sciences suggested it was this hyena-like animal called **Pachyaena** that evolved into a whale.* [20]

B: *In 1999, evolution scientists were "100% confident" it was a hippo-like animal that evolved into a whale.* [21]

C: *In September 2001, evolution scientist Dr. Phillip Gingerich appearing on PBS suggested it was this cat-like animal called **Sinonyx** that evolved into a whale.* [22]

D: *In September 2001, this same scientist suggested in **Science** it was this wolf-like land animal called **Pakicetus** that evolved into a whale.* [23]

E: *In 2007, evolution scientist Dr. Hans Thewissen suggested it was a deer-like animal called **Indohyus**—similar in appearance to the modern mouse deer—that evolved into a whale.* [23]

From Land Animal to Whale?

What are the differences in the DNA of a whale and the DNA of the land animal from which it may have evolved? Scientists will probably never be able to decode the DNA sequence of the proposed land animal that, theoretically, eventually evolved into the whale. This is because DNA is usually degraded or destroyed in the fossilization process. Nonetheless, by listing the anatomical differences between any particular land animal and a whale, and estimating the number of new proteins that would be required to bring about these changes, scientists are able to estimate the number of chance mutations in the DNA that would have had to occur for whales to evolve.

Evolution scientists are not in agreement regarding which land animal evolved into the whale. For this example, we will use the hyena-like animal called *Pachyaena*. If you were to carry out this same analysis by substituting any other land animal that supposedly evolved into the whale, such as the deer-like animal (*Indohyus*) or the wolf-like animal (*Pakicetus*), your results would be the same!

How many parts of a hyena would have to change by chance mutations to become a whale?

1. The hyena would have to develop a dorsal fin.

Above: *Whales have dorsal fins which provide rotational stability in the water. Many mutations in the DNA letters would be necessary for a hyena-like animal* (**above, right**) *to form a dorsal fin by chance.*

2. The bony tail of the hyena would have to change into a cartilaginous fluke.

There are many differences between a hyena's tail and a whale's tail. A hyena's tail is made of mostly bones and fur and is not involved in locomotion. A whale's tail is wide, made of mostly cartilage and large muscles, and is the primary body part used for propulsion through water.

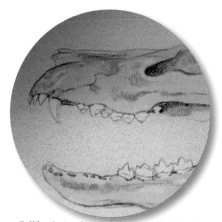

California Academy of Sciences, San Francisco
© 2007 AVC Inc., Photo by Debbie Werner

3. The hyena's teeth would have to develop into a huge baleen filter.

Above: *A hyena has teeth for chewing meat. Toothless whales* (**right**) *have no teeth, only a fine filter called a baleen for filtering plankton. How many chance mutations would it take to lose all the teeth and then form this huge filter? What are the odds of this happening?*

Harvard Museum of Paleontology
© 2007 AVC Inc., Photo by Debbie Werner

4. The hyena's hair would have to nearly disappear and be replaced by blubber for insulation through chance mutations in the DNA.

The hyena (left) is covered by hair for warmth. Hair does not function to warm the body in water. Whales and dolphins instead have a thick layer of blubber.

5. *The nostrils would have to move from the tip of the hyena's nose to the top of the whale's head, disconnect from the mouth passage, and form a strong muscular flap to close the blowhole.*

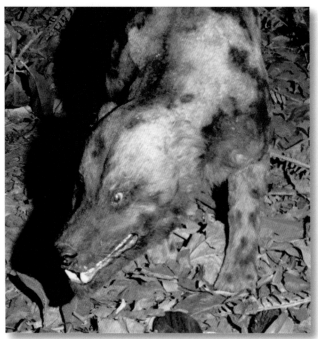

California Academy of Sciences, San Francisco
© 2007 AVC Inc., Photo by Debbie Werner

Above: *Hyenas and other land mammals breathe through their nose and mouth.*
Below: *Whales have a blowhole on the top of their head through which they breathe. The blowhole connects their lungs directly to the outside without air going through the mouth.*

Whales also have a strong muscular flap, which covers the blowhole, and prevents saltwater from rushing into their lungs as they descend into deep, high-pressure water. What are the odds of these features occurring by mutations?

6. *The hyena's front legs would have to change into pectoral fins.*

Humpback whales do not have front legs but have pectoral fins.

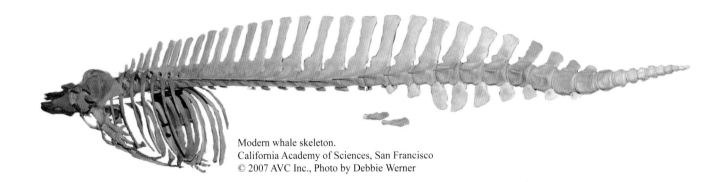

Modern whale skeleton.
California Academy of Sciences, San Francisco
© 2007 AVC Inc., Photo by Debbie Werner

College of the Atlantic, Maine © 2007 AVC Inc., Photo by Debbie Werner

7. The hyena's body would have to increase in size from 150 pounds to 400,000 pounds.

The skull would have to change from less than a foot long to 14 feet long. The eyes and brain would have to enlarge. The thickness of the eyes would have to increase to withstand pressure and the eye lenses would need to become enormous. The hyena's heart would have to change from the size of a human fist to the size of a compact car. [14] *The heart valves would have to change from the size of a dime to the size of a hubcap.* [24]

Visitor standing next to a 14-foot-long whale skull at the College of the Atlantic Museum in Maine.

8. *The hyena's external ears would have to disappear and then develop to compensate for high-pressure diving to 1,640 feet deep.*

9. *The hyena's back legs would have to disappear.*

What Are the Differences?

	Land Mammal	Blue Whale
Length:	Less than 6 feet	100 feet [13]
Weight:	Less than 150 pounds	400,000 pounds [13]
Diving capability:	Less than 8 feet	1,640 feet [25]
Teeth:	Teeth	Filter for eating plankton
Tail:	Tubular, used to show emotion	Wide fluke, used for propulsion
Front legs:	Legs for running	Flipper for steering
Back legs:	Legs for running	Absent
Air passage:	Tip of nose	Top of head
Dorsal fin:	None	Present for rotational stability
Water intake:	Freshwater only	Salt water only
Heat regulation:	Fur	Blubber
Ears:	External	Internal and can withstand high-pressure diving
Propulsion:	Legs	Tail

Could a land animal evolve into a whale by chance mutations? What are the odds of this happening?

Chances or Odds Can Be Calculated by the Number of Possibilities.

1 out of 2 chance

Left hand or right hand? There is one chance out of two possibilities in selecting the correct hand.

1 out of 3 chance

Left shell, middle shell or right shell? There is one chance out of three possibilities in selecting the correct shell.

1 out of 52 chance

Which one is the ace of spades? There are 52 unique playing cards in a deck. There is one chance out of 52 possibilities in selecting a particular card.

1 out of 80,000,000 chance

What is the chance of winning the lottery? There is one chance out of 80 million in selecting the winning Powerball Lottery numbers.

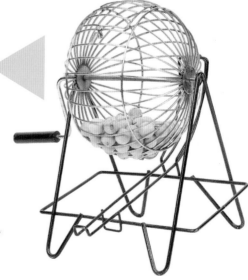

Calculating the Odds of a Land Animal Mutating into a Whale

The exact number of DNA letters that must be changed to reflect the evolution of one animal into another could never be known without the genetic codes of both animals. Even without the exact codes, the number of changes can be *tentatively* calculated as shown below. (**Author's Note:** It must be kept in mind that this is an educated guess, not an exact answer. There are a number of factors that have to be estimated, including: How many *new* proteins would be needed for each body change? How *long* would each of these *new* proteins be? How many *other* proteins would have to be *altered* and how many amino acids were changed in these altered proteins? How many amino acids are called on by multiple codons? etc. This calculation conservatively proposes that only one new protein is needed for each of the major changes listed on page 50 and no other proteins would have to be added or changed.)

The number of DNA letters that must be added to change one animal into another can be calculated using the following formula:

# of body changes	X	# of *new* proteins needed per change	X	# of amino acids in each new protein	X	3 new letters of DNA needed for each new amino acid added	=	Total # of DNA letters that must be added

So What Is the Answer?

If only one new protein was added for each of the nine body changes described in this chapter, and, on average, each new protein was only 100 amino acids long, then 2,700 new letters of DNA would have to be added to the existing DNA of the hyena, over millions of years, for a whale to evolve from a land animal. (Scientists who oppose evolution would argue that more than 2,700 letters of DNA would be required to accidentally form these new body parts; whereas scientists who support evolution would argue that less than 2,700 would be needed.)[26]

Using the above assumptions and formula, 2,700 new letters of DNA would have to be added to the existing DNA:

9 body changes	X	1 new protein per change	X	100 amino acids per new protein	X	3 letters of DNA for each new amino acid added	=	2,700 DNA letters

Since DNA is comprised of only four letters, namely A, C, G, and T, the odds of adding the correct single letter of DNA for any one position on the DNA strand are 1 out of 4 possibilities or ¼. The odds then of adding 2,700 new letters of DNA would be ¼ times ¼ times ¼ times and so on, 2,700 times, or $¼^{2,700}$. So what exactly does this mean? What is the answer to this calculation?

Before revealing the answer, it is helpful to review the odds of other chance events. For example:

The odds of being struck by lightning in your lifetime are 1/5,000 (**3 zeros**).[27] The odds of winning the Powerball Lottery are 1/80,000,000 (**7 zeros**).[28] The odds of winning the Powerball Lottery **two times** in a row are 1/6,400,000,000,000,000 (**14 zeros**). The odds of throwing 100 dice (at once) and all coming up as the number "3" are 1/6,533 followed by **74 zeros**. The odds of throwing 2,000 dice (at once) and all coming up as the number "3" are 1/2,006 followed by **1,553 zeros**. The odds of one individual winning the Powerball Lottery once every year, *for 200 years in a row*, would be 1/1,149 followed by **1,577 zeros**.

Now for the answer: By taking the equation of $¼^{2,700}$ (as explained above) and multiplying it out to the end, the odds of a land mammal becoming a whale by random mutations are 1/364 followed by **1,625 zeros** or (see next page):

1/364,000,000,000,000,000,000,000,000,000,000,000,000,000,000,000,000,000,000,000,
000,000,000,000,000,000,000,000,000,000,000,000,000,000,000,000,000,000,000,000,000,
000,000,000,000,000,000,000,000,000,000,000,000,000,000,000,000,000,000,000,000,000,
000,000,000,000,000,000,000,000,000,000,000,000,000,000,000,000,000,000,000,000,000,
000,000,000,000,000,000,000,000,000,000,000,000,000,000,000,000,000,000,000,000,000,
000,000,000,000,000,000,000,000,000,000,000,000,000,000,000,000,000,000,000,000,000,
000,000,000,000,000,000,000,000,000,000,000,000,000,000,000,000,000,000,000,000,000,
000,000,000,000,000,000,000,000,000,000,000,000,000,000,000,000,000,000,000,000,000,
000,000,000,000,000,000,000,000,000,000,000,000,000,000,000,000,000,000,000,000,000,
000,000,000,000,000,000,000,000,000,000,000,000,000,000,000,000,000,000,000,000,000,
000,000,000,000,000,000,000,000,000,000,000,000,000,000,000,000,000,000,000,000,000,
000,000,000,000,000,000,000,000,000,000,000,000,000,000,000,000,000,000,000,000,000,
000,000,000,000,000,000,000,000,000,000,000,000,000,000,000,000,000,000,000,000,000,
000,000,000,000,000,000,000,000,000,000,000,000,000,000,000,000,000,000,000,000,000,
000,000,000,000,000,000,000,000,000,000,000,000,000,000,000,000,000,000,000,000,000,
000,000,000,000,000,000,000,000,000,000,000,000,000,000,000,000,000,000,000,000,000,
000,000,000,000,000,000,000,000,000,000,000,000,000,000,000,000,000,000,000,000,000,
000,000,000,000,000,000,000,000,000,000,000,000,000,000,000,000,000,000,000,000,000,
000,000,000,000,000,000,000,000,000,000,000,000,000,000,000,000,000,000,000,000,000,
000,000,000,000,000,000,000,000,000,000,000,000,000,000,000,000,000,000,000,000,000,
000,000,000,000,000,000,000,000,000,000,000,000,000,000,000,000,000,000,000,000,000,
000,000,000,000,000,000,000,000,000,000,000,000,000,000,000,000,000,000,000,000,000,
000,000,000,000,000,000,000,000,000,000,000,000,000,000,000,000,000,000,000,000,000,
000,000,000,000,000,000,000,000,000,000,000,000,000,000,000,000,000,000,000,000,000,
000,000,000,000,000,000,000,000,000,000,000,000,000,000,000,000,000,000,000,000,000,
000,000,000,000,000,000,000,000,000,000,000,000,000,000

In other words, the chance of a land animal becoming a whale may be less likely than the chance of winning the national Powerball Lottery every year in a row for 200 *straight years*. Or the odds may be less likely than throwing 2,000 dice *(at once)* and all coming up as a "3."

Because the statistical odds of one animal evolving into another by a series of chance mutations are so unfavorable, some scientists are now reexamining the theory of evolution. They suggest that if this sort of evolution is so unlikely, did it even occur?

But other scientists bristle at such "proofs" or "odds" calculations using such broad pre-suppositions. They point out there is no way to know how many letters of DNA actually mutated without the actual genetic codes for the land mammal and the whale.

Watch DVD

Can you think of other factors to make the odds calculation more accurate?

SIMILARITIES:
A BASIC PROOF OF EVOLUTION?

A Fish with Fins

A Mammal with Fins

Many Scientists Believe That Similarities in Animals Are Evidence for the Theory of Evolution.

Evolution teaches the following: The universe was formed 10 to 20 billion years ago as a result of a big-bang explosion in space. Ultimately, as an indirect consequence of this explosion, life began in the ocean in the form of a single-cell organism about 4 billion years ago. Evolution scientists call this event "the origin of life." Then, around 650 million years ago, a single-cell organism evolved into a multicellular invertebrate. Millions of years later, this invertebrate then evolved into a fish. Then one fish slowly evolved into another and another until one fish eventually evolved into a semiaquatic amphibian. After one amphibian evolved into another and so on, one amphibian eventually evolved into a reptile. Then, one reptile evolved into another and another, until eventually one reptile evolved into the first mammal 225 million years ago, and another reptile evolved into the first bird around 150 million years ago.

Scientists favoring evolution base their belief in the theory on many evidences, which, to name a few, include the fossil record, radioactive dating, and the human fossil record. They also offer *similarities among animals* as one more evidence.

To better understand the concept of similarities, we must first define the terms "related animals" and "unrelated animals." These terms are frequently used in evolution science and assume that all animals are related to one another since they ultimately evolved from a single-cell organism.

The term "related animals" theoretically means that two or more animals evolved from a common ancestor and are thus closely related to one another to the extent that they inherited similar body features, such as the same number of bones in the arm or the same number of fingers in the hand. For example, all dinosaurs, birds, whales, and apes (shown on the next page) have a single bone in the upper arm, two bones in the lower part of the arm, and multiple bones in the wrist/hand/fin regions. To some scientists, these similarities suggest that all of these animals are closely related to one another. According to the theory of evolution, all four of these animals evolved from a theoretical common ancestor that also had one bone in the upper arm, two bones in the lower arm, and multiple bones in the wrist/hand/fin regions.

Conversely, the term "unrelated animals" theoretically means that two or more animals are only distantly related to one another since they do not share a common ancestor that has similar body features. For example, both a shark and a dolphin (below) have dorsal fins. But one is a fish and one is a mammal, and neither evolved from a theoretical common ancestor with a dorsal fin.

Scientists who oppose evolution (and even some scientists who support evolution) believe that similarities in different animals do not prove evolution. They suggest this line of evidence is, at best, circumstantial. This chapter will deal with the pitfalls of using similarities as a proof for evolution.

A shark (left) and a dolphin (right) look very similar in some aspects, but are unrelated.

A dinosaur, a bird, a whale, and an ape have one bone in the upper arm, two bones in the forearm, and multiple bones in the wrist. According to evolution scientists, their theoretical common ancestor is a lizard-like reptile, which also had one upper arm bone, two bones in the forearm, and multiple bones in the wrist.

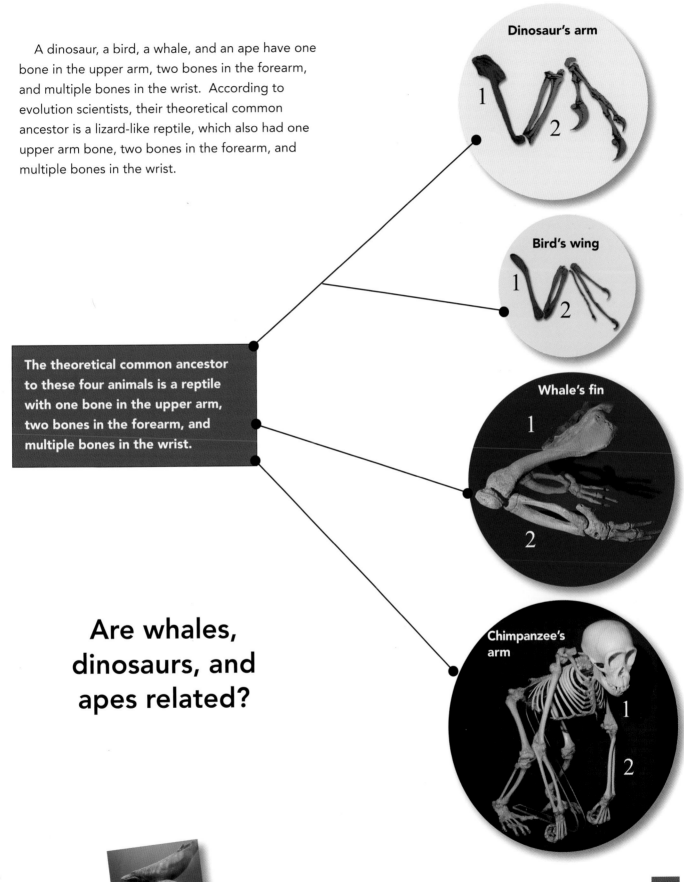

Dinosaur's arm

1

2

Bird's wing

1

2

The theoretical common ancestor to these four animals is a reptile with one bone in the upper arm, two bones in the forearm, and multiple bones in the wrist.

Whale's fin

1

2

Are whales, dinosaurs, and apes related?

Chimpanzee's arm

1

2

Many Times, Scientists Have Been Proven Wrong Using "Similarities" As Evidence for Evolution

Giant Panda

Red Panda

Pandas and Red Pandas

Scientists once firmly believed the red panda (above, center) and the giant panda (above, right) were closely related to each other because they have very similar anatomies.[1] Both have an extra thumb on their hands (above, left). Both have a V-shaped jaw (below, left). Both have similar teeth (below, left), and both have similar skulls (below, right). But when scientists tested the DNA from these two animals, they were surprised. The giant panda belongs to the bear family and the red panda is related to raccoons. In this instance, similarities were misleading and scientists were fooled.

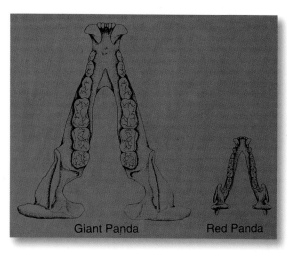

Giant Panda   Red Panda

Left and right:
*Both the panda and the red panda have a V-shaped jaw, similar teeth, similar skulls, and extra thumbs. Yet, they are **not** closely related.*

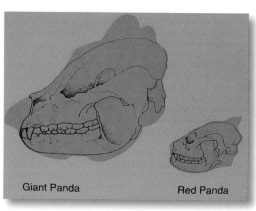

Giant Panda   Red Panda

All photos from St. Louis Zoo (except giant panda)
© 2007 AVC Inc., Photos by Debbie Werner

Seals and Sea Lions

Seals and sea lions are very similar in appearance. Both have front flippers and finned feet. They are so similar it is difficult to tell them apart. Because of their similarities, it was logical for scientists to believe they shared a common ancestor with similar features, namely front flippers and finned feet. Now some proponents of evolution believe seals descended from a skunk or otter, and sea lions evolved from a dog or bear, meaning they do not share a common ancestor after all.

Scientists who oppose evolution argue that these types of contradictions are precisely the reason why similarities cannot be used to prove evolution in other animals as well. If the similarities of seals and sea lions do not equate to evolution, then one can argue that similarities in other animals cannot be used as proof of evolution.

Seal

Sea Lion

Do Similarities Prove Evolution?

What Do You Think?

Similarities Are Subject to Observer Bias

Even scientists who support evolution have disagreements regarding which similarities are evidence for evolution and which are not. The hyrax, for example (as shown in center of next page), is a small, nine-pound furry mammal. Its teeth are similar to an elephant and a sea cow. Because of this, some scientists who advocate evolution believe the hyrax, the elephant, and the sea cow are "closely related" to each other, sharing a common ancestor with similar teeth. Other experts who endorse evolution focus on the ears of the hyrax instead, saying the ears of the hyrax are similar to those of a horse or a rhinoceros and is, therefore, more "closely related" to horses and rhinos.

Scientists opposing evolution do not believe that any of these animals shared a common ancestor. They propose that the similarities are either coincidental or the result of intentional design, as in the previous examples of the seal/sea lion and the red panda/giant panda. For them, the whole process of comparing similarities is highly subjective and open to observer bias.

Dr. Domning: *"Some scientists have challenged the hyrax, elephant, sea cow connection on the grounds of special anatomical features, like the shape of the teeth in the hyraxes, which is much like that of elephants. A particular sac-like structure inside the neck related to the eustachian tube, which resembles what you see in horses and tapirs, is not found in sea cows or elephants or other mammals. So you can find pieces of evidence like that, characters as we call them, that associate hyraxes with the horse, rhino, and tapir group. You can find other features that associate them with the elephants and the sea cows. In one commonly used approach, it boils down to a matter of counting characters on both sides and using what we call parsimony, the simplest explanation being that the relationship is wherever there is a greater number of characters in common.*

There are other ways of approaching the analysis as well. When we come to molecular evidence, likewise, it tends to be a matter of counting characters, counting resemblances in the molecules on both sides and see[ing] where the greater number of resemblances lies. Right now, I think the consensus is leaning towards putting the hyraxes with the elephants and the sea cows. But that can always change as we develop more sophisticated ways of analyzing the data." [2]

Above: *Dr. Daryl Domning, Paleontologist and Anatomist at Howard University, is an expert on the evolution of sea cows.*

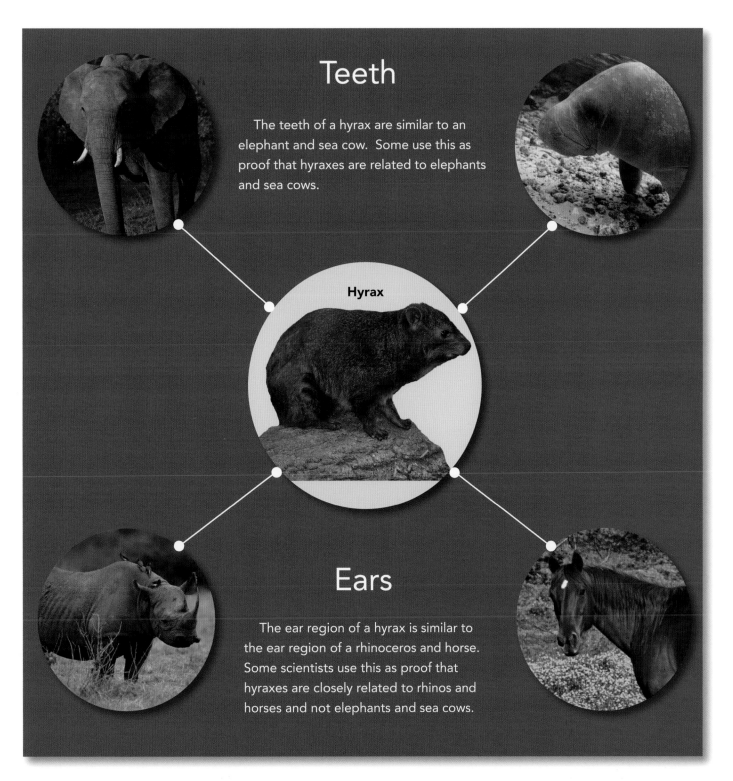

Teeth

The teeth of a hyrax are similar to an elephant and sea cow. Some use this as proof that hyraxes are related to elephants and sea cows.

Hyrax

Ears

The ear region of a hyrax is similar to the ear region of a rhinoceros and horse. Some scientists use this as proof that hyraxes are closely related to rhinos and horses and not elephants and sea cows.

Do similarities equate to evolution?

What Do You Think?

Why Do Unrelated Animals Also Have Similarities?

Scientists who oppose evolution ask how similarities can be used as evidence for evolution if so many "unrelated" animals also have similarities. How can you have it both ways? You cannot claim that similarities in animals are evidence for evolution in the face of unrelated animals also possessing similar features.

Scientists who support evolution explain similarities in disparate animals with the term "convergent" evolution. Dr. William Clemens, Professor of Integrated Biology and Curator of the Museum of Paleontology at the University of California Berkeley, calls convergent evolution a phenomenon and defines it in the caption below.

The following pages display other examples of totally unrelated animals with similarities. As shown on the next page, a shark (a fish), the extinct ichthyosaur (a reptile), and a dolphin (a mammal) all look very similar in their body forms. They all have a dorsal fin, a pectoral fin, and a finned tail. But, the theoretical common ancestor of two of these animals did not have a dorsal fin. According to evolutionists, ichthyosaurs evolved from a land reptile, similar to a lizard, and dolphins evolved from a hippopotamus-like animal. In this case, scientists ignored similarities in the dorsal fins and instead focused on other features such as fur, mammary glands, and the type of teeth.

Dr. Clemens: *"We speak of convergent evolution to describe phenomena where two groups of organisms, possibly distantly related, evolve into similar patterns and come to look like one another."* [3]

What does it mean when "unrelated" animals have similar features?

What Do You Think?

Unrelated Animals with Dorsal Fins

U. of Wisconsin, Madison, Geological Museum
© 2007 AVC Inc., Photo by Debbie Werner

A *fish* with fins

*Sharks (fish) are thought to have evolved from an unknown fish **with** a fin.*

St. Louis Zoo © 2007 AVC Inc.

A *reptile* with fins

*Ichthyosaurs (extinct aquatic reptiles) are thought to have evolved from an unknown land reptile **without** a fin.*

Milwaukee County Zoo, Wisconsin
© 2007 AVC Inc., Photo by Debbie Werner

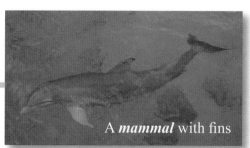

A *mammal* with fins

*Dolphins (aquatic mammals) are thought to have evolved from a hippopotamus-like animal **without** a fin.*

Unrelated Animals with Wings

Pterosaur with wings

Jura Museum, Germany
© 2007 AVC Inc., Photo by Debbie Werner

Bat with wings

South Australian Museum, Adelaide
© 2007 AVC Inc., Photo by Debbie Werner

Bird with wings

If unrelated animals have similar features, how can you use the evidence of similar features to support evolution?

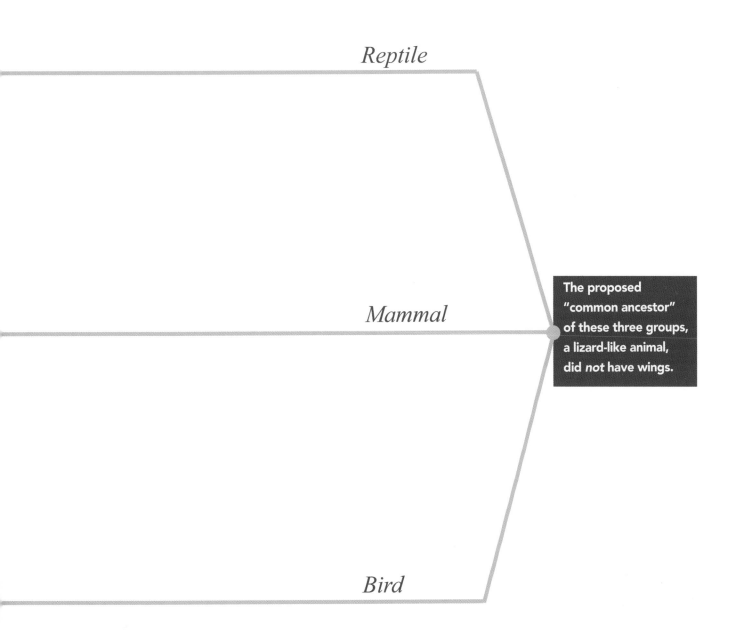

Reptile

Mammal

The proposed "common ancestor" of these three groups, a lizard-like animal, did *not* have wings.

Bird

What Do You Think?

Unrelated Animals with Eyes

The eye is a complex organ with a lens to focus light on the retina, a retina to receive the light on the back of the eye and convert it to an electrical impulse, and a nerve going to the brain to conduct the nerve impulses from the eye. Some eyes also have pupils to control the amount of light coming into the eye. The eye of an animal is more complex than the most sophisticated digital camera available today.

Evolution science teaches that more than 40 types of animals *independently* evolved eyes from a common ancestor without eyes, even in different phyla groups (such as molluscs, vertebrates, and arthropods).[4] According to the theory of evolution, the similarity of possessing an eye should be ignored and has nothing to do with evolution from a common ancestor with a similar trait.

Nautilis

Mollusc

Human

Vertebrate

The theoretical "common ancestor" did *not* have eyes.

Arthropod

Hoverfly

Unrelated Animals with Duckbills

Duckbills appear in unrelated animals, such as the duck-billed platypus (mammal), the duck-billed dinosaurs (reptile), and ducks (bird). Proponents of evolution believe that none of these animals evolved from a common ancestor with a duckbill. They believe these animals evolved from a common ancestor without a duckbill.

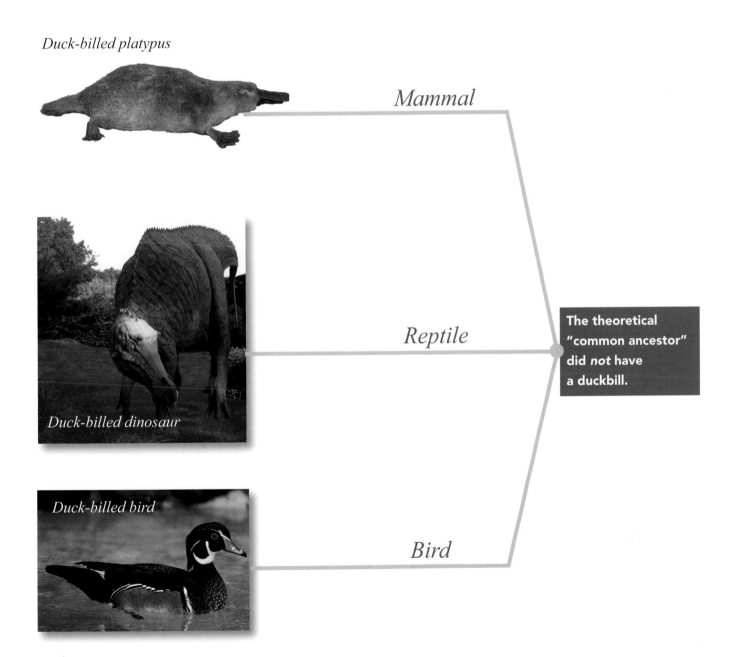

Duck-billed platypus

Mammal

Duck-billed dinosaur

Reptile

Duck-billed bird

Bird

The theoretical "common ancestor" did *not* have a duckbill.

Unrelated Animals with Eye Rings

Another example of similarities in unrelated animals is the bony eye ring present in some birds, some aquatic reptiles, and some fish. Scientists who champion evolution do not believe these animals evolved from a common ancestor with a bony eye ring.

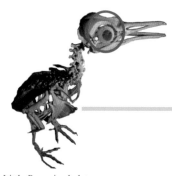

Bird

Little Penguin skeleton,
South Australian Museum
© 2007 AVC Inc., Photo by Debbie Werner

Reptile

The theoretical "common ancestor" did *not* have an eye ring.

Ichthyosaur fossil, Museum Victoria, Melbourne
© 2007 AVC Inc., Photo by Debbie Werner

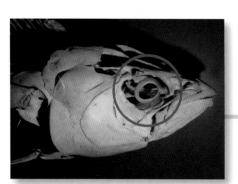

Fish

Bluefin Tuna skeleton, South Australian Museum
© 2007 AVC Inc., Photo by Debbie Werner

Unrelated Animals with Head Crests

The southern cassowary bird is a large flightless bird with a head crest that lives today in the dense rain forests in Queensland, Australia. *Oviraptor*, a dinosaur, also had a crest on the top of its head. Scientists who support evolution believe that these animals evolved from an animal *without* a head crest.

Do similarities equate to evolution from a common ancestor?

A cassowary, a modern bird with head crest

Bird

The theoretical "common ancestor" of these two animals did *not* have a head crest.

An oviraptor, a dinosaur with head crest

Reptile

CHAPTER 5

Which of These Three Animals Do Evolution Scientists Believe Are Most Closely Related?

Placental Mole

South Australian Museum, Adelaide
© 2007 AVC Inc., Photo by Debbie Werner

Pouched Mole

Humpback whale

Answer: The whale and the (placental) mole.

Which of These Three Animals Do Evolution Scientists Believe Are Most Closely Related?

Placental Mouse

South Australian Museum, Adelaide
© 2007 AVC Inc., Photo by Debbie Werner

Marsupial Mouse

Horse

Answer: The horse and the (placental) mouse.

As can be seen in these pictures, the appearance of a placental mouse (which does not have a pouch) and a marsupial mouse (which has an external pouch to raise and suckle its young) are strikingly similar in appearance, yet evolution scientists do not consider these animals to be closely related. The same is true for the placental mole and the marsupial mole. Instead, evolution scientists believe a placental horse is more closely related to a common, placental mouse, and a placental whale is more closely related to a common placental mole. It is examples such as these that prompt scientists who oppose evolution to suggest that body similarities cannot be used as evidence for evolution.

Play Video!

Since Darwin's Time Until Now, Scientists Have Debated the Meaning of Similarities in Animals

Charles Darwin, father of the modern theory of evolution

"But it would in most cases be extremely rash to attribute to convergence a close and general similarity of structure in the modified descendants of widely distinct forms." [5]

— **Charles Darwin**

"In other words, each investigator decides on the basis of an assumed evolutionary pathway which, a priori, he or she prefers, and then interprets the evidence accordingly, invoking whatever reversals, parallel evolution, or convergent evolution, as the scheme may require. Such theories are so plastic that they are rendered non-falsifiable even if false, and thus they cannot be called scientific theories." [6]

— **Dr. Duane Gish**

Dr. Duane Gish, modern opponent of the theory of evolution

THE FOSSIL RECORD AND DARWIN'S PREDICTION

Darwin Recognized That the Fossil Record in His Day Did Not Match What His Theory Predicted.

The fossil record is the documented collection of animal and plant fossils known worldwide. Darwin recognized that this particular body of evidence was of pivotal importance for eventually proving his theory. For that reason, a closer look at the fossil record is necessary to better assess the theory of evolution.

When Charles Darwin wrote *The Origin of Species*, he surprisingly included a two-chapter apology (*Difficulties of the Theory* and *On the Imperfection of the Geological Record*) in which he recognized that the fossils collected by scientists prior to 1859 did *not* correspond with his theory of evolution. While fossils of invertebrates, fish, reptiles, birds, mammals, and humans had been discovered, the fossil record still lacked sufficient evidence of invertebrates changing into fish; of fish changing into

amphibians; and of reptiles changing into birds and mammals. In other words, there were "gaps" in the fossil record. The transitional forms between the animal groups (also referred to as intermediates or ancestors) were, in large part, missing.

Darwin acknowledged this discrepancy in *The Origin of Species*. He wrote: *"Why then is not every geological formation and every stratum full of such intermediate links? Geology assuredly does not reveal any such finely-graduated organic chain; and this, perhaps, is the most obvious and serious objection which can be urged against the theory."* [1]

Interestingly, Darwin formulated his theory despite what the fossils disclosed. Ideally, a scientist develops a theory from patterns of "known" data, but Darwin did the opposite. He predicted the data would be found later.

Watch DVD!

From *Evolution*: *The Grand Experiment* video series, Episode 1

Dr. Andy Knoll
Harvard University

Dr. Andrew Knoll, Professor of Biology, Harvard University

*"Darwin devotes two chapters of **The Origin** [of Species] to the fossil record. And you might think that's because Darwin, like most of his intellectual descendants, would have seen the fossil record as the confirmation of his theory. That you could really see, directly document, the evolution of life from the Cambrian to the present. But, in fact, when you read **The Origin** [of Species], it turns out that Darwin's two chapters are a carefully worded apology in which he argues that natural selection is correct despite the fact that the fossils don't particularly support it."* [2]

—— **Dr. Knoll**

Previous page: *Several acres of fossil rhinoceros bones were found in Agate Springs, Nebraska. These fossils are on display at the Harvard Museum of Paleontology.*

What Should the Fossil Record Show if Evolution Is True?

The fact that Darwin predicted the fossil record would eventually bear out his theory of evolution is of great importance because it gives us a framework by which to judge evolution. The fossil record will never be complete, but if it were, what should be found if Darwin's theory was right?

If evolution *did* occur, and if the fossil record was nearly complete, the fossil record would reflect many of the intermediate or ancestral forms of an animal slowly changing into a different type of animal over time. In essence, the theory of evolution "predicts" such evidence will be found in the fossil record.

In order to use the fossil record to prove or dis-prove evolution, one would have to choose two very dissimilar appearing animals and then look for fossil intermediates. Finding intermediate ancestors between two disparate animals, such as a mouse and a bat, would be of more significance than finding intermediate ancestors of already similar appearing animals, such as a dog and a wolf. Darwin's theory predicted that very dissimilar animals changed from one into another.

For the sake of discussion, let's say that mice evolved into bats. If this occurred, you would expect to find fossil mice and fossil bats, along with all the transitional forms (or intermediate animals) between the two, in the fossil record. A hypothetical example follows:

Animal A (below) is the first step of a mouse changing into a bat. The animal looks like a mouse, but its arms are now longer than its legs. It will need these long arms to form the wings. **Animal B** is very unusual looking. It looks something like a mouse, but its fingers are longer than its elongated arms. These fingers will act as struts for the eventual wings of the bat. **Animal C** is developing enlarged muscles in new locations on its arms. A flying animal needs its strongest muscles for the movement of the wings. **Animal D** is developing a membrane on each arm. The membrane is not developed enough to allow the animal to fly because it is not yet attached to the body and back legs. Rather, the membrane is more like a loose cape. (See the picture of a bat's wing membrane below.) **Animal E** is halfway to becoming a bat. It has wings, which are attached to the body, but the animal still cannot fly because the muscles for flying have not yet completely developed. **Animal F's** knees are starting to turn outward, like a modern bat's knees. Walking is getting more difficult than before because of this awkward change in the legs and the extremely long fingers and arms. **Animal G's** knees are facing backward like a bat's knees. **Animal H** is nearly all bat, but not quite. Its bones are still solid, rendering the animal too heavy to fly. Flying animals have hollow bones to make them lighter. This process has yet to take place before the final step of evolution into a bat.

Predicted Intermediates
A   B   C   D   E   F   G   H

Mouse

Theoretical animals A through H evolving over millions of years.

Bat

What Should the Fossil Record Show if Evolution Is False?

I f evolution did *not* occur, and if the fossil record was essentially complete, only mice and bats would appear in the fossil record. There would be no intermediate animals between mice and bats.

Fossil bat, Messel Museum, Germany
© 2007 AVC Inc., Photo by Debbie Werner

Fossil Layers
Millions of years ago (MYA)*

Bat	Many Fossils
Animal H	No Fossils
Animal G	No Fossils
Animal F	No Fossils
Animal E	No Fossils
Animal D	No Fossils
Animal C	No Fossils
Animal B	No Fossils
Animal A	No Fossils
Mouse	Many Fossils

Fossil Layers

Gap
(No intermediates)

*Scientists do not agree on the age or number of years it took to deposit these fossil layers. This is a theoretical construct to evaluate the theory of evolution.

Fossil mice and fossil bats have been found all over the world.

Fossil mammal, Carnegie Museum of Natural History
© 2007 AVC Inc., Photo by Carl Werner

Since Darwin's Time, Close to "One Billion" Fossils Have Been Collected.

Fossil Counts:

Number of fossils in museums worldwide: [3]	1,000,000,000-
Fossils in Natural History Museum, London: [3]	9,000,000
Fossils in University of Nebraska State Museum: [3]	8,500,000
Fossils in American Museum of Natural History: [3]	5,000,000+
Fossils in Natural History Museum, Melbourne: [4]	4,000,000

Fossil Invertebrates:

Fossil invertebrates in museums worldwide: [3]	750,000,000+
Fossil invertebrates, University of Nebraska State Museum: [5]	7,500,000
Fossil invertebrates, American Museum of Natural History: [3]	4,000,000
Fossil invertebrates, Yale Peabody Museum: [6]	4,000,000
Fossil invertebrates, University of Michigan Museum of Paleontology: [7]	2,000,000
Fossil invertebrates, Florida Museum of Natural History: [8]	1,060,000+
Fossil insects in museums worldwide. [3]	1,000,000+

Fossil Vertebrates:

Fossil vertebrate specimens, University of Nebraska State Museum: [9]	1,000,000+
Fossil vertebrate specimens, American Museum of Natural History: [3]	1,000,000+
Fossil vertebrate specimens, Florida Museum of Natural History: [10]	335,000
Fossil vertebrate specimens, University of California, Berkeley: [11]	189,000
Fossil vertebrate specimens, University of Michigan Museum of Paleontology: [12]	80,000
Fossil vertebrate specimens, Yale Peabody Museum: [13]	70,000
Fossil vertebrate specimens, Raymond M. Alf (High School) Museum, California: [14]	44,000
Fossil whale specimens in museums worldwide: [3]	2,000,000
Fossil fish in museums worldwide: [3]	500,000+/-
Fossil bird specimens in museums worldwide: [3]	200,000+
Fossil dinosaurs in museums worldwide: [3]	100,000+/-
Fossil turtle specimens in museums worldwide: [3]	100,000
Fossil bats in museums worldwide: [3]	1,000+
Fossil flying reptiles (pterosaurs): [3]	1,000+/-

Fossil Plants:

Fossil plants in museums worldwide:	1,000,000+
Fossil plant specimens, Florida Museum of Natural History: [15]	300,000
Fossil plant specimens, Yale Peabody Museum: [16]	150,000+

The Fossil Record: Soft-bodied Organisms

Thousands of Fossil Bacteria

Used with permission,
Dr. Andrew Knoll,
Harvard University

1,000,000 Fossil Plants

Ulrich's Fossil Quarry, Fossil Butte,
Wyoming © 2007 AVC Inc.,
Photo by Debbie Werner

Fossil Leaf

South Dakota School of
Mines & Technology,
Museum of Geology
© 2007 AVC Inc.,
Photo by Debbie Werner

Fossil Embryos

Used with permission,
Dr. Andrew Knoll,
Harvard University

> Since Darwin's time, millions of "difficult to fossilize" bacteria, soft-bodied animals, and plants have been discovered.

Background photo of dinosaur skin from South Dakota
School of Mines & Technology, Museum of Geology
© 2007 AVC Inc., Photo by Carl Werner

Fossil Worms

[WORM CA

Museum Victoria, Melbourne,
Australia © 2007 AVC Inc.,
Photo by Debbie Werner

Fossil Cattails

Fossil Fish Eggs

Milwaukee Public Museum, Wisconsin
© 2007 AVC Inc., Photo by Debbie Werner

Chicago Field
Museum, Illinois
© 2007 AVC Inc.,
Photo by Debbie Werner

Fossil Flowers

Fossil Jellyfish

U. of Wisconsin, Madison,
Geological Museum
© 2007 AVC Inc.,
Photo by Debbie Werner

Sam Noble Oklahoma Museum of Science and Natural History,
Oklahoma © 2007 AVC Inc., Photo by Debbie Werner

Even "difficult to fossilize" embryos, worms, fish eggs, jellyfish, and soft-petaled flowers have been collected.

The Fossil Record: Invertebrates

Blastoids

Carnegie Museum of Natural History © 2007 AVC Inc., Photo by Carl Werner

Marine Snails

U. of Wisconsin, Madison,
Geological Museum
© 2007 AVC Inc.,
Photos by Debbie Werner

Cockles

Ammonites

Scallops

Carnegie Museum of Natural History
© 2007 AVC Inc.,
Photo by Carl Werner

So far, over 750,000,000 of the most representative invertebrates have been collected.

See Appendix A:
The Number of Fossils

Museum Victoria, Melbourne,
Australia © 2007 AVC Inc.,
Photo by Debbie Werner

Shellfish

Trilobites

Sea Star

U. of Wisconsin, Madison, Geological Museum
© 2007 AVC Inc., Photo by Debbie Werner

U. of Nebraska State Museum, Lincoln © 2007 AVC Inc., Photo by Debbie Werner

**1,000,000
Insects**

Jura Museum, Germany
© 2007 AVC Inc.,
Photo by Debbie Werner

Crinoids

**Fossilized insects, clams,
sea stars, trilobites, and
crinoids have been found
in great abundance.**

Milwaukee Public Museum, Wisconsin
© 2007 AVC Inc., Photo by Debbie Werner

The Fossil Record: Vertebrates

1,000 Fossil Bats

Messel Museum, Germany
© 2007 AVC Inc., Photo by Debbie Werner

Exhibit Museum of Natural History,
U. of Michigan, Ann Arbor © 2007 AVC Inc.,
Photo by Debbie Werner

4,000 Fossil Whales

500,000 Fossil Fish

Ulrich's Fossil Quarry, Fossil Butte, Wyoming
© 2007 AVC Inc., Photo by Debbie Werner

Over one million of the most representative vertebrates have been collected.

200,000+ Fossil Bird Specimens

Jura Museum, Germany
© 2007 AVC Inc.,
Photo by Debbie Werner

Background photo of fossil rhinoceros bones
from Harvard Museum of Paleontology
© 2007 AVC Inc., Photo by Debbie Werner

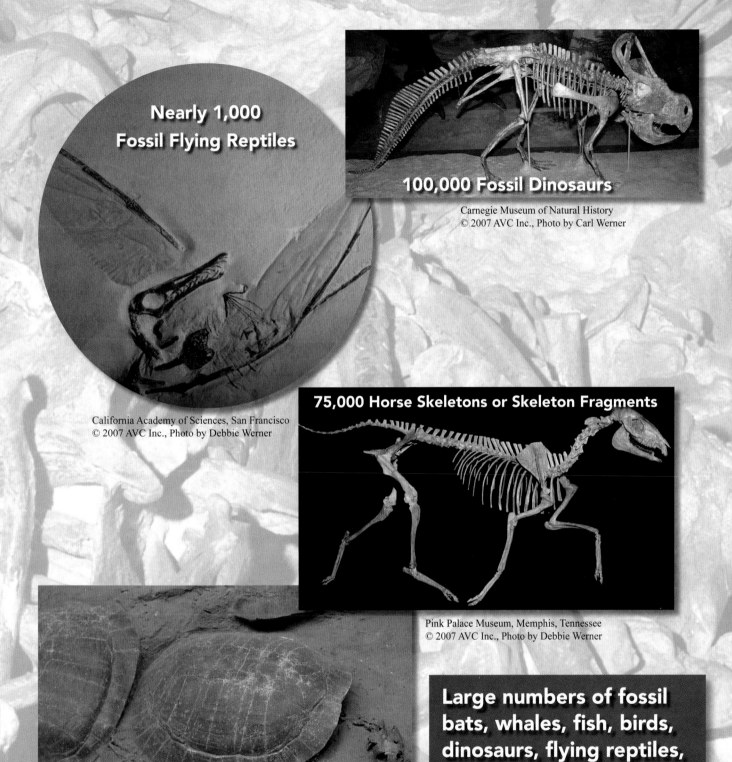

Nearly 1,000 Fossil Flying Reptiles

100,000 Fossil Dinosaurs

Carnegie Museum of Natural History
© 2007 AVC Inc., Photo by Carl Werner

California Academy of Sciences, San Francisco
© 2007 AVC Inc., Photo by Debbie Werner

75,000 Horse Skeletons or Skeleton Fragments

Pink Palace Museum, Memphis, Tennessee
© 2007 AVC Inc., Photo by Debbie Werner

100,000 Fossil Turtle Specimens

U. of Nebraska State Museum, Lincoln © 2007 AVC Inc., Photo by Debbie Werner

Large numbers of fossil bats, whales, fish, birds, dinosaurs, flying reptiles, land mammals, and turtles have been collected.

**See Appendix A:
The Number of Fossils**

What Are Scientists Today Saying about the Fossil Record?

"In spite of the many factors that prevent fossilization, the fossil record is remarkably comprehensive. On the basis of this impressive record, paleontologists have been able to piece together a history of past life that is balanced and largely accurate." [17]

— Dr. Harold Levin, Professor of Geology, Washington University

Dr. James Kirkland, Utah's State Paleontologist, digging for fossil dinosaur bones

At Bone Cabin Quarry in eastern Wyoming: *"Fossils were so plentiful that he [a sheepherder who lived at this site], had built his cabin out of the long bones of dinosaurs."* [19]

— Richard Milner, author of *The Encyclopedia of Evolution: Humanity's Search for Its Origins*

"This is one of the most amazing things for the layperson...the extent of the fossil record...Now in any museum around the world you can see millions of fossils. This museum alone has four million fossils in its paleontology collection, and we're only one museum in Australia." [4]

— Dr. John Long, Paleontologist and Chief of Science, Museum Victoria, Melbourne, Australia

At the Gobi Dessert: *"For a paleontologist, it was truly like being a kid in a candy store. The ground was littered with fossils of dinosaurs, primitive mammals, lizards, and nests of eggs."* [20]

— Dr. Michael Novacek, Curator of Vertebrate Paleontology, American Museum of Natural History, New York

"At Landslide Butte, the abundance is almost embarrassing. We already have hundreds and hundreds of baby [dinosaur] bones. There are spots where, without even digging, you can literally shovel up the baby bones." [18]

— Dr. John Horner, Paleontologist, Curator of Paleontology, Museum of the Rockies, Montana

"In the Judith River formation, [near Glacier National Park]...you step on fossils all the time, and you can see them when you're standing up." [21]

— Dr. John Horner, Paleontologist, Curator of Paleontology, Museum of the Rockies, Montana

The Fossil Record Is Comprehensive, Balanced, Accurate, and Impressive.

*"The fossil record, as held in all the world's major museums, government organisations, universities and private collections, now tallies **close to a billion** fossil specimens."*[22]

**— Dr. John Long, Paleontologist and Chief of Science,
Museum Victoria, Melbourne, Australia**

"Judging from the concentration of bones in various pits, there were up to thirty million fossil fragments in that area. At a conservative estimate, we had discovered the tomb of 10,000 dinosaurs."[23]

— Dr. John Horner, Paleontologist, Curator of Paleontology, Museum of the Rockies, Montana

"The Karroo formation in South Africa alone contains fossil remains of about 800 billion animals."[25]

— Richard Milner, author of The Encyclopedia of Evolution: Humanity's Search for Its Origins

The Green River formation in Wyoming *"covers hundreds of square miles and literally contains billions and billions of fishes that have yet to be excavated."*[24]

— Dr. Lance Grande, Curator, Department of Geology, Chicago Field Museum

"...Mary Leakey and her team excavated 55,000 square feet [at Olduvai site in Africa]. A total of 37,127 artifacts and 32,378 fossils were recorded — that second figure does not include over 14,000 rodent fossils, plus fragmentary finds of birds and frogs!"[26]

— Delta Willis, author of The Leakey Family: Leaders in the Search for Human Origins

How Good Is the Fossil Record?

In order to satisfactorily answer this question, one would have to evaluate the completeness of the fossil record. One possible way to do this is to count how many fossils from each type of animal have been collected to date.

Another possible way to assess the completeness of the fossil record is to calculate the percentage of those animals living today that have also been found as fossils. In other words, if the fossil record is comprised of a high percentage of animals that are living today, then the fossil record could be viewed as being fairly complete; that is, most animals that have lived on the earth have been fossilized and discovered.

The chart below depicts the percentage of fossilization for two classifications of land animals living today. Of the 43 living land animal *orders*, such as carnivores (Carnivora), rodents (Rodentia), bats (Chiroptera), and apes (Primates), nearly all, or 97.7 percent, have been found as fossils. This means at least one example from each animal order has been collected as a fossil. Of the 178 living land animal *families*, such as dogs (Canidae), bears (Ursidae), hyenas (Hyaenidae), and cats (Felidae), 87.8 percent have been found as fossils. The percentages of fossilization depicted below were calculated prior to 1985. The fossil record has improved dramatically since that time; therefore, the percentages would obviously increase.

The question remains: Are nearly a billion collected fossils adequate to judge whether evolution is true or not true?

The next nine chapters will provide a more in-depth investigation of the fossil record for individual animal groups, such as invertebrates, fish, bats, seals and sea lions, flying reptiles, dinosaurs, whales, birds, and flowering plants. In each chapter, you will be given a chance to evaluate if the fossil record matches Darwin's prediction, that as more fossils were discovered, more intermediate animals would also be found to support his theory of one animal slowly changing into another.

Number of living orders of terrestrial vertebrates.	43
Number of living orders of terrestrial vertebrates *found as fossils*.	42
Percentage fossilized.	97.7%
Number of living families of terrestrial vertebrates.	329
Number of living families of terrestrial vertebrates *found as fossils*.	261
Percentage fossilized.	79.1%
Number of living families of terrestrial vertebrates, excluding birds.	178
Number of living families of terrestrial vertebrates *found as fossils*, excluding birds.	156
Percentage fossilized.	87.8%

Chart information from *Evolution: A Theory in Crisis* by Michael Denton, 1985.[27]

THE
FOSSIL RECORD
OF INVERTEBRATES

A

B

Invertebrates

C

E

Clockwise from top left:
A: Crinoid sheet, Kansas
B: Crinoid, Iowa
C: Trilobite, Utah
D: Lobster-like crustacean,
Solnhofen, Germany
E: Crayfish, Solnhofen,
Germany

D

Invertebrates are animals without a backbone or spinal cord. The six major invertebrate phyla groups include shellfish (clams, oysters, etc.), arthropods (shrimp, trilobites, etc.), echinoderms (sea stars, sea urchins, etc.), corals, sponges, and worms. Although more than 750,000,000 invertebrate fossils have been collected [1]—including fossils of bacteria, soft-bodied jellyfish, worms, soft sponges, and soft corals—there are no evolutionary ancestors for any invertebrate phyla group. [2] The sudden appearance of the phyla groups in the lower (Cambrian/Ediacaran) fossil layers is called the "Cambrian Explosion" and is a major problem for the theory of evolution. [2]

Scientists who support evolution suggest ancestors of the invertebrate phyla groups existed but were soft-bodied animals and less likely to fossilize; this is why these invertebrate groups appear without ancestors.

Scientists who oppose evolution point out that thousands of fossils of soft-bodied animals (jellyfish, worms, sponges, soft corals, etc.) have been found in the lowest fossil layers (Cambrian/Ediacaran) plus fossils of microscopic bacteria. They cite the absence of theoretical evolutionary ancestors of the invertebrate phyla groups—in light of a vast fossil record, including fossils of soft-bodied animals (and bacteria)—as evidence that evolution did not occur.

Previous page: *Fossil sea stars on display at the Carnegie Museum of Paleontology, Pittsburgh.*

CHAPTER 7

California Academy of Sciences,
San Francisco © 2007 AVC Inc.,
Photo by Debbie Werner

California Academy of Sciences,
San Francisco © 2007 AVC Inc.,
Photo by Debbie Werner

California Academy of Sciences,
San Francisco © 2007 AVC Inc.,
Photo by Debbie Werner

Clockwise from top left:
F: Gastropod shellfish
G: Sea star, Butte
    County, California
H: Sand dollar,
    Baja, California
I: Trilobite
J: Ammonite shellfish,
    Germany
K: Crab, Verona, Italy
L: Sand dollar, Egypt

California Academy of Sciences,
San Francisco © 2007 AVC Inc.,
Photo by Debbie Werner

U. of Wisconsin, Madison, Geological Museum
© 2007 AVC Inc., Photo by Debbie Werner

Mississippi Petrified Forest and Museum
© 2007 AVC Inc., Photo by Debbie Werner

California Academy of Sciences,
San Francisco © 2007 AVC Inc.,
Photo by Debbie Werner

*More than 750,000,000 invertebrate fossils
have been collected by museums.*

What's the Problem with Trilobites?

Fossil Layers
Millions of years ago (MYA)*

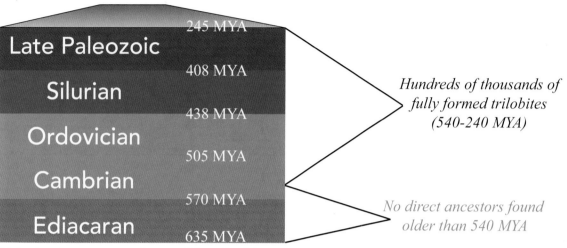

Late Paleozoic	245 MYA
Silurian	408 MYA
Ordovician	438 MYA
Cambrian	505 MYA
Ediacaran	570 MYA
	635 MYA

Hundreds of thousands of fully formed trilobites (540-240 MYA)

No direct ancestors found older than 540 MYA

*Scientists do not agree on the age of these fossil layers.

Trilobites are representative of one of the major problems with the fossil record in that they appear suddenly in the Cambrian fossil layers without a trace of an evolutionary ancestor. Yet over 15,000 species of trilobites have been collected. [2,3,4] If evolution occurred and if the fossil record is reflective of the past, then the animals that evolved into trilobites should have been discovered by now. Proponents of evolution imagine that the ancestors of trilobites would have had soft bodies. Despite finding thousands of other unrelated soft-bodied fossilized invertebrates in the lowest layers, not one soft-bodied fossil has been declared the uncontested ancestor of trilobites. [2,5,6] Remember, Darwin believed his theory would be upheld as more fossils were found. But now, hundreds of thousands of fossil trilobites, possibly millions, have been collected by museums, but no direct ancestors have been found. [2,5,6] Does this indicate there is a problem with the theory of evolution? Or is there a problem with the fossil record?

Dr. Andy Knoll
Harvard University

"What bothered Darwin about the fossil record more than anything else was the pattern of paleontology that we've been talking about... the oldest fossils you see are both diverse and complex, [such as] fabulously complicated things like trilobites." [5]

— **Dr. Knoll**

Dr. Andrew Knoll, Paleontologist and Professor of Biology, Harvard University.

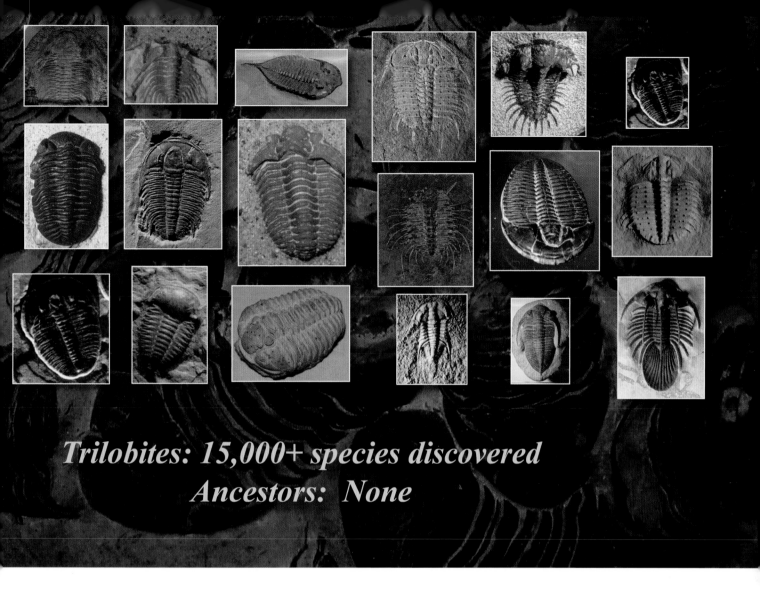

Trilobites: 15,000+ species discovered
Ancestors: None

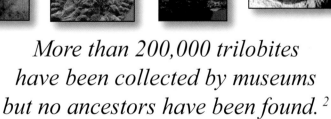

More than 200,000 trilobites
have been collected by museums
but no ancestors have been found. [2]

At the *"beginning of the Cambrian Explosion proper...one finds brachiopods* [shellfish] *and gastropods* [shellfish]*...We also see trilobites for the first time."* [6]

— Dr. Valentine

Dr. James Valentine, Professor Emeritus, University of California, Berkeley, Department of Integrated Biology.

Brachiopod shellfish

Gastropod shellfish

Fossil Layers
Millions of years ago (MYA)*

Devonian	
Silurian	408 MYA
Ordovician	438 MYA
Cambrian	505 MYA
Ediacaran	570 MYA

Hundreds of millions of invertebrates appear fully formed in these layers.

No direct ancestors found in Ediacaran layer below

*Scientists do not agree on the age or number of years it took to deposit these fossil layers. This is a theoretical construct to evaluate the theory of evolution.

Author's Note: Bacteria, sea pens, and other soft-bodied fossils are found in the Ediacaran layers. But these fossils also appear fully formed, without ancestors, and are not the ancestors of the fossils in the Cambrian layer above.

Darwin's Enigma: No Ancestors

Below, left: *Large numbers of these huge fossil sea pens (soft corals) have been discovered in Australia, in the Ediacaran layer — the layer in which fossil multicellular organisms first appear. No ancestors for these soft corals have ever been found, thus creating a large gap in the fossil record. Compare this fossil to a modern sea pen* (**below, right**).

South Australian Museum, Adelaide © 2007 AVC Inc., Photo by Carl Werner

Did Invertebrates Evolve?

"Despite 30 years of research on Ediacaran fossils, there are very few, if any, unambiguous ancestors of things that appear in the Cambrian." [5]

— Dr. Knoll

The problem of the sudden appearance of invertebrates occurs not only for hard-bodied animals, such as trilobites and shellfish, but also for soft-bodied animals, including jellyfish, sea pens, and sponges.

U. of Nebraska State Museum, Lincoln
© 2007 AVC Inc., Photo by Debbie Werner

U. of Wisconsin, Madison, Geological Museum
© 2007 AVC Inc., Photo by Debbie Werner

Above, left: *This jellyfish was found in the Cambrian layers. No ancestors were found below this layer.* **Above, right:** *This sponge, also found in the Cambrian layer, appears without ancestors.*

THE
FOSSIL RECORD
OF FISH

Fossilized fish are rather abundant. The number of fossil fish collected by museums totals 500,000.[1] Many of these fossils are exquisitely preserved with all of the bones, scales, and fins readily apparent. Even the boneless stingrays and sharks are found beautifully preserved at times. (See stingray on next page.)

According to many experts, each fish family appears suddenly in the fossil record. (See interview on page 98 and Appendix C.) The immediate appearance of each family is a difficulty for evolution. Fish, which are vertebrates, are thought to have evolved from the invertebrates. To date, more than 750,000,000 fossil invertebrates and nearly 500,000 fossil fish are represented in the fossil record.[1] Yet, given these amazing numbers, the formation of a vertebral column has not been observed in the fossil record. Animals are either vertebrates or invertebrates, and no transitional forms have been found between the two groups.

Scientists who support evolution give examples of fish *within* a family that appear to be ancestors of each other. Scientists who oppose evolution point out that lining up different types of fish within the same fish family in order to demonstrate evolution is presumptuous because you are lining up similar types of fish. They suggest that if the evolution truly occurred, one should be able to witness the transformation from invertebrates to vertebrate fish. One should also see one fish family slowly changing into another.

Proposed Fish Evolution

Common ancestor of fish not found.

"0" on chart means fossils not found
(See Appendix C)

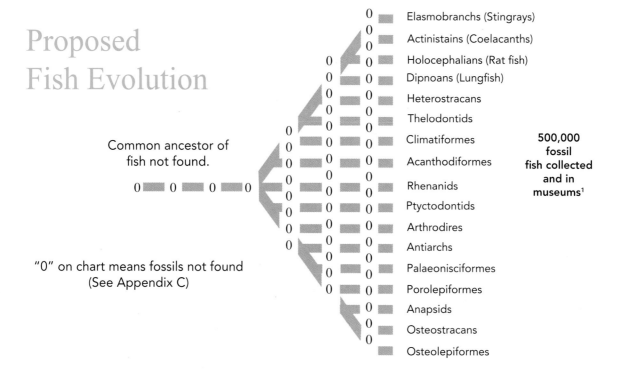

500,000 fossil fish collected and in museums[1]

- Elasmobranchs (Stingrays)
- Actinistains (Coelacanths)
- Holocephalians (Rat fish)
- Dipnoans (Lungfish)
- Heterostracans
- Thelodontids
- Climatiformes
- Acanthodiformes
- Rhenanids
- Ptyctodontids
- Arthrodires
- Antiarchs
- Palaeonisciformes
- Porolepiformes
- Anapsids
- Osteostracans
- Osteolepiformes

Dr. Duane Gish,
"Evolution, The Fossils Still Say No"

"Every major kind of fish that we know anything about appears fully formed; there is not a trace of an ancestor for any of these creatures, and there are no transitional forms suggesting that these major kinds of fishes evolved from a common ancestor." [2]

— **Dr. Gish**

Dr. Duane Gish is an opponent of evolution and is the author of ***Evolution: The Fossils Still Say No!***

Previous page: *Fossil fish on display at the Wyoming Dinosaur Center, Thermopolis.*

A

Ulrich's Fossil Quarry,
Fossil Butte, Wyoming
© 2007 AVC Inc.,
Photo by Debbie Werner

B

Ulrich's Fossil Quarry,
Fossil Butte, Wyoming
© 2007 AVC Inc.,
Photo by Debbie Werner

J

Wyoming Dinosaur Center, Thermopolis
© 2007 AVC Inc., Photo by Debbie Werner

500,000 Fish
in Museums

C

Ulrich's Fossil Quarry, Fossil Butte, Wyoming
© 2007 AVC Inc., Photo by Debbie Werner

I

Jura Museum, Germany © 2007 AVC Inc.,
Photo by Debbie Werner

Clockwise from top left:
A: Sheet of fossil fish,
Knightia and *Diplomystus*
B: *Priscacara*
C: Garfish
D: Stingray
E: Coelacanth, *Holophagus*
F: Guitar fish
G: *Gyrodus*
H: Pycnodont,
Eomesodon gibbosus
I: Pycnodont,
Mesturus verrucosus
J: *Amblypterus*
macropterus,
Germany

D

Fossil Butte National Monument, Wyoming
© 2007 AVC Inc., Photo by Debbie Werner

H

Jura Museum, Germany © 2007 AVC Inc.,
Photo by Debbie Werner

E

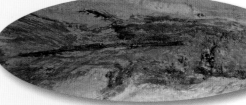

California Academy of Sciences,
San Francisco © 2007 AVC Inc.,
Photo by Debbie Werner

G

Wyoming Dinosaur Center, Thermopolis
© 2007 AVC Inc., Photo by Debbie Werner

F

Jura Museum, Germany
© 2007 AVC Inc.,
Photo by Debbie Werner

*The ancestors of each
fish group are missing.*

Dr. John Long, Paleontologist and Head of Science at the Museum Victoria, Melbourne, Australia. Dr. Long is a strong proponent of evolution and author of the book *The Rise of Fishes: 500 Million Years of Evolution.*

Watch DVD!

Dr. Long's Comments on the Evidence for Fish Evolution

Museum Victoria, Melbourne, Australia
© 2007 AVC Inc., Photo by Debbie Werner

How good is the fossil record of invertebrates?

Dr. Long: *"The fossil record of invertebrates back 500 million years ago is very good, with soft-bodied organisms."* [3]

How good is the fossil record of fish?

Dr. Long: *"I've visited some of the biggest museums in the world to study their fossil fish collections, such as the Natural History Museum in London and the American Museum of Natural History, and I'd say, conservatively, there'd be hundreds of thousands, probably maybe up to half a million [fossil fish in these museum collections]."* [3]

What is the evidence of fish (vertebrates) evolving from invertebrates?

Dr. Long: *"...the transition from spineless invertebrates to the first backboned fishes is still **shrouded in mystery**, and many theories abound as to how the changes took place."* [4] *"There are still many different opinions as to which invertebrate group may have given rise to the first vertebrates or first fishes...I'm sure that in the next 10 years or so we'll answer this mystery."* [3]

Which jawless fish evolved into the first jawed fish?

Dr. Long: *"Well, there's a lot of debate over the origins and diversity of the first fishes...That's still one of the **great mysteries** and problems to be solved in vertebrate evolution, the origins and interrelationships of these early jawed fishes."* [3]

What fish did sharks (cartilaginous fish) evolve from?

Dr. Long: *"The **mystery** remains as to how sharks first evolved...The current fossil evidence is too incomplete to answer this question."* [5] *"The origin of sharks are still a **mystery**."* [6]

What fish did the spiny fin fish evolve from?

Dr. Long: *"The structure of the head and the shape of the body in the earliest complete acanthodian [spiny fin] fossils tell us little about which other group of fishes they may have evolved from or collaterally with."* [7]

Where did the bony fish come from?

Dr. Long: *"The origin of the bony fishes is also **shrouded in mystery**...So, there's still **mystery** and some debate over where the true bony fishes came from...The **controversy** is that the origins of the bony fishes could be linked to either the [spiny fin] acanthodian fishes or the sharks or the placoderms...So, all we really know at the moment is that the bony fishes came from one of these primitive groups, but we don't really know which one."* [3]

After 150 years of research and collecting 500,000 fish, have the origins of fish been elucidated?

Dr. Long: *"The evolution of fish is still very much **debated** amongst paleontologists...I think that within the next ten years, we'll probably get some resolution on the origin and interrelationship of the major groups of fishes."* [3]

THE
FOSSIL RECORD
OF BATS

No Evolutionary Ancestors of Bats Have Been Discovered!

Scientists have found over 1,000 fossil bats. [1] If evolution is true, and with such an abundant fossil record, one would expect to find fossil ancestors showing the evolution of the bat, such as the formation of a bat's wing membrane over time or the slow elongation of the mammal's fingers to support a wing membrane. (See Chapter 6.) But all fossilized bats discovered to date are fully developed and capable of flying. (See interviews on next page.)

There is disagreement among scientists as to the significance of these fossil finds. Evolutionists believe that since fossilization is a chance event and rarely occurs, the fossil record can, at times, be incomplete. Therefore, the absence of bat ancestors does not necessarily imply they did not exist.

Scientists who oppose evolution argue that if the ancestors existed, surely *some* of them should have been fossilized. They believe it is inconsistent to blame the lack of bat ancestors on the processes of fossilization since millions of other fossils from the time period of bat evolution have been fossilized and collected by museums. [2] They suggest this pattern of absence of ancestors is strong evidence that evolution did *not* occur.

Fossil Layers
Millions of years ago (MYA)*

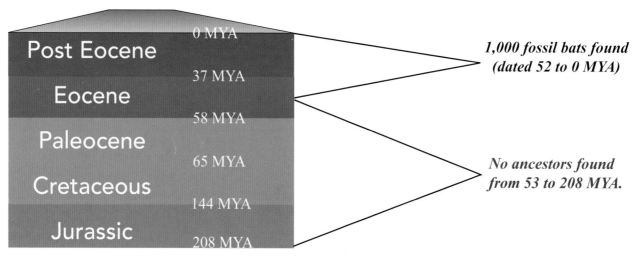

Post Eocene	0 MYA
Eocene	37 MYA
Paleocene	58 MYA
Cretaceous	65 MYA
Jurassic	144 MYA
	208 MYA

1,000 fossil bats found (dated 52 to 0 MYA)

No ancestors found from 53 to 208 MYA.

*Scientists do not agree on the age or number of years it took to deposit these fossil layers. This is a theoretical construct to evaluate the theory of evolution.

Previous Page: *Fossil bat, Jura Museum, Germany. Ghost bat, South Australian Museum, Adelaide.*

From *Evolution: The Grand Experiment* video series

Dr. Gary Morgan is Assistant Curator of Paleontology, New Mexico Museum of Natural History and Science. He specializes in bat evolution.

"There's a ten-million-year period of early mammal evolution where you would guess that there'd be some sort of bat precursor, but once again, nothing. Bingo, they just show up...We don't have any precursor and that's sort of the major problem with bat evolution is that you get this perfectly formed bat that shows up at the earliest time period, in the Eocene, fifty to fifty-five million years ago...There are certain people who think they were specially created. They actually are kind of a problem with the creationists who like to [think] if things were created, here's a very highly complex mammal with all these adaptations and bingo, they just show up at some particular moment in time, fully formed as a bat. Obviously, we evolutionary biologists and paleontologists don't believe that. But at this point, we don't have a good fossil ancestor for them." [3]

— Dr. Morgan

See
*Evolution:
The Grand
Experiment*
DVD

"We have no evidence for this evolution. The bats appear perfectly developed in the Eocene." [4]

— Dr. Viohl

Dr. Gunter Viohl, Curator of the famous Jura Museum in Eichstatt, Germany.

Dr. Gunter Viohl
Curator Jura Museum, Germany

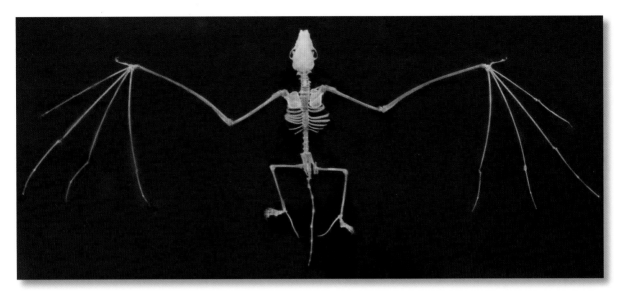

Bats have extremely long forearms and digits to support their wing membranes. The digits (fingers) act as struts in the wings. **Above:** *Skeleton of a modern Vesper bat (Myotis auriculus).* **Below, left:** *Fossil bat (Onychonycteris finneyi).* **Below, right:** *Fossil bat (Palaeochiropteryx tupaiodon). Impressions of the wing membranes can be seen as black discoloration in this fossil.*

Onychonycteris finneyi on display at Royal Ontario Museum, Toronto, Canada. © ROM, 2011, used by permission.

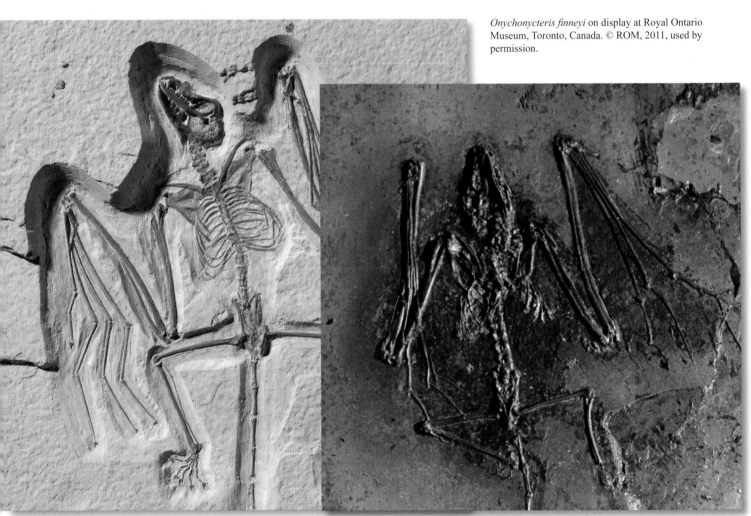

Jura Museum, Germany © 2007 AVC Inc., Photo by Debbie Werner

Palaeochiropteryx tupaiodon, Messel Museum, Germany © 2007 AVC Inc., Photo by Debbie Werner

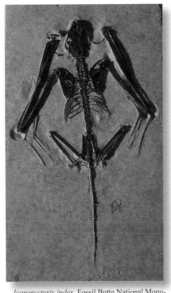

Icaronycteris index, Fossil Butte National Monument © 2007 AVC Inc., Photo by Carl Werner

Archaeonycteris trigonodon, Messel Museum, Germany © 2007 AVC Inc., Photo by Debbie Werner

New Mexico Museum of Science and Natural History © 2007 AVC Inc., Photo by Debbie Werner

Palaeochiropteryx spiegeli, Messel Museum, Germany © 2007 AVC Inc., Photo by Debbie Werner

Senckenberg Museum, Frankfurt, Germany © 2007 AVC Inc., Photo by Debbie Werner

Senckenberg Museum, Frankfurt, Germany © 2007 AVC Inc., Photo by Debbie Werner

Senckenberg Museum, Frankfurt, Germany © 2007 AVC Inc., Photo by Debbie Werner

Senckenberg Museum, Frankfurt, Germany © 2007 AVC Inc., Photo by Debbie Werner

An Amazing 1,000 Fossil Bats Have Been Discovered but None of the Predicted Evolutionary Ancestors Have Been Found!

From *Evolution: The Grand Experiment* video series

"We don't have any non-flying bats, and so we can't pull something out of that, any kind of information out of that, that tells us how they might have evolved." [5]

— **Dr. Czeplewski**

Dr. Nicholas Czeplewski, Staff Curator of Paleontology, Sam Noble Oklahoma Museum of Science and Natural History. Dr. Czeplewski specializes in bat evolution.

Left: Smithsonian Museum drawing of *Icaronycteris index,* the "oldest fossil bat in the world." [6] Compare to photograph of a modern Ghost bat **(below)**.

Is There Evidence That Bats Evolved? What Do You Think?

Dr. Joerg Habersetzer
Senckenberg Museum, Frankfurt

"We have found more than 650–670 specimens so far [at this one location alone in Germany]. We have no fossil records of bats during the Cretaceous period. This means that we are only depending on speculation, when it [bat evolution] started and what happened in that time." [6]

— **Dr. Habersetzer**

Dr. Joerg Habersetzer of the Senckenberg Museum of Natural History in Frankfurt, Germany, specializes in bat evolution.

Author's Note: After the first edition of this book was published in the fall of 2007, a new fossil bat, *Onychonycteris finneyi,* was reported in the February 2008 edition of the journal *Nature.* Turn now to Appendix D: Bat Evolution Update for a detailed discussion of this important fossil bat.

THE
FOSSIL RECORD
OF PINNIPEDS:
SEALS AND SEA LIONS

Sea Lions

Sea lions can be distinguished from seals by the presence of a visible external ear. There are various forms of sea lions living today, such as the California sea lion, the Australian sea lion, and the Stellar sea lion.

Sea lions are highly streamlined and can swim at speeds of up to 25 miles per hour.[1] They can hold their breath for up to 15 minutes. Their front extremities are fin-like and are used during the swimming power stroke.[2] The back feet are webbed and also provide propulsion. California sea lions can readily dive up to 360 feet deep and occasionally dive to an amazing 800 feet.[3] At these depths, most land mammals would be crushed by the intense pressures of the deep, but these creatures have body features which allow them to withstand such high pressures.

Some scientists who advocate evolution believe it was a dog-like animal that evolved into the sea lion.

Others believe it a was a bear-like animal that evolved into a sea lion. These scientists theorize this dog or bear-like creature evolved flippers over millions of years. Since a dog or bear could not have willed itself to grow flippers, these flippers would have had to form by pure chance, by genetic mistakes in the reproductive cells of the land animal. (See Chapter 4.)

Scientists who oppose evolution ask: Where is the evidence for this evolution? They point out the proposed bear-like or dog-like animal has never been found, nor have any fossils of the animals evolving into a sea lion, despite the fact that many fossil sea lions have been found.

Evolutionary scientists respond to such questions and challenges with the hope that one day these fossils will be discovered, given enough time and money to search for these fossils.

Previous Page: *Australian sea lion.* **Above:** *California sea lions.*

Sea lions can be distinguished from seals by the presence of external ears.

Top, right: *Australian sea lion basking in the sun on Kangaroo Island, Australia.*
Above, left: *California sea lion with visible external ear flap.*
Right: *A Stellar sea lion swims by a visitor at the Alaska Sea Life Center.*

What Animal Evolved into a Sea Lion?

Australian scientists believe that a *dog or dog-like* animal evolved into a sea lion. (See museum display at right.) But scientists at Howard University in Washington, D.C. think a *bear* evolved into a sea lion. Could they both be right? What is the evidence for their beliefs? Is it possible that sea lions did not evolve from a dog or a bear? Could they both be wrong? What do you think?

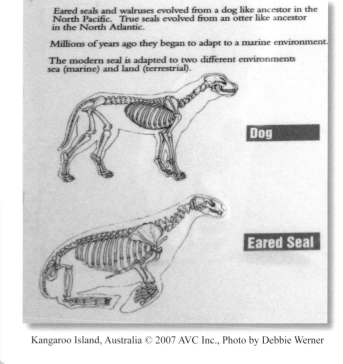

Eared seals and walruses evolved from a dog like ancestor in the North Pacific. True seals evolved from an otter like ancestor in the North Atlantic.

Millions of years ago they began to adapt to a marine environment.

The modern seal is adapted to two different environments sea (marine) and land (terrestrial).

Dog

Eared Seal

Kangaroo Island, Australia © 2007 AVC Inc., Photo by Debbie Werner

A dog? A bear? Or neither?

Despite an Abundant Fossil Record, Scientists Have Not Found the Proposed Evolutionary Ancestors for Sea Lions.

From *Evolution: The Grand Experiment* video series

Question: *What animal did sea lions evolve from?*
Dr. Koretsky: *"Eared seals came from bear-like animals."* [4]

Question: *"Do they know which bear-like creature it was?"*
Dr. Koretsky: *"No, no, no."* [4] [Shaking head.]

Question: *Have you found any fossils between the proposed bear-like animal and sea lions?*
Dr. Koretsky: *"We could not find, we could not name it, the exact animal which make it this missing link between bear-like animal and an eared seal or sea lion."* [4]

Dr. Irina Koretsky, Paleontologist and Research Associate, Smithsonian Museum of Natural History, and Assistant Professor of Anatomy, Howard University. Dr. Koretsky specializes in seal and sea lion evolution.

Only fossil sea lions have been found.

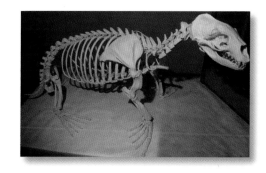

"And the earliest animal that we've recognized has the name Pithanotaria. It's very similar in terms of its body size and morphology to the modern sea lions." [5]

— Dr. Berta

Dr. Annalisa Berta, Professor at San Diego State University, specializes in aquatic mammal evolution.

Thousands of Fossil Sea Lions Have Been Found.

Fossil Layers
Millions of years ago (MYA)*

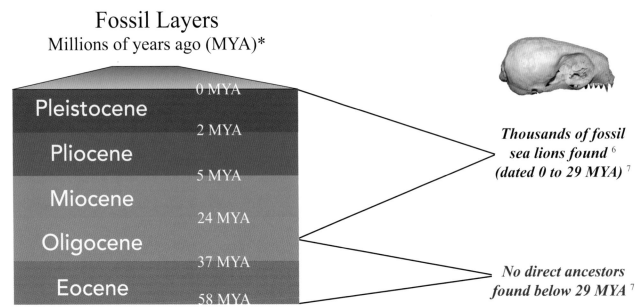

Pleistocene	0 MYA
	2 MYA
Pliocene	
	5 MYA
Miocene	
	24 MYA
Oligocene	
	37 MYA
Eocene	
	58 MYA

Thousands of fossil sea lions found [6] *(dated 0 to 29 MYA)* [7]

No direct ancestors found below 29 MYA [7]

*Scientists do not agree on the age of these fossil layers.

Author's Note: Below the Miocene layers there are many fossil land mammals, but none have been identified as the ancestors of sea lions. (See interviews on previous page.)

Despite this peculiar imbalance in the fossil record, scientists continue to hold out hope.

"Far from being hopeless, there is every reason to expect that similarly exciting pinniped missing links are out there waiting quietly [to be discovered], *who knows where or when."* [8]

— Dr. Ray

Dr. Clayton Ray graduated from Harvard University in 1955, magna cum laude, Phi Beta Kappa, with double majors in geology and biology; M.A., Harvard, 1958, and Ph.D., 1962. He was Curator at the Smithsonian National Museum of Natural History from 1963 to 1994, and currently is Curator Emeritus at the Smithsonian.

Seals

Watching seals play on the beach or frolicking in the water is a beautiful sight. Seals are highly streamlined. They can dive to extreme depths, sometimes diving nearly a mile deep, and can hold their breath for an amazing two hours at a time. [9] To put this in perspective, a Los Angeles class nuclear attack submarine can dive only 800 feet deep, [10] but a seal can dive over six times that depth to around 5,200 feet. Because of some similarities among seals, skunks, and otters, proponents of evolution believe seals evolved from either a skunk or an otter-like animal. (See interview below.)

Scientists who oppose evolution do not believe that seals evolved. They disagree with the concept that similarities between two animal groups prove evolution because many other animals appear similar but are *unrelated*. (See Chapter 5.) Therefore, animals having similar features is not a justifiable proof of evolution. They also suggest the fossil record does not correlate with the idea of a skunk or otter evolving into a seal. They ask: If evolution occurred, where are the fossils of a skunk or otter slowly changing into a seal?

Left and above:
Elephant seals on a California beach.

From *Evolution: The Grand Experiment* video series

Dr. Annalisa Berta
San Diego State University

"Seals are allied to a completely separate group of carnivores... the skunks and the otters." [5]

— **Dr. Berta**

What Animal Evolved into a Seal?

From *Evolution: The Grand Experiment* Video Series

Question: *Which mustelid (skunk or otter-like animal) evolved into the seal?*
Dr. Koretsky: *"I don't have evidence or material yet."* [4]
Question: *Do you have fossils between the mustelid (skunk or otter-like animal) and seals?*
Dr. Koretsky: *"We don't have such material...There is not a time when we can find the missing link."* [4]
Dr. Koretsky also indicated that all fossils found to date have been true seals. No intermediate animals have been found:
Dr. Koretsky: *"We have material from South Carolina [as] I mentioned before...but we can say this is true seals. We already can say this is true seals according to morphology of the bones. We cannot say I don't know what this is."* [4]

5,000 Fossil Seals Have Been Found, but the Proposed Evolutionary Ancestors of Seals Have Not Been Found.

Fossil Layers
Millions of years ago (MYA)*

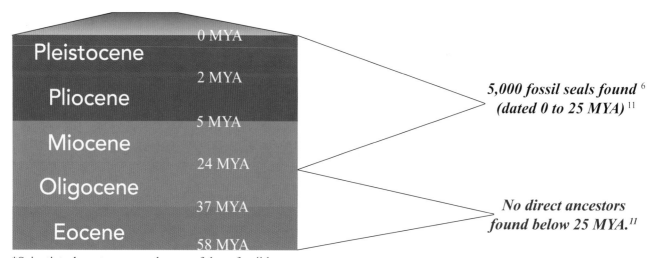

Pleistocene	0 MYA
	2 MYA
Pliocene	
	5 MYA
Miocene	
	24 MYA
Oligocene	
	37 MYA
Eocene	
	58 MYA

5,000 fossil seals found [6] (dated 0 to 25 MYA) [11]

No direct ancestors found below 25 MYA.[11]

*Scientists do not agree on the age of these fossil layers.

Author's Note: Two years after the first edition of this book was published in the fall of 2007, a new fossilized "walking seal," named *Puijila darwini*, was reported in the April 2009 edition of the journal *Nature*. It was heralded as the missing link. Turn now to Appendix E: Pinniped Evolution Update for a more detailed discussion of this most important fossil!

THE
FOSSIL RECORD
OF FLYING REPTILES

Pterosaurs

Pterosaurs are flying reptiles which lived during the time of the dinosaurs. To date, nearly 1,000 fossilized pterosaurs have been found[1] from all over the world, including over 100 different species.[2] Some of these fossils are exquisitely preserved with detailed impressions of the soft membranes of the wing. (See Fossils B and C below.)

Pterosaurs can be divided into two varieties, the short-tailed Pterodactyls (Fossils A, G, H, I, J, K below) and the long-tailed *Rhamphorhynchus* (Fossils B, C, D, E, F below). Pterosaurs range in size from that of a tiny sparrow to larger than a fighter jet. The wingspan of the largest known pterosaur was two feet wider than that of a U.S. F-4E Phantom II fighter jet.[2, 3]

Scientists recognize that the evolutionary ancestors of pterosaurs have not been found. But what does this mean? Evolution scientists believe the fossil record is incomplete and hope one day to find these ancestors. Scientists who oppose evolution believe pterosaurs did not evolve and suggest the fossil record supports their position.

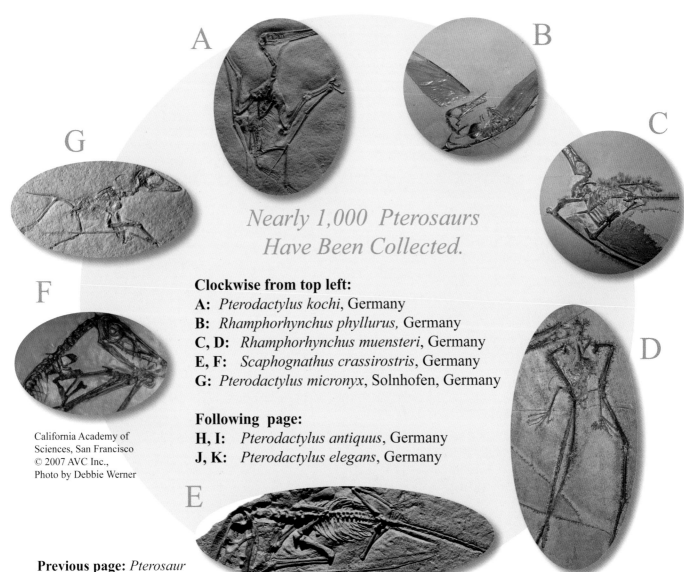

Nearly 1,000 Pterosaurs Have Been Collected.

Clockwise from top left:
A: *Pterodactylus kochi,* Germany
B: *Rhamphorhynchus phyllurus,* Germany
C, D: *Rhamphorhynchus muensteri,* Germany
E, F: *Scaphognathus crassirostris,* Germany
G: *Pterodactylus micronyx,* Solnhofen, Germany

Following page:
H, I: *Pterodactylus antiquus,* Germany
J, K: *Pterodactylus elegans,* Germany

California Academy of
Sciences, San Francisco
© 2007 AVC Inc.,
Photo by Debbie Werner

Previous page: *Pterosaur model on display at the Jura Museum, Germany.*

Fossils A, C, D, E, G, I, and K from the Jura Museum, Germany. © 2007 AVC Inc., Photos by Debbie Werner

"I would say the specimen numbers go at least in the hundreds or close to a thousand or so, or something like that. So we have a fairly good record of pterosaur fossils and pterosaurs worldwide." [4]

— Dr. Wellnhofer

Dr. Peter Wellnhofer, Curator Emeritus of the Bavarian State Collection of Paleontology in Munich, and author of **The Illustrated Encyclopedia of Prehistoric Flying Reptiles**.

Fossil pterosaurs have been found on every continent, including Antarctica.

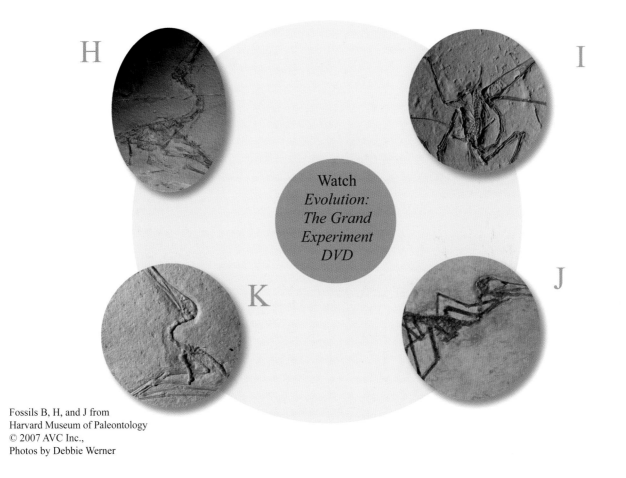

H

I

Watch
*Evolution:
The Grand
Experiment*
DVD

K

J

Fossils B, H, and J from
Harvard Museum of Paleontology
© 2007 AVC Inc.,
Photos by Debbie Werner

Despite a Rich Fossil Record, Not a Single Ancestor of Pterosaurs Has Been Found!

"We know only little about the evolution of pterosaurs. The ancestors are not known...When the pterosaurs first appear in the geological record, they were completely perfect. They were perfect pterosaurs." [5]

— **Dr. Viohl**

Dr. Gunter Viohl, Curator of the famous Jura Museum, Eichstatt, Germany.

"As for the ancestors, the possible ancestors of pterosaurs, there are only theories, hypotheses of course...In fact, it is a mystery which group of reptiles, prior to the Triassic, might have given rise to the pterosaurs." [4]

— **Dr. Wellnhofer**

Fossil Layers
Millions of years ago (MYA)*

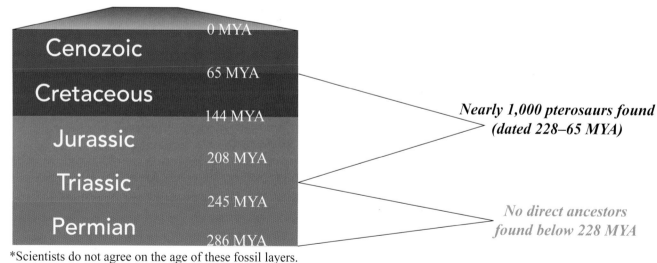

0 MYA	
Cenozoic	
65 MYA	
Cretaceous	
144 MYA	
Jurassic	
208 MYA	
Triassic	
245 MYA	
Permian	
286 MYA	

Nearly 1,000 pterosaurs found (dated 228–65 MYA)

No direct ancestors found below 228 MYA

*Scientists do not agree on the age of these fossil layers.

Did Pterosaurs Evolve? What Do You Think?

THE
FOSSIL RECORD
OF DINOSAURS

Tyrannosaurus rex

Of all the dinosaurs, *Tyrannosaurus rex* is probably the most familiar to us. This dinosaur walked on its hind legs and could run up to 25 miles per hour.[1] It stood 18 feet tall, was 42 feet in length, and weighed over 14,000 pounds.[2] It was the largest meat-eating dinosaur to have ever lived.[3] Although *T. rex* was huge, its arms were tiny. They were so short, they could not even reach its mouth. The arms were probably used to stabilize its prey while the large teeth ripped into its food.

According to Dr. David Weishampel, the Lead Editor of the book *The Dinosauria*, 24 *T. rex* specimens have been found, 12 of which are nearly complete. Eight additional *T. rex* dinosaurs were discovered by John Horner, curator of paleontology at the Museum of the Rockies, as recently as 2001.

The theory of evolution suggests that a four-legged reptile, similar to an alligator, slowly changed into this 14,000-pound dinosaur over millions of years. While 32 *T. rex* dinosaurs have been found, according to evolution experts, *not a single* direct ancestor of *T. rex* has ever been uncovered in any of the fossil layers preceding it. It was once thought that other meat-eating dinosaurs, such as *Coelophysis, Herrerasaurus, Allosaurus* and *Eoraptor*, were the direct

Milwaukee Public Museum, Wisconsin © 2007 AVC Inc., Photo by Debbie Werner

ancestors of *T. rex*. But when scientists began studying the fossil bones of these dinosaurs, each of them had either the wrong *number* of bones or the wrong-*shaped* bones and were eliminated as possible direct ancestors of *T. rex*. Interestingly, when scientists cannot find evidence that a dinosaur is the direct ancestor of another, they label these dinosaurs as cousins.

"Wherever we try to put Tyrannosaurs in the phylogeny of the branching history of the therapod dinosaurs, they have a long missing record. And we are going to find that record one of these days."[4]

— **Dr. Sereno**

Dr. Paul Sereno, Paleontologist and Professor at the University of Chicago, is one of the world's leading experts on dinosaur evolution.

Previous and following page: *T. rex on display at the University of California, Berkeley, Museum of Paleontology.*

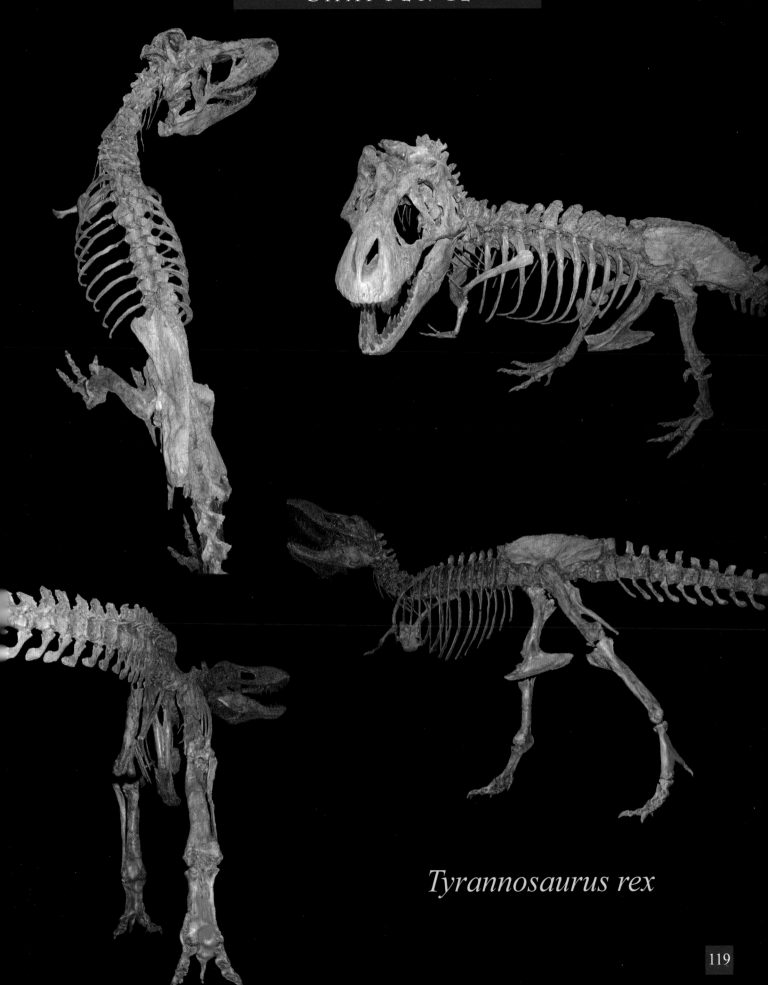

Tyrannosaurus rex

No direct ancestors for *Tyrannosaurus rex*

Scientists who oppose evolution ask: How is it possible that so many fossil *T. rex* dinosaurs appear suddenly in the fossil record? Given the fact that dinosaurs lived over a period of 180 million years, they suggest the lack of direct ancestors means they never existed in the first place and that evolution never occurred.

U. of Wyoming Geological Museum
© 2007 AVC Inc., Photo by Debbie Werner

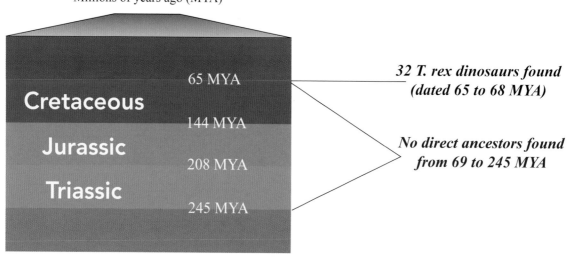

Dinosaur Age Fossil Layers
Millions of years ago (MYA)*

65 MYA

Cretaceous

144 MYA

Jurassic

208 MYA

Triassic

245 MYA

*32 T. rex dinosaurs found
(dated 65 to 68 MYA)*

*No direct ancestors found
from 69 to 245 MYA*

*Scientists do not agree on the age of these fossil layers.

Triceratops

Triceratops was a plant-eating dinosaur which lived at the end of the dinosaur era alongside *T. rex*. This dinosaur weighed 10,000 pounds and was 25 feet long.[5] It is the largest and best known of the horned dinosaurs.[5] Its skull was distinctive with a pair of long horns above the eyes and a small horn located over the nose. *Triceratops* literally means "three horned face."

Triceratops is a member of the ornithischian group of dinosaurs. Dinosaurs are divided into two groups, the ornithischians and the saurischians. Ornithischians, such as *Triceratops,* have a pelvis shape similar to a bird's pelvis whereas the saurischians, like *T. rex*, have a pelvis shape similar to a lizard's pelvis.

Scientists have found hundreds of *Triceratops*, but have not found any direct ancestors of this species. Evolution scientists believe there were direct ancestors, but they were not preserved as fossils. Or they were preserved, but simply have not been discovered yet.

Those who do not accept the theory of evolution point out that if the direct ancestors of *Triceratops* existed, they should have been discovered by now. For them, the lack of ancestors is evidence that the theory of evolution is a myth.

Utah Field House of Natural History State Museum
© 2007 AVC Inc., Photo by Carl Werner

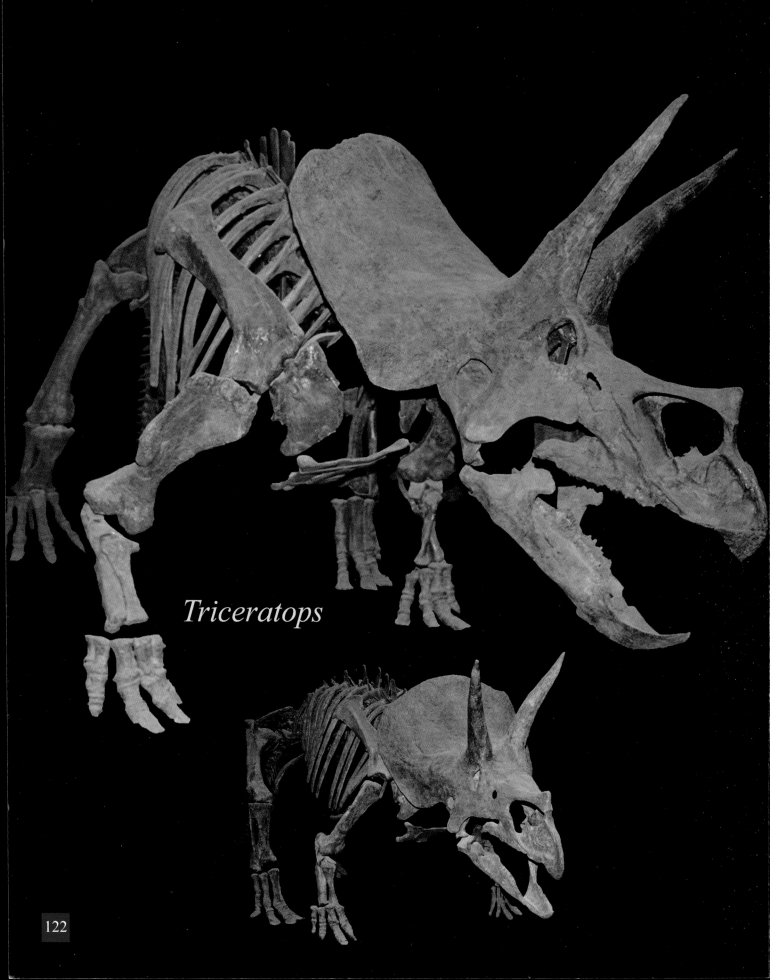

Triceratops

Hundreds of *Triceratops*, yet no direct ancestors

"I suspect we probably know a hundred or hundreds of Triceratops from their skulls." [6]

— Dr. Weishampel

Dr. David Weishampel, Anatomist and Paleontologist, Johns Hopkins University and Lead Editor of the encyclopedic reference book **The Dinosauria**.

From *Evolution: The Grand Experiment* Video Series

"We are certainly lacking information that ties together meat-eating dinosaurs and all the rest of the dinosaurs. We certainly [don't know]. *We really don't have any idea how the whole other group of dinosaurs, called ornithischians,* [evolved from the meat-eating dinosaurs]. [We really do not know] *exactly the timing and the way they branched off. We've got nothing there yet. There is a huge gap."*[7]

— Dr. Milner

Dr. Angela Milner, Paleontologist and Head of Vertebrate Paleontology, Natural History Museum of London.

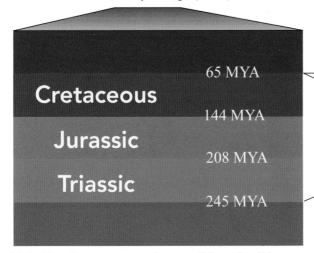

Dinosaur Age Fossil Layers
Millions of years ago (MYA)*

65 MYA

Cretaceous

144 MYA

Jurassic

208 MYA

Triassic

245 MYA

Hundreds of Triceratops dinosaurs (dated 65–68 MYA)

No direct ancestors found from 69 to 245 MYA

*Scientists do not agree on the age of these fossil layers.

Previous page: *Triceratops on display at the Wyoming Dinosaur Center, Thermopolis.*

Apatosaurus

*A*patosaurus, formerly called *Brontosaurus,* was a long-necked (sauropod), plant-eating dinosaur that used its long neck to eat leaves high up in trees. *Apatosaurus* averaged 70 to 90 feet in length [8] and weighed up to 30 tons. It was roughly two times longer than the average home. Their limb bones were huge with some longer than four feet.

Sam Noble Oklahoma Museum of Science and Natural History, Oklahoma © 2007 AVC Inc., Photo by Debbie Werner

So far, nearly 30 of these dinosaurs have been found throughout the world. Thirteen of these are nearly complete. Dr. David Weishampel, Lead Editor of the encyclopedic reference book *The Dinosauria,* recounts the current collection of these dinosaurs: *"Apatosaurus is probably one of the better represented of all sauropods. It's known from at least 13, more or less, complete skeletons and then from a lot of individual bones as well. So the minimum number of individuals of Apatosaurus is probably 20 to 30, possibly more."* [6]

Specimens of this spectacular dinosaur are on display in museums, most notably at the American Museum of Natural History in New York City, the Carnegie Museum of Natural History in Pittsburgh, and the Sam Noble Oklahoma Museum of Science and Natural History.

Sam Noble Oklahoma Museum of Science and Natural History, Oklahoma © 2007 AVC Inc., Photo by Debbie Werner

Similar to *T. rex* and *Triceratops*, not a single direct ancestor has been found for *Apatosaurus*. Because of its tremendous size, one would expect ancestors of *Apatosaurus* to be visible in the fossil record. However, this is not the case. While dinosaur experts once claimed *Eoraptor* and the prosauropods as direct ancestors, they subsequently found these dinosaurs are not related to *Apatosuarus*, except as cousins, due to their peculiar anatomy.

Sam Noble Oklahoma Museum
of Science and Natural History, Oklahoma
© 2007 AVC Inc., Photo by Debbie Werner

From *Evolution: The Grand Experiment* video series

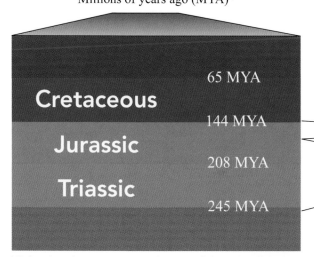

Dr. David Weishampel
Johns Hopkins University

"Prosauropods actually are not on the direct line to get to sauropods, like Diplodocus and Apatosaurus and Brachiosaurus. ...They have their own evolutionary history that is independent of the evolutionary history of sauropods." [6]

— **Dr. Weishampel**

Dinosaur Age Fossil Layers
Millions of years ago (MYA)*

65 MYA
Cretaceous
144 MYA
Jurassic
208 MYA
Triassic
245 MYA

*30 Apatosaurus dinosaurs found
(dated 145–156 MYA)*

*No direct ancestors found
from 157 to 245 MYA*

*Scientists do not agree on the age of these fossil layers.

How Many Direct Ancestors
of Dinosaurs Have Been Found?

According to one of the world's leading experts in dinosaur evolution, direct ancestors have yet to be discovered for *any* of the known 700 dinosaur species. This statement is an apparent gross contradiction to Darwin's prediction that as more fossils were found, there would, in turn, be more evidence for the changing of species to confirm his theory.

"From my reading of the fossil record of dinosaurs, no direct ancestors have been discovered for any dinosaur species. Alas, my list of dinosaurian ancestors is an empty one." [9]

— Dr. Weishampel

From *Evolution: The Grand Experiment* video series

"Early on, again, I think researchers and even maybe lay people really felt that we had more ancestors in the fossil record than we actually do…we don't have a lot of ancestors, we have a lot of twigs." [4]

— Dr. Sereno

Pink Palace Museum, Memphis, Tennessee
© 2007 AVC Inc., Photo by Debbie Werner

Museum Diagrams Demonstrating Dinosaur Evolution.

By and large, the public is not aware of the recurrent pattern of ancestral gaps in the fossil record of dinosaurs. Current museum displays usually do not indicate there are such gaps. For example, the illustration on the right from the Chicago Field Museum is not a record of discovered dinosaur fossils, but is actually a theoretical model representing evolution. Only when the number of discovered fossils are included in this diagram does one get a more clear and factual picture which, according to some, contradicts the theory of evolution. (See amended diagram on the next page.)

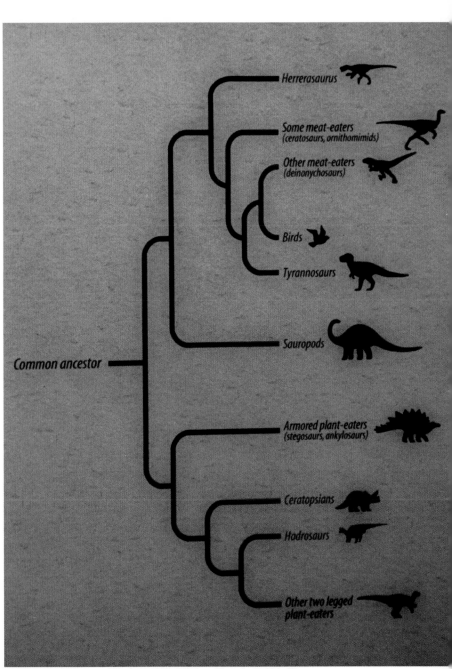

Chicago Field Museum, Illinois © 2007 AVC Inc., Photo by Debbie Werner

Same diagram displaying actual number of dinosaurs found.

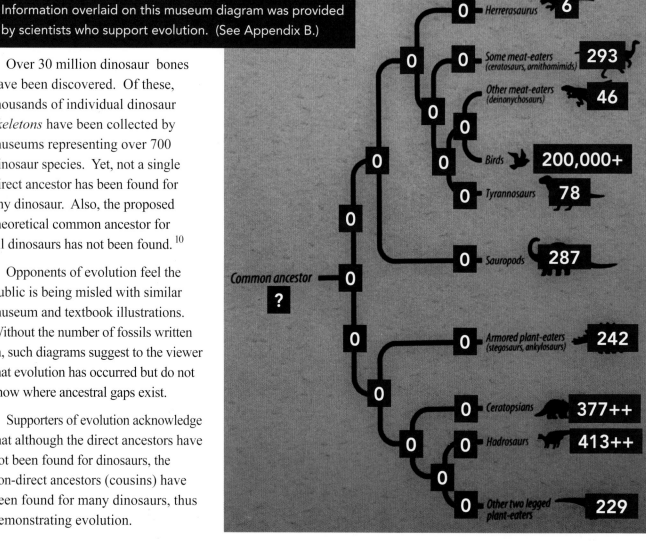

Information overlaid on this museum diagram was provided by scientists who support evolution. (See Appendix B.)

	Herrerasaurus	6
	Some meat-eaters (ceratosaurs, ornithomimids)	293
	Other meat-eaters (deinonychosaurs)	46
	Birds	200,000+
	Tyrannosaurs	78
	Sauropods	287

Common ancestor — **?**

	Armored plant-eaters (stegosaurs, ankylosaurs)	242
	Ceratopsians	377++
	Hadrosaurs	413++
	Other two legged plant-eaters	229

Over 30 million dinosaur bones have been discovered. Of these, thousands of individual dinosaur *skeletons* have been collected by museums representing over 700 dinosaur species. Yet, not a single direct ancestor has been found for any dinosaur. Also, the proposed theoretical common ancestor for all dinosaurs has not been found. [10]

Opponents of evolution feel the public is being misled with similar museum and textbook illustrations. Without the number of fossils written in, such diagrams suggest to the viewer that evolution has occurred but do not show where ancestral gaps exist.

Supporters of evolution acknowledge that although the direct ancestors have not been found for dinosaurs, the non-direct ancestors (cousins) have been found for many dinosaurs, thus demonstrating evolution.

What Do You Think?

University of Chicago © 2007 AVC Inc., Photo by Debbie Werner

Skull (above) and skeleton (right) of the dinosaur Eoraptor. This dinosaur was recently thought to be the common ancestor to all dinosaurs. Further analysis by Dr. Sereno revealed it was actually an advanced meat-eating dinosaur.

Sam Noble Oklahoma Museum of Science and Natural History, Oklahoma © 2007 AVC Inc., Photo by Debbie Werner

THE
FOSSIL RECORD
OF WHALES

How Did Whales Get Here?
How Good Is the Evidence?

Whales are warm-blooded, give birth to live young, suckle their young, and have some body hair around their face used for tactile sensation. Based on these characteristics, whales are classified as mammals. Because they live in water, whales are classified as aquatic mammals. Whales are members of a larger group of aquatic mammals called Cetaceans, which also includes dolphins and porpoises.[1]

The theory of evolution maintains that land mammals evolved from reptiles approximately 220 million years ago and then, around 50 million years ago, one species of land mammal went back into the water and evolved into a whale. If this is true, what evidence is there to prove this whale evolution?

Today, many evolution experts believe the fossil evidence for the evolution of whales is overwhelming and is actually one of the best demonstrations of animal evolution. While it is generally acknowledged as rare to have fossils showing one animal group slowly evolving into a completely different animal type, evolution scientists suggest that whales are the exception to this rule. These scientists believe that nearly all of the pertinent fossils demonstrating a four-legged land mammal changing into a walking whale, and subsequently changing into a fully modern whale, have been found. As Dr. Clayton Ray of the Smithsonian Museum explains: *"Fifteen years ago, the origin and early evolution of whales was even more hopeless than that of pinnipeds* [seals and sea lions] *and gave the creationists much to crow about. Now, suddenly, the paleontology of early whales is one of our most widely and justly trumpeted success stories."*[2]

Dr. Ray is not alone in his view. One advocate for the theory of evolution has boldly suggested that if you cannot see whale evolution after examining the whale fossils on display at the University of Michigan's Exhibit Museum of Natural History, you are either blind or three days dead. (See interview below.)

From *Evolution: The Grand Experiment* video series

Dr. Kevin Padian
University of California, Berkeley

Dr. Kevin Padian, Professor and Curator, University of California, Berkeley.

Discussing whale exhibit at University of Michigan:
"We now have whales with legs, whales with reduced legs, whales with little tiny legs, whales with no legs at all, and their heads are getting bigger and their teeth are getting stranger...They have a big exhibit on it out in Michigan, in Ann Arbor. Yeah, I was just there. They have all these things just sitting out there. They're all there. I mean, you really have to be blind or three days dead not to see the transition among these. You know, you have to not want to see it. And, a big part of the question, why doesn't everybody agree on these things, is that it comes down to what you bring to the questions to begin with. If you don't want to see things, you're not going to see them. And we are all guilty of not wanting to see certain things."[3]

— **Dr. Padian**

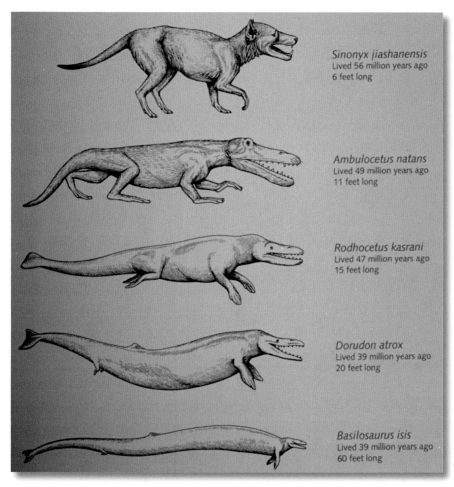

Sinonyx jiashanensis
Lived 56 million years ago
6 feet long

Ambulocetus natans
Lived 49 million years ago
11 feet long

Rodhocetus kasrani
Lived 47 million years ago
15 feet long

Dorudon atrox
Lived 39 million years ago
20 feet long

Basilosaurus isis
Lived 39 million years ago
60 feet long

Evidence for whale evolution on display at the University of Michigan, Ann Arbor

Exhibit Museum of Natural History,
University of Michigan, Ann Arbor
© 2007 AVC Inc., Photo by Debbie Werner

From *Evolution: The Grand Experiment* video series

"What is good to show about these particular fossil whale specimens is that they do show us intermediates in the evolution of whales. We don't often get fossil intermediates so we can actually trace the development of characters, say, for example, the evolution of swimming in whales. We don't often have that opportunity." [4]

— Dr. Berta

Dr. Annalisa Berta, Professor at San Diego State University, specializes in aquatic mammal evolution. Dr. Berta has held the position of president of the prestigious Society of Vertebrate Paleontology.

The fossil evidence for the evolution of whales is considered both strong and unique by scientists who support evolution.

Not All Scientists Agree

Not all scientists agree that the fossil record proves whale evolution. In fact, scientists who oppose evolution believe the fossil evidence demonstrating whale evolution is simply wishful thinking on the part of evolution scientists. They suggest that museum diagrams demonstrating whale evolution, including walking whales, are flawed. They further propose that the fossil record of whale evolution is so *bad* the entire theory of evolution should be rejected just on this one purported case alone.

How could two groups of scientists have such different opinions? How could the same fossil evidence lead to such disparate ideas? The following pages detail some of the best evidence for and against whale evolution. The reader is left to decide if evolution is or is not demonstrated in this "best case for evolution."

Author's Note: Since the first edition of this book was released, museums have changed their whale evolution displays to correct the serious problems revealed in this chapter. The reader is encouraged to first read this chapter then immediately read Appendix F: Whale Evolution Update for the latest information on whale evolution.

From *Evolution: The Grand Experiment* video series

Dr. Duane Gish,
"Evolution, The Fossils Still Say No"

"I'd like to challenge these people to describe the series of intermediates. [Also], why would [this land mammal] leave the land for which it was highly adapted, abundant food supply, good drinking water available there, venture into the water, the ocean or whatever, and evolve into whales? They never come up with any explanation for something like that." [5]

— Dr. Gish

*Dr. Duane Gish, author of **Evolution: The Fossils Still Say No!***

The First Step: The Land Mammal

One of the most basic questions concerning whale evolution is this: If whales evolved from a land mammal, which one was it? You might be surprised to learn that if you asked different experts this question, you will get widely different answers. For example, if you asked scientists at the prestigious California Academy of Sciences Natural History Museum in San Francisco, they would show you a museum display that suggests a hyena-like animal evolved, over millions of years, into a whale. [6] If you went to the premier whale evolution exhibit at the University of Michigan's Exhibit Museum of Natural History, Ann Arbor, you would see a display suggesting a cat-like animal eventually evolved into a whale. [7] If you interviewed biologists in Japan, they would tell you it was a hippopotamus relative that evolved into a whale. [8] In forming their conclusions, scientists often focus on shared features between animals. In this instance, each of these three land mammals shared common features with whales, such as similar teeth or similar DNA.

Scientists who oppose evolution point out that just because an animal has similar features does not necessarily indicate they are evolutionary ancestors to one another. Many animals that are not related have nearly identical body plans, such as the marsupial mole and the placental mole, as discussed in Chapter 5. They maintain that the lack of consensus among scientists who support evolution regarding which land animal evolved into a whale indicates the story of whale evolution is just that, a story. They ask: Why can't the supporters of the theory of evolution agree on the ancestor of whales, given the "fact" that whale evolution is so clear to them using the fossils?

Hyena-like whale ancestor?

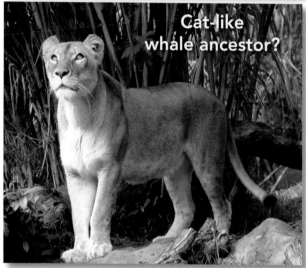

Cat-like whale ancestor?

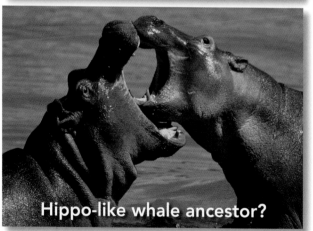

Hippo-like whale ancestor?

Proponents of evolution are not sure what land animal whales evolved from.

Meat-Eating Teeth or Plant-Eating Teeth?

All whales are meat-eaters. Even large filter-feeding baleen whales eat small crustacean animals called krill. Evolution scientists have chosen certain meat-eating land mammals, such as the cat-like *Sinonyx* or the hyena-like *Pachyaena,* as the land animal precursor of whales because of the similarities of their meat-eating teeth when compared to the teeth of the oldest fossil whales.

From *Evolution: The Grand Experiment* video series

"The main thing that is similar between hoofed hyenas and the archaic whales are the teeth." [9]

— **Dr. Gingerich**

Dr. Phil Gingerich, Professor of Geological Sciences, Professor of Geology, and Director of the Museum of Paleontology, University of Michigan. Dr. Gingerich is recognized as one of the world's leading authorities on whale evolution.

Whale teeth (*Rodhocetus*)

Exhibit Museum of Natural History,
University of Michigan, Ann Arbor
© 2007 AVC Inc., Photo by Debbie Werner

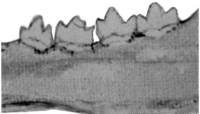

Hyena-like teeth (*Pachyaena*)

California Academy of Sciences, San Francisco
© 2007 AVC Inc., Photo by Debbie Werner

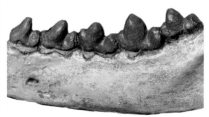

Cat-like teeth (*Sinonyx*)

Exhibit Museum of Natural History,
University of Michigan, Ann Arbor
© 2007 AVC Inc., Photo by Debbie Werner

Even though some have built their case for whale evolution around animals with meat-eating teeth, it is important to note that scientists at the Tokyo Institute of Technology have recently found evidence that hippopotamus DNA is the closest match to the DNA of whales (when compared to all of the other mammal groups). [8] This presents somewhat of a quandary because hippos are plant-eaters and their teeth are not even remotely similar to meat-eating whale teeth.

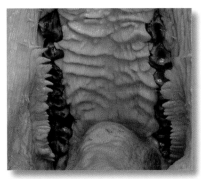

Rodhocetus (whale) teeth: Sharp for meat eating.

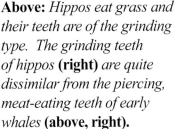

Above: *Hippos eat grass and their teeth are of the grinding type. The grinding teeth of hippos (right) are quite dissimilar from the piercing, meat-eating teeth of early whales (above, right).*

Hippo teeth: Flat for plant eating.

From *Evolution: The Grand Experiment* video series

"We still have the problem, if we are talking about whales evolving from these even-toed hoofed mammals [hippos], they are all plant-eaters. Whales today are all carnivores." [9]

— **Dr. Gingerich**

DNA evidence suggests a *plant*-eating hippo-like mammal evolved into a meat-eating whale. Fossil evidence suggests it was a *meat*-eating cat-like or hyena-like mammal.

What Do You Think?

The Missing Hippo Fossil Problem

In addition to the controversy over DNA evidence suggesting hippos to be the closest land ancestor of whales, there is another problem. The fossil layers show that hippos did not live before whales. If hippos were not living before whales, how then could they evolve into whales? At times, even evolution scientists express frustration with these contradictory lines of evidence.

> *"To a paleontologist, this is nonsense because whales have been around in the fossil record about five times as long as hippos have. Hippos were very late on the scene, at which time whales had already been around for tens of millions of years...And to associate those two is really an absurdity to anyone who takes the fossil record seriously."* [10]
>
> **— Dr. Domning**

Dr. Daryl Domning, Paleontologist and Professor of Anatomy, Howard University. Dr. Domning specializes in aquatic mammal evolution.

Scientists who oppose evolution ask how the evidence for whale evolution can be so fluid. First, it was either a meat-eating hyena-like or a cat-like mammal that was the predecessor of whales, and then it was a plant-eating hippopotamus. The teeth were once the salient point of comparison, then it was the DNA. The fossil record was supposed to demonstrate the best proof for whale evolution, but now there are no fossils of hippos that lived prior to whales. In their estimation, identifying the land animal that eventually became a whale seems to be elusive.

Scientists who support evolution note that although they have differences of opinion as to which land animal evolved into a whale, the evidence of walking whales (next page) is so convincing that this one detail may be ignored until further fossil evidence is discovered.

The Second Step of Whale Evolution:
Ambulocetus, a Walking Whale?

Exhibit Museum of Natural History,
University of Michigan, Ann Arbor
© 2007 AVC Inc., Photo by Debbie Werner

As depicted in the whale evolution diagram provided earlier in this chapter, *Ambulocetus* is considered to be the second whale intermediate in the ancestral line of whale evolution. *Ambulocetus* was discovered in the mountains of Pakistan in 1993 by Dr. Hans Thewissen and Dr. Taseer Hussain, and is believed to have been a "walking whale." The fossil discovery provided strong evidence to (some) scientists that whales evolved from a land mammal because *Ambulocetus* could both walk on land and swim *and* had whale-like, meat-eating teeth.

When one looks at the above drawing of *Ambulocetus*, it is difficult to understand why it is even called a whale. What evidence do scientists have that proves *Ambulocetus* was a whale? According to Dr. Annalisa Berta, an expert in aquatic mammal evolution, "*Ambulocetus is a whale by virtue of its inclusion in that lineage.*"[11] In other words, *Ambulocetus* was defined as a "walking whale" not because it had a whale's tail or a whale's flippers or a blowhole, but because (some) evolution scientists believed it evolved into a whale. Once evolution scientists believed it was on the line to becoming a whale, it became a "whale." And since it was a land animal with four legs, it was then called a "walking whale." Scientists who oppose evolution are quick to point out that this reasoning is circular and therefore specious.

Site in Pakistan where the walking whale, Ambulocetus, was discovered

From *Evolution: The Grand Experiment* video series

"*They claim they found a whale with legs. Frankly, I don't know why they could call that creature a whale. I have never seen a walking whale, and I've never seen a pig that flies. These things just don't exist. And, the idea that there's a whale that walked, well, we have marine organisms today — seals and these other creatures, sea lions and so forth — that can get up and maneuver on the land a little bit. But they're made for that. They're not intermediate between anything else at all.*"[5]

— **Dr. Gish**

Dr. Duane Gish,
"Evolution, The Fossils Still Say No"

The Eye Problem of *Ambulocetus*

The eyes of whales living today are on the *side* of their head. The same is true for the proposed hyena-like (*Pachyaena*) and cougar-like (*Sinonyx*) whale ancestors. In contrast, *Ambulocetus* had eyes on the *top* of its head, more like a crocodile. Some evolutionary scientists now suggest that *Ambulocetus*

may not be an ancestor to whales because of the location of its eyes (see picture below). If *Ambulocetus* is not on the line of whale evolution, it could no longer be called a "walking whale" and would have to be reclassified simply as a mammal with legs.

Model of *Ambulocetus*, College of the Atlantic, Maine
© 2007 AVC Inc., Photo by Debbie Werner

"*Ambulocetus has its eyes raised up on top of its head in a very strange way, and it is unusually large for an early whale...maybe it's not on the main line* [in whale evolution]."[9]

— **Dr. Gingerich**

Dr. Phil Gingerich
University of Michigan

Was it bad science to call Ambulocetus a "walking whale"?

The Third Step: *Rodhocetus* — Legs, Flippers, and a Whale's Tail

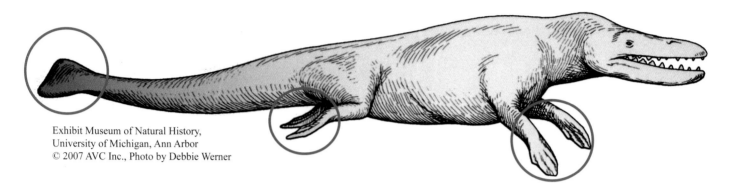

Exhibit Museum of Natural History,
University of Michigan, Ann Arbor
© 2007 AVC Inc., Photo by Debbie Werner

When the evolution of whales is taught in high school or college textbooks, or displayed in museums, important details are sometimes unavailable or limited. Only by interviewing scientists involved in the discovery of the fossils, or by visiting the dig sites where the fossils were found, or by talking with museum curators where the fossils are on display, can one gather the critical details essential to fully understanding the proposed case for the evolution of whales. Unfortunately, very few have the time and resources to participate in such an in-depth review of the subject. Thus, we are left with exhibits, textbooks and science writers to tell the story.

The fossil evidence for whale evolution seems straightforward and compelling, with four intermediates provided between the land animal and a modern whale. However, as seen with the two intermediates introduced thus far, there have been discrepancies. The third intermediate, *Rodhocetus*, is no exception.

For years, scientists have promoted the idea that *Rodhocetus* had a whale's tail (called a fluke) and four legs with flippers. This animal was unique because it had arms and legs but it could also swim like a whale. A typical description of what scientists thought *Rodhocetus* looked like and how it functioned is detailed below.

From *Evolution: The Grand Experiment* video series

Dr. Annalisa Berta
San Diego State University

"*Rodhocetus...*[was] *using its **tail fluke** for propulsion through the water and not using the hind limbs.*"[4]

— Dr. Berta

Walking Whales — Real or Imagined?

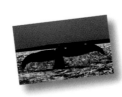

New Details Are Beginning to Emerge about the *Tail* of *Rodhocetus*.

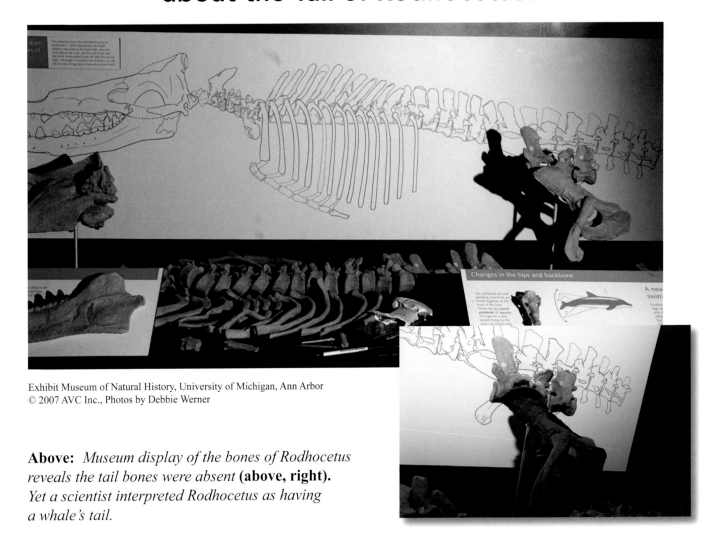

Exhibit Museum of Natural History, University of Michigan, Ann Arbor
© 2007 AVC Inc., Photos by Debbie Werner

Above: *Museum display of the bones of Rodhocetus reveals the tail bones were absent* **(above, right).** *Yet a scientist interpreted Rodhocetus as having a whale's tail.*

At the University of Michigan, the original bones of *Rodhocetus* are on display (above). This is one of the few places in the world where a person can actually see the fossil bones of *Rodhocetus*. In this display, the end of the tail of *Rodhocetus* is missing, the part where a whale's fluke would be attached.

A scientist can tell if an animal had a whale's widened tail fluke by looking at the bones of the tail. A whale's tail has a special round "ball" vertebrae, followed by several flat bones where the cartilaginous fluke tail attaches.[12] (See ball vertebrae in photo on next page.) Without a ball vertebrae, a scientist could not be sure if *Rodhocetus,* in fact, had a fluked tail.

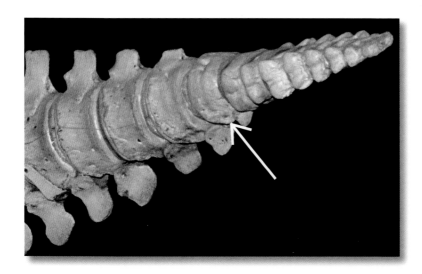

Above: *This dolphin's tail shows the typical ball vertebrae (arrow) followed by flattened vertebrae indicating a fluke was present.*
Right: *Dolphin showing fluke (widened tail). All Cetaceans (whales, dolphins, and porpoises) have a fluked tail (* **top, right** *)*.

Dr. Gingerich, who discovered *Rodhocetus* and promoted the idea that *Rodhocetus* had a whale's tail, was asked how he knew this to be true since the end of the tail was missing in the original fossil bones. That is, he had never found the ball vertebrae. (If the whale tail was removed from *Rodhocetus* and replaced with a land animal's tail, it would dramatically affect the animal's appearance.) Dr. Gingerich's answer was surprising. (See interview below.)

From *Evolution: The Grand Experiment* video series

"I speculated that it might have had a fluke...I now **doubt** *that Rodhocetus would have had a fluked tail."* [9]

— **Dr. Gingerich**

New Details Are Beginning to Emerge about the *Flippers* of *Rodhocetus.*

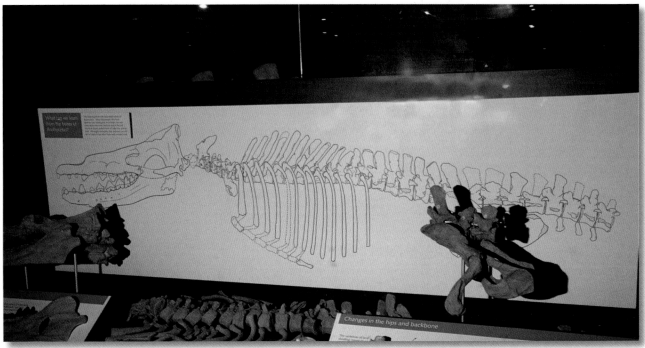

Exhibit Museum of Natural History, University of Michigan, Ann Arbor © 2007 AVC Inc., Photo by Debbie Werner

Above: *Museum display of the bones of Rodhocetus reveals the front and back flipper bones were absent. The museum placard at the top left says: "When discovered, this fossil skeleton was missing the front limbs, the rear limbs below the knee, and the end of the tail." Despite the missing fossils, the scientist at this museum interpreted Rodhocetus as having a whale's fluke and front and back flippers.*

In addition to the tail problem, a second discrepancy regarding *Rodhocetus* was revealed in the interview for the video series that accompanies this book. The drawings of *Rodhocetus,* which appeared in the University of Michigan's museum exhibit (next page) and many national science magazines, indicate that *Rodhocetus* had both front and back *flippers.* When the author of this book visited the museum to see the original fossils of *Rodhocetus,* he observed there were no hand or feet bones of this animal. (See display above.) Without the hand and feet bones, it would be difficult to know if the animal actually had

flippers. During the interview, Dr. Gingerich was asked how he knew *Rodhocetus* had front and back flippers, since these bones had not been found. Dr. Gingerich indicated the flippers were also based on scientific speculation and were added to the drawings. However, he explained that he subsequently found the hand bones and now believes that *Rodhocetus* did *not* have flippers. (**Author's Note:** His response was curious because the University of Michigan's Exhibit Museum of Natural History still displayed the drawings with the flippers and the tail fluke too.)

The front and back flippers of Rodhocetus were also a mistaken speculation.

From *Evolution: The Grand Experiment* video series

*"Since then, we have found the forelimbs, the hands, and the front arms of Rodhocetus, and we understand that it **doesn't** have the kind of arms that can be spread out like flippers are on a whale."* [9]

— **Dr. Gingerich**

Dr. Phil Gingerich
University of Michigan

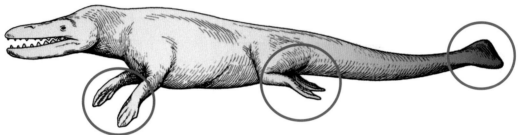

Drawing of Rodhocetus at the University of Michigan, where Dr. Gingerich works, indicating Rodhocetus had flippers and tail fluke similar to a whale. (Red circles added by author for emphasis.) The interview with Dr. Gingerich contradicted this museum display.

None of the scientists interviewed either before or after Dr. Gingerich's interview indicated there was a problem with *Rodhocetus* and its whale flipper or whale tail reconstruction. All spoke excitedly about this fossil, as if there were no doubts about the placement of the whale's flippers or whale's tail on the reconstructions of this fossil.

Dr. Taseer Hussain
Howard University

*"We have a **complete, modern whale-type structure in Rodhocetus**...There are not many modifications from Rodhocetus to the modern whale, other than changes in size of the structures."* [13]

— **Dr. Hussain**

Dr. Taseer Hussain, Paleontologist and Professor of Anatomy, Howard University, and Research Associate at the Smithsonian National Museum of Natural History. Dr. Hussain was the co-discoverer of Ambulocetus and sub-specializes in the evolution of whales.

The Last Step: *Basilosaurus*

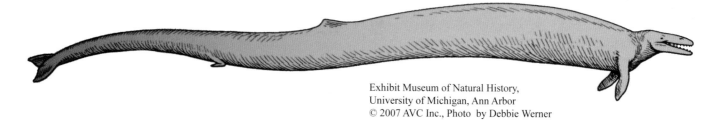

Exhibit Museum of Natural History,
University of Michigan, Ann Arbor
© 2007 AVC Inc., Photo by Debbie Werner

Basilosaurus was a very long and unusual looking whale with tiny back legs. Some have suggested that its back legs indicate it could walk, while others think the back appendages were instead used for reproduction.

According to the previously shown whale evolution diagram, *Basilosaurus* was the precursor to modern whales, one of the missing links.

Others disagree. Dr. Lawrence Barnes, a whale evolution expert from the Natural History Museum in Los Angeles, does not believe *Basilosaurus* was an ancestor to modern whales because this whale lived at the same time as the more modern forms of whales and, therefore, could not be the precursor. As Dr. Barnes explains: "...*Basilosaurus existed at a time when baleen-bearing mysticetes* [baleen whales] *are known to have existed, and echolocating odontocetes* [toothed whales] *are presumed to have existed.*"[14] Apparently, not all agree on *Basilosaurus* being the last ancestor prior to the evolution of the modern forms of whales.

Basilosaurus Skull

Exhibit Museum of Natural History,
University of Michigan, Ann Arbor
© 2007 AVC Inc., Photo by Debbie Werner

Summary:
The Fossil Evidence for Whale Evolution

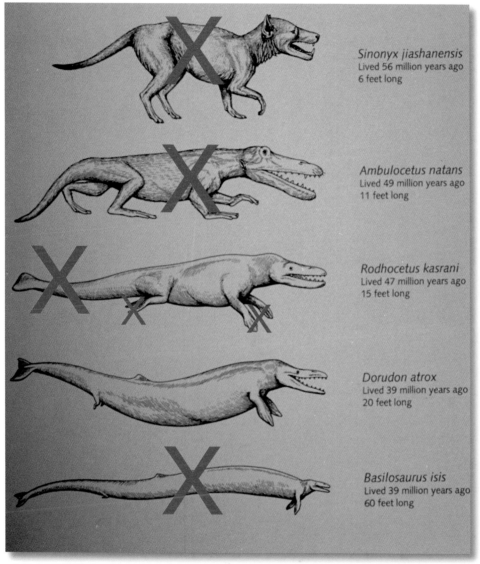

Sinonyx jiashanensis
Lived 56 million years ago
6 feet long

Ambulocetus natans
Lived 49 million years ago
11 feet long

Rodhocetus kasrani
Lived 47 million years ago
15 feet long

Dorudon atrox
Lived 39 million years ago
20 feet long

Basilosaurus isis
Lived 39 million years ago
60 feet long

Dr. Gingerich: *"...the [cat-like Sinonyx and the hyena-like Pachyaena]...will have to be put on a side branch... I doubt that they have any special relationship to whales."* [9]

Dr. Gingerich: *"Maybe [Ambulocetus] is not on the main line [of whale evolution]."* [9]

Dr. Gingerich: *"I now doubt that Rodhocetus would have had a fluked tail...Rodhocetus doesn't have the kind of arms that can be spread out like flippers."* [9]

Dr. Barnes suggests *Basilosaurus* was not on the line to modern whales. He believes it lived at the same time as more modern forms. [14]

Above: *Whale diagram on display at the University of Michigan where Dr. Gingerich works. Diagram was on display at the same time the interviews in this chapter were conducted. Red x's were added by author based on interviews with Dr. Gingerich and Dr. Barnes.*

What Do You Think?

Conclusions

Many evolution scientists agree that whales offer the ultimate example (best fossil proof) of evolution, but few of these scientists are aware of the discrepancies uncovered here. None of the experts interviewed mentioned or seemed to be aware of the problems with *Rodhocetus*.

Scientists who oppose evolution believe whale evolution is nothing but a story on paper, a story developed by scientists and artists eager to prove evolution. They suggest that if diagrams of whale evolution are examined critically, the same pattern is revealed as in other types of animal evolution, i.e., there are large ancestral gaps in the fossil record indicating that animals did not evolve. Instead, there is a sudden appearance of animal types in the fossil record. These same scientists suggest that if whale evolution is the *best* example of evolution, then for

all practical purposes, the theory is dead — especially in light of the fact that over two million fossil whale bones have been discovered representing thousands of whales. [15]

Scientists who support evolution suggest science is always changing and self-correcting. New discoveries cause scientists to modify their ideas and theories. You cannot toss out the good parts of a theory because of a few mistakes. They suggest that instead of throwing out the theory of evolution, a new invigorated search should be undertaken. Even though millions of fossil whale bones have been discovered, the fossil record of whales is not complete. New fossil whales are being discovered every year. They believe that one day all of the missing links for whales, including the land animal that evolved into a whale, will be found.

Do whales appear suddenly in the fossil record?

Whale skeleton, Kangaroo Island, Australia © 2007 AVC Inc., Photo by Debbie Werner

Author's Note: Since the first edition of this book was released, museums have changed their whale evolution displays to correct the serious problems revealed in this chapter. The reader is highly encouraged to now turn to Appendix F: Whale Evolution Update to learn about the latest changes and updates on walking whales.

THE FOSSIL RECORD OF BIRDS — PART 1:
ARCHAEOPTERYX

Bird Evolution and *Archaeopteryx*

Birds are amazing creatures. They can overcome gravity and fly for miles at a time. Some can swim underwater for great distances. Where did they come from?

With the nineteenth century discovery of the oldest known fossil bird, *Archaeopteryx,* some scientists believed they had found the missing link proving the evolution of birds from dinosaurs. Today, scientists who support Darwin consider the evolution of birds one of the three best fossil proofs for the theory of evolution (the other two being the evolution of whales from a land mammal and the evolution of men from apes). Many scientists believe *Archaeopteryx* is a hybrid animal, possessing traits similar to a dinosaur (dinosaur tail, scaly reptilian head, and claws) and a bird (feathers and wings).

There is, however, a controversy surrounding *Archaeopteryx.* Reconstructions of *Archaeopteryx* have varied over the years, and there have been recent disagreements within the scientific community regarding how *Archaeopteryx* should be artistically

Archaeopteryx lithografica, (negative fossil plate), Jura Museum, Germany © 2007 AVC Inc., Photo by Debbie Werner

recreated beyond its skeletal frame. This chapter will address these issues concerning this ancient bird fossil. The next chapter will then continue with the mysterious "feathered dinosaurs" discovered in China in the mid-1990s.

From *Evolution: The Grand Experiment* video series

"Archaeopteryx is a classical example of a connecting link between two high systematic categories, namely the classes of birds and reptiles...The discovery of the first specimens of Archaeopteryx met the expectations of the Darwinians and had an enormous impact on the scientific community... Its skeleton is still dinosaur-like, whereas it had already fully developed feathers...and obviously it was capable of powered flight." [1]

— Dr. Viohl

Dr. Gunter Viohl is Curator of the famous Jura Museum in Germany where one of the original Archaeopteryx fossils is kept.

Previous page: *Archaeopteryx model at a "feathered dinosaur" exhibit at the Museum Victoria, Melbourne, Australia.*

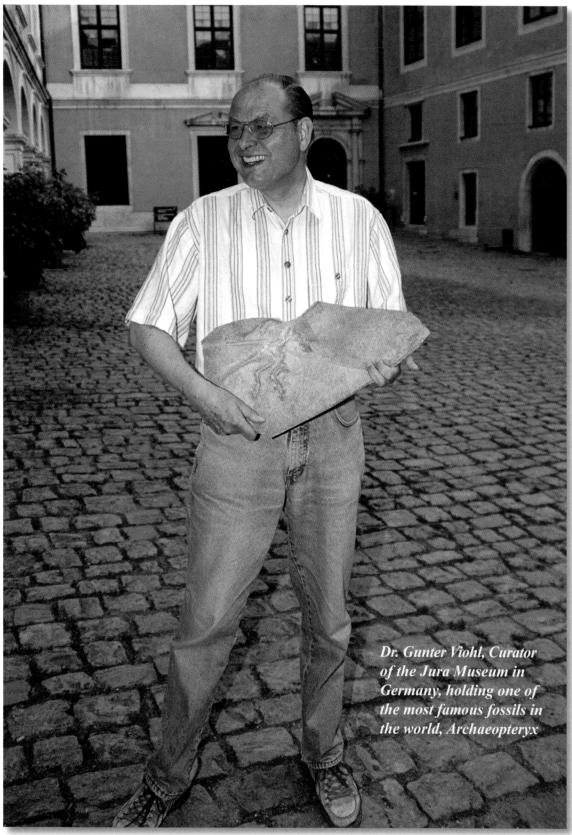

Dr. Gunter Viohl, Curator of the Jura Museum in Germany, holding one of the most famous fossils in the world, Archaeopteryx

A

B

Archaeopteryx Fossils

All of the fossil *Archaeopteryx* birds have been found in a small area surrounding the town of Solnhofen, Germany, just north of Munich. Most of these fossils are found not by paleontologists but by quarry workers mining the rock for tile floors and lithographic plates. (See following page.) Because the limestone is made up of very fine grains, it preserves the fossils in exquisite detail.

The fossils of *Archaeopteryx* are extremely rare. Over the past 140 years, only nine specimens have been found.

H

C

Clockwise from top left:
A: *Archaeopteryx lithografica*, 1956, Maxberg Museum, Solnhofen
B: *Archaeopteryx lithografica*, 1987, Burgermeister Muller Museum, Solnhofen
C: *Archaeopteryx lithographica*, 1861, British Museum, London
D: *Archaeopteryx lithografica*, 1951, (positive fossil plate), Jura Museum, Eichstaat
E: *Archaeopteryx lithografica*, 1951, (negative fossil plate), Jura Museum, Eichstaat
F: *Archaeopteryx lithografica*, 1876, Natural History Museum, Berlin
G: *Archaeopteryx bavarica*, 1992, Munich Paleontologic Museum
H: *Archaeopteryx lithografica*, 1855, Teylers Museum, Haarlem, Netherlands

G

D

F

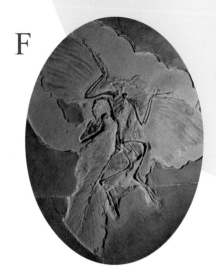

E

Photos on this page:
Jura Museum, Germany
© 2007 AVC Inc.,
Photos by Debbie Werner

Solnhofen Quarry, Germany
© 2007 AVC Inc., Photos by Debbie Werner

*The Solnhofen tile quarry where fossils of the famous bird Archaeopteryx were found.
Quarry workers split the limestone rock to make thin floor tiles. These floor tiles, coveted
by architectural designers, are shipped all over the world.*

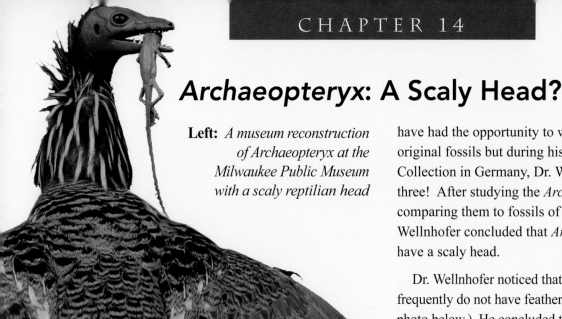

Archaeopteryx: A Scaly Head?

Left: *A museum reconstruction of Archaeopteryx at the Milwaukee Public Museum with a scaly reptilian head*

The interpretation of what *Archaeopteryx* actually looked like is a matter of debate today. Was it halfway between a dinosaur and a bird — a true missing link? Or was it just a bird?

The answer to this question has varied over the years due to the fluid nature of how different scientists and artists have reconstructed *Archaeopteryx* based on the skeletal fossil evidence. Early reconstructions of *Archaeopteryx* (above) suggested that this animal was half dinosaur/half bird with a scaly, featherless, reptilian head. The rationale for this model was the fact that imprints of head feathers were not seen on any of the fossils found. Scientists assumed the lack of feathers around the head of *Archaeopteryx* fossils meant the animal did not have feathers on its head during life. They took this interpretation one step further and concluded that this animal must have had scales on the head (even though they did not see scales in the fossils). Recently, some prominent evolution scientists have expressed strong reservations about this scaly-headed interpretation.

Dr. Peter Wellnhofer, Curator of the State Collection in Munich, Germany, had the unprecedented opportunity to examine and describe three of the original *Archaeopteryx* fossils. Very few scientists have had the opportunity to work with just one of the original fossils but during his tenure at the State Collection in Germany, Dr. Wellnhofer worked with three! After studying the *Archaeopteryx* fossils and comparing them to fossils of modern birds, Dr. Wellnhofer concluded that *Archaeopteryx* did *not* have a scaly head.

Dr. Wellnhofer noticed that fossils of modern birds frequently do not have feathers around the head. (See photo below.) He concluded that after a bird dies, but before it is fossilized, there is a tendency for the smaller feathers on the head to become detached and lost. The larger feathers on the wings tend to stay attached after death. Dr. Wellnhofer reasoned that if modern birds frequently fossilize without feather imprints around the head, then *Archaeopteryx* probably had feathers on its head too. Many other scientists now agree with Dr. Wellnhofer. Modern reconstructions of *Archaeopteryx,* such as the one on display at the Chicago Field Museum (bottom of next page), show *Archaeopteryx* with a feathered head.

Adding feathers to the head of *Archaeopteryx* poses a problem for the evolution of birds: With this simple reinstallation of feathers, *Archaeopteryx* no longer looks reptilian, nor does it look like a hybrid animal. Rather, it looks more like a modern bird.

Above: *A more modern fossil shore bird from Florissant Fossil Quarry. Note that this bird also does not have feather imprints preserved around the head.*

Older model
Archaeopteryx

Right: *An older museum reconstruction of Archaeopteryx at Jura Museum in Germany with a scaly reptilian head.*

© 2007 AVC Inc., Photo by Debbie Werner

From *Evolution: The Grand Experiment* video series

"It doesn't mean that the lack of feather imprints [around the head] means that there were no feathers. It's well possible that finer feathers and short and more delicate feathers [around the head] just were not preserved as fossils." [2]

— **Dr. Wellnhofer**

Dr. Peter Wellnhofer, Curator Emeritus of the Bavarian State Collection of Paleontology in Munich, worked on three of the original specimens of Archaeopteryx.

Right: *A newer reconstruction of Archaeopteryx at the Chicago Field Museum. With a feathered head, Archaeopteryx looks much more like a modern bird.*

© 2007 AVC Inc., Photo by Debbie Werner

Newer model
Archaeopteryx

Newer models of Archaeopteryx have changed: Feathers have replaced scales.

The Significance of the Wing Claws of *Archaeopteryx.*

Another feature noted by scientists is that *Archaeopteryx* had claws on its wings. (See fossil on right.) Many evolution scientists have suggested that claws on the wings indicate *Archaeopteryx* was the progeny of meat-eating dinosaurs (also with claws), such as *Deinonychus.*

Scientists who oppose evolution disagree, contending that claws on the wings do not necessarily link *Archaeopteryx* to meat-eating dinosaurs. They point out that other flying vertebrates also have claws on their wings. For example, modern bats have claws on their wings, but bats are mammals. Mammals are not thought to be the progeny of dinosaurs. Also, the ancient flying reptiles, called pterosaurs, had claws on their wings. Again, pterosaurs are not thought to be the descendants of dinosaurs. Modern birds, such as ostriches, hoatzins, and juvenile touracos, also have claws on their wings.[3] Yet these modern birds are not thought of as being the direct descendants of animals with claws. If flying vertebrates, in general, have claws on their wings, why do the claws of *Archaeopteryx* suggest evolution from meat-eating dinosaurs?

Archaeopteryx fossil and Pterosaur model
Jura Museum, Germany © 2007 AVC Inc.,
Photo by Debbie Werner

Pterosaur with claws on wings

Modern bird (ostrich) with claws on wings

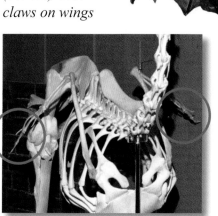

U. of Nebraska State Museum, Lincoln
© 2007 AVC Inc., Photo by Debbie Werner

Modern bat with claws on wings

The Significance of the Tail of *Archaeopteryx.*

When looking at the fossil of *Archaeopteryx*, you can see that its tail is very long compared to the rest of its body. By comparison, modern birds have short tails. This long, dinosaur-like tail leads proponents of evolution to believe that *Archaeopteryx* is the missing link between dinosaurs and birds.

Opponents of evolution differ. They suggest that a side-by-side comparison of the skeleton of *Archaeopteryx* with a skeleton of a modern bird shows few differences. They contend that *Archaeopteryx* was simply a bird. They also believe that the differences between *Archaeopteryx's* tail and a dinosaur's tail are so dramatic it would be difficult to consider them related. The tails of meat-eating dinosaurs are 4 to 5 *feet* long and covered with scales while the tail of *Archaeopteryx* is 4 to 5 *inches* long and is covered with feathers. Also, the tail of the reconstructed models of *Archaeopteryx* look rather like a modern bird's tail. (See photos at bottom of page.)

Archaeopteryx

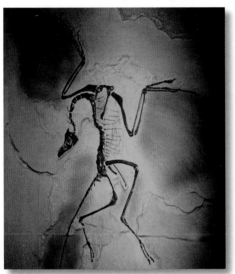

Archaeopteryx, Jura Museum, Germany
(post-production color enhanced)
© 2007 AVC Inc., Photo by Debbie Werner

Cormorant (Modern Bird)

Fossil Cormorant skeleton, Wyoming Dinosaur Center,
Thermopolis © 2007 AVC Inc., Photo by Debbie Werner

Carnegie Museum of Natural History
© 2007 AVC Inc., Photo by Carl Werner

*If one disregards the controversial scaly head covering depicted in this painting (**left**), Archaeopteryx looks more bird-like than a modern cormorant (**right**).*

The Significance of the Teeth of *Archaeopteryx*.

Photos Jura Museum, Germany
© 2007 AVC Inc., Photo by Debbie Werner

Evolution scientists point out that *Archaeopteryx* had teeth, a unique feature not seen in any modern bird. This trait, along with the dinosaur-like tail, the scaly reptilian head, and the dinosaur-like claws confirms, beyond a shadow of a doubt, that this animal was a true missing link between two distinct animal groups, namely dinosaurs and birds.

Opponents of evolution suggest the teeth of *Archaeopteryx* are not similar to meat-eating dinosaurs, their proposed ancestor. Meat-eating dinosaurs have teeth that are serrated, like a steak knife, but the teeth of *Archaeopteryx* are smooth. [4] These differences infer that the teeth of *Archaeopteryx* were not passed down from a meat-eating dinosaur but are simply a unique characteristic of this bird. They point out that every bird type, such as ostriches, humming-birds, and even *Archaeopteryx,* is unique, but unique traits do not imply evolution. Some birds, such as the Great Hornbill, have unusually large bills. Others, such as the ostrich, have unusually long necks. And still others, like the puffin, can dive deep in the water and use their wings to "fly" underwater. They also assert that similar features do not necessarily imply relatedness. For example, an ostrich is not related to a giraffe because it has a long neck. A duck is not related to the duck-billed platypus because it has a billed beak. A puffin bird is not related to a fish because it can swim deep in the water. By the same token, *Archaeopteryx* is not related to dinosaurs just because it has teeth. They argue that similarities between animals are circumstantial and inconclusive evidence. (See Chapter 5: Similarities.) Only a whole series of fossils, showing a dinosaur slowly changing into a flying bird, such as *Archaeopteryx*, would prove the evolution of birds.

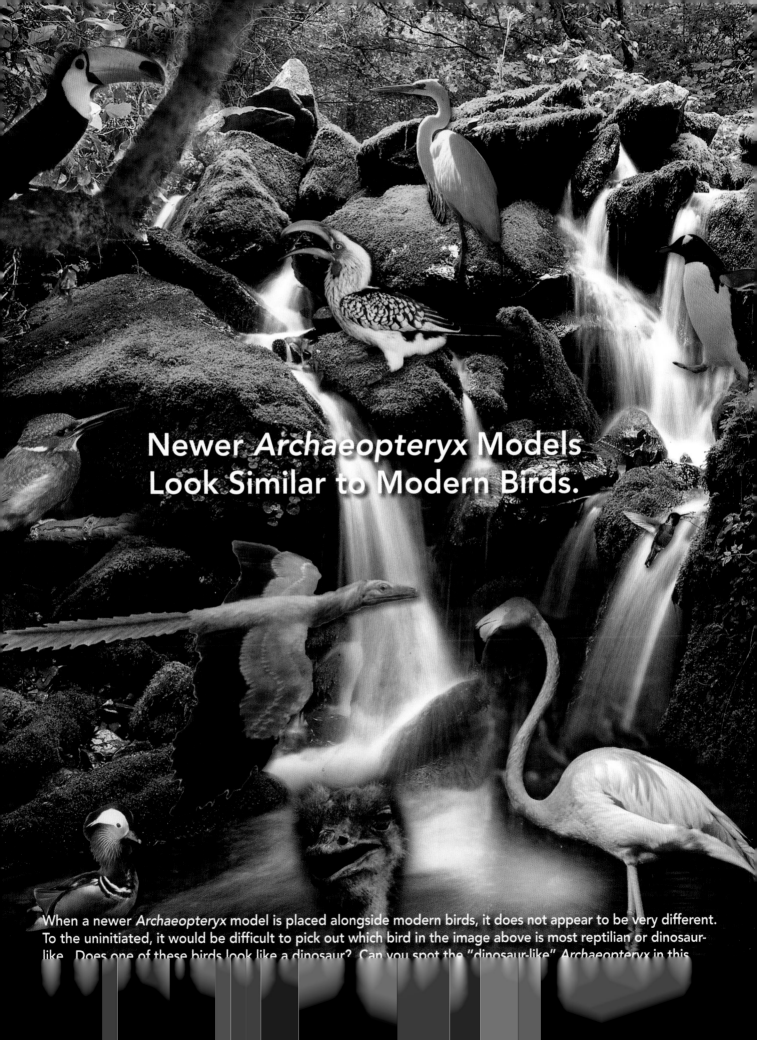

Newer *Archaeopteryx* Models
Look Similar to Modern Birds.

When a newer *Archaeopteryx* model is placed alongside modern birds, it does not appear to be very different. To the uninitiated, it would be difficult to pick out which bird in the image above is most reptilian or dinosaur-like. Does one of these birds look like a dinosaur? Can you spot the "dinosaur-like" *Archaeopteryx* in this

A

B

C

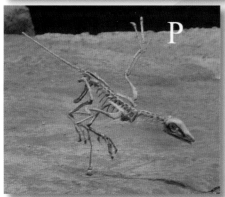

P

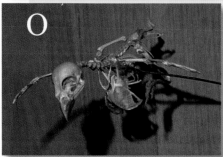

O

Does the Skeleton of *Archaeopteryx* Appear Any More Dinosaur-like Than These Other Bird Skeletons?

Can you spot Archaeopteryx?
(Answer on next page.)

M

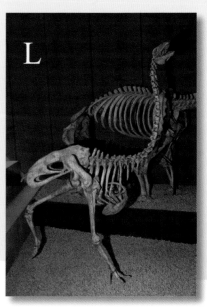

L

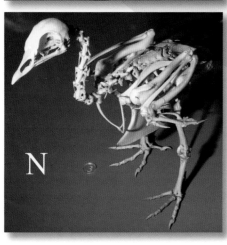

N

Previous page: *Archaeopteryx is flying in foreground, just above the ostrich.*

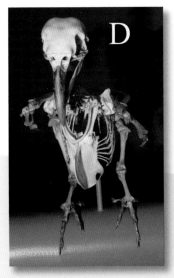

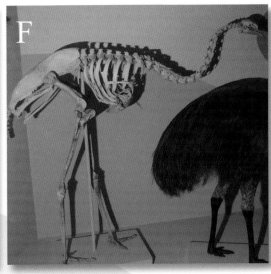

Clockwise from top left:

A: Modern Malleefowl
B: Modern Nicobar Pigeon
C: Modern English Sparrow
D: Modern New Zealand Kea
E: Modern Hummingbird
F: Modern Emu
G: Modern Little Penguin
H: Modern Ostrich
I: Modern American
   Great Horned Owl

J: Modern Sandhill Crane
K: Modern Chicken
L: Extinct flightless bird,
   Genyornis newtoni
M: Modern Turkey
N: Modern Malleefowl
O: Modern English Sparrow
P: *Archaeopteryx*

See Photo Credits for photo source locations.

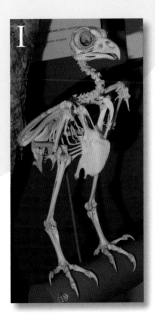

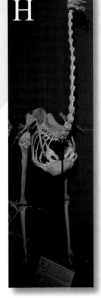

The Dinosaur Ancestor for Birds Is Unknown!

Scientists who believe that birds evolved from dinosaurs cannot decide from which dinosaur *Archaeopteryx* evolved. In the past, many have suggested that the meat-eating *Deinonychus* dinosaur was the ancestor to *Archaeopteryx*. But this is problematic since this dinosaur lived ***after*** *Archaeopteryx*. (See diagram next page.)

"So we don't know exactly the dinosaurs from which the birds evolved." [1]

— Dr. Viohl

Below: *Scientists and museums often suggest this dinosaur, Deinonychus, as the animal that may have evolved into birds because Deinonychus had arm bones similar to those of Archaeopteryx.* [5] *But Deinonychus lived 30 million years **after** Archaeopteryx and, therefore, could not be the ancestor of birds.*

California Academy of Sciences, San Francisco
© 2007 AVC Inc., Photo by Debbie Werner

Dinosaur Age Fossil Layers
Millions of years ago (MYA)*

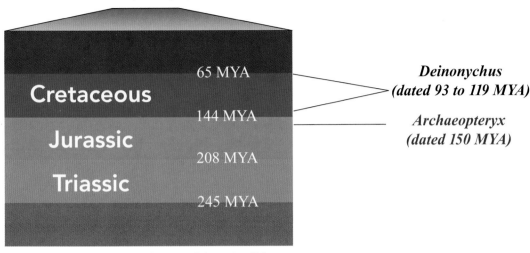

Cretaceous	65 MYA		*Deinonychus*
	144 MYA		*(dated 93 to 119 MYA)*
Jurassic			*Archaeopteryx*
	208 MYA		*(dated 150 MYA)*
Triassic	245 MYA		

*Scientists do not agree on the age of these fossil layers.

Did *Archaeopteryx* Even Evolve from a Dinosaur?

Although textbooks and museum displays[5] suggest birds evolved from dinosaurs, possibly *Deinonychus,* some scientists specializing in bird evolution are not sure if this is true. Some experts believe birds may have evolved from another type of reptile called an archosaur. This is referred to as the reptile ancestor problem of birds.

"Of course there are still two groups. The one supports the origin of birds from Triassic archosaurs, which are not directly dinosaurs. And the other group supports the idea that birds are closely related to dinosaurs and originated from dinosaurs directly… You see it is not so easy, not so black or white."[2]

— **Dr. Wellnhofer**

Since evolution scientists are not sure what type of animal evolved into birds, opposing scientists find the case for bird evolution dubious, at best. They ask: What does this say for the theory of evolution, as a whole, if bird evolution is touted as one of the three best fossil proofs for evolution?

Given the extraordinarily rich bird and dinosaur fossil records, they argue that the ancestral gaps between reptiles and *Archaeopteryx* is too great.

Scientists who support evolution disagree with this assessment and maintain that the evidence is overwhelming for the evolution of birds from dinosaurs.

Bird Evolution Conclusions:
If *Archaeopteryx* Was a Bird, Then
There Are *No* Ancestors to Birds.

The theory of evolution predicted that when enough fossils were found, evidence would emerge showing a reptile slowly forming wings over millions of years and eventually changing into *Archaeopteryx*. (See Chapter 6.) To date, 100,000 fossil dinosaurs and 200,000 fossil bird specimens have been collected,[6] yet evolution science cannot demonstrate a single reptile (dinosaur or archosaur) evolving into a bird.

If *Archaeopteryx* was a bird that could fly and if no direct reptilian ancestors of *Archaeopteryx* have been found to date, then there is a large gap in the fossil record between these two groups. Once again, some who oppose evolution charge that the repeated lack of direct ancestors for all animals, including birds, challenges the validity of the theory of evolution. They also suggest that museum diagrams depicting bird evolution are misleading. Only by placing fossil numbers on these diagrams do they tell the whole story.

Chicago Field Museum diagram demonstrating the evolution of birds.

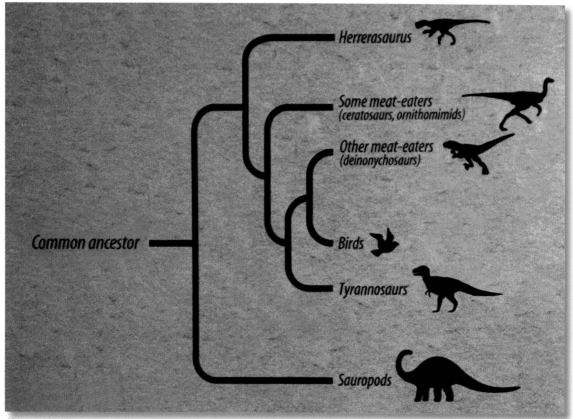

Chicago Field Museum, Illinois © 2007 AVC Inc., Photo by Debbie Werner

From *Evolution: The Grand Experiment* video series

"What we actually find in the fossil record is a systematic absence of the transitional forms between the major divisions. Even as Richard Goldschmitt, a very definite evolutionist, pointed out, that at the level of the phyla, the classes, the orders, and he said down to almost every family, each one appears fully formed with no transitional forms." [7]

— **Dr. Gish**

Dr. Duane Gish opposes evolution and is the author of the book **Evolution: The Fossils Still Say No!**

What Do You Think?

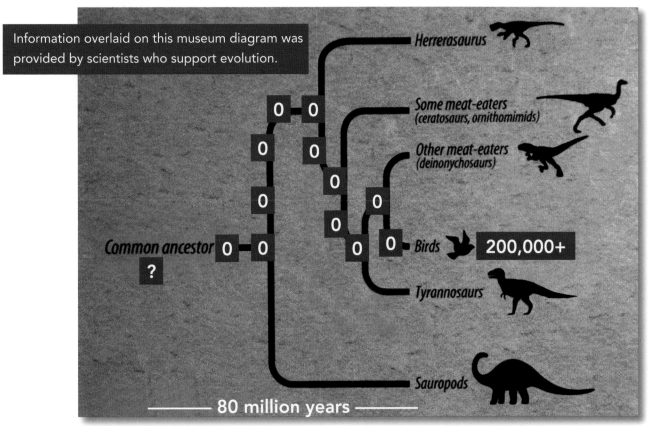

Information overlaid on this museum diagram was provided by scientists who support evolution.

*Same diagram superimposed with the **actual number of fossils** found.*

Postscript: *Archaeopteryx* Found with Fossils of *Modern* Animals.

The information presented thus far has certainly cast doubt on bird evolution, but there is still another important aspect to consider. Over the last century, the rock layers that have given up *Archaeopteryx* have also given up numerous fossils of *modern-appearing* animals, such as sharks, guitar fish, horseshoe crabs, dragonflies, turtles, lizards, lobsters, crayfish, shrimp, cockroaches, woodwasps, waterbugs, grasshoppers, beetles, scorpion flies, water skeeters, sea urchins, sea stars, and prawns. These fossils appear similar to modern animals. Scientists who oppose evolution suggest these modern-appearing animals laying next to *Archaeopteryx* are yet another reason for questioning the theory of evolution. They believe that these fossils indicate that life has not evolved, simply some animals, such as *Archaeopteryx* and dinosaurs, have gone extinct.

Scientists who support evolution explain these modern-appearing animals as "living fossils." In other words, these types of animals were so well-adapted to the environment that they did not need to change and have therefore remained the same for over a hundred million years.

Because of the noticeably large number of living fossils that have been discovered alongside *Archaeopteryx* and dinosaurs, this topic will be addressed in the second book and video in this series, *Living Fossils*.

Does this mean that evolution did not occur?

What Do You Think?

Fossil photos from Jura Museum, Germany.
© 2007 AVC Inc., Photos by Debbie Werner.

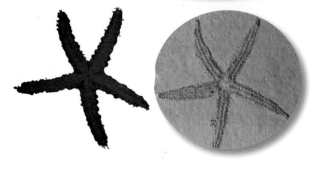

Above, left: *Fossil grasshopper found in the same layer as Archaeopteryx. Compare to modern variety.*
Above, right: *Horseshoe crab fossil found near Archaeopteryx. Compare to the undersurface of a modern horseshoe crab.*
Left: *Compare this modern starfish to the fossil starfish found with Archaeopteryx.*

THE FOSSIL RECORD OF BIRDS — PART 2: FEATHERED DINOSAURS

A model of a "feathered dinosaur" on display at the Museum Victoria in Melbourne, Australia.

Bird Evolution and "Feathered Dinosaurs"

In the mid 1990s, fossils of "dinosaurs with feathers" were found in the Liaoning Province of China which, according to some, added further evidence that birds evolved from dinosaurs. These new fossils are considered by many scientists who support evolution to be the missing links between dinosaurs and modern birds.

Although many scientists are excited about these fossils, problems are emerging concerning their feathers, their age, and their authenticity. Criticisms have been voiced, not just from scientists who oppose evolution, but from those who support it as well.

Dinosaurs or birds?

Although many newspaper headlines have reported the discovery of these fossils as "feathered dinosaurs," some evolution experts are quietly reconsidering these claims and questioning if these fossils are even dinosaurs at all. These paleontologists believe the "feathered dinosaur" fossils from China are actually flightless birds, similar to ostriches or emus of today.

It is hard to imagine that one would have trouble distinguishing whether a fossil was a dinosaur or a bird, but this seems to be the case. Those who believe the Chinese fossils are *birds* base their interpretation on the anatomy of the feathers and the size of the wings. The feathers look like those of modern flightless birds. Those evolution scientists who consider these fossils as *dinosaurs* with feathers base their impression on the fact that some of these specimens have teeth and some have other dinosaur-like features, such as a long tail. At the moment, the only conclusion one can draw from these fossils is that scientists who support evolution have not decided yet what these fossils represent.

Are the "feathered dinosaurs" flightless birds?

"There is the problem. Are these dinosaurs with feathers? The other possibility would be they are not dinosaurs; they are very primitive birds...The feathers of flightless birds of today are as well-reduced in structure, are not as complicated as bird feathers [that] are used for...flight. So this again is a...problem." [1]

— **Dr. Wellnhofer**

Dr. Peter Wellnhofer, Curator Emeritus of the Bavarian State Collection of Paleontology in Munich, who worked on three of the original specimens of Archaeopteryx.

Feathered Dinosaurs from China

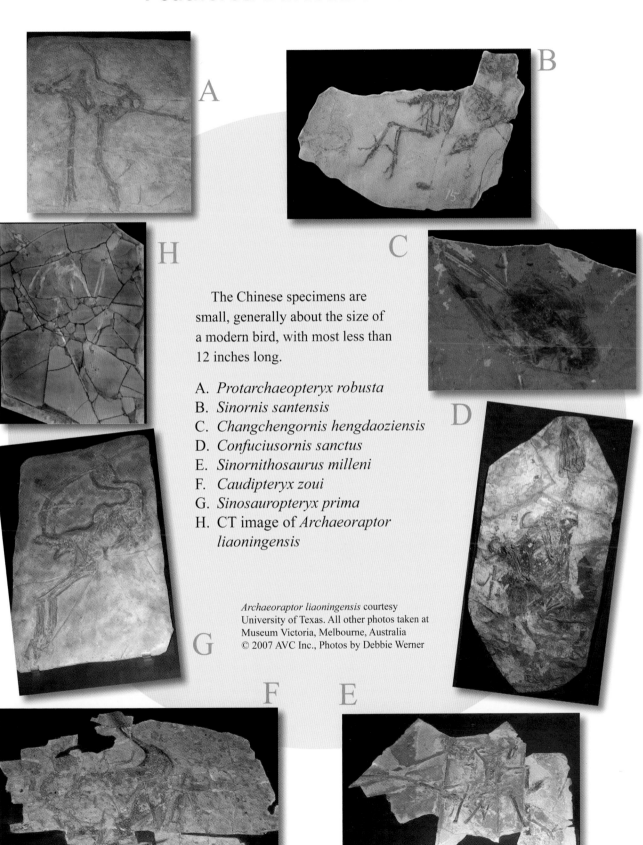

The Chinese specimens are small, generally about the size of a modern bird, with most less than 12 inches long.

A. *Protarchaeopteryx robusta*
B. *Sinornis santensis*
C. *Changchengornis hengdaoziensis*
D. *Confuciusornis sanctus*
E. *Sinornithosaurus milleni*
F. *Caudipteryx zoui*
G. *Sinosauropteryx prima*
H. CT image of *Archaeoraptor liaoningensis*

Archaeoraptor liaoningensis courtesy University of Texas. All other photos taken at Museum Victoria, Melbourne, Australia
© 2007 AVC Inc., Photos by Debbie Werner

To understand why some evolution scientists have concluded the Chinese "feathered dinosaurs" are actually flightless birds, one must first know the difference between the feathers of modern birds that can fly and the feathers of modern flightless birds. Feathers from *birds that can fly*, such as cardinals or blue jays, are *asymmetrical*, meaning the quill (rachis) does not run down the center of the feather. It is instead off-centered. (See photo below, left.) In contrast, the feathers of modern *flightless birds*, such as an ostrich or emu, have *symmetrical*

feathers; that is, the quill (rachis) does run down the center of the feather. (See photograph below, right.) Besides this obvious difference, feathers from modern flightless birds are also less dense, less organized, and do not have barbules.

Some of the fossils from China have feathers similar to modern flightless birds. It is these features that cause some to believe that these animals are actually flightless birds and not "feathered dinosaurs."

The Chinese "feathered dinosaurs" had feathers similar to today's emu or ostrich.

Far left: *Feather of a modern flying bird. The quill (rachis) is off-center forming an asymmetrical feather. The barbs are dense and are held tightly in place by barbules. Compare this feather to the feather of a modern* **flightless** *bird (emu). In flightless birds (and some of the Chinese fossils), the quill (rachis) runs down the center of the feather making the feather symmetrical. Also, in flightless birds and some of the Chinese specimens, the barbs are not tightly held in place by barbules but are instead loose and less dense.*

"But [the Chinese specimens] *are not capable of powered flight. You can see this from the feather structures. The wing feathers had still a symmetric structure."* [2]

— Dr. Viohl

Dr. Gunter Viohl is Curator of the famous Jura Museum in Germany where one of the original Archaeopteryx fossils is kept.

Chinese "Feathered Dinosaurs" Are the Wrong Age To Be the Ancestors of Flying Birds.

An even more basic problem with the fossils from China has to do with their age. These "feathered dinosaurs" (or flightless birds as some believe) lived 25 million years *after* the first bird *Archaeopteryx*. In other words, the rock layers containing the "feathered dinosaurs" are younger in age than the rock layers where the bird *Archaeopteryx* was found.

Scientists who oppose the idea that birds evolved from dinosaurs ask this: How could the "feathered dinosaurs" be the *ancestors* of birds if they lived *after Archaeopteryx,* a bird that could already fly?

They suggest that these fossils could not be the missing link between dinosaurs and *Archaeopteryx.*

Scientists who support the idea that birds evolved from dinosaurs believe that feathered dinosaurs also probably lived before *Archaeopteryx*, although none have been found in these layers yet. They hope one day they will find feathered dinosaurs in rock layers older than *Archaeopteryx* to prove bird evolution (for anyone who would doubt that birds evolved from dinosaurs).

> *"The dinosaurs in China are not the ancestors of birds, of course. They couldn't be because they are later than Archaeopteryx...There must have been older dinosaurs with feathers, yet we haven't any evidence for them, unfortunately."* [2]
>
> **— Dr. Viohl**

Fossil Layers
Millions of years ago (MYA)*

The "feathered dinosaurs" came *after* the first bird!

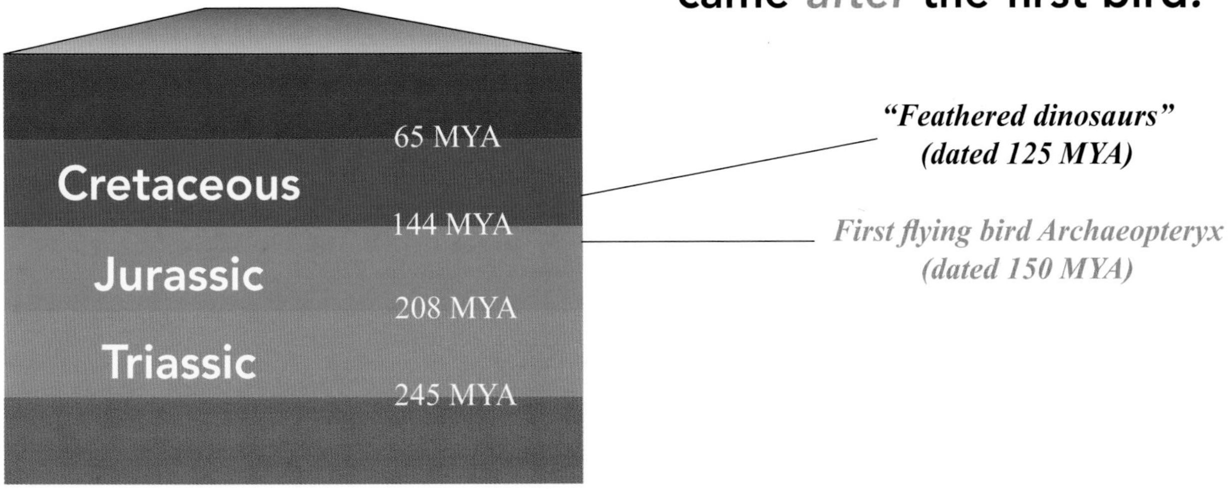

"Feathered dinosaurs"
(dated 125 MYA)

Cretaceous

65 MYA

144 MYA

First flying bird Archaeopteryx
(dated 150 MYA)

Jurassic

208 MYA

Triassic

245 MYA

*Scientists do not agree on the age of these fossil layers.

Are the Chinese Fossils Even Real?

In addition to the discrepancies involving the feathers and the age of these fossils, some evolution scientists have raised pointed questions regarding the authenticity of these fossils from China.

If you were ever allowed to pick up any of these rare specimens at a museum, you would be very impressed. They feel very heavy and solid. Scientists who have held these Chinese fossils in their hands have had these same thoughts, while marveling at the evidence for the evolution of birds from dinosaurs. Little did they know that there was a fundamental problem with these fossils; namely, that many of these Chinese fossils had been altered. These scientists were unaware that the Chinese fossils did *not* come out of the ground as they appeared. Understanding how these fossils were found and then "assembled" is a key factor when considering their significance and reliability.

When the original Chinese "feathered dinosaurs" were discovered by quarry workers, they were dug out of the ground in sheets of very fragile, thin rock. If the fossil was broken, the pieces were gathered and later reassembled in a most unusual manner, like a mosaic using mortar. It appears that in some cases, fragments of the original fossil were missing, and quarry workers and scientists substituted fossils or other rocks to fill in the gaps. In order for the completed specimen not to look fake or reassembled, the mortar was painted.

In light of this process, certain fossil specimens, which at first looked and felt so believable and solid, now beg a series of questions. Who was there when the fossils were found? Who kept the pieces before it was reassembled? Who assembled the fossil? Did a scientist oversee the assembly process? Are any of the imprints of the feathers missing because of rock substitutions? Were the buyers of these fossils aware of how they were assembled? Are all of the fossil bones contained in the specimens original? Were any

Jura Museum, Germany
© 2007 AVC Inc., Photo by Debbie Werner

Above: *Scientist holding a fossil of Confuciusornis found in China. Although the fossil looks real, the white paint on the upper edge of the fossil indicates that repairs were made and the fossil is a composite.*

of the fossil bones added from another specimen? Why was the mortar painted to hide the repairs?

Dr. Timothy Rowe had an eye-opening experience when he examined what appeared to be a perfect, museum-quality specimen from China called *Confuciusornis*. Although the fossil *Confuciusornis* looked genuine upon initial inspection, when Dr. Rowe CT scanned the fossil, substitutions of fossil and rock became obvious. Dr. Rowe recounts his uneasy

Dr. Rowe Scans First Chinese
"Feathered Dinosaur" Specimen.

feelings when he first realized the fossil "feathered dinosaur" was not what it first appeared to be: *"And this was brought to me, and I thought this was how it came out of the ground. And I thought, 'Wow, what an awesome specimen.' It's complete and massive and easy to handle and only by scanning it, did I learn, in fact, how it had been repaired. Many of the paleontologists who have visited the site understand how these things are repaired and they already knew this. But I've never been to China. I've never seen Liaoning for myself. And, by scanning it though, we thought, 'Oh, so that's what's going on here.' And, it was a little bit of a jolt because that repair process was hidden in this specimen and, to be honest, at that time, I hadn't really thought in such length of what all the conflicts are between commercial and scientific objectives in these specimens. And so, this really started me thinking, 'Well, there's hmm, there's a little more here than meets the eye.'"*

Dr. Rowe continued to discuss the oddities he encountered with the Chinese specimen *Confuciusornis*: *"This specimen* [of *Confuciusornis*], *when it was collected, was fractured into many pieces. The rock that contains them is very thin...And, the repair method that's used in this case, that's customary in this region, involves finding another stone that's solid, that has no fractures in it, another massive piece of shale. It's like having a piece of wood, something like that, a plate of wood to back this, and you smear some grout or glue of some kind over that and then you press the pieces into place. And so, it's like building a mosaic.*

"But, given that that's the process of repair, you can also see how easy it is to do a better or worse job...And, then if the object is being prepared for commercial sale...the last step...would be to do the cosmetic work on it, to disguise the fractures, to hide the fractures, to hide the blemishes, and to make it look better...Well, if the pieces that are glued together don't fit together naturally, often there are gaps that are left. And so, you can imagine how someone would be able to press grout in from the top or lay it in with a palette knife or something like this. And that would fill the fractures and it also serves to make the specimen more solid and more stable...It's a simple matter to take some paint and touch that up to make the fractures go away. And, that's exactly what's happened in this specimen. When you look at it, when I first held it and looked at it, I didn't see very many fractures at all. And, in fact, I didn't really know how it was built until we did the CT scanning and could see it in cross-sections."

"The edges of the Confuciusornis specimen had been painted and so I couldn't see this cross-section when I was handling the specimen...It looked like a single, massive piece of rock...Only by looking at it in cross-section [by CT scanning] *could I see that it was built in three layers, two of which were natural and the intervening layer was made by humans."* [3]

— **Dr. Rowe**

Dr. Timothy Rowe, Professor of Biology and Geology at the University of Texas, and also the Director of the Vertebrate Paleontology Laboratory of the Texas Memorial Museum.

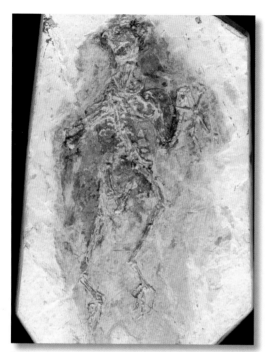

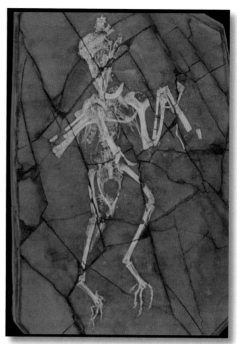

Above, left: *The Chinese fossil Confuciusornis appears to be part of a solid piece of rock with no hint of tampering. Only when Dr. Rowe put this fossil under a CT scanner did he realize separate pieces of rock and bone had been assembled to form the fossil. (CT scan image of same fossil on right.)*

Not only did the CT scanner show that the fossil, *Confuciusornis*, was assembled from dozens of separate pieces of rock and bone (see CT scan above), but it also revealed the grout that was used to assemble the fossil. The grout was obvious because it had air bubbles and chips of steel in it. (See cross-sectional CT scan image below.) Dr. Rowe: *"But*

once we scanned it, we could understand that there was this massive shale backing, a solid piece of rock without fractures. [On top of that layer] *we could see the grout layer. And, the grout layer is a human construct, okay. It's like mixing cement or mixing plaster of Paris. And, it has a unique human signature, a unique human thumbprint, and that*

Photo, CT scan images, and diagram on this page courtesy of the University of Texas CT Scan Lab, Austin.

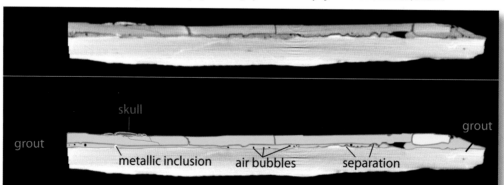

Above: *CT scan image showing the three layers that made up this Chinese feathered dinosaur fossil. The bottom layer, a piece of shale, was used as an artificial backing for the fossil. Grout was then placed on top of this shale backing and then the fossils were laid on top of the grout. A steel fragment (metallic inclusion) and air bubbles can be seen in the CT scan image on the top. None of this was apparent to the naked eye.*

One of the arm bones was upside down in the fossil.

is the presence of air bubbles. Normally, these would all be squeezed out over the millions of years that this thing was lying in the ground. And, we would also find metallic fragments. In all of the kinds of cements and grouts and things, a little bit of metal finds its way in there because the machinery that digs these things up, you know, metal wears off it. Well, metal fragments are just a part of our environment. They're kind of like fibers in a murder case. You know, they're just out there. And, I can guarantee that there was no steel in the Cretaceous. And so, when we see steel objects in these things, we know that it's got to be made by humans. It's a simple, simple thing."

An even more significant finding occurred as Dr. Rowe continued with his examination of the *Confuciusornis* fossil using the CT scanner. Parts

were, in fact, not from the original fossil. They had been substituted. There were fossil fragments from one or more other fossils that did not belong to this animal. One of the disputed fragments pertained to the jaw bone. Dr. Rowe: *"Well, I have no idea what animal this piece came from. It's just a very small fragment of bone, and it was probably chipped out to fit this space…And, from more complete specimens, we know that the back end of the jaw of Confuciusornis doesn't look like this. So, I have no idea where this extraneous piece came from…And there are some other odd pieces around the edges, too, that don't fit on this…There's a little piece of the radius* [wing bone] *that's upside down."*

Dr. Rowe's CT scan discoveries of fossil substitutions would not end here and soon he found himself in the middle of a scientist's worst nightmare.

Below: *Although fossils of Confuciusornis appear solid and unaltered, this is far from the truth.*

Jura Museum, Germany © 2007 AVC Inc., Photo by Debbie Werner

Dr. Rowe Scans Second Chinese "Feathered Dinosaur" Specimen and Finds Fraud.

As Dr. Rowe's work on the Chinese specimen *Confuciusornis* soon became known by other scientists, it was logical that other specimens from China would be brought to him for analysis. The next specimen brought to Dr. Rowe for CT scanning was an exciting fossil called *Archaeoraptor (*full name *Archaeoraptor liaoningensis),* a fossil thought to prove the evolution of birds from dinosaurs. *Archaeoraptor* was unusual because it had the appearance of two different animals blended together, just as Darwin predicted. Some of the features of *Archaeorpator,* such as the feathers and the wings, were similar to birds. But other features, such as the tail, looked reptilian. Yet, unlike *Archaeopteryx,* there were no feathers on the tail of this specimen. It appeared even more dinosaur-like than *Archaeopteryx.* This fossil was touted as the missing link that scientists had been looking for to prove the evolution of birds from dinosaurs. Months later, *National Geographic* magazine would write this: "[*Archaeoraptor liaoningensis*] *is perhaps the best evidence since Archaeopteryx that birds did, in fact, evolve from certain types of carnivorous dinosaurs."* [4]

At the request of a *National Geographic* scientist, Dr. Rowe performed a CT scan on this evolutionary breakthrough fossil on July 29, 1999 (three months before it was to be published). Rowe's earlier experience of CT scanning helped him to interpret this new fossil specimen rather rapidly. Again, what he saw on the computer screen of the CT scanner left him speechless.

First, Dr. Rowe noticed irregularities in the CT scan images of *Archaeoraptor.* There were problems with the surrounding pieces of rock. Some were thick pieces of rock; others were thin. Some were dense rock; others were less dense. The rock pieces in the fossil obviously didn't come from the same rock layer. Also, the fracture lines that appeared in the CT scanned images did not line up. It looked as if some of the rocks and fossils had

been substituted. Where fractures should have been, they were not and vice versa. There were also problems with the bones. The tail didn't exactly fit onto the pelvis. The foot bones were *exact* copies of each other, mirror images of the same foot. The leg bones couldn't have been from the same animal because they didn't fit either. In all, 39 of the rock pieces did not belong. Additionally, 26 fossil bones were not from this bird but were from *four* other animals, including a dinosaur tail. Dr. Rowe and his team at the University of Texas were shocked this fossil had gotten this far without having its authenticity validated. It was only three months away from being published in a leading public science magazine.

After further analysis of the CT scan images, Dr. Rowe and his team were able to determine, step by step, how the fossil was *fraudulently* constructed. Dr. Rowe: *"It was built from a new species of a Cretaceous bird and a new species of a Dromaeosaur* [dinosaur]… *We could find no verifiable fit between the tail, the most spectacular part of this specimen…and any of the other parts of the* [fossil] *block. And, we found other irregularities as well…The two shinbones were glued in. And, likewise, these have no verifiable associations. The next thing that happened is that the foot was glued on, and I say foot rather than feet because this is a single foot. This is a slab and counter-slab that were split and separated and glued in place to make it look as though there are right and left feet there. It's a clever use of materials. You know, if you're limited, you take a single foot and turn it into two, you know, very, very creative… And, that's how Archaeoraptor was built. And, from the anatomical clues and from the clues from the fractures in cross-section, what I can say about it is that these twenty-three pieces really do go together and there's no verifiable fit between these* [other 65 pieces]."

CHAPTER 15

Archaeoraptor liaoningensis: A Feathered Fraud

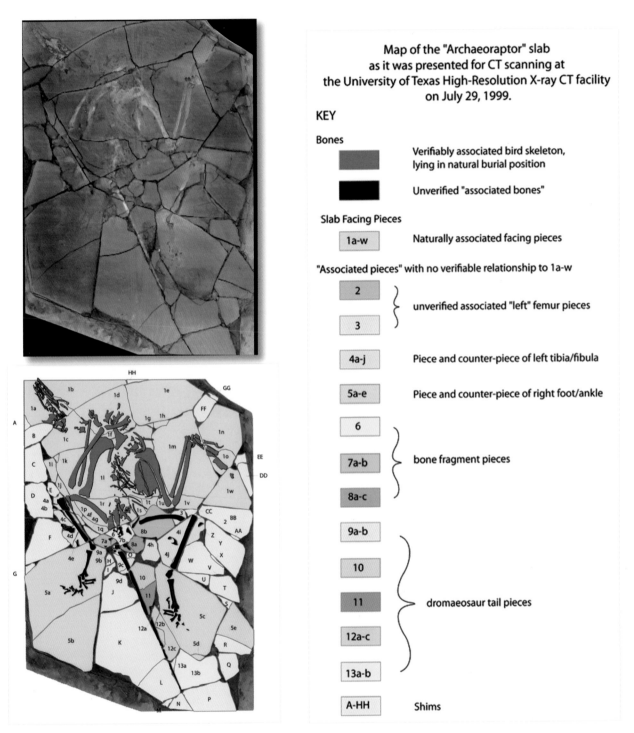

Map of the "Archaeoraptor" slab
as it was presented for CT scanning at
the University of Texas High-Resolution X-ray CT facility
on July 29, 1999.

KEY

Bones

| | Verifiably associated bird skeleton, lying in natural burial position |
| | Unverified "associated bones" |

Slab Facing Pieces

| 1a-w | Naturally associated facing pieces |

"Associated pieces" with no verifiable relationship to 1a-w

2	} unverified associated "left" femur pieces
3	
4a-j	Piece and counter-piece of left tibia/fibula
5a-e	Piece and counter-piece of right foot/ankle
6	} bone fragment pieces
7a-b	
8a-c	
9a-b	} dromaeosaur tail pieces
10	
11	
12a-c	
13a-b	
A-HH	Shims

Top, left: *CT scan image of Archaeoraptor liaoningensis showing it was composed of 88 pieces of rock and bone. Without the CT scan, one would never have realized this specimen was a fraud. Compare the CT scan (**top, left**) to the diagram (**bottom, left**) showing which rocks and bones came from different sources. Each different color represents a fossil or rock from a different source. Only the rock in yellow and the bones in red are original. Everything else was fraudulently placed and hidden with mortar and paint.* CT scan image, diagram and chart courtesy of the University of Texas CT Scan Lab, Austin.

What Would You Do if You Found Yourself in This Position?

Now, imagine if you were the lead scientist working for *National Geographic* magazine on this story and you were told that all the pieces didn't fit, and that something was wrong with the fossil tail. How would you react? Put yourself in this position for a moment. What would *you* do? Your entire scientific career is on the line, as well as your credibility with this magazine. You have three months before the story is to be published. Luckily, no damage has been done, since only a few people even know about this fossil. With one (embarrassing) call to the magazine's headquarters, you could cancel the story and regroup. Maybe you could salvage some of the information and repackage it for another day, another article. But this scientist pushed ahead.

In spite of being made aware of the CT scan results, he published the find anyway and did not mention the CT scan irregularities found by Dr. Rowe. It was written up as a spectacular new "feathered dinosaur" with a two-page photo spread of the fossil and models showing what this "feathered dinosaur" looked like. (See November 1999 issue of *National Geographic*.) The scientist still thought this "feathered dinosaur" from China was real and proved the evolution of birds from dinosaurs. In retrospect, knowing this background information, it is quite interesting to read. Below are a few quotes from this article. [4]

"A Flying Dinosaur?"

"It's a missing link between terrestrial dinosaurs and birds that could actually fly."

"This fossil is perhaps the best evidence since Archaeopteryx that birds did, in fact, evolve from certain types of carnivorous dinosaurs."

"Preliminary studies show that this specimen has startling similarities to both dinosaurs and birds."

"New Birdlike Fossils are Missing Links in Dinosaur Evolution."

"Scientists funded by National Geographic...used CT scans to view parts of the animal obscured by rock. Preliminary study of the arms suggests that it was a better flier than Archaeopteryx, the earliest known bird. Its tail, however, is strikingly similar to the stiff tails of a family of predatory dinosaurs called dromaeosaurs. This mix of advanced and primitive features is exactly what scientists would expect to find in dinosaurs experimenting with flight."

[**Author's Note:** Negative CT evidence is not mentioned here.]

The Scientist Was Told That Archaeoraptor Was Problematic... but He Published the Story Anyway.

Dr. Rowe recounts how he felt when *National Geographic* announced in a news conference that the fossil *was* the missing link, even though he had told them it was problematic: *"National Geographic paid for the CT scanning. We knew that they were writing an article and that some of our information would be used in that article...We presented our interpretation, original copies of the data to all parties, and it was a total shock when the news conference came that they were announcing that this was a valid specimen...The questions really didn't come [up] until after the specimen had been published. We provided the data and our interpretation to the representatives of Geographic. And, the scientist in charge, as he walked out of the building, his last comment to me was, 'Well, all of these Chinese things have been fiddled with'...But he understood that there were profound [problems] surrounding this, and we'd been brought in as consultants simply to scan the specimen, which we did...He was a scientist...He was the one that represented National Geographic. He was the one that accompanied the National Geographic reporters. He was the one that guaranteed payment. He was the one that the story was about. He was the lead on it. He was National Geographic during this episode. He represented himself as such, as the lead on the story. And so he was our client and so we reported everything back to him very directly, and it was not conveyed further up the channels...National Geographic, I believe, did a disservice in a subsequent article by whitewashing the story."*

National Geographic later printed a two-sentence retraction in the infrequently read *Forum* section of the March 2000 *National Geographic* magazine. (The original November 1999 article was 10 pages long.) The retraction gives an account that seems to contradict the timeline of events elucidated by Dr. Rowe. The magazine implied that *National Geographic* knew nothing about the CT scan results until March, after the fact. Here is what the magazine printed in the *Forum* section eight months after the CT scanning was completed: *"As we go to press, researchers in the U.S. report that CT scans of the fossil seem to confirm the observations cited in his letter. Results of the society-funded examination of Archaeoraptor and details of new techniques that revealed anomalies in the fossil's reconstruction will be published as soon as the studies are completed."* [5] The retraction implies to the reader that *National Geographic* did not know anything about the CT scans until March, four months *after* the original story was printed. But, in fact, the scientist was told about the anomalies months *before* the original article was published in November.

Lessons Learned

So what was reported to the public as proof that birds evolved from dinosaurs turned out to be a sham. More important than the details of this story is what can be learned from these events.

Both scientists and the public should approach every fossil, and every scientific idea CAUTIOUSLY. You cannot necessarily trust a fossil until it has undergone extensive, painstaking analysis, over decades of time. Also, you cannot necessarily trust evidence being offered for a theory even though it is from a scientist. Lastly, you cannot necessarily trust a popular science magazine or science institution to report all the facts it has in its possession, especially those facts that may be of a negative nature about the evidence.

Scientists are human. Humans, by nature, are tempted to go beyond the facts and follow their biases. We should be careful to stay as close to the facts as possible and not over-interpret what we see. Skepticism should be a large part of our intellectual diet.

Since the Chinese "feathered dinosaur" fossils are relatively new, it may take decades before coming to any firm conclusions about them. Will they turn out to be just flightless birds? Or will they turn out to be feathered dinosaurs? The process of interpreting what the Chinese fossils truly looked like should not be undertaken until all of the specimens have been confirmed by CT scanning. Once the CT scans are completed, the *range of interpretations* should then be presented to the public. Individuals should be allowed to form an opinion, rather than having others offer their single, best interpretation, which may be partial to the theory that birds evolved from dinosaurs.

Postscript: Who Carried Out the Hoax?

Dr. Rowe was asked *who* perpetrated this act of fossil forgery on *Archaeoraptor liaoningensis*. He said he did not know who the perpetrator was, but indirectly suggested that it may have been a scientist. Dr. Rowe: *"But whoever put this specimen together had access to the rarest components of the fauna, had anatomical knowledge. They had knowledge of evolutionary theory to be able to construct an interme-diate form that seemed credible at first blush, and then the last thing is that this person also had access to someone that could smuggle the specimen out of the country* [China]...*But what I believe is that the forger in this case was somebody of privileged scientific position that had knowledge of what he or she was doing and that was very well connected and has profited from this venture."*

Is It Scientific to Add Feathers to Dinosaurs If None Have Been Found?

In the 1993 movie *Jurassic Park,* a young boy and girl were being chased through a kitchen area by two *Velociraptor* dinosaurs. (Luckily, these children escaped this close encounter and the audience collectively took a sigh of relief.) These *Velociraptors* of *Jurassic Park* looked like any other meat-eating dinosaurs, were about six feet tall and had thick reptilian skin and large claws. The producer of this movie, Stephen Spielberg, and his scientific advisors recreated these dinosaurs based on the fossils that had been found by scientists over the last century.

But now, some scientists want to change what *Velociraptor* looked like. These scientists are so convinced that dinosaurs evolved into birds, they have put feathers on museum models of dinosaurs *even though they have never found feathers on the original fossils.* (See museum display to right.)

Scientists who oppose evolution ask if adding feathers to dinosaurs, when none have been found, is true science? Opponents ask how anyone can evaluate the validity of the theory of evolution when scientists (and museums) are adding feathers to dinosaurs, adding dinosaur tails to birds, and altering models of fossils to support one particular view of science. They charge that there is a common recurrent theme throughout the history of evolution — scientists altering fossils and evidence to make evolution more believable. They offer the following examples to support their position: Ernst Haeckel's nineteenth century altering of embryo drawings to prove evolution; a museum scientist at the Natural History Museum in London altering human and ape fossils and planting them in the field for the discovery of a new "ape-man"; biologist Paul Kammerer faking experiments to prove adaptation; modern scientists adding a whale's tail and flippers to *Rodhocetus*; and ending with these latest modern examples of bird evolution. They ask: If evolution is true, why would scientists have to do this?

These examples embarrass supporters of evolution. Yet they contend it is inappropriate to suggest that the theory of evolution is wrong or is in some way in trouble. Instead, they believe that rarely will scientists use poor judgment and go beyond the norms of science because of preconceived ideas or because of other external pressures. Usually, they argue, these separate incidents are not a matter of a scientist trying to mislead the public but rather a scientist mistakenly taking his ideas to the next logical conclusion.

Velociraptor and sign from Museum Victoria, Melbourne, Australia © 2007 AVC Inc., Photos by Debbie Werner

Velociraptor has many features found on birds, though no fossil of it has yet been found that shows traces of feathers. This does not necessarily mean it never had feathers—skin and feathers often decay before an animal starts to fossilise.

However the Liaoning discoveries have shown that the closest relatives of *Velociraptor* had feathers. For this reason, the maker of the *Velociraptor* model decided to add them. By comparison, in the 'Jurassic Park' movies the velociraptors were featherless.

Above: *Museum Victoria's sign indicating that scientists have added feathers to this dinosaur reconstruction even though there is no fossil evidence that this creature had feathers.*

Problems with Museum Interpretations of the Fossils.

On the following pages are various interpretations given by evolution scientists and museum artists regarding feathered dinosaurs and related fossils. It is evident from these wildly different interpretations of the same fossil that scientists could support any one of a number of ideas about evolution. If you pick and choose your artist, you could conclude that birds did evolve from dinosaurs or that birds did not evolve from dinosaurs. One thing is clear: Scientists and museum artists employ wide latitude in interpreting the fossil evidence.

Above, left: *Archaeopteryx at the Oklahoma Museum of Science and Natural History.* **Above, right:** *Archaeopteryx at a "feathered dinosaur" exhibit at the Museum Victoria, Melbourne, Australia. The model of Archaeopteryx (on the left) looks more like a pheasant and suggests it uses its wings to fly. The painting of Archaeopteryx from the "feathered dinosaur" exhibit in Melbourne suggests that Archaeopteryx was using its wings to catch prey. It also portrays Archaeopteryx as having a dinosaur-like, reptilian, scaly head.*

Above, left: *Sinornis santensis, on display at the Chicago Field Museum, looks similar to a modern songbird.* **Above, right:** *Same animal on display at a "feathered dinosaur" exhibit at the Museum Victoria, Melbourne, Australia, showing scales painted on the head and wings in attack mode, both of which make it look more dinosaur-like.*

All photos © 2007 AVC Inc., Photos by Debbie Werner

Above, left: *Painting of Caudipteryx from the American Museum of Natural History in New York. This bird looks similar to a modern grouse* **(above, center insert)**. *Compare this painting of Caudipteryx to a model of this same bird used in a "feathered dinosaur" exhibit at the Museum Victoria in Melbourne* **(above, right)**. *The model on right has a scaly, reptilian head, a longer dinosaur-like tail, and unusual proto-feather fibers around the neck. Its arms are positioned in an attack mode as a dinosaur would hold its arms to attack prey. Compare the arms in this model to the wings on the first specimen.*

Above, left: *The dinosaur Velociraptor on display at the Missouri Botanical Gardens in St. Louis. The dinosaur looks nothing like a bird. Now compare this model with the model of the same dinosaur* **(above, right)** *from a "feathered dinosaur" exhibit at the Museum Victoria in Melbourne.*

Evolution's "Best Proof" Is Under Attack from Top Scientists!

Some evolution scientists have been critical of how news organizations have reported the theory of bird evolution to the public. One of those critics is Dr. Storrs Olson, Curator of Birds at the Smithsonian Museum. In an open letter to the National Geographic Society (below), he chided this organization for articles that were excessively supportive of the dinosaur-to-bird evolutionary theory. The letter clearly points out the interpretation problems associated with the Chinese "feathered dinosaur" fossils that have now plagued scientists dealing in this area of science for over a decade. (Letter truncated for space considerations.)

National Museum of Natural History
Smithsonian Institution
Washington, D. C. 20560

1 November 1999

OPEN LETTER TO:

Dr. Peter Raven, Secretary
Committee for Research and Exploration
National Geographic Society
Washington, DC 20036

Dear Peter,

I thought that I should address to you the concerns expressed below because your committee is at least partly involved and because you are certainly now the most prominent scientist at the National Geographic Society.

With the publication of "Feathers for T. rex?" by Christopher P. Sloan in its November issue, National Geographic has reached an all-time low for engaging in sensationalistic, unsubstantiated, tabloid journalism.

... Prior to the publication of the article "Dinosaurs Take Wing" in the July 1998 National Geographic, Lou Mazzatenta, the photographer for Sloan's article, invited me to the National Geographic Society to review his photographs of Chinese fossils and to comment on the slant being given to the story. At that time, I tried to interject the fact that strongly supported alternative viewpoints existed to what National Geographic intended to present, but it eventually became clear to me that National Geographic was not interested in anything other than the prevailing dogma that birds evolved from dinosaurs.

Sloan's article takes the prejudice to an entirely new level and consists in large part of unverifiable or undocumented information that "makes" the news rather than reporting it. His bald statement that "we can now say that birds are theropods just as confidently as we say that humans are mammals" is not even suggested as reflecting the views of a particular scientist or group of scientists, so that it figures as little more than editorial propagandizing. This melodramatic assertion had already been disproven by recent studies of embryology and comparative morphology, which, of course, are never mentioned.

More importantly, however, none of the structures illustrated in Sloan's article that are claimed to be feathers have actually been proven to be feathers. Saying that they are is little more than wishful thinking that has been presented as fact. The statement on page 103 that "hollow, hairlike structures characterize protofeathers" is nonsense considering that protofeathers exist only as a theoretical construct, so that the internal structure of one is even more hypothetical.

The hype about feathered dinosaurs in the exhibit currently on display at the National Geographic Society is even worse, and makes the spurious claim that there is strong evidence that a wide variety of carnivorous dinosaurs had feathers. A model of the undisputed dinosaur Deinonychus and illustrations of baby tyrannosaurs are shown clad in feathers, all of which is simply imaginary and has no place outside of science fiction.

The idea of feathered dinosaurs and the theropod origin of birds is being actively promulgated by a cadre of zealous scientists acting in concert with certain editors at Nature and National Geographic who themselves have become outspoken and highly biased proselytizers of the faith. Truth and careful scientific weighing of evidence have been among the first casualties in their program, which is now fast becoming one of the grander scientific hoaxes of our age—the paleontological equivalent of cold fusion. If Sloan's article is not the crescendo of this fantasia, it is difficult to imagine to what heights it can next be taken. But it is certain that when the folly has run its course and has been fully exposed, National Geographic will unfortunately play a prominent but unenviable role in the book that summarizes the whole sorry episode.

Sincerely,

Storrs L. Olson
Curator of Birds
National Museum of Natural History
Smithsonian Institution
Washington, DC 20560

*The evidence of birds evolving from dinosaurs is **not** clear for some scientists working in this area.*

Does the Promotion of "Feathered Dinosaurs" Involve Financial Gain?

Other scientists offer financial gain as the motive for promoting feathered dinosaurs. Dr. Wellnhofer was asked why newspapers reported the story of the Chinese fossils as "feathered dinosaurs" even though some scientists think they may be flightless birds. He believes the term "feathered dinosaur" may have been a way to grab press attention or to obtain financial support for scientists.

"Sometimes science needs a headline, a nice headline — 'Feathered Dinosaur,' and 'The Oldest Bird in the World,' or 'The Largest Pterosaur in the World' — things like that in order to get attention and, in the end, to get support, to get financial support, to get funds from different sites/organizations." [1]

— Dr. Wellnhofer

Watch Evolution: The Grand Experiment DVD!

"[National Geographic magazine] is a marvelous operation, but it's a commercial operation and so, they need to sell magazines. They need to get the copy out. And, as a commercial operation, they didn't question the potential conflicts between the commercial purchase of this specimen, which they were aware of, and the fellow who purchased it who had an investment of eighty thousand dollars in this specimen. They didn't question the potential for scientific conflict there." [3]

— Dr. Rowe

Author's Note: The BBC has uncovered a fossil-faking industry in China in the same area of the world where most of the "feathered dinosaurs" have been found. Equally important, fossils of many modern birds (parrots, ducks, albatross, etc.) have been discovered alongside dinosaurs, seemingly contradicting the theory of evolution. This was reported in the second volume of this book and video series, *Living Fossils*. Turn now to Appendix G: Bird Evolution Update for this most important information!

THE FOSSIL RECORD
OF FLOWERING PLANTS

Darwin's "Abominable Mystery"

The plant kingdom is composed of flowering and non-flowering plants. An astounding 250,000 out of the known 300,000 plant species are flowering plants, also called angiosperms. This group includes roses, tomatoes, rhododendrons, the various grasses, and the flowering trees, such as sassafras, oak, palm, and apple.

How flowering plants originated has puzzled scientists ever since Darwin's day. In the late nineteenth century, Darwin highlighted the question of where flowering plants came from when he called their origin an "*abominable mystery*."[1] Even though there were plant fossils during Darwin's time (see fossil drawing on this page), there were no fossils showing the development of the flower and its structures. Darwin attributed the lack of fossil evidence, meaning no intermediate ancestors demonstrating flower evolution, to the poor fossil record of his day.

Seventy years later, in the mid-twentieth century, botanists continued to lament the few answers concerning plant evolution. In his book, *An Introduction to Paleobotany*, Dr. Chester Arnold, Professor of Botany and Curator of Fossil Plants at the University of Michigan, wrote: "*It has long been hoped that extinct plants will ultimately reveal some of the stages through which existing groups have passed during the course of their development, but it must freely be admitted that this aspiration has been fulfilled to a very slight extent, even though paleobotanical research has been in progress for more than one hundred years.*"[2]

Now, nearly 150 years after Darwin put forth his theory, and after hundreds of thousands of the most significant and representative plant fossils have been collected by museums worldwide, the evolutionary steps of flowering plants are still seemingly absent. According to *The Encyclopedia of Evolution*,

Ruth Hall Museum of Paleontology, Ghost Ranch
© 2007 AVC Inc., Photo by Carl Werner

Darwin had at his disposal plant fossils and drawings similar to the one above dated 1876.

flowering plants "*seemed to appear suddenly during the Cretaceous period...*"[1]

One of the world's leading authorities on plants, Dr. and Professor Sir Peter Crane, Director of the Royal Botanic Gardens in England, also speaks in terms of "*mystery*" when discussing flowering plants (see next page). Surprisingly, little is known about the origin of the reproductive structure of flowers and the origin of fruits.

Scientists who support evolution believe the fossils demonstrating plant evolution have yet to be collected or these plants were not fossilized.

Scientists who oppose evolution believe there is an abundant record of flowering plants, including microscopic pollens, delicate flowers showing the sepals, petals, stamens and pistils, as well as seeds, leaves, branches and trees. They believe the lack of flowering plant ancestors speaks for itself — that plant evolution did not occur.

Previous page: *Fossil angiosperm leaf on display at the Sam Noble Oklahoma Museum of Science and Natural History, Oklahoma.*

CHAPTER 16

The Origin of Flowering Plants Remains a Mystery Today.

From *Evolution: The Grand Experiment* video series

"There are still many things we don't understand about the early evolution of flowering plants, particularly how the detailed reproductive structures of the flowers were constructed [evolved], *how you get fruits* [how fruits evolved]*...We don't really understand those kinds of things so well yet. So there is still an element of mystery."* [3]

— Dr. Crane

Professor Sir Peter Crane, Director of the Royal Botanic Gardens in London, England and formerly the Director and Curator at the Field Museum in Chicago, is one of the world's leading experts in plant evolution. Dr. Crane holds academic appointments in the Department of Botany at the University of Reading and the Department of Geology at the Royal Holloway College.

A Plethora of Fossil Flowering Plants Has Been Found

A

Chicago Field Museum, Illinois
© 2007 AVC Inc., Photo by Debbie Werner

B

South Dakota School of Mines
& Technology, Museum of Geology
© 2007 AVC Inc.,
Photo by Carl Werner

J

Chicago Field Museum, Illinois
© 2007 AVC Inc., Photo by Debbie Werner

Clockwise from top left:
  A : Delicate fossil cattail seed head
  B : Fossil poplar leaf
  C : Fossil plant with limbs and fine fruit
  D : Fossil sassafras leaf
  E : Fossil flowers
  F : Fossil leaf
  G : Fossil maple seed
  H : Fossil palm
  I : Fossil petals
  J : Sycamore fruits

I

Ulrich's Fossil Quarry, Fossil Butte, Wyoming
© 2007 AVC Inc., Photo by Debbie Werner

H

Chicago Field Museum, Illinois
© 2007 AVC Inc., Photo by Debbie Werner

C

D

Sam Noble Oklahoma Museum of Science and Natural History,
Oklahoma © 2007 AVC Inc., Photo by Debbie Werner

E

*Hundreds of thousands
of fossil plants have been
collected, but plant
evolution still remains
a "mystery."*

Sam Noble Oklahoma Museum of Science
and Natural History, Oklahoma
© 2007 AVC Inc., Photo by Debbie Werner

Ulrich's Fossil Quarry, Fossil Butte, Wyoming
© 2007 AVC Inc., Photo by Debbie Werner

F

G

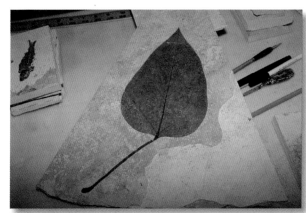

Ulrich's Fossil Quarry, Fossil Butte, Wyoming
© 2007 AVC Inc., Photo by Debbie Werner

University of Nebraska State Museum, Lincoln
© 2007 AVC Inc., Photo by Debbie Werner

Despite a Seemingly Abundant Fossil Record, the Evolution of Flowering Plants Is Still Not Well Understood by Scientists!

University of Nebraska State Museum, Lincoln
© 2007 AVC Inc., Photos by Debbie Werner

Above, left: *Fossil flower found in a dinosaur-bearing fossil layer in Nebraska.*
Above, right: *Museum reconstruction of what this flower once looked like based on the fossil flower's sepals, petals, stamens, and pistils (as revealed through a microscope).*

Did Flowering Plants Evolve?

What Do You Think?

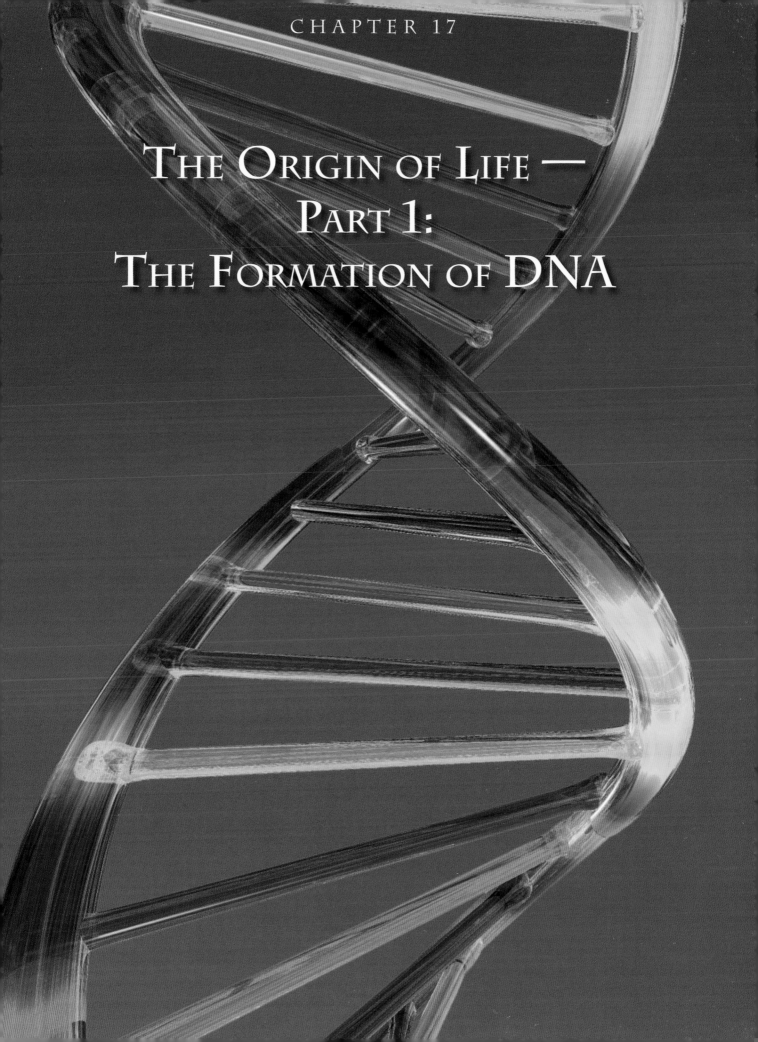

THE ORIGIN OF LIFE — PART 1: THE FORMATION OF DNA

Evolution scientists believe that life began naturally about 4 billion years ago, [1] with the formation of a microscopic organism [2] from a series of spontaneous chemical reactions. [3] They refer to this theoretical event as "the origin of life," and it is from this point that the evolutionary chain of life began. [2] According to the theory of evolution, over billions of years of time, this single, spontaneously-formed organism mutated into all the bacteria, fungi, plants and animals that have lived on earth. In keeping with the theory, all matter that existed prior to the spontaneous formation of the first living organism was comprised of nonliving chemicals.

For more than a half century, scientists have successfully formed some simple organic molecules (molecules containing the element carbon) in the laboratory using sophisticated equipment, but they have not been able to create an actual living organism. Unfortunately, the public has often misunderstood the laboratory formation of simple organic molecules (such as amino acids) to mean that scientists had created life itself or that scientists understand how life could form from chemicals. This is not true. The production of life by a spontaneous, natural process from chemical elements is still not understood.

In order to grasp the *enormous* difficulties associated with the theoretical spontaneous formation of the first living organism from chemicals, it is necessary to understand the essential components for life to exist.

All living organisms today (bacteria, fungi, plants, and animals) are comprised of cells that contain *DNA* and *proteins*, and are enclosed by a *cell membrane*. *DNA* contains the genetic blueprint of life and a copy is passed to the next generation. *Proteins* provide the chemical catalysts and the structure of the cell, and the *cell membrane* holds all of these together. This chapter, the first of three discussing the origin of life, addresses the formation of DNA from chemicals.

(**Author's Note:** All forms of life today have DNA. To be credible, a spontaneous origin of life theory must demonstrate how DNA forms directly from chemicals or how it forms through a series of steps. Some scientists who support the idea of life from non-life theorize that RNA formed first from chemicals. Theorizing that RNA first formed from chemicals does not solve the problem because RNA is similar to DNA in its structure. Both DNA and RNA are extremely complicated molecules and neither forms from chemicals naturally or spontaneously. Suggesting that RNA formed first simply moves the problem to a different but equally complicated molecule.)

All plants and animals contain DNA, the chemical compound which carries the genetic code. DNA is made up of a combination of four different letters (A, C, G, and T) located on a spiral helix.

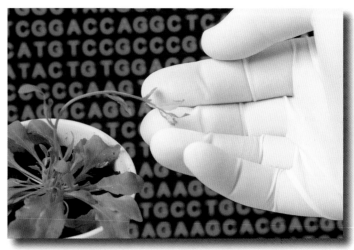

DNA: A Necessary Component for Life

Scientists agree that all living organisms, including bacteria, fungi, plants and animals, have DNA (deoxyribonucleic acid) as their genetic blueprint. No organism living today can function or reproduce without DNA. DNA has two functions: It gives instructions to the rest of the cell to make proteins, and it passes this same information on to the next generation. Even if a simple organism formed by the accidental assembly of all the other necessary components (such as proteins and a cell membrane) but did not have DNA (or RNA), it could not reproduce and would eventually die.

(**Author's Note:** For simplicity, the phrase "DNA or RNA" will be henceforth described as "DNA" since forming RNA from chemicals has the same problems or roadblocks as forming DNA from chemicals.)

Many scientists who oppose evolution look at DNA as a feature of design, implying that there was a designer who not only made the complex DNA molecule but also programmed it with information.

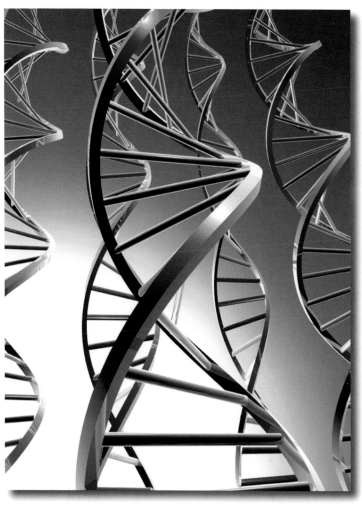

Above: *DNA looks like a twisted ladder. DNA contains the genetic information of an organism.*

"DNA is the instruction book for living organisms. It contains the information necessary to allow an organism to grow, develop, and mature...Information in DNA (such as how to make a protein) could not arise naturally. All information requires an intelligent, immaterial source." [4]

— **Dr. Purdom**

Dr. Georgia Purdom has her Ph.D. in molecular genetics, and is a Researcher and Speaker for Answers in Genesis, Petersburg, Kentucky, near Cincinnati, Ohio.

The Structure of DNA

Conceptually, DNA looks like a twisted ladder (called a double helix). Holding the rungs of the ladder together are the "letters" A, C, G, and T. These four complex chemical "letters" (known as bases) bond to one another to hold the two strands of the DNA molecule together. In DNA, the base letter A always bonds to T (see below) and the base letter G always bonds to C. Three contiguous letters on the DNA molecule (called a codon) instruct the cell to place one particular amino acid into a protein chain. To accomplish this, the DNA is unzipped and a copy of the DNA is made using a special protein which carries out this copying process. RNA carries this template of the DNA and along with other proteins assembles proteins by attaching amino acids together in a chain.

This presents a problem for the spontaneous origin of life theory. *DNA is needed to make proteins, yet many different proteins are involved in copying and translating the information of DNA into proteins.* Scientists who oppose the spontaneous origin of life theory are quick to point out this problem and challenge their colleagues with this question: Which came first, the DNA or the proteins? If life originated by chance, then this problem must have a solution. Scientists who support the spontaneous origin of life theory have proposed several ideas that attempt to explain how to solve this paradox. Those who oppose the spontaneous origin of life theory point to this "chicken and egg" problem as another reason why evolution could not have happened as the result of random chemical interactions.

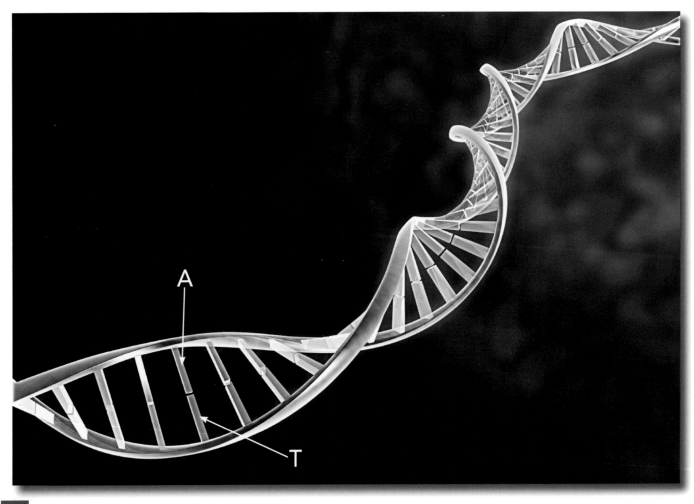

A

T

Calculating the Length of DNA for a Single Protein

How long of a piece of DNA (or its theoretical precursor RNA) would be necessary to encode the information of one protein? Since three letters of DNA are required to instruct the cell to place a single amino acid into a protein chain, and since most proteins today are, on average, 300 amino acids long, the DNA strand needed to make just one protein would have to be approximately 900 letters long.

A single protein containing 300 amino acids **X** 3 letters of DNA needed for each amino acid in this protein **=** 900 letter DNA strand needed for a single protein

The DNA Length Problem

If a large quantity of pre-assembled complex chemical "letters" of DNA are placed in a beaker, strands of up to only 20 letters form, but not any longer. [5] After 20 letters coalesce, the DNA begins to break apart. (RNA is even more unstable.) Herein lies another major stumbling block for scientists trying to understand how life could form spontaneously. Strands of DNA approximately 900 letters long are needed to make a single protein, but DNA strands of only 20 letters long form in the laboratory. Twenty letters is not long enough to create a protein.

The Total Amount of DNA for Life to Begin

How much total DNA would be necessary to start life as a single-cell organism? Today, the most rudimentary bacterium has hundreds of unique proteins. Scientists believe that the first living organism would have required, at the very least, 20 or so basic proteins to function. [6] If each of these 20 basic necessary proteins requires 900 letters of DNA, then strands of DNA containing a total of 18,000 letters would be needed to theoretically form the proteins necessary for the first single-cell organism.

20 proteins needed for life to begin **X** 900 letters of DNA needed for each protein **=** 18,000 letters of DNA needed for life to begin

The DNA Order Problem

Even if 18,000 letters of DNA (or its theoretical precursor RNA) could form into strands naturally or spontaneously, there is another problem. The 18,000 letters needed to start life in the simplest theoretical first organism also have to be in a correct *order* to make any sense. They cannot be in any random order. (**Author's Note:** Not only do the letters have to be in the correct *order*, but they also require distinct sequences before and after the instructions to control the production of the protein. These sequences are essential. You can imagine what would happen if your cells constantly made every protein they had instructions for without stopping.)

Random letters of DNA do not convey meaning just as random letters typed onto a page do not make sentences. For example, if the DNA letters need to read ACC—TAC—CGT—GAG, etc. but instead read CCC—TCG—CAG—TTC, the DNA would not produce the necessary functional protein. The 18,000 DNA letters have to be lined up in a *particular order* to call for *particular amino acids* in a *particular set of proteins* for life to begin.

The odds of 18,000 letters lining up in the correct order for life to begin in the most simple theoretical single-cell organism can be calculated. The odds for any particular letter of DNA to be inserted into any one position are one out of four, since there are only four possible DNA letters. The odds of accidentally arranging *two* consecutive letters of DNA in correct order would be $1/4 \times 1/4 = 1/16$. The odds of accidentally arranging *three* consecutive letters in correct order would be $1/4 \times 1/4 \times 1/4 = 1/64$. (The odds of multiple random events occurring are simply the odds of each event multiplied by the odds of the other events occurring.) What would be the odds of lining up *18,000* letters of DNA in the correct order for life to begin by chance? The answer may surprise you.

The odds of 18,000 DNA (or RNA) letters lining up in proper order would be: $1/4^{18,000}$ or one out of 1,201,000,
000,000,000,000,000,000,000,000,000,000,000,000,000,000,000,000,000,000,000,000,000,
000,000,000,000,000,000,000,000,000,000,000,000,000,000,000,000,000,000,000,000,000,
000,000,000,000,000,000,000,000,000,000,000,000,000,000,000,000,000,000,000,000,000,
000,000,000,000,000,000,000,000,000,000,000,000,000,000,000,000,000,000,000,000,000,
000,000,000,000,000,000,000,000,000,000,000,000,000,000,000,000,000,000,000,000,000,
000,000,000,000,000,000,000,000,000,000,000,000,000,000,000,000,000,000,000,000,000,
000,000,000,000,000,000,000,000,000,000,000,000,000,000,000,000,000,000,000,000,000,
000,000,000,000,000,000,000,000,000,000,000,000,000,000,000,000,000,000,000,000,000,
000,000,000,000,000,000,000,000,000,000,000,000,000,000,000,000,000,000,000,000,000,
000,000,000,000,000,000,000,000,000,000,000,000,000,000,000,000,000,000,000,000,000,
000,000,000,000,000,000,000,000,000,000,000,000,000,000,000,000,000,000,000,000,000,
000,000,000,000,000,000,000,000,000,000,000,000,000,000,000,000,000,000,000,000,000,
000,000,000,000,000,000,000,000,000,000,000,000,000,000,000,000,000,000,000,000,000,
000,000,000,000,000,000,000,000,000,000,000,000,000,000,000,000,000,000,000,000,000,

000,000,000,000,000,000,000,000,000,000,000,000,000,000,000,000,000,000,000,000,000,000,000,000,
000,000,000,000,000,000,000,000,000,000,000,000,000,000,000,000,000,000,000,000,000,000,000,000,
000,000,000,000,000,000,000,000,000,000,000,000,000,000,000,000,000,000,000,000,000,000,000,000,
000,000,000,000,000,000,000,000,000,000,000,000,000,000,000,000,000,000,000,000,000,000,000,000,
000,000,000,000,000,000,000,000,000,000,000,000,000,000,000,000,000,000,000,000,000,000,000,000,
000,000,000,000,000,000,000,000,000,000,000,000,000,000,000,000,000,000,000,000,000,000,000,000,
000,000,000,000,000,000,000,000,000,000,000,000,000,000,000,000,000,000,000,000,000,000,000,000,
000,000,000,000,000,000,000,000,000,000,000,000,000,000,000,000,000,000,000,000,000,000,000,000,
000,000,000,000,000,000,000,000,000,000,000,000,000,000,000,000,000,000,000,000,000,000,000,000,
000,000,000,000,000,000,000,000,000,000,000,000,000,000,000,000,000,000,000,000,000,000,000,000,
000,000,000,000,000,000,000,000,000,000,000,000,000,000,000,000,000,000,000,000,000,000,000,000,
000,000,000,000,000,000,000,000,000,000,000,000,000,000,000,000,000,000,000,000,000,000,000,00
0, 000,000,000,000,000,000,000,000,000,000,000,000,000,000,000,000,000,000,000,000,000,000,000,
000,000,000,000,000,000,000,000,000,000,000,000,000,000,000,000,000,000,000,000,000,000,000,000,
000,000,000,000,000,000,000,000,000,000,000,000,000,000,000,000,000,000,000,000,000,000,000,000,
000,000,000,000,000,000,000,000,000,000,000,000,000,000,000,000,000,000,000,000,000,000,000,000,
000,000,000,000,000,000,000,000,000,000,000,000,000,000,000,000,000,000,000,000,000,000,000,000,
000,000,000,000,000,000,000,000,000,000,000,000,000,000,000,000,000,000,000,000,000,000,000,000,
000,000,000,000,000,000,000,000,000,000,000,000,000,000,000,000,000,000,000,000,000,000,000,000,
000,000,000,000,000,000,000,000,000,000,000,000,000,000,000,000,000,000,000,000,000,000,000, 00
0,000,000,000,000,000,000,000,000,000,000,000,000,000,000,000,000,000,000,000,000,000,000,000, 000
,000,000,000,000,000,000,000,000,000,000,000,000,000,000,000,000,000,000,000,000,000,000,000, 000,
000,000,000,000,000,000,000,000,000,000,000,000,000,000,000,000,000,000,000,000,000,000,000, 000,0
00,000,000,000,000,000,000,000,000,000,000,000,000,000,000,000,000,000,000,000,000,000,000, 000,00
0,000,000,000,000,000,000,000,000,000,000,000,000,000,000,000,000,000,000,000,000,000,000, 000,000
,000,000,000,000,000,000,000,000,000,000,000,000,000,000,000,000,000,000,000,000,000,000, 000,000,
000,000,000,000,000,000,000,000,000,000,000,000,000,000,000,000,000,000,000,000,000,000, 000,000,0
00,000,000,000,000,000,000,000,000,000,000,000,000,000,000,000,000,000,000,000,000,000, 000,000,00
0,000,000,000,000,000,000,000,000,000,000,000,000,000,000,000,000,000,000,000,000,000, 000,000,000
,000,000,000,000,000,000,000,000,000,000,000,000,000,000,000,000,000,000,000,000,000, **followed by
additional zeros for 10,837 zeros total**.

To put this number in perspective, keep in mind that the odds of being struck by lightning in your lifetime are 1/5,000 **(3 zeros)**.[7] The odds of winning the national Powerball Lottery are 1/80,000,000 **(7 zeros)**.[8] The odds of winning the national Powerball Lottery *every day for 365 days* are 1/4,244 followed by 2,881 zeros.[9] If winning the national lottery 365 times in a row seems unlikely **(2,881 zeros)**, then how much more unlikely are the chances of DNA forming spontaneously with the proper letter sequence **(10,837 zeros)**? With such odds, some have suggested life could never have formed naturally.

The DNA Shape Problem

If the length and order problems were not enough, there is a third problem with DNA forming naturally. When the complex, pre-assembled chemical DNA "letters" are placed in a glass beaker (as in origin of life experiments), the strands of DNA that coalesce are *deformed*. Specifically, they connect in the wrong "corners" of the sugar molecules which make up the DNA backbone, resulting in non-spiraled DNA. Spiraling is very important because it compacts and protects the DNA.

Right: *A conceptual model of DNA created in the laboratory. It is only 20 letters long, not spiraled, and distorted in shape.*

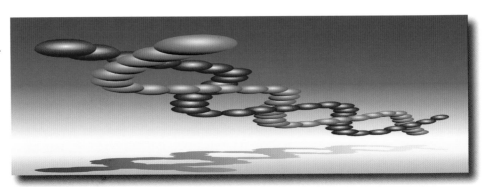

Could DNA Form Naturally to Start Life?

Scientists who oppose evolution contend that if DNA (or its theoretical precursor RNA) cannot spontaneously assemble in the proper length to produce a *single* protein, the proper order to produce the needed 20 functional proteins to begin life, and the proper shape to protect the DNA from breaking up, then life could never have started from chemi-

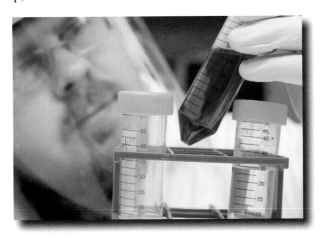

cals. For them, the evidence speaks for itself. They challenge their evolution colleagues to show the formation of just *one* molecule of DNA or RNA from chemical elements that is capable of producing one functional protein.

Scientists who support evolution believe such suggestions are presumptuous. Ignorance of a process (how DNA forms naturally) does not necessarily mean it did not happen. Rather, the lack of knowledge in this area of science should spur further research and investigation. If scientists simply quit every time they did not understand a process, they would never make discoveries. For them, the search must continue.

What Do You Think?

THE ORIGIN OF LIFE — PART 2: THE FORMATION OF PROTEINS

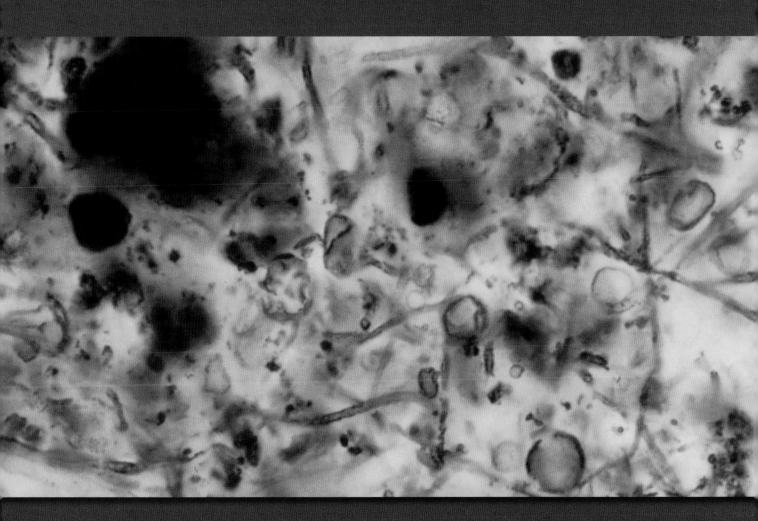

Proteins: A Second Necessary Component for Life

All living organisms are made up of and use proteins to carry out the basic functions of the cell, such as producing energy, developing structures, and assisting in copying the DNA (for reproduction). Living organisms simply cannot perform and reproduce without proteins.

Conceptually, proteins can be thought of as a chain. Amino acids are the individual links which make up the protein chain. Typically, proteins consist of hundreds of individual links.

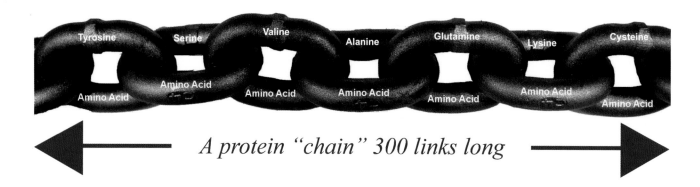

A protein "chain" 300 links long

Since proteins are necessary for life, scientists who support evolution want to know how proteins may have formed naturally. They believe that life, in the form of a single-cell organism, began in the *ocean* billions of years ago. Yet, it has been shown that *water prevents amino acids from linking together to form a protein.*

Scientists studying the origin of life were initially discouraged with the prospect of not knowing how proteins formed, but now they think they have a breakthrough. By taking dried amino acids and super heating them to 300 degrees Fahrenheit, they have produced an unnatural congealing of amino acid links, which they call a "proteinoid."

From *Evolution: The Grand Experiment* video series

"No one has ever seen or witnessed a protein molecule form naturally." [1]

— **Dr. Gish**

Duane Gish, Ph.D., Biochemist, opposes evolution.

Previous page: *Photo of fossil bacteria. Courtesy of Dr. Andrew Knoll, Harvard University.*

Proteinoids: A Proposed Bridge to Proteins

A proteinoid does not look like a natural protein chain. Rather, it looks like a bunch of chain links welded together in a clump. The links of a proteinoid are not connected properly (below, right) compared to a true protein (previous page).

Scientists who support evolution believe proteinoids, which may have acted like proteins, came first and then eventually converted to proteins by an unknown mechanism. Advocates of evolution have also suggested that the process of heating dried amino acids to form a proteinoid did not occur in the ocean but rather on the heated surface of a volcano.[2] They postulate that the heat of the volcano caused the amino acids to congeal. Later, rain washed these proteinoid chemicals back into the ocean at which point they interacted with DNA and other chemicals floating in the water and eventually formed the first living organism.

Some scientists, however, question whether this scenario of pure, dried amino acids accumulating on the side of a volcano is plausible. They ask: How could significant quantities of pure, dried amino acids randomly occur in nature?[3] Some experiments have shown how proteinoids can come about in other conditions and then form microspheres. It has been suggested that these microspheres may have acted as a chamber to collect the molecules necessary to form the first life. These microspheres are believed to be a possible source for the first cell membranes.

However, there is still no explanation for how the complex cell membranes could have come from these primitive microspheres or sacs in the water.

Other scientists who support evolution have suggested that clay minerals acted as catalysts for forming life or that bubbles from volcanic vents in the oceans were the laboratories where life began. However, after nearly a century of study in this area, scientists still do not understand how life began.

Those who oppose evolution believe that the ideas of a proteinoid acting like a protein or clay minerals forming the first life are preposterous. Proteinoids do not have any significant functionality, such as the ability to copy DNA or form any of the known structures in bacteria living today. They also point out that proteinoids have never been observed to form outside of a laboratory nor have they ever been observed to convert to proteins. If proteinoids cannot convert to proteins, which are part of all life forms today, how could life begin?

Above: *A proteinoid has an unnatural connection of the links.*

"Although researchers have debated whether the thermal synthesis of proteins [proteinoids] *could occur extensively in present natural surroundings...the exact conditions encountered on the primitive Earth are certainly not known."*[4]

— **Dr. Strickberger**

Dr. Monroe Strickberger is the author of the college textbook **Evolution**.

Dr. Strickberger on proteinoids:

"...proteinoids engage in a number of enzyme-like activities that can increase the rates of various organic reactions. For example, they help split apart certain molecules by addition of water (hydrolysis), they catalyze the condensation of nucleotides, such as ATP into di- and trinucleotides, and they help to remove carboxyl groups or amino groups from various structures. Moreover, they can improve catalytic activity of molecules, such as heme, that aid hydrogen peroxide in removing hydrogen from reduced compounds in oxidation reactions."[5]

— Dr. Strickberger

*Dr. Monroe Strickberger received his Ph.D. at Columbia University under the famed evolution scientist, Theodocius Dobzhansky, and is the author of the college textbook **Evolution** (Jones and Bartlett Publishers). Currently, Dr. Strickberger is a Research Associate at the Museum of Vertebrate Zoology, University of California, Berkeley.*

The de novo formation of proteins is necessary for life to begin, but this process has never been observed in nature.

Dr. Gish on protein synthesis:

"No one has ever seen or witnessed a protein molecule form naturally. To combine two amino acids, you have to put energy into that chemical bond. The chemical bond does not want to form. It resists this. So you add energy...Now if these amino acids are floating around in an ocean of water, and you have to split-out water to form the bond, that is contrary to the mass action law. The idea that you could form a protein molecule with 50 or 60 or 100 amino acids, without these things breaking apart. No, that would never happen. You just don't see that happening."[1]

— Dr. Gish

Dr. Duane Gish received his Ph.D. in biochemistry from the University of California, Berkeley. He spent 18 years in biochemical research at Cornell University Medical College, the University of California, Berkeley, and the Upjohn Company.

The Sequence Problem

A second problem, dealing with the *sequence* of the amino acids, also exists. Not only do amino acids need to be properly linked to form a protein chain, they also need to be arranged in a very specific *order.* There are 20 different kinds of amino acids found in living organisms and each amino acid is unique. Substituting just one incorrect amino acid for another frequently causes a protein to malfunction. Diseases, such as sickle cell anemia, hemophilia, and cystic fibrosis, originate from a single erroneous substitution of one amino acid for another in a protein. The most simple bacterium living today has hundreds of necessary proteins. Evolution scientists theorize that only 20 protein chains would have been necessary for life to begin. If each of these 20 proteins were 300 amino acids long, 6,000 amino acids would need to line up in the correct *order* by *chance.*

> **20 proteins needed for life to begin**   X   **300 amino acids in each protein chain**   =   **6,000 amino acids lined up in the correct order**

The odds of that many amino acids accidentally lining up in the correct order leave many scientists in doubt. Even if a protein chain was only 100 amino acids long, billions and billions of years would not have been enough time to form just one protein, much less 20 necessary proteins. Even Dr. Strickberger, who supports the traditional evolutionary theory, questions how this could occur. He writes: *"Thus, if we randomly generated a new 100-amino-acid-long sequence each second, we could expect such a given enzyme to appear only once in 4 x 10^{122} years!"* [6] (**Author's Note:** Dr. Strickberger is saying it would take 10^{122} years [or 10 followed by 122 zeros] to make just one specific protein by accident. Given the assumption that the earth is 4 billion years old [9 zeros], there would *still* not be enough time [in the history of the earth] to generate even one specific protein by accident.)

Dr. Strickberger also suggests that there is not enough space in the entire universe to generate even one specific protein: *"By similar reasoning, the chances for most complex organic structures to arise spontaneously are infinitesimally small. Even a small enzymatic sequence of 100 amino acids would have only one chance in 20^{100} (=10^{130}) to arise randomly, since there are 20 possible kinds of different amino acids for each position in the sequence...In terms of the volume necessary to generate all such possibilities, the difficulty appears just as immense: If an entire universe, 10 billion light years in diameter, were densely packed with randomly produced polypeptide...the number of such molecules 10^{103} would not equal their 10^{130} possibilities."* [6] In other words, there would not be enough room in the universe to form one specific protein naturally, much less the 20 proteins needed for life to begin.

Scientists who oppose evolution suggest no further proof is needed. If proteins do not form naturally, but are necessary for life to begin, then the theory of evolution is dead. Proponents of evolution acknowledge the extreme difficulties in this area of science, but they feel that one day they will be able to understand how proteins formed.

Criticisms of Proteinoids

Some scientists who advocate the theory of evolution have conjectured that proteinoids were a theoretical intermediate step in the origin of life, and these later converted into proteins. [7] But many other scientists voice serious disapproval over proteinoids. Here is a summary of some of their criticisms:

1. A proteinoid has never been shown to convert into a protein, a necessary component in the formation of life.

2. A proteinoid has never possessed the ability to copy DNA, an essential step in the formation of life.

3. Dried, purified amino acids used to form proteinoids do not occur in nature. As one biochemist wrote: *"The central question...is where did all those pure, dry, concentrated, and optically active amino acids come from in the real, abiological world?"* [3]

4. To be created, proteinoids depend upon investigator interference. [8] They have never been observed to form under *natural* circumstances. They are the result of a biochemist's formulation/intervention.

5. Heating amino acids to 300 degrees Fahrenheit to form a proteinoid destroys any proteins in the area since most proteins denature at such high temperatures.

6. Proteinoids do not resemble proteins. *"...studies using nuclear magnetic resonance (NMR) have shown that thermal proteinoids 'have scarce resemblance to natural peptidic material because beta, gamma and epsilon-peptide bonds largely predominate over* [the normal] *alpha-peptide bonds.'"* [9]

7. Proteins are assembled mainly with left-handed amino acids, the "L" form, in nearly all living organisms today. (Exceptions being some venoms such as those found in marine cone snails and the cell walls of some bacteria.) Using right-handed amino acids in the formations of a protein (the "D" form), frequently renders the protein non-functional. This is a problem because proteinoids are composed of approximately equal numbers of left- and right-handed amino acids. [10] How could a proteinoid with both left- and right-handed amino acids convert, by chance, to proteins with only lefthanded amino acids?

8. It has been postulated that at least 20 complex proteins would be necessary to carry out the functions of the first cell. Proteinoids have not been shown to carry out any of these essential functions, such as copying DNA, assisting in the formation of other proteins, and energy management.

Are proteinoids sufficient to start life?

What Do You Think?

THE ORIGIN OF LIFE —
PART 3:
THE FORMATION OF AMINO ACIDS

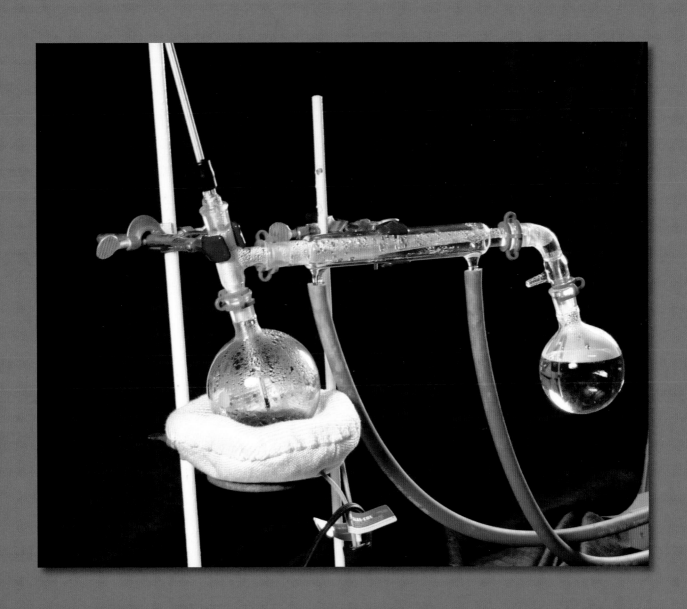

Amino Acids: A Third Necessary Component for Life

Proteins are necessary for all living organisms. They carry out the functions of the cell. Amino acids are the molecules that make up the individual links of a protein chain. If life began naturally around 4 billion years ago, amino acids would have had to form spontaneously. Although much progress has been made in understanding the formation of amino acids under natural conditions, there are still unresolved issues.

The first success in creating amino acids under "natural settings" occurred in 1953 when Dr. Stanley Miller produced a mixture of simple amino acids with a specially designed piece of laboratory equipment.[1] (See photo below.) The device was a complex piece of glassware filled with water and chemicals. Miller produced amino acids by sparking the water and chemicals with a tungsten electrode. To prevent the amino acids from breaking down quickly, he then separated and removed the amino acids with a glass distillation device. He heated and sparked the chemicals in the first section of the device and through the process of condensation, he removed the amino acids using the second section of the device and collected the amino acids in a third section, a glass container. Dr. Miller theorized his experiment emulated how amino acids may have formed in nature billions of years ago.

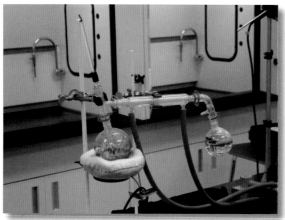

Title page and above: *A model of the apparatus used to create amino acids under "natural conditions."*

Criticisms of this experimental model have been growing since the original findings were reported in 1953. The main objection to the experiment is that it was carried out using a sophisticated three-part glassware device specifically designed for the purpose of producing amino acids. Although this experiment did provide insight regarding how to produce amino acids in the laboratory, it still left a large void in understanding how amino acids could form in nature, spontaneously.

Many scientists who support evolution, including Dr. Miller, believe this experiment may have mimicked the formation of amino acids in nature billions of years ago. They suggest that the tungsten electrode used to create a spark could have been similar to an electrical charge emitted from a lightning bolt striking the ocean. After lightning struck the ocean, amino acids formed, and they then washed up onto the side of a volcano where they were heated into proteinoids. Later these proteinoids may have been washed back into the ocean where they met up with the other necessary molecules for life and formed the first living organism. Since oxygen had to be removed from the air for Miller's apparatus to work, it has been suggested that the earth did not have oxygen when life first began.

Scientists who oppose evolution believe these are fanciful ideas. Producing amino acids in a controlled environment (a laboratory), with sophisticated multi-sectional equipment designed by a scientist, under very specific conditions, does not equate to the production of amino acids in nature. Rather, it is merely a laboratory experiment. Opponents challenge those who support evolution to demonstrate the production of the 20 essential amino acids without such sophisticated equipment and without these extreme amounts of intervention. They argue that since the essential amino acids needed for life do not form spontaneously, by the same token, then life could never have begun spontaneously.

Criticisms of the Stanley Miller Experiment

There are many other criticisms of the Miller experiment, (also called the Miller-Urey experiment in recognition of the other scientist involved, Harold Urey). Detailed below are a summary of these criticisms.

1. The Miller-Urey experiment required extreme amounts of "investigator interference." This outside intervention by a scientist invalidated the experiment. [2] The amino acids did not form *naturally*.

2. Stanley Miller removed oxygen from his device because he knew oxygen was poisonous to the formation of amino acids. [3] If trace amounts of oxygen are present, amino acids cannot form. [3] Because of this experimental requirement, some have suggested the earth did not have oxygen in the atmosphere when life began. But some evidence suggests that oxygen was present on the earth at the theoretical time when life began around 4 billion years ago. Iron oxide minerals have been found in Greenland, dating to 3.8 billion years ago. [4] The presence of *oxides* suggests that oxygen was present at that time. [4] If this evidence proves to be true, then Miller's model and apparatus would be nullified since oxygen was artificially removed from the device.

3. Miller removed oxygen to produce amino acids, yet oxygen is necessary to protect proteins and DNA from the sun. Dr. Charles Thaxton, a Biochemist and author of *The Mystery of Life's Origin: Reassessing Current Theories,* writes: *"Since living organisms* [bacteria] *and organic molecules* [amino acids, proteins, and DNA] *need the protection from ultraviolet radiation provided by an ozone screen* [which is derived from oxygen]*, yet the presence of oxygen* [in the atmosphere] *prevents the development of such living systems and biological molecules* [amino acids]*, this would constitute a catch-22 in the model."* [5] (Words in brackets added by author for clarification.)

4. The amino acids produced in Miller's apparatus were both right- and left-handed amino acids. [6, 7] In contrast, nearly all living organisms today use only left-handed amino acids. Right-handed amino acids usually render a protein nonfunctional. To be credible, the theory of evolution would need to explain how life came to be a nearly exclusively left-handed world — starting with the equally mixed right- and left-handed amino acids that the Miller apparatus produced.

5. Miller's experiment produced only a few rudimentary amino acids, not the full complement of the 20 essential amino acids that are used by living organisms today. Other scientists have subsequently designed additional laboratory experiments and have produced the remaining amino acids, but the same problem persists. The necessary 20 amino acids needed for life to exist do not form spontaneously, *without* investigator interference and complex equipment.

Rocks with alternating red bands of oxidized iron suggest that oxygen was present in the atmosphere in pre-Cambrian times. Miller's experiment presumed oxygen was not *present at the time life began.*

Milwaukee Public Museum, Wisconsin © 2007 AVC Inc., Photo by Debbie Werner

Summary of Origin of Life Problems

In summary, scientists who oppose the spontaneous origin of life suggest the following problems contradict the theory that life started from chemicals.

DNA

1. DNA and RNA does not form spontaneously, or naturally, from chemicals.

2. Strands of DNA (or RNA) hundreds of letters long are needed to make a single functional protein but DNA strands of only 20 letters long form in the laboratory when the complex preassembled chemical "letters" are placed in a beaker.

3. Even if DNA (or RNA) could assemble spontaneously, or naturally, the letters needed to create the 20 necessary proteins to begin life would have to be in the correct *order* to be functional. The odds of 18,000 letters of DNA (or RNA) — the required number of letters to code for the 20 necessary proteins to begin life — assembling in the correct order are 1/1,200 followed by 10,837 zeros. To put this number in perspective, the odds of winning the national Powerball Lottery every day for 365 days are 1/4,244 followed by 2,881 zeros. [8]

Proteins

1. Proteins are necessary for life, but they do not form spontaneously, or naturally, from chemicals.

2. The theory of evolution suggests that life may have begun in the ocean, yet water prevents the formation of proteins.

3. Oxygen, in the form of ozone, is necessary to protect DNA from the sun, yet oxygen prevents amino acids from forming spontaneously from chemicals. This is a paradox for the theory of evolution.

4. Heat is necessary to form proteinoids, but heat destroys (denatures) proteins.

5. Amino acids would have to assemble in a specific order to form a functional protein spontaneously, or naturally. The odds of 6,000 amino acids lining up in the proper order to form the 20 proteins necessary for life to begin are infinitesimally small. The odds would be 1/1,500 followed by *13,006* zeros. To put this number in perspective, the odds of winning the national Powerball Lottery every day for 365 days are 1/4,244 followed by 2,881 zeros. [8]

Amino Acids

1. The 20 essential amino acids necessary for life, do not form spontaneously, or naturally, from chemicals.

2. The amino acids formed by the Miller experiment were a mixture of D- and L-amino acids, yet today nearly all living things use L-amino acids. Scientists who support evolution would need to demonstrate how the first form of life could use both D- and L-amino acids and later change into life forms which use exclusively L-amino acids.

Cell Membrane

1. *Functional* cell membranes are neccessary for life, but they have never been shown to form naturally from chemicals.

2. In order for the first single-cell organism to form in the ocean by a chance occurrence, enormous quantities of DNA and proteins would be required. In essence, billions of pounds of DNA and billions of pounds of proteins (both of which do not form naturally) would have had to be floating in the oceans in order to randomly bring enough of these materials in close proximity to each other to form a single-cell organism inside of a functional cell membrane, which also does not form naturally. If these materials do *not* form spontaneously, or naturally, from chemicals, how could this happen?

The Proposed First Form of Life:

A Typical Prokaryote Cell

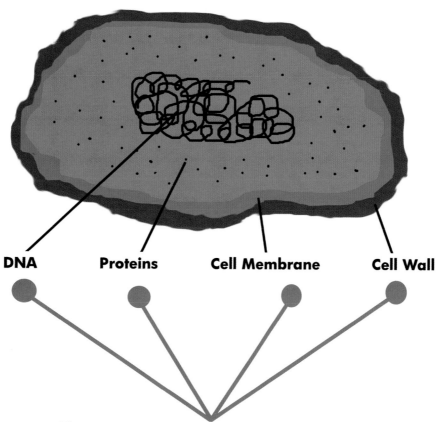

DNA **Proteins** **Cell Membrane** **Cell Wall**

These components have never been produced in a laboratory from a mixture of chemicals.

Could Life Begin Spontaneously?

Proponents of Evolution View

Many evolution scientists suggest the problems regarding the origin of life are not insurmountable. They believe, a priori, that since life exists on earth, this means that life formed spontaneously. They contend that even though they don't yet understand the mechanism, it does not mean spontaneous life did not occur. They ask, how many times in the past has persistence eventually led to a discovery after decades or centuries of research? To give up the search now, and say that evolution is not true, would be unthinkable.

Opponents of Evolution View

Scientists who oppose evolution ask: What further evidence is needed to prove that evolution and the spontaneous origin of life is just a story? Since the 1950s, universities from around the world have performed thousands of experiments and spent millions of dollars in an attempt to produce life from non-life. Despite large degrees of scientific intervention and use of sophisticated laboratory equipment, the work thus far has produced nonfunctional fragments of DNA, proteinoids (but not proteins), and a poisonous mixture of amino acids. Not one living organism has been formed in the laboratory using a mixture of chemicals. If the top scientists from around the world cannot demonstrate that life formed spontaneously, then the theory of evolution is, for all practical purposes, dead.

What Do You Think?

CONCLUSIONS —
EVOLUTION: POINTS
OF CONTROVERSY

espite significant advances in biochemical and paleontological research, the theory of evolution is one of the most controversial topics of our day. While scientists, both for and against evolution, continue to promote their points of view, the public appears to be divided over the issue. There are still many who are at a loss as to what is true and what is untrue.

The following is a final summary of some of the key points addressed in the previous chapters. After each point is a summary of the criticisms (counterpoints) made by those who oppose evolution.

Points of Controversy

Many Americans, 46 percent, believe God created man less than 10,000 years ago!

32 percent of Americans believe evolution did occur but that God guided the process.

Point One: *Many Americans believe and accept evolution, which is evidence that the theory is true.*

Counterpoint: *Only 15 percent of Americans believe the theory of evolution in its current form.*

Only 15 percent believe in pure evolution.

7 percent No opinion.

See Chapter 1: Two Opposing Views

Source: Gallup poll, May 2012

Previous page: *Charles Darwin. Down House, England.*

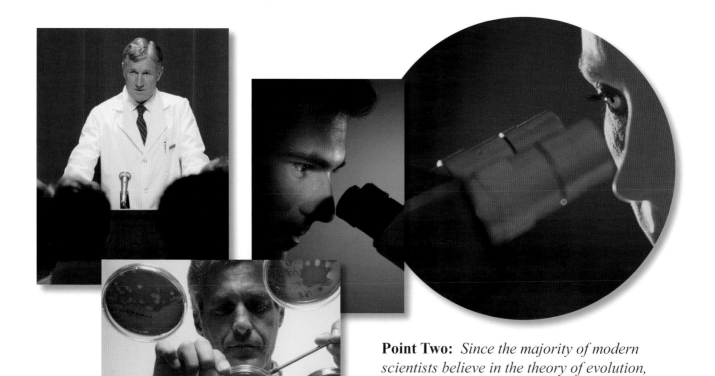

Point Two: *Since the majority of modern scientists believe in the theory of evolution, it is evident (to most) that the theory is true.*

Counterpoint: *Many scientists also believed in the theory of spontaneous generation and the law of acquired characteristics, both of which were disproved after thousands of years of acceptance. Scientific theories and even laws, no matter how well accepted, are not necessarily true.*

See Chapter 2: Spontaneous Generation
Chapter 3: Acquired Characteristics

Points of Controversy

Point Three: *A series of chance mutations in the DNA is one of the major mechanisms by which evolution (theoretically) occurs.*

Counterpoint: *The odds of chance mutations causing an animal to develop new body parts are astronomically high. The odds of a land animal evolving into a whale are statistically impossible.*

See Chapter 4: Natural Selection and Chance Mutations

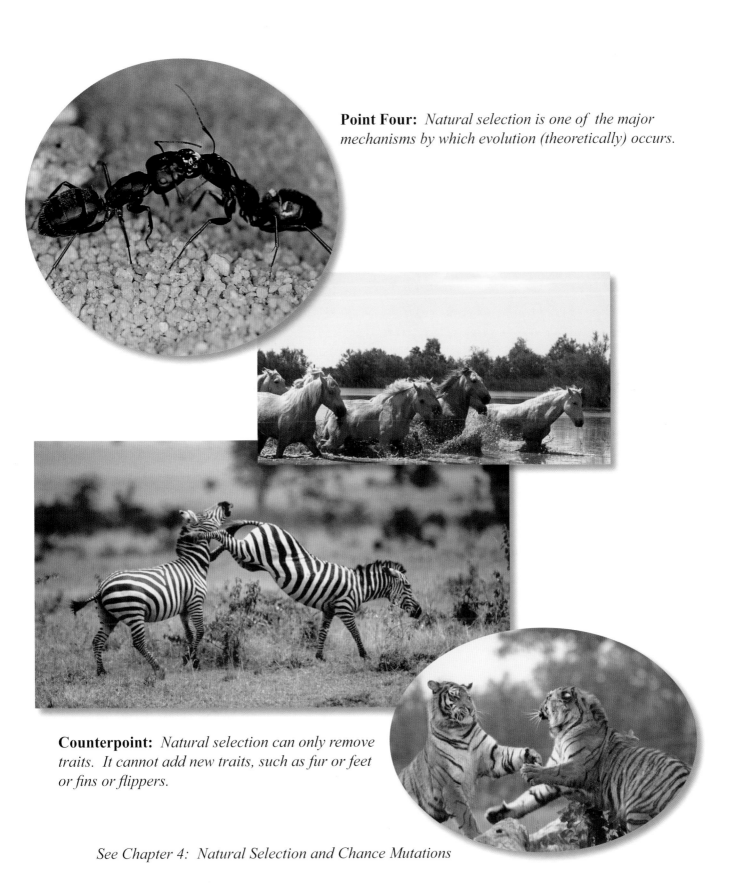

Point Four: *Natural selection is one of the major mechanisms by which evolution (theoretically) occurs.*

Counterpoint: *Natural selection can only remove traits. It cannot add new traits, such as fur or feet or fins or flippers.*

See Chapter 4: Natural Selection and Chance Mutations

Points of Controversy

Point Five: *A series of chance mutations in the DNA causes animals to fortuitously adapt to the environment. This is one of the major mechanisms by which evolution (theoretically) occurs.*

Counterpoint: *Many scientists believe the word "adaptation" is misleading and should be eliminated. An individual animal cannot directly adapt to the environment. Any changes that occur to an animal must be by accidental mutations. Some scientists still incorrectly use the term or concept of adaptation in a context that suggests that an individual animal can respond directly to the environment, which is genetically impossible.*

See Chapter 4: Natural Selection and Chance Mutations

Point Six: *Some animals have similar anatomy, and this demonstrates that these animals evolved from a common ancestor which also had this same anatomy.*

Counterpoint: *Completely **unrelated** animals also have similar anatomy, such as sharks and dolphins, birds and bats, and marsupial and placental mice. With so many examples of unrelated animals with similarities, this evidence is, at best, circumstantial.*

See Chapter 5: Similarities: A Basic Proof of Evolution?

Points of Controversy

Point Seven: *The fossils clearly demonstrate evolution. When missing links do occur, it is only because the fossil record is poor.*

Number of animals discovered	*Expected* number of direct ancestor fossils found [1]	*Actual* number of direct ancestor fossils found
Apatosaurus 20–30+	1,750	0
Tyrannosaurus rex 32	4,800	0
Pterosaur 1,000+/-	22,000	0
Bat 1,000+	14,000	0

See Chapters 6–16: The Fossil Record

Counterpoint: *The fossil record is rich. Nearly one billion fossils have been collected by museums. Despite this, the direct ancestors of most animal groups are still missing.* [1]

Point Eight: *Recent discoveries of walking whales have proved, beyond a shadow of a doubt, that whales evolved from a land mammal. (**This is one of the three best fossil proofs for evolution.**)*

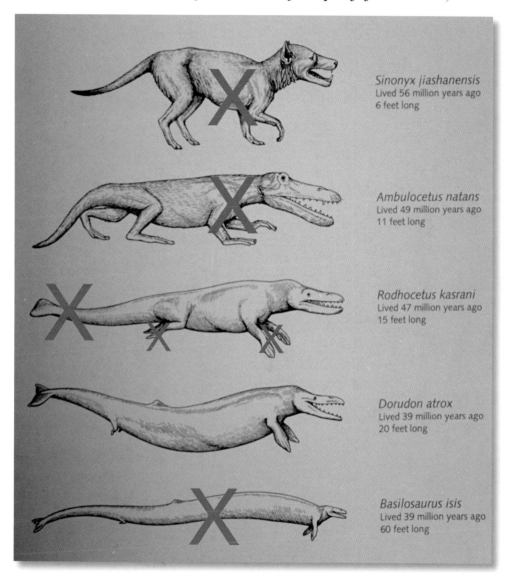

Sinonyx jiashanensis
Lived 56 million years ago
6 feet long

Ambulocetus natans
Lived 49 million years ago
11 feet long

Rodhocetus kasrani
Lived 47 million years ago
15 feet long

Dorudon atrox
Lived 39 million years ago
20 feet long

Basilosaurus isis
Lived 39 million years ago
60 feet long

Counterpoint: *If whales evolved from a land animal, which one was it? A bear as Charles Darwin believed? A hyena-like animal as scientists from the California Academy of Sciences suggested? A cat-like animal as scientists from the University of Michigan promoted? A wolf-like mammal as scientists at the American Museum of Natural History suggested? A hippo-like animal as Japanese scientists believed? Or was it a deer-like animal as Dr. Hans Thewissen recently suggested?*

Scientists have added a whale's tail and flippers to a land animal when no such fossils were found. They have called land animals "walking whales" even though they are not whales at all.

See Chapter 13: The Fossil Record of Whales and Appendix F

Points of Controversy

Point Nine: *Archaeopteryx and the feathered dinosaurs from China prove that birds evolved from dinosaurs.* ***(This is considered, by some, to be one of the three best fossil proofs for evolution.)***

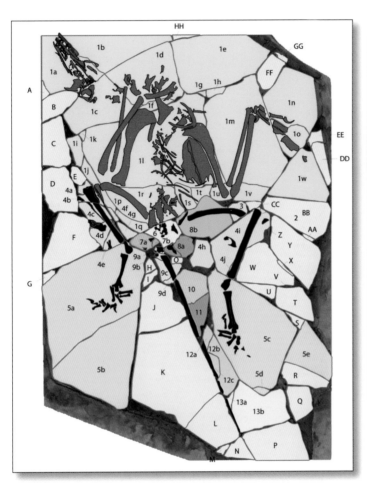

Counterpoint: *Far from proving evolution, these examples show that some scientists have gone to extreme measures to prove evolution including: Hiding CT evidence from the public, falsifying fossils, creating wild artistic models inconsistent with the fossil evidence, ignoring dating inconsistencies, and adding feathers to dinosaur models when none have been found in the fossils. Also, there is an entire fossil-faking industry in China, the same country where most of the" "feathered dinosaurs" have been found. Lastly, modern birds are supposed to have evolved from dinosaurs, but modern birds have been discovered in the same layers as dinosaurs. Evolution scientists have ignored this evidence for years.*

See Chapters 14, 15, and Appendix G

Point Ten: *Around 4 billion years ago, through a series of chemical reactions, a single-cell organism formed spontaneously.*

A Typical Prokaryote Cell

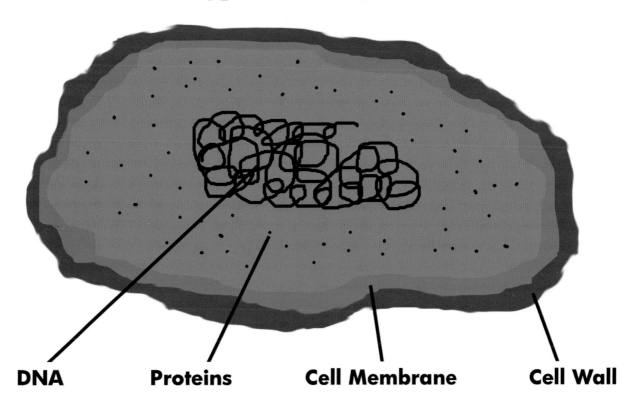

DNA   **Proteins**   **Cell Membrane**   **Cell Wall**

Counterpoint: *The three necessary components of a single-cell organism — spiraled functional DNA, proteins, and a cell membrane — do not form naturally, or spontaneously. Since this is true, then the first form of life could not arise from a spontaneous interaction of chemicals.*

See Chapters 17–19: The Origin of Life

Evolution: More Questions Than Answers?

After reviewing all of these facts, where should we go from here? It seems that we are left with more questions than answers. Here are some final questions for you, the reader.

Should the origin of life from chemicals be taught as a fact to students even though DNA, proteins, and functional cell membranes do not form naturally from chemicals?

In your opinion, could mutations cause one animal to change into a completely different type of animal? Could a complicated specialized animal, such as a whale, come about by random mutations in the DNA of a land mammal?

Does the fossil record support evolution? If there are nearly one billion fossils in our museums today, why are there gaps in the fossil record? Could the scientific experts have been wrong to embrace the theory of evolution before the fossil record was fully developed? How could a 60,000-pound dinosaur appear in the fossil record without a direct ancestor? A bat? A pterosaur? How could *all* of the animal phyla groups appear in the fossil record without direct ancestors?

If Darwin saw the fossil record today, with all of the gaps still present, would he still believe in his theory? Will finding more fossils prove evolution or will it simply reiterate the fossil record's gaps? How many fossils would be enough to prove or disprove evolution?

Are the best fossil examples of evolution (whales and birds) so compelling that we disregard the problem of the absence of transitional forms in the other animal groups?

Did animals evolve from simpler forms, as Darwin suggested, or is his theory a fantasy as others have suggested? Has evolution been proven groundless, just as the theory of spontaneous generation was, or is it scientifically sound? Should evolution be accepted as a fact? A theory? Or should it be discarded? Is it scientifically acceptable to question the theory of evolution?

Referring back to the poll depicted in the beginning pages of this book, approximately 46 percent of Americans reject the idea of evolution being the answer to the origin of life. With all the controversies and problems surrounding the theory of evolution, as presented in this text, do you think they are justified in their disbelief? If people were given the opportunity to read this text, do you think the percentage would increase or decrease? And, just as importantly, what do you think?

What Do You Think?

Watch DVD
*Evolution:
The Grand
Experiment*

The Number of Fossils

Museum Collections: Nearly a Billion

In the first edition of this book, Dr. John Long, Paleontologist and Head of Science at the Museum Victoria, Melbourne, Australia estimated the total number of fossils in museums worldwide as "hundreds of millions." In 2008, he revised this number upwards to *"close to a billion fossil specimens."* [1]

It is not unusual for a single museum to have millions of fossils. For instance, The Natural History Museum of London has 9,000,000 total fossils; [2] the University of Nebraska State Museum has a total of 8,500,000 fossils of which 7,500,000 are fossil invertebrates; [3] the American Museum of Natural History has 4,000,000 invertebrate specimens and 1,000,000 vertebrate specimens; [4] the Yale Peabody Museum has 4,000,000 fossil invertebrates; the Museum Victoria in Melbourne has 4,000,000 total fossils; [5] the University of Michigan has 2,000,000 fossil invertebrates; [6] the Florida Museum of Natural History has 1,060,000 fossil invertebrates; [7] and the University of Nebraska State Museum has 1,000,000 fossil vertebrate specimens. [8]

Number of Fossil Fish: Up to 500,000

Fossil fish have been found throughout the world and can be bought from fossil dealers for as little as a few dollars, reflecting their abundance.

Dr. John Long, Head of Science at the Museum Victoria, Melbourne, Australia and author of the book *The Rise of Fishes: 500 Million Years of Evolution,* estimates there are half a million fossil fish in museums today: *"I've visited some of the biggest museums in the world to study their fossil fish collections, such as the Natural History Museum in London and the American Museum of Natural History, and I'd say, conservatively, there'd be hundreds of thousands, probably maybe up to half a million."* [5]

Dr. Lance Grande, Curator, Department of Geology, Chicago Field Museum: *"There are literally hundreds of thousands of complete fish skeletons in museums around the world today."* [9]

Ulrich's Fossil Quarry, Fossil Butte, Wyoming
© 2007 AVC Inc., Photo by Debbie Werner

There are over 40 fossil fish, perfectly preserved, on this one fossil slab of rock from the Green River Formation in Wyoming. Museums have collected 500,000 of the best fossil fish specimens and hundreds of thousands of these are complete fish skeletons.

Scientists have collected close to 1,000,000,000 fossils, including 500,000 fossil fish!

Over 2,000,000 fossil whales specimens have been collected!

Number of Dinosaurs: 100,000

There are fossils from 100,000 *individual dinosaurs* in museums today. Of these 100,000 individuals, 3,050 are articulated dinosaur *skeletons*.[10] An articulated dinosaur skeleton means that a large number of the bones from an individual dinosaur were collected, enough to reassemble the dinosaur at the museum. These dinosaurs are "the cream of the crop" since museums collect only the best examples of a particular dinosaur species and leave the rest in the ground. Collecting hundreds of the same species of dinosaurs is unproductive and costly.

The following reflects dinosaur fossils found at only *some* of the North American dinosaur sites. The numbers do *not* include any of the dinosaur sites outside North America: Over 10,000 dinosaurs were discovered in Montana[11] (uncollected for the most part); 10,000 *Centrosaurus* dinosaurs were buried at Dinosaur Provincial Park in Alberta, Canada[12] (many eroded away and were uncollected for the most part); 1,000 *Coelophysis* dinosaurs were found at Ghost Ranch, Arizona[13] (some collected but many still lie in the ground); over a hundred *Triceratops* skulls have been found;[14] hundreds of dinosaurs have been found in the Morrison Formation,[15] including 85 dinosaurs from Dinosaur National Monument;[16] and 70 dinosaurs[17] were discovered at the Cleveland-Lloyd Quarry in Utah. And lastly, there are an estimated 250,000 dinosaur *bones* in the ground at Thermopolis, Wyoming,[18, 19] but paleontologists do not know how many individual dinosaurs are actually buried there.

The 1990 edition of the encyclopedic reference book *The Dinosauria*[20] lists 2,610 individual dinosaurs that have been reported in scientific articles. Again, these dinosaurs reflect only the tip of the iceberg of those fossils which remain in the field and are available for collection.

Rodent Fossils: 14,000

At the Olduvai site in Africa, Mary Leakey's team excavated 32,378 fossils, of which 14,000 were rodents.[21]

Fossil Horses: 75,000

"The American Museum of Natural History alone has over 75,000 skeletons or skeleton fragments." (Source: American Museum of Natural History horse display, July 2011.)

Fossil Rhinoceros: 100s

At just one location in western Nebraska, hundreds of fossil rhinoceros skeletons were found.[22]

Fossil Whales: 4,000

Dr. Lawrence G. Barnes, Curator of Vertebrate Paleontology at the Natural History Museum of Los Angeles County reports that over 2 million fossil whale bones have been found. *"It is difficult to estimate the numbers of fossil cetacean specimens that have been recovered, and even a compilation of the computerized inventories of the major museums of the world would not give an accurate total count. I would venture a guess that there are probably 2 million fossil cetacean specimens now in the care of all museums. Of these, I have personally collected several thousand fossil cetacean specimens."*[23]

Dr. Phil Gingerich from the University of Michigan in Ann Arbor and an expert on whale fossils reports that at least 4,000 fossil whales have been discovered so far.[24]

Fossil Seals: 5,000

Dr. Lawrence G. Barnes, Curator of Vertebrate Paleontology at the Natural History Museum of Los Angeles County, was asked how many fossil seals have been found. **Question:** *"Excluding recent non-fossilized specimens and recent ice age specimens, how many fossil seals have been found, thus far, worldwide? This would assume you found either one single bone of a fossil seal or a complete fossil seal, in both cases they would be counted as one fossil seal."* **Dr. Barnes:** *"I cannot give an exact count, but would estimate that perhaps 5,000 fossil seal specimens have been found worldwide, counting isolated bones and partial skeletons."*[23] **Question:** *"Of these fossil seals, what percent are more than 50 percent complete?"* **Dr. Barnes:** *"I would estimate much less than 1 percent, with partial associated skeletons only being known for three or four species."*[23] **Question:** *"Where are some of the biggest finds for fossil seals? How many fossil seals*

Over 5,000 fossil seals have been discovered!

have been found at some of these important seal sites?" **Dr. Barnes:** *"Antwerp Basin, Belgium, maybe several hundred specimens; Lee Creek Mine, North Carolina, maybe 3,000; Langebaanweg, South Africa, several hundred; coastal Peru, a few dozen; and a few more from eastern Europe, southeastern U.S., western North America, [and] Japan."* [23]

Dr. Annalisa Berta, Professor at San Diego State University and seal evolution expert, was asked the following question: *"Approximately how many fossil seals have been found worldwide? Assume if you found one bone of a seal or if you found an entire skeleton of a fossil seal, these would both be counted as one."* **Dr. Berta:** *"Here I assume you mean earless seals (Phocidae) — approximately 20 species — perhaps 50 individuals (a guess)."* [25] **Question:** *"Of these known fossil seals, what percent are more than 50 percent complete?"* **Dr. Berta:** *"Only four species are more than 50 percent complete — Homiphoca, Piscophoca, Acrophoca, Leptophoca. Each of these species is represented by multiple specimens, perhaps as many as 12–15 individuals (again, this is a guess)."* [25]

Fossil Sea Lions and Walruses: 15,000+

Dr. Lawrence G. Barnes, Curator of Vertebrate Paleontology at the Natural History Museum of Los Angeles County, was asked how many fossil sea lions have been found. **Question:** *"Excluding recent non-fossilized specimens and recent ice age specimens, how many fossil sea lions have been found, thus far, worldwide? This would assume you found either one single bone of a fossil sea lion or a complete fossil sea lion, in both cases they would be counted as one fossil sea lion."* **Dr. Barnes:** *"Counting fossil walruses, walrus-like animals, and diverse extinct groups that are related to them and to the sea lions, which we call the otarioid pinnipeds (Enaliarctines, Desmatophocines, Allodesmines, Imagotariines, Dusignathines, etc.), I would estimate that 15,000 specimens have been found, much more abundant than the phocid true seal fossil record. I personally have collected more than a thousand such fossils."* [23] **Question:** *"Of these fossil sea lions, what percent are more than 50 percent complete?"* **Dr. Barnes:** *"Probably no more than 17 specimens*

represent skeletons that were found 50 percent complete. While that is probably twice the number of such phocid true seal specimens, that is still less than 1 percent of the known record. I have personally collected about four such partial skeletons and many less complete specimens."* [23] **Question:** *"Where are some of the biggest finds for fossil sea lions? How many fossil sea lions have been found at some of these important sea lion sites?"*

Dr. Barnes: *"Lumping together sea lions, walruses, and their diverse fossil relatives: Sharktooth Hill Bonebed, central California, maybe 8,000 specimens; Southern Orange County, southern California, perhaps 1,500 specimens; Isla Cedros, Baja California, Mexico, perhaps 400 specimens; [and] Lee Creek Mine, North Carolina, perhaps 300 specimens. Of these, I have collected probably 10 percent of the specimens, and have named 14 of the presently recognized extinct species of otarioid pinnipeds, which is approximately 25 percent of the known extinct species."* [23]

Dr. Annalisa Berta, Professor, San Diego State University, was asked the following question: *"Approximately how many fossil sea lions have been found worldwide? Be as specific as possible. Assume if you found one bone of a sea lion or if you found an entire skeleton of a fossil sea lion, these would both be counted as one."* **Dr. Berta:** *"Here I assume that you mean fur seals and sea lions (Otariidae) and do not include walruses in this grouping Otariidae as some do — approximately 13 species and perhaps as many as 30–35 individuals."* [25] **Question:** *"Of these known fossil sea lions, what percent are more than 50 percent complete?"* **Dr. Berta:** *"A much smaller number — two species Thalassoleon mexicanus and Pithanotaria starri, perhaps five individuals."* [25]

Fossil Birds: 200,000+ "Specimens"

Dr. Larry Martin, Professor and Senior Curator at the University of Kansas, states that fossil birds are rather common: *"In fact, fossil birds are not really as rare as has been supposed. There are thousands of specimens and nearly the whole skeleton is known for many species."* [26]

Dr. Storrs Olson, Senior Zoologist for the Division of Birds at the Smithsonian Institution, was interviewed

The fossil collections of flying vertebrates are staggering!

to clarify the number of fossil birds that have been found. **Question:** *"Excluding recent ice age and non-fossilized bird specimens, how many fossil birds have been collected by museums worldwide? Assume if you found one whole bird, this would count as one. Or if you found just one bone of a bird, this would also count as one. Please try to be as specific as possible. I would also be curious to know approximately what percent of these were more than 50 percent complete."*

Dr. Olson: *"I gather what you mean is individual specimens of fossil birds. I am not sure what you mean, however, by recent ice age. Regardless, the number would be in the 100s of thousands. We must have between 10 and 20 thousand bird fossils from the Lee Creek Mine in North Carolina alone. The Tertiary fissure fills in France have yielded many more fossils than that, I would imagine."* [27]

Fossil Bats: 1,000

One of the richest fossil bat sites is at Riversleigh, Australia, where hundreds of fossil bats have been collected.[28, 29] In Messel, Germany, 650+ individual fossil bats were found.[30] In Florida, 100 fossil bats were found.[31] Fossil bats are known from all over the world.

Flying Reptiles (Pterosaurs): Nearly 1,000

Dr. Peter Wellnhofer, author of *Pterosaurs, The Illustrated Encyclopedia of Prehistoric Flying Reptiles,* was asked how many pterosaurs have been found worldwide? **Dr. Wellnhofer:** *"It is difficult to calculate or give an answer [to] how many pterosaurs have been found worldwide because many are housed in private collections and not known to scientists. There might be much more than have been published and described, I am sure. I would say the specimen numbers go at least in the hundreds or close to a thousand or something like that...One of the most important localities always has been the Solnhofen in Bavaria. The Solnhofen limestone has yielded hundreds of specimens. So we have a fairly good record of pterosaur fossils and pterosaurs worldwide from the Triassic up to the late Cretaceous."* [32]

Fossil Butte National Monument, Wyoming © 2007 AVC Inc., Photo by Debbie Werner

Above: *Dozens of fossil birds were found at Fossil Butte National Monument, Wyoming.* [28]

Sam Noble Oklahoma Museum of Science and Natural History, Oklahoma © 2007 AVC Inc., Photo by Debbie Werner

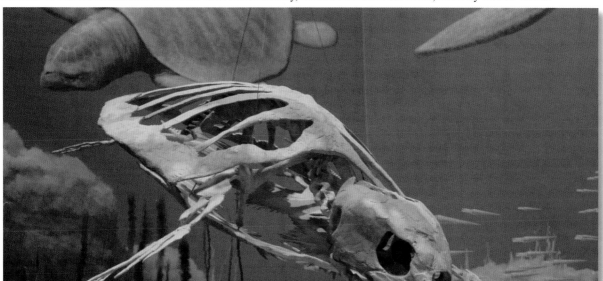

Fossil Turtles: 100,000

Fossil turtles are known throughout the world and are on display at many of the museums visited by the author. Two scientists who specialize in fossil turtles were interviewed concerning the number of fossil turtles collected by museums.

Dr. Jim Parham, Paleontologist from the University of California, Berkeley, is the Editor of *Fossil Turtle Research,* Associate Editor of *Asiatic Herpetological Research*, and Editor of *Fossil Turtle Newsletter.* **Question:** *"Approximately how many fossil turtles are in museum collections worldwide now? This would be a liberal definition of a fossil turtle and would assume that if a museum had a complete turtle skeleton, this would count as one turtle. Or if they had only one bone or one piece of shell from a different fossil turtle in their collection, this would also count as one turtle. Please be as specific as possible, such as between 15,000 and 25,000, or more than 10,000."* **Dr. Parham:** *"Unfortunately, most turtle fossils consist of mere fragments. Although there are probably over a hundred thousand of such specimens in museums around the world (many of them uncatalogued),* *relatively complete turtle specimens are exceedingly rare with less than one hundred being known to science."* [33]

Dr. Eugene S. Gaffney is a Vertebrate Paleontologist at the Department of Vertebrate Paleontology, American Museum of Natural History in New York. Dr. Gaffney specializes in turtle evolution. **Question:** *"Approximately how many fossil turtles were in museum collections worldwide when Darwin published **The Origin of Species** [in] 1859, and how many fossil turtles are in museum collections worldwide now? Both of these questions would assume that if a museum had a complete turtle skeleton, this would count as one turtle. Or if they had only one bone or one piece of shell from a different fossil turtle in their collection, this would also count as one turtle. Please be as specific as possible, such as between 15,000 and 25,000, not thousands."* **Dr. Gaffney:** *"Unfortunately, I haven't the slightest clue; presumably more, but I haven't an order of magnitude even."* [34]

Over 1,000,000 fossil insects have been collected!

Number of Fossil Insects: 1,000,000+

Fossil insects are commonly found throughout the world. Some insects are preserved in rock while others are preserved in amber.

Dr. Conrad C. Labandeira, Curator of Paleoentomology, Smithsonian National Museum of Natural History, was interviewed concerning the number of fossil insects. **Question:** *"How many fossil insects have museums collected over the last century? Hundreds? Thousands? Millions?"* **Dr. Labandeira:** *"Undoubtedly one to a few million, particularly if one includes the effects that insects have had on fossil plant organs, such as leaf mines, chew marks, galls, wood borings, egg-laying structures, and piercing-and-sucking marks. Some individual museums — such as the Paleontological Institute in Moscow, Capital Normal University in Beijing, the American Museum of Natural History in New York, and the National Museum of Natural History in Washington, D.C. — each have at least 50,000 fossil insects. Many new deposits have been discovered and quarried within the past ten years and have provided approximately 20 major pristine sites for fossil insect collections."* [35]

Number of Fossil Invertebrates: 750,000,000

There are "close to a billion" fossil specimens in museums today. It is conservatively estimated (by the author) that at least seventy-five percent of the nearly one billion fossils in museums are invertebrates.

Mesalands Community College's Dinosaur Museum, Tucumcari, New Mexico © 2007 AVC Inc., Photo by Carl Werner

Right: *Fossil cricket from dinosaur fossil layers.*
Below: *Ants preserved in amber found in Miocene fossil layers in Africa.*

Houston Museum of Natural Science
© 2007 AVC Inc., Photo by Carl Werner

Dinosaur Evolution Chart

The theory of evolution predicts that one type of dinosaur evolved into another type of dinosaur. Then, this new type of dinosaur, yet again, evolved into another type of dinosaur and so on, during what is known as the dinosaur period from 220 million years ago to 65 million years ago. Accordingly, dinosaur evolution charts should demonstrate a continuous evolution of dinosaur families, one family evolving into another dinosaur family and so forth, during this vast period of 155 million years.

The dinosaur evolution chart depicted on the right (which appeared in its original form in Chapter 12), has been superimposed with the actual number of discovered dinosaurs. These numbers are based on interviews with the following dinosaur evolution experts: Dr. Paul Sereno, University of Chicago; Dr. David Weishampel, Editor of the encyclopedic reference book *The Dinosauria*; Dr. Phillip Currie, Curator of the Royal Tyrell Museum in Alberta, Canada; and Dr. Angela Milner, Head of Vertebrate Paleontology at the Natural History Museum in London. Information was also obtained from Dr. Weishampel's encyclopedic reference book, *The Dinosauria,* [1] and dinosaur evolution charts from the Museum Victoria, Melbourne, Australia, and *The Ultimate Dinosaur* by Preiss and Silverberg. [2]

If one dinosaur evolved into another and so on, and if 100,000 dinosaurs have been collected

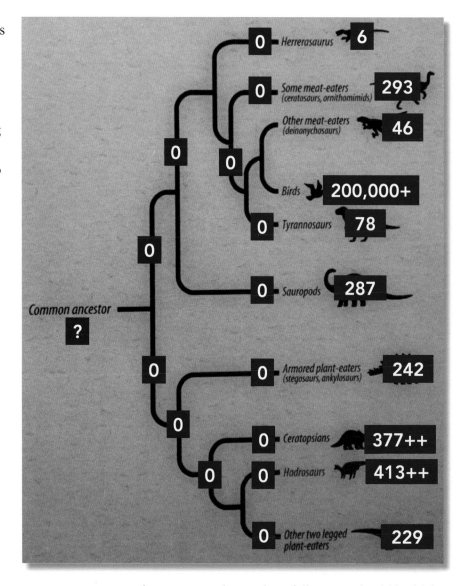

by museums, the number of dinosaurs should be fairly evenly distributed on the evolution chart above. But this is not the case. Dr. Weishampel suggested that no dinosaur was ancestral to any other dinosaur. In other words, the ancestors for every type of dinosaur are, in fact, missing. Even the very first theoretical dinosaur called the "common ancestor" of dinosaurs is absent. Dr. Weishampel: *"From my reading of the fossil record of dinosaurs, no direct ancestors have been discovered for any dinosaur species. Alas, my list of dinosaurian ancestors is an empty one."* [3]

Numbers on the Dinosaur Chart

The following interviews and citations detail how the numbers on the chart were derived.

Herrerasaurus: Interview with Dr. Sereno. **Question:** How many *Herrerasaurus* skeletons have been found at the Valley of the Moon and worldwide? **Dr. Sereno:** *"We found parts of five skeletons and odd bones of many others. I think that is the most of any herrerasaurid ever found. The one from North America is known from one partial skeleton, so these animals are fairly rare."* [4] This would be a total of six *Herrerasaurus*, five from Argentina and one from North America.

Some meat-eaters (ceratosaurs and ornithomimids): The number of "Some meat-eaters" on the Dinosaur Evolution Chart is a sum of ceratosaurs and ornitho-mimids, as taken from the book *The Dinosauria*. Page 152 of the 1990 edition of *The Dinosauria* lists 261 individual ceratosaurs. It lists the number of *Coelophysis* dinosaurs at Ghost Ranch as "several hundred." (This number was entered as 200 but is probably a conservative estimate. Others have estimated this number to be 1,000. [5]) Page 226 of *The Dinosauria* lists 32 known Ornithomimosauria. In summary, the "Some meat-eaters" category includes 32 Ornithomimosauria, plus 261 ceratosaurs, for a total of 293.

Other meat-eaters (deinonychosaurs): *The Dinosauria* quotes John Ostrom: *"Sometimes dromaeosaurs are allied with members of the Troodontidae, formerly the Saurornithoididae of Barsbold's 1974 systematic scheme, although not everyone is convinced. Together, these two constitute to many the core of the Deinonychosauria which are distinctive in foot structure and hand and wrist construction."* [6] *The Dinosauria* lists 22 Dromaeo-sauridae on page 270, including the eight *Deinony-chus* and 24 Troodontidae on page 260, for a total of 46.

Tyrannosaurs: *The Dinosauria* lists 78 Tyrannosauridae, including Albertosaurs, Tyranno-saurs and Tarbosaurs, but excluding 70 allosaurids. [7]

Sauropods: There are 287 sauropods reported on pages 346–352 of *The Dinosauria*.

Armored plant-eaters (stegosaurs and ankylosaurs): There are 133 Stegosauria listed on page 450 of *The Dinosauria* and 109 Ankylosauria listed on pages 475–477, for a total of 242 armored plant-eating dinosaurs.

Ceratopsians: *The Dinosauria* suggests that Ceratopsians "consist of the Psittacosauridae and the Neoceratopsia." [8] One-hundred-twenty Psittacosauridae are listed on page 589 of *The Dinosauria* and 257 Neoceratopsia are listed on pages 611–612, for a total of 377 Ceratopsians.

(**Author's Note:** This is a gross underestimate. Neoceratopsia consists of many horned dinosaurs, such as *Centrosaurus* and *Triceratops*. Discoveries of *Centrosaurus* bone beds in Alberta, Canada, have led paleontologists to conclude there are as many as 10,000 *Centrosaurus* dinosaurs buried at Dinosaur Provincial Park. [9] Yet, *The Dinosauria* lists only 19 *Centrosaurus* from this area. Similarly, *The Dinosauria* reports 50 complete or partial *Triceratops*, but Dr. Weishampel indicated in an interview that hundreds of *Triceratops* skulls had been discovered, not to mention the other *Triceratops* skeletons without skulls that had been found. [10])

Hadrosaurs: Pages 556–558 of *The Dinosauria* list 413 Hadrosauridae, which consist of dinosaurs, such as Maiasaurs and Lambeosaurs.

(**Author's Note:** The number of 413 is also a gross underestimate because it does not reflect the number of known Hadrosaurs which are still in the ground. *The Dinosauria* lists only 200 Maiasaurs found by Horner, but in his book, *Digging Dinosaurs*, Horner reports finding 10,000 Maiasaurs: *"At a conservative estimate, we had discovered the tomb of 10,000 dinosaurs."* [11] Adding these 10,000 Maiasaurs to the list yields a total of 10,213 Hadrosauridae.)

Other two-legged plant-eaters: Eighty-nine Iguanodontidae and related ornithopoda are listed on pages 530–531 of *The Dinosauria*. Approximately 104 Hypsilophodontidae, Tenontosaurs, Dryosauridae are listed on page 500; 31 Pachycephalosauria are listed on page 566; and 5 Heterodontosauridae are listed on page 487, for a total of 229 "other two-legged plant-eaters."

These numbers from *The Dinosauria* probably represent a gross underestimate because many dinosaur finds are not reported or are underreported in a text such as *The Dinosauria*.

Has the Common Ancestor to All Dinosaurs Been Discovered?

In the past, different reptiles/dinosaurs, such as *Eoraptor*, *Lagosuchus*, *Staurikosaurus* and *Herrerasaurus,* have been suggested as being *the* common ancestor to all dinosaurs. These ideas were recently rejected as indicated in the following interviews with Dr. Sereno, Dr. Milner and Dr. Weishampel. The common ancestor to all dinosaurs has not yet been found.

Question: Was *Eoraptor* the common ancestor to all other dinosaurs? **Dr. Sereno:** *"Eoraptor, we believe, is off to the side* [not on the line to all later dinosaurs] *because it has a few features that we believe are advanced. A few features suggest that it was already along the predatory dinosaur line and had moved away from the common ancestor."* [4]

Question: What features in the skull tell you that *Eoraptor* cannot be the common ancestor to all dinosaurs? **Dr. Sereno:** *"If we look at the skull of Eoraptor...there is a little sliding joint in the lower jaw. That sliding joint allowed the toothed portion of the jaw, the front part, to flex around prey. This is a basic trapping mechanism in the jaws of all predatory dinosaurs from little Eoraptor to big T. rex...We don't think that the primitive dinosaur ancestor had it because the herbivores and the sauropod lines don't have it."* [4] **Question**: What other features in *Eoraptor* lead you to conclude that

it can't be the basal dinosaur? **Dr. Sereno:** *"It has a narrow scapular blade. The blade is narrower than we would suspect in more primitive things — in the other types of dinosaurs we find. We find changes in the ankle joint. They are all suggesting one thing — that it is a primitive theropod and not the dinosaur ancestor. It took us a long time to actually realize* [this]*."* [4]

Dr. Milner: *"There is some controversy of exactly what we got in the way of early dinosaur remains. Eoraptor and Herrerasaurus are certainly the earliest probable dinosaurs,* [although] *they are not accepted as true dinosaurs by everybody. But if you take this one stage further back, you really haven't got a linking form between those possible early dinosaurs and what went before. So we are lacking information at that level."* [12]

Question: Are recent dinosaur discoveries, such as *Eoraptor* and *Staurikosaurus* and *Herrerasaurus,* on the direct line to *T. rex* or are they a sister group? **Dr. Weishampel:** *"There have been a number of important recent discoveries in South America. These include some of the earliest dinosaurs, like Eoraptor and Herrerasaurus and Staurikosaurus. Initially, these dinosaurs — they were called dinosaurs at the time — were actually thought to be outside this major group called the saurischian (or lizard-like) pelvis dinosaurs and bird pelvis type dinosaurs. More recent study of new material, really beautiful specimens, very complete skeletons, suggests that they are actually theropod dinosaurs — that they are actually meat-eating dinosaurs."* [13]

Question: Is *Lagosuchus* on the direct line to early dinosaur evolution? **Dr. Weishampel:** *"Lagosuchus is not directly on the line because it doesn't have all the right bits. By the right bits, I mean all the right characteristics that are found in the skeletons of these guys. The anatomical parts of Lagosuchus suggests that it is off the direct line. Some* *of the features of Lagosuchus, and things like Coelophysis, some of the common characteristics suggests that some of those common characteristics would also be found in this yet-to-be-found ancestor."* [13]

Are Dinosaur Families Ancestral to One Another?

Prosauropods

Dr. Weishampel was interviewed concerning the previously accepted idea that prosauropod dinosaurs were on the direct line to sauropod dinosaurs.

Question: Are prosauropods directly on the line to sauropods, such as *Apatosaurus?* **Dr. Weishampel:** *"Like other sorts of dinosaurs we have been talking about, prosauropods actually are not on the direct line to get to sauropods, like Diplodocus and Apatosaurus and Brachiosaurus. They [prosauropods] are grouped together because they have their own evolutionary history that is independent of the evolutionary history of sauropods."* [13]

Preiss's phylogeny chart (bottom of next page) in *The Ultimate Dinosaur* [14] indicates that dinosaur families are, in fact, not ancestral to each other except for *possibly* two dinosaur families — Hadrosaurs and allosaurids. Hadrosaurs are shown to be ancestral to Iguanodons (although this is indicated by a light green line indicating "limited fossil records") and allosaurids are the direct ancestors of tyrannosaurids. (Again, a light line indicates this relationship is based on "limited fossil records.") These two ideas were disputed by all that were interviewed and other authors as follows.

Are Allosaurids Ancestral to *T. rex*?

Concerning Preiss's diagrams implying the evolution of *Allosaurus* into *T. rex,* Dr. David Weishampel and Dr. Phillip Currie were interviewed. **Question:** Is *Allosaurus* on the direct line to *T. rex* (as indicated by Preiss's phylogeny chart)? **Dr. Weishampel:** *"Allosaurus and Acrocanthosaurus are not ancestors to T. rex in any form. So they sit off the line. They have their own evolutionary history, their own*

evolutionary destiny. That is indicated to us by having these unique features that could only be accounted for by their separate evolution." [13]

Dr. Currie: *"Until recently, we thought of Tyrannosaurs as being animals that were derived from big meat-eating dinosaurs, like Allosaurus. But there is a lot of things wrong with that. There are a lot of characters in Tyrannosaurus that don't fit with that kind of a model."* [15]

Question: Are there any known animals on the actual direct ancestry of *T. rex*? **Dr. Sereno:** *"Not exactly. When you go out fishing as a paleontologist for these new species, you'll find one that happens to come to rise to dominance and dominates the landscape. But that's not necessarily the common ancestor to two later species. It's a twig that became very common and successful. But evolution is complex enough, you have enough lineages evolving, that your chance of picking one that is directly ancestral to a later branch is relatively small. I know of only a couple instances in dinosaurs where we think we actually have a common ancestor that gave rise to all later members of a particular group. There is one in prosauropods, and one in the small contemporary theropods — Coelophysis and Syntarsus. Coelophysis looks exactly ancestral to Syntarsus. Syntarsus has a little crest. Otherwise, it's virtually identical to Coelophysis. And you could argue that the former, Coelophysis, is ancestral to the latter, but that's very rare."* [4]

In an interview with Dr. Dave Weishampel, the following question was asked: **Question:** In constructing a phylogeny chart of *T. rex,* starting with the pre-dinosaur phytosaur or thecodont, which animals can be placed on the direct line as a direct ancestor to *T. rex*? **Dr. Weishampel:** *"I think that will happen in each case* [that we will not find the direct ancestor of any dinosaur], *and that is based on the improbability of finding the ancestor, and then the improbability of recognizing it as the ancestor. So in each case, they* [all of the dinosaurs we have found] *will be a little off the* [direct ancestral] *line."* [13] (Information in brackets was added by author based on Dr. Weishampel's previous comments in the interview.)

Are Hadrosaurs Ancestral to Iguanodons?

Concerning Preiss's diagrams [14] indicating that Hadrosaurs were the direct descendents from Iguanodonts (see diagram below), Norman in 1984, Cooper in 1985, Sereno in 1986, and Weishampel in 1990, suggest that both evolved from a "proposed" earlier dinosaur rather than Iguanodonts evolving into Hadrosaurs. [16]

How Are Ornithischians Related to Saurischians?

In an interview with Dr. Angela Milner, she states: *"We are certainly lacking information that ties together meat-eating dinosaurs and all the rest of the dinosaurs. We certainly* [don't know]. *We really don't have any idea how the whole other group of dinosaurs, called Ornithischians* [evolved from the meat-eating dinosaurs]. [We really do not know] *exactly the timing and the way they branched off. We've got nothing there yet. There is a huge gap."* [12]

Evolution Chart adapted from Preiss and Silverberg's *The Ultimate Dinosaur.*

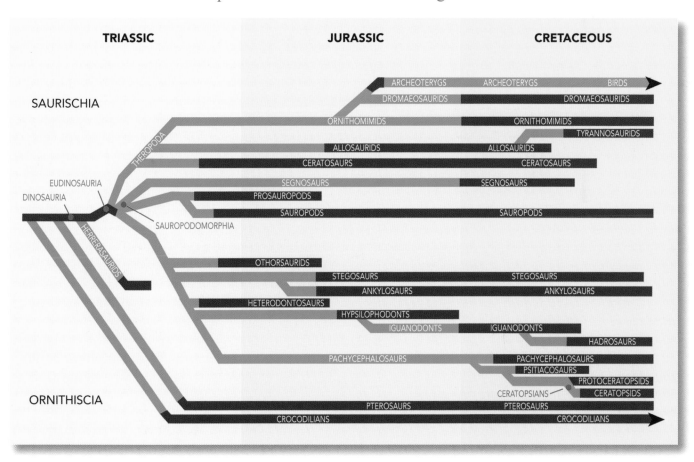

Fish Evolution Chart

The theory of evolution proposes that an invertebrate animal evolved into a fish. Later, over the course of millions of years, one fish family evolved into another, which subsequently evolved into yet another fish family and so on, until we get to modern fish families.

The proof for the evolution of fish would be the demonstration of an invertebrate evolving into the first fish. This would, of course, include multiple intermediate forms between this invertebrate, without a backbone, and the first fish with a vertebral column. The proof for evolution would then entail showing which fish family evolved into which subsequent fish family, and so on and so on.

The fish evolution chart on page 96 of Chapter 8 was a compilation of multiple resources, including Dr. Long's book *The Rise of Fishes: 500 Million Years of Evolution,* [1] the fish evolution chart from *The Macmillan Illustrated Encyclopedia of Dinosaurs and Prehistoric Animals* [2] (see adapted/modified version below), and an interview conducted with Dr. John Long for the accompanying video series. [3] Dr. Long is a paleontologist and Head of Science at the Museum Victoria, Melbourne, Australia, and is also considered to be one of the world's leading experts on fish evolution.

The original fish evolution diagram in *The Macmillan Illustrated Encyclopedia of Dinosaurs and Prehistoric Animals* shows lines of fish evolution as either solid lines or dotted lines. Solid lines depict the "known fossil record of a group," while dotted lines denote "possible evolutionary relationships." Wherever dots are located on the chart below, they have been replaced with the number 0 on the chart in Chapter 8 based on the suggestion that the fossil record is not known. This interpretation was reinforced during an interview with Dr. Long, also found in Chapter 8, during which he indicated that evolutionary relationships between fish groups were still not well understood, nor did scientists know what invertebrate evolved into vertebrates.

The groups (semionotiformes, pycnodontiformes, aspidorhynchiformes and teleosts) are shown by Macmillan to be derived from the group called palaeonisciformes. But again, the fossil record documenting this relationship is unknown. Because of space considerations for printing, these radiations were omitted from the chart in Chapter 8.

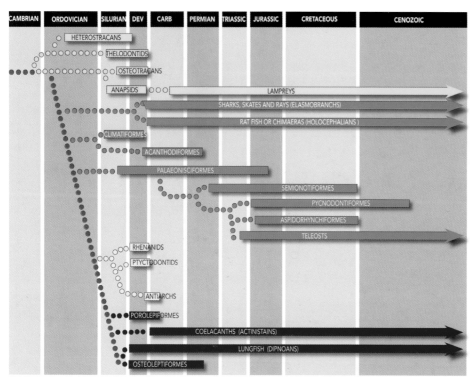

Fish Evolution Chart adapted from *The Macmillan Illustrated Encyclopedia of Dinosaurs and Prehistoric Animals*

Bat Evolution Update

Shortly after the first edition of this book was published, evolution scientists reported the discovery of a new fossil bat, *Onychonycteris finneyi*, in the prestigious journal *Nature*. The editors of *Nature* thought the fossil was of such great importance they placed it on the front cover with the headline "*FIRST FLIGHT, Solving the mysteries of bat evolution.*"[1] This appendix will examine this newest fossil bat in detail.

All Bats Could Fly

If you compare the photograph of this newly discovered bat, *Onychonycteris finneyi*, to all of the other bats in Chapter 9, both living and fossil, you will notice they look very similar. (See photos below and Chapter 9.)

The theory of evolution suggests a bat evolved from a non-flying mammal about the size of a mouse or a shrew, over millions of years, through slow accidental mutations. If evolution is true, one should find various examples of fossilized mammals slowly evolving into a bat as the fossil record becomes more complete. In other words, scientists should find a

ground mammal with partially developed wings, not yet capable of flying. Nearly one billion fossils have now been collected, including over 1,000 fossil bats,[2] but no partially evolved bat ancestors have been found. All fossil bats found, even *Onychonycteris finneyi*, were fully formed and could fly.

All Bats Have the Same Bone Pattern

All bats have the same pattern of bones in the wings: a long upper arm bone (humerus), even longer forearm bones (radius and ulna), and very long digits. The digits (fingers) act as struts in the membranous wings. A bat, like a bird or an airplane, needs very large wings for lift in the flight process, hence the need for such long fingers and arm bones.

The scientists who reported the discovery of *Onychonycteris finneyi* wrote: "*The limb proportions of Onychonycteris are unique among bats, being intermediate between all other known bats and forelimb dominated non-volant [non-flying] mammals.*"[1] This statement implies that *Onychonycteris* was a partially developed bat with arm bones halfway between a ground mammal and a bat. But to arrive at this conclusion, these evolution scientists excluded the all-important digits from their limb-proportion calculations. Instead, they simply

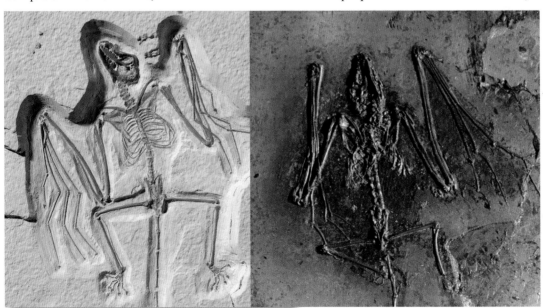

The fossil bat Onychonycteris finneyi **(far left)** *does not look significantly different from other fossil or living bats, such as this fossil bat from Germany* **(left)**.

Mouse-tailed bat

echolocate to catch insects at night. Megabats, such as the fruit bat seen on this page (below), are fruit eaters and generally do *not* need or possess the ability to use echolocation.

The authors of the *Nature* article reported the fossil bat *Onychonycteris* had small ear bones (cochlea), implying that this bat did not have the ability to echolocate. Because of this particular trait in *Onychonycteris*, they concluded that bats evolved the ability to fly before they could echolocate, implying evolution.

Scientists who oppose evolution argue that the absence of echolocation in a fossil bat, such as *Onychonycteris,* is not significant. Some fossil bats could echolocate, others could not. The same applies to bats living today.

After 150 years of searching, there is still no evidence of a partially developed bat ancestor. Instead, bats appear in the fossil record fully formed and capable of flying and *Onychonycteris* is no exception.

compared the arm-to-leg ratio of *Onychonycteris* to the arm-to-leg ratio of tree sloths, gibbons, and flying lemurs, animals with long arms that have nothing to do with bat evolution. They then declared *Onychonycteris* a missing link.

This conclusion stands in stark contrast with reality. Meaning, if one compares *Onychonycteris finneyi* to any other bat in Chapter 9, it is obvious that it is a typical bat, and not an intermediate ancestor. In fact, the authors of the same article report that *Onychonycteris* could fly in a manner similar to living mouse-tailed bats (above).

Onychonycteris Could Not Echolocate

Echolocation is a sonar-like sound system used by bats to "see" in the dark. Using echolocation, bats can fly in complete darkness and catch insects in mid-flight. They do this by making a series of clicks which bounce off of their surroundings, allowing them to form a sonar-like "picture" in their mind of what lies ahead.

There are two types of bats living today, microbats and megabats. Most microbats, such as the Ghost Bat shown in Chapter 9, have the ability to

Above: *Fruit bats, such as this one hanging in a tree in downtown Cairns, Australia, do not have sonar-like echolocation.*

Pinniped Evolution Update

Pinnipeds are carnivorous marine mammals that have "finned back feet," similar to the fins used by a scuba diver. The Latin-derived word "pinniped" literally means "finned-foot." Pinnipeds include three groups of mammals living today; namely, sea lions, seals, and walruses.

By 2007, when the first edition of this book was published, scientists had discovered 20,000 fossil pinnipeds. (See Appendix A.) Despite this plethora of fossils, evolution scientists have not found any definitive fossils showing a land mammal evolving into a seal, sea lion, or walrus.

Canadian paleobiologist and professor, Dr. Natalia Rybczynski of the Canadian Museum of Nature, wrote this candid assessment in 2009: The "*fossil evidence of the morphological steps leading from a terrestrial ancestor to the modern marine forms has been weak or contentious.*" [1]

Sea lion

All three types of pinnipeds living today, sea lions (**left**)*, walruses* (**bottom left**)*, and seals* (**below**)*, have finned back feet, the telltale sign of a pinniped.*

Seal

Walrus

Enaliarctos—The Oldest Pinniped

Enaliarctos, characterized by evolution scientists as "the oldest fossil pinniped," looks like a sea lion, and not a missing link. [2] (See photos below.) Dr. Natalia Rybczynski highlights this missing link problem—the absence of evolutionary intermediate fossils between a land mammal and the first pinniped—when she wrote: "*With Enaliarctos considered the earliest pinniped,* *there exists a major transformational gap between a terrestrial ancestor and the appearance of flippered pinnipeds. Indeed, most studies of pinniped relationships and evolution do not consider the critical first evolutionary stages, that ultimately gave rise to this successful group of marine carnivores.*" [1]

Fossil bones of Enaliarctos

Museum painting of Enaliarctos

Sea lion

Puijila—A New Discovery

In April 2009, a team of evolution scientists reported the discovery of a missing link—a fossil pinniped with *webbed* feet, not flippers, and dubbed this animal *Puijila darwini* (in honor of Charles Darwin). [1, 3, 4, 5]

Dr. Natalia Rybczynski, the lead scientist of the discovery team, wrote, "*Puijila is a morphological intermediate in the land-to-sea transition of pinnipeds and provides new evidence concerning the evolution and biogeography of the earliest pinnipeds.*" [1]   According to these scientists, this new fossil solves a conundrum for the theory of evolution that has existed for over 150 years.

In September 2009, an iconic evolution scientist named Dr. Richard Dawkins highlighted this fossil in his book *The Greatest Show on Earth: The Evidence for Evolution* when he wrote, "*Puijila neatly straddles the gap between land and water in the ancestry of pinnipeds. It is yet another delightful addition to our growing list of 'links' that are no longer missing.*" [6]

Scientists who oppose evolution question whether *Puijila is* a missing link or even a pinniped. The reasons for their skepticism are discussed in the following 11 pages.

Above: *Research assistant at the Canadian Museum of Nature preparing Puijila darwini.*

Problems with *Puijila*

Puijila Found with a Rabbit

Opponents of evolution would suggest that *Puijila* could not be a "prehistoric" animal since it was found with fossils of a rabbit, a shrew, and a duck? [7, 8] How could *Puijila* be that old if it was found with modern types of animals?

Problems with Fossil Numbers

If evolution is true, why would you find only a single fossilized intermediate animal (*Puijila*) in the ancestral line of pinnipeds? The fossil record should be evenly distributed and representative of animals that lived in the past. Since 20,000 pinnipeds have been found, one should find thousands of each of the evolving animals between a land animal and pinnipeds, not just one fossil of one animal. Because of this odd pattern of fossil numbers, *Puijila* requires closer scrutiny.

Problems with Miocene Layer

Although *Puijila* was reported to be the ancestor of pinnipeds, it was discovered in the *same* rock layer in which pinnipeds were found (Miocene).[1] In fact, pinnipeds (seals and sea lions) have been found in rock layers *below Puijila* (Oligocene).[9, 10] Opponents of evolution ask how *Puijila* could be an "ancestor" to seals and sea lions if it was found above them? This would be equivalent to calling your younger cousin your "great-great-great-great-great-great-great-great grandfather." (See chart below.)

Was *Puijila* Even a Pinniped?

The last and most serious charge about *Puijila* is the use of the scientific classification of "pinniped" by the scientists who discovered this fossil. [4, 5] Opponents of evolution ask: Why call *Puijila* a pinniped if it does not have the classic pinniped characteristics of finned back feet, front flippers, large eye sockets, and pinniped dental patterns?

Fossil Layers
Millions of years ago (MYA)*

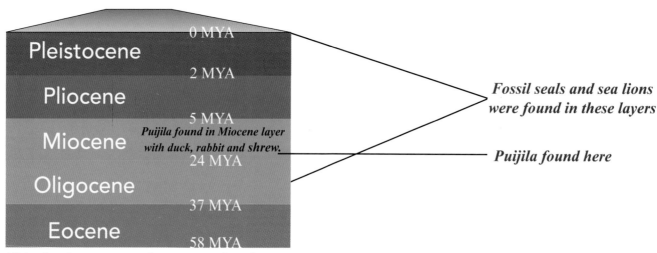

Fossil seals and sea lions were found in these layers

Puijila found here

Puijila found in Miocene layer with duck, rabbit and shrew.

Pleistocene	0 MYA
	2 MYA
Pliocene	
	5 MYA
Miocene	
	24 MYA
Oligocene	
	37 MYA
Eocene	
	58 MYA

*Scientists do not agree on the age or number of years it took to deposit these fossil layers. This is a theoretical construct to evaluate the theory of evolution.

Is *Puijila* a Pinniped?

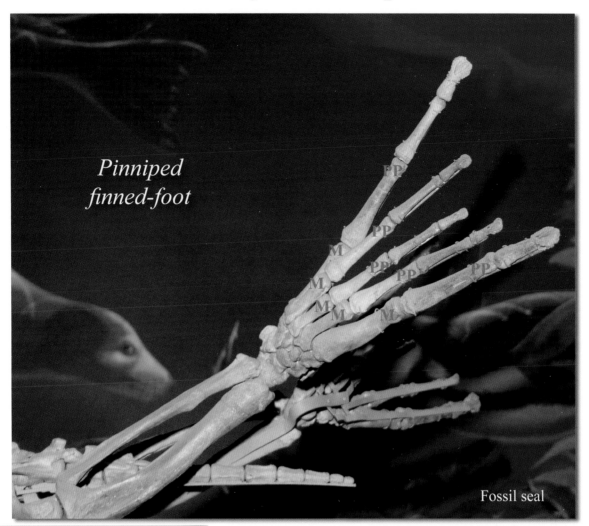

Pinniped
finned-foot

Fossil seal

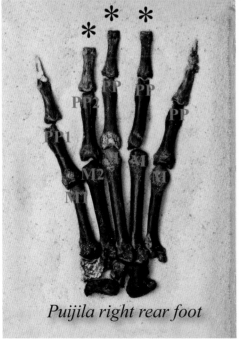

Puijila right rear foot

Did *Puijila* Have Finned Back Feet?

Pinnipeds have a distinct bone pattern in their finned back feet. The first and last digits (toes) are longer, giving the end of the foot a V-shaped appearance as shown above.[11] This V-shaped pattern can be seen not only in the tips of the toes but also in the length of the proximal phalanges (**PP**) and in the length of the metatarsals (**M**).

In *Puijila* (left), the middle digits are longer than the first and fifth toes—the *opposite* of pinnipeds. This can be seen in the length of the proximal phalanges (**PP**) and in the length of the metatarsals (**M**). (The author has provided asterisks* to show where distal toe bones are missing on *Puijila*.)

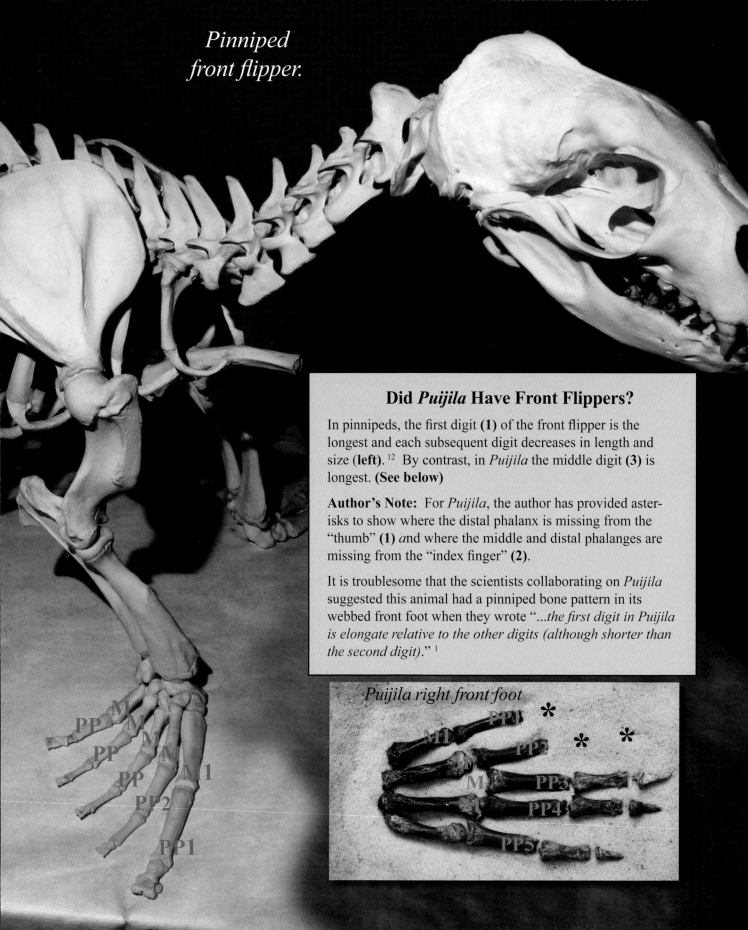

Pinniped front flipper.

Modern Australian sea lion

Did *Puijila* Have Front Flippers?

In pinnipeds, the first digit **(1)** of the front flipper is the longest and each subsequent digit decreases in length and size **(left)**. [12] By contrast, in *Puijila* the middle digit **(3)** is longest. **(See below)**

Author's Note: For *Puijila*, the author has provided asterisks to show where the distal phalanx is missing from the "thumb" **(1)** *a*nd where the middle and distal phalanges are missing from the "index finger" **(2)**.

It is troublesome that the scientists collaborating on *Puijila* suggested this animal had a pinniped bone pattern in its webbed front foot when they wrote "*...the first digit in Puijila is elongate relative to the other digits (although shorter than the second digit).*" [1]

Puijila right front foot

North American river otter

Puijila Pinniped or Otter?

Surprisingly, nearly all of the features of *Puijila* are similar to modern otters, not pinnipeds: *Puijila* did not have the typical oversized back finned feet or front flippers of a pinniped. Rather, *Puijila* had four small webbed feet similar to a North American river otter.[1] (See photos this page) Also, the limb proportions of *Puijila* were similar to a modern otter.[1] The overall length of *Puijila* was *about* 110 cm, nearly the same length as the living North American river otter (112 cm).[1,13] *Puijila*

had a long tail like a river otter, not a short tail typical of pinnipeds.[1,14] *Puijila* had an upturned ridge on the back end of the skull, but male North American river otters have this same feature. According to the official Canadian Museum of Nature website, *Puijila* had six upper incisors, the same as river otters.[15,16,17,18] *Puijila* may have had four lower incisors.[19] Sea otters have four lower incisors,[20,21] while river otters have six lower incisors,[17,18] whereas pinnipeds have either two or four.[22]

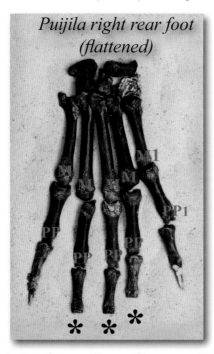

Puijila right rear foot (flattened)

River otter right rear foot (natural position)

Puijila right front foot (flattened)   *River otter right front foot (natural)*

Puijila Skeleton
Pinniped or Otter?

Although scientists who support evolution refer to *Puijila* as a "*walking seal*" or an otter with "*the head of a seal*," its skeletal appearance is very similar to a river otter, as shown in the photographs below.[3, 23]

Puijila skeleton

River otter skeleton

OTTER
Lutra canadensis

Top: *Recreated model of Puijila. Actual bones found are brown and missing bones are white. Starting with the tail and moving forward, compare the brown bones of Puijila to the bones of the river otter.* **Author's Note:** *The museum artist did not place cartilaginous endings on Puijila's ribs, which would connect them to the sternum. Disregard the subjective positioning of the feet chosen by the artist, placing Puijila on its heels rather than its toes.*

Could *Puijila* be an otter?

Puijila darwini

What do you think?

When one compares the artistic rendition of *Puijila* (above) with the living North American river otter (below), their uncanny similarities challenge the scientific interpretation that *Puijila* was a walking seal. Evolution opponents ask: If *Puijila* looked like an otter and had the same bone anatomy as an otter, shouldn't it simply be called an otter and not a missing link?

For an even more technical discussion on the skull anatomy of *Puijila*, you are invited to continue on and read the last section or visit: www.TheGrandExperiment.com/Puijila.pdf for an analysis of the article which appeared in *Nature*.

North American river otters

Puijila's Eye Socket

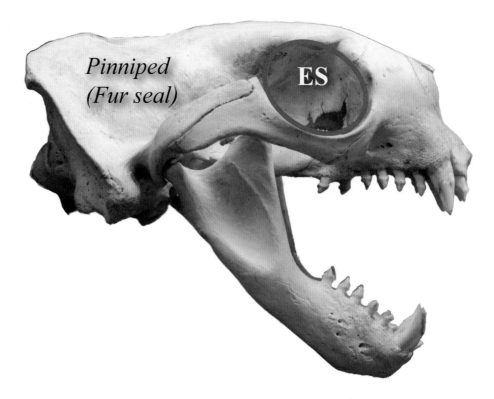

Pinniped
(Fur seal)

One key feature of a pinniped is the enormous eye socket relative to the size of the skull.

Examine the relative size of the eye sockets of *Puijila*, a river otter, and a pinniped.

Did *Puijila* have a large eye socket as the scientists suggested when they reported the discovery? [24, 25] Or did *Puijila* have a small eye socket similar to a river otter?

Author's Note:
The fur seal skull on this page was reduced to the same size as *Puijila* in order to make the eye socket comparisons. In reality, *Puijila's* skull and the modern river otter skull are both small, about the size of your palm.

The shape of *Puijila's* skull, especially the back segment, is speculative and should be taken into account when comparing *Puijila's* skull to the river otter skull. The white areas of *Puijila's* skull indicate where bone is missing.

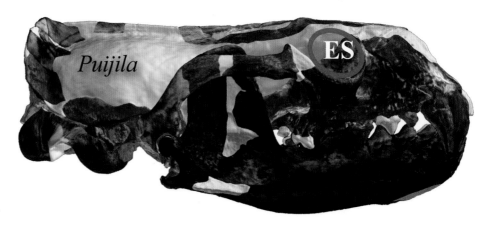

Puijila

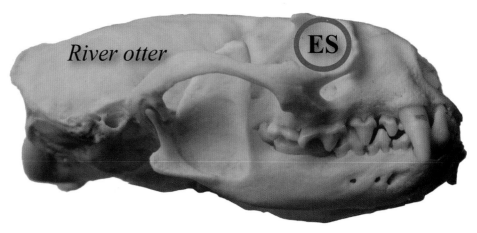

River otter

*Pinniped
(Harbor seal)*

Puijila's Infraorbital Foramen

Pinnipeds have a large passage just below the eye, which carries nerves out to the surface of the face, called an infraorbital foramen (labeled IOF). [26] River otters have this same feature.

Scientists who support evolution report that *Puijila's* large infraorbital foramen implies *Puijila* was a pinniped. [27] Could this feature just as well imply that *Puijila* was an otter?

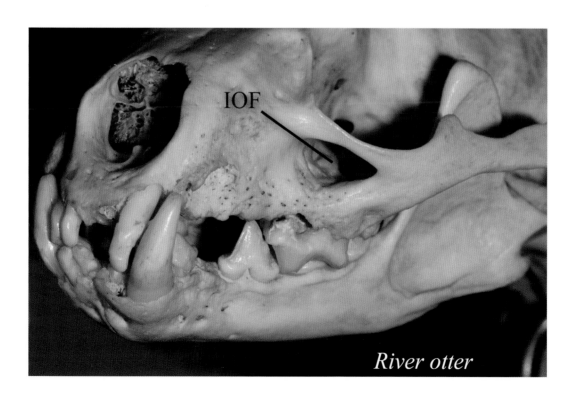

River otter

Puijila's Teeth

Another reason scientists classified *Puijila* as "a pinniped" is because they believed *Puijila* had a pinniped tooth pattern. They wrote, "*Each upper 'end-molar' in pinnipeds is very small and located slightly towards the midline of the skull. This molar pattern is normal for pinnipeds, but unusual in other mammals. Puijila's molars follow the pinniped pattern.*" [28]

For verification of this claim, let's compare the skulls of a pinniped, an otter, and *Puijila*. The following three photos were taken from the bottom of the skull looking up after the lower jaws were removed.

Do you agree that *Puijila's* last tooth is smaller and closer to the skull midline, as in pinnipeds? Or do you think *Puijila's* "end-molar" compares more favorably—size, shape and position—with a common river otter?

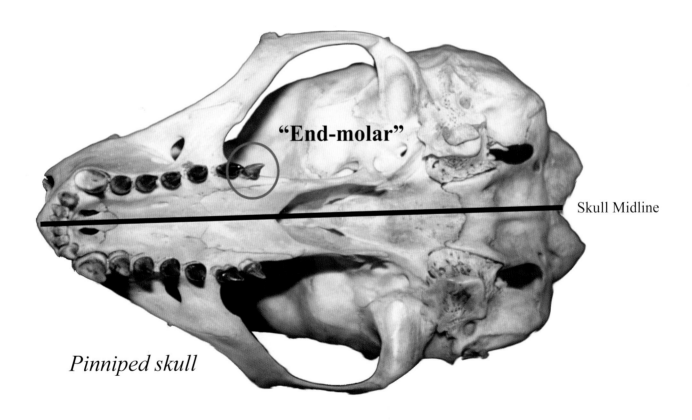

"End-molar"

Skull Midline

Pinniped skull

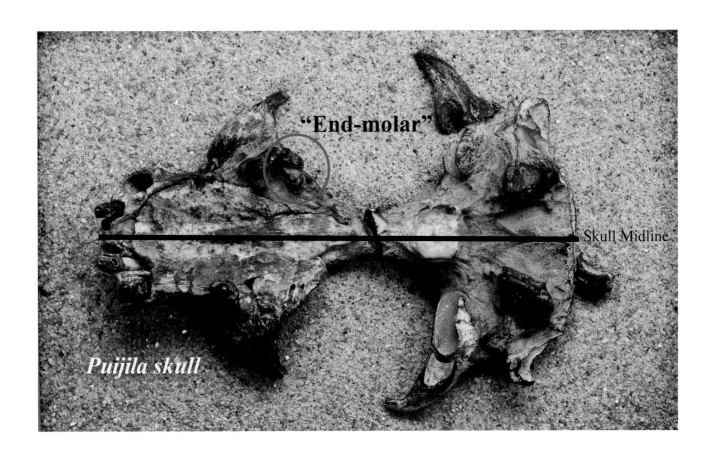

"End-molar"

Skull Midline

Puijila skull

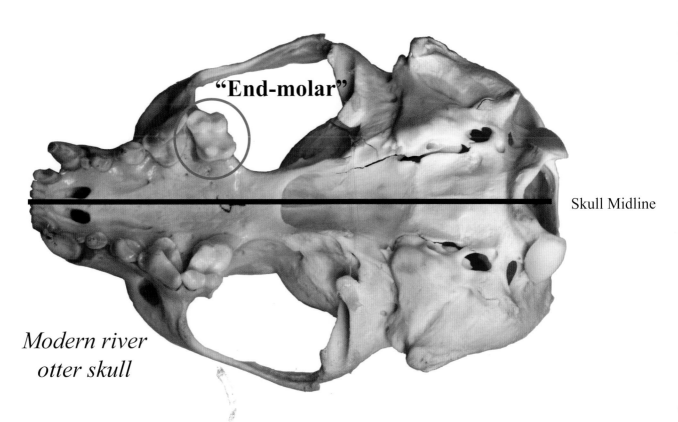

"End-molar"

Skull Midline

*Modern river
otter skull*

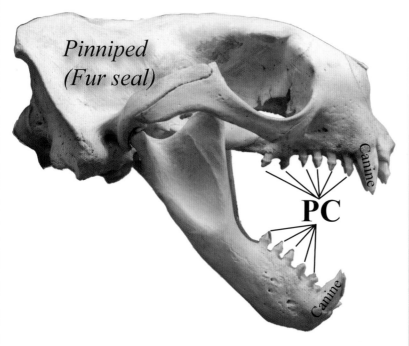

Pinniped (Fur seal)

Canine

PC

Canine

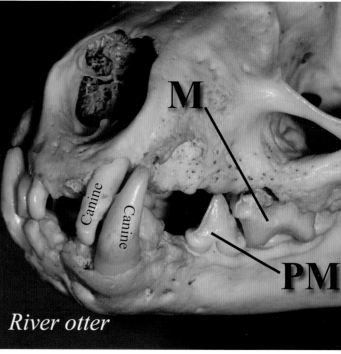

M

Canine

Canine

PM

River otter

Pinniped Post-Canine Teeth

Pinnipeds are very unusual mammals because they have only *one type* of tooth in the back of their jaw, called post-canine teeth **(PC)**.[29] This can clearly be seen in this fur seal skull above.

Most other mammals have *two different types* of teeth in their back jaw, namely premolars **(PM)** and molars **(M)** as seen in this modern otter skull (above right).

Scientists reported that *Puijila* had a pinniped head. If so, one would expect it to also have the pinniped teeth; namely, only one type of tooth (post-canine) in the back jaw, but this is not the case. *Puijila* has two distinct types of back teeth, premolars and molars, like an otter.[1]

After reading this appendix, do you agree that *Puijila* was a pinniped? Or did scientists get it wrong?

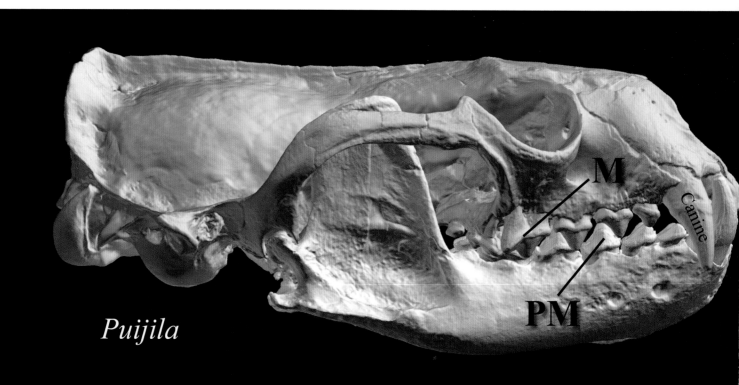

Puijila

M

Canine

PM

Whale Evolution Update

Despite the fact that nearly one billion fossils have been collected by museums (including fossils of soft-bodied animals and bacteria), there is no fossil evidence to support Darwin's premise that a microscopic bacteria-like organism slowly changed into any of the animal phyla groups. [1,2] In other words, shellfish, corals, sponges, worms, arthropods (shrimp), and even the first vertebrates (fish), suddenly appear—without evolutionary ancestors—in the lowest rock layers. Even within the phyla groups, most classes and orders of animals, such as fish classes, dinosaur orders, etc., appear in the fossil record without any evolutionary ancestors being found, again seemingly contradicting the theory of evolution. [3,4] An iconic evolution scientist, the late Dr. Steven Jay Gould from Harvard University, referred to the extreme rarity of transitional evolutionary fossils as a "*trade secret*" of paleontology. [5]

Since Dr. Gould wrote this stinging assessment of the fossil record in 1977, evolution scientists often cite the early evolution of whales as an exception to Dr. Gould's observation. In fact, whale evolution is considered "*one of the best examples of macroevolution as documented by the fossils.*" [6,7,8,9] In 2001, eight science organizations wrote an executive paper on evolution and used the early record of whales as its best fossil example to demonstrate macroevolution. [10] That same year a PBS television documentary, entitled *Evolution: Great Transformations*, also cited whale evolution as its best example to demonstrate macroevolution using fossils. [11] Since the first edition of this book was released, more information has emerged casting a dark shadow over this evidence.

In order to gain insight into the significance and reliability of the evidence for whale evolution, it is essential that the reader understand the *chronology* of the *discoveries* and the interpretations of the evidence over time. Only by stepping back and watching this evidence unfold through the lens of history—how fossils were interpreted and presented to the public and their final outcome—can one appreciate the full impact of this story. What is about to be detailed for the first time may be one of the most fascinating stories in the history of science.

2002: *"The origin and early evolution of Cetacea (whales, dolphins, and porpoises) is one of the best examples of macroevolution as documented by fossils."* [6]

— **Dr. Hans Thewissen**
Northeast Ohio Medical University

1859
Black Bears as Whale Ancestor

When Charles Darwin wrote the *Origin of Species* in 1859, he suggested whales may have evolved from bears because bears feed on insects with widely open mouths, like a whale. [12] After his book was released, he was chastised by zoologists for his "*preposterous*" idea. [13] He decided to remove the bear-to-whale story from subsequent editions of the *Origin of Species* but regretted giving in to his critics. "*Years later he still thought the example 'quite reasonable.'*" [13]

1883
"Hoofed Mammal" as Whale Ancestor

Twenty-four years later, Dr. William Flowers, President of the Zoological Society of London, suggested that whales evolved from a *hoofed* mammal, not a carnivorous *clawed* mammal as Darwin thought. [14, 15] He could not say which hoofed mammals became a whale. The following year, in 1884, Dr. Flowers became the Director of the British Museum in London.

Sir William Henry Flower, K.C.B.

1966
Mesonychids as Whale Ancestor

In 1966, Dr. Leigh Van Valen (right), a biologist from the American Museum of Natural History in New York took Dr. Flowers' ideas one step further and suggested that whales evolved from an extinct order of hoofed land mammals called mesonychids. [16] (See photos of mesonychids next page.) Subsequent generations of evolution scientists embraced Dr. Van Valen's ideas. They noted that the teeth of mesonychids were *very* similar to the teeth of the extinct group of whales called Archaeocetes. "*...the teeth of these early whales are dead ringers for mesonychid teeth.*" [17] Although evolution scientists were confident that mesonychids gave rise to whales, they were unable to arrive at a consensus regarding *which* mesonychid was *the* whale ancestor. [10, 18, 19, 20, 21, 22] Each scientist and each museum offered a different mesonychid as the true ancestor of whales. Frequently museum scientists cited one of the fossil mesonychids that they had found as the true ancestor. [23, 24, 25, 26, 27, 28, 29]

The mesonychid-to-whale theory peaked in 2001. That year, Dr. Phillip Gingerich, a leading expert in

whale evolution, appeared in the PBS television show *Evolution: Great Transformations* in which he promoted the idea that *Sinonyx*, a wolf-like carnivorous mesonychid, evolved into a whale. [11]

Tragically, three days *before* the show aired on September 24, 2001, Dr. Gingerich retracted the entire idea of whales evolving from mesonychids. [11, 30, 31] In *Science* he wrote that he and other whale experts had overstated the similarities between the teeth of mesonychids (such as *Sinonyx*) and the teeth of extinct whales and have rejected this entire line of reasoning. [30] He now believed that a different order of mammals, the artiodactyls, were the true ancestor of whales, not the mesonychids. [30] Dr. Hans Thewissen, another whale expert agreed, and told the press that the entire idea of mesonychids evolving into whales should be sent "*out the window.*" [32] As you might imagine, some were quite disappointed with the timing of Dr. Gingerich's announcement. (See below.) [33] Surprisingly, some museums still promote the idea that mesonychids evolved into whales (as can be seen on the next page). [26, 27, 28, 29]

NABT
National Association of Biology Teachers

"The very day I viewed the segment "Great Transformations," wherein P. D. Gingerich firmly stated that whales evolved from wolf-like carnivores, he [Dr. Gingerich] and several colleagues published a paper in Science showing that, in fact, whales evolved from ancestral artiodactyls." [33]

Wayne Carley
President National Association of Biology Teachers

2001 Mesonychids Fall From Grace

2001 *Science*: *"Although there is a general resemblance of the teeth of archaeocetes to those of mesonychids, such resemblance is sometimes overstated and evidently represents evolutionary convergence."* [30]

— **Dr. Gingerich**

Dr. Phil Gingerich
University of Michigan

Dr. Phil Gingerich, University of Michigan, is recognized as one of the world's leading authorities on whale evolution.

2001 *Nature*: *"Earlier fossil studies related them [whales] to the mesonychians, an extinct group of meat eaters. The new discoveries send this idea "out the window," says Thewissen."* [32]

— **Dr. Thewissen**

Dr. Hans Thewissen from Northeast Ohio Medical University discovered the walking whale Ambulocetus.

Museum Whale Evolution Displays Containing Mesonychids: Should they be thrown "out the window"?

Fossil evidence suggests that whales and dolphins evolved from a group of mammals that lived on land—the mesonychids. Here you can see *Mesonyx*, a mesonychid that hunted in North America some 46 million years ago.

Fossils show that one line of mesonychids became adapted to life in the water, eventually leading to the modern cetaceans familiar to us today. Similarities between the teeth and bones of mesonychids and those of the earliest known fossil whales provide the strongest evidence for this relationship.

Sinonyx was a meat-eater.

Its general body shape and teeth superficially resemble those of other carnivores, like cats and dogs. Although not closely related to them, *Sinonyx* has many similar features because it had a similar way of life.

cat skeleton ▶

C

Clockwise from top left:

A: *Surprisingly, the American Museum of Natural History in New York issued a press release in 2013 suggesting that this lion-like mesonychid called Andrewsarchus, discovered by one of the museum scientists (Andrews), was "the land-dwelling relative of whales" and a "whale cousin."* [25, 26, 27]

B: *While in 2013, the Natural History Museum in London suggested whales evolved from the mesonychid called Mesonyx.*

C: *In 2001, the University of Michigan Museum of Paleontology whale evolution exhibit suggested the mesonychid Sinonyx evolved into a whale. This Sinonyx skeleton was featured as the ancestor of whales in the 2001 PBS documentary Evolution: Great Transformations.* [11, 23, 24]

Pachyaena (PAK-ee-ee-na)
(life-size models)
This extinct, wolf-like mammal is closely related to modern whales.
Pachyaena had hoofed feet, and its teeth were modified for shearing and holding meat.
57 to 52 million years ago; Europe, North America

D: *Museum sign from the College of the Atlantic Whale Museum suggesting mesonychids evolved into whales (1998).*

E: *The California Academy of Sciences in San Francisco suggested it was this hyena-like mesonychid called Pachyaena that evolved into a whale (1998).*

According to Dr. Thewissen and Dr. Gingerich, all of these museum displays are wrong.

D

Mesonychid
Mesonychids were land mammals that existed approximately 60 million years ago (MYA), not long after the extinction of the dinosaurs. They were hoofed animals (ungulates) believed to have been the earliest ancestors of the modern whale. As competition for food on land increased, the *Mesonychids* were probably forced to feed along the shores of ancient seas.

1983
The First Whale Missing Link Discovered: *Pakicetus*

During the first 120 years of studying whale evolution, much of the focus was centered on discovering the *land animal* that evolved into whales. But in the early 1980s, Dr. Gingerich and others began finding evidence of *transitional forms*, intermediate animals in the evolutionary line to whales. In 1983, Dr. Phil Gingerich published a report stating he had found an amphibious whale halfway evolved between a land mammal and a whale.[34] This animal called *Pakicetus* (right) was a four-legged "whale" that could walk on land and swim in the sea. According to Dr. Gingerich, *Pakicetus* was *"the oldest and most primitive cetacean* [whale] *known"* and *"the 'perfect missing link' between whales and their terrestrial forebears."*[34,35] The story of a walking whale was so prominent that in 1983 it made the cover story of *Science*, the official publication for the American Association for the Advancement of Science (right).

When Dr. Gingerich published this article, he had only a few fragments of the skull and jaw and a few teeth (see diagram right). From these fragments, Dr. Gingerich and an artist from the University of Michigan Natural History Museum created a watercolor painting of *Pakicetus*, which appeared on the 1983 cover of *Science* (right).[36,37] Soon, a team of like-minded scientists created a skull of *Pakicetus* based on these few fragments (bottom right).

If one compares the fossils that were found (shown in solid charcoal grey in the skull diagram on the right) to the skull that was created by the scientists (bottom right) and the full body watercolor painting, which appeared on the cover of *Science*, it is difficult to imagine that so much information could have been obtained from these few fossil skull fragments. For example, the created skull and the watercolor painting show *Pakicetus* with a (partially evolved) blowhole positioned partway up the snout (red arrows) even though this part of the skull had not been recovered. The recreated skull and painting placed the eyes of *Pakicetus* on the side of the head (as in modern whales) even though the eye region of the skull had not been found (white arrows). In like manner, *Pakicetus* was envisioned to lack a visible neck (as in modern whales) even though the neck bones had not been found. *Pakicetus* was thought to have paddle-like feet and hands capable of diving in the ocean; but no fossils of flippers, arm, or leg bones had been found.[34]

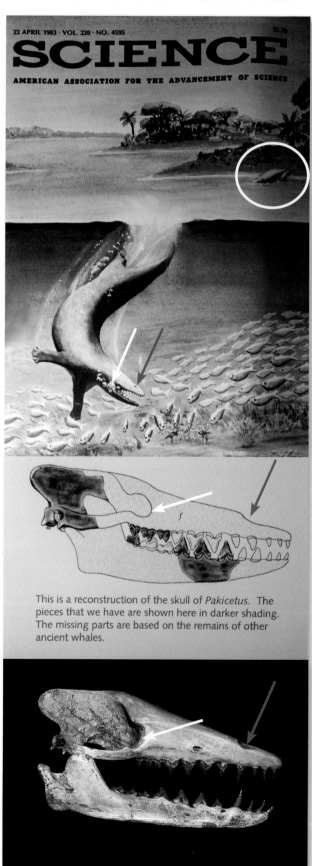

22 APRIL 1983 · VOL. 220 · NO. 4595

SCIENCE
AMERICAN ASSOCIATION FOR THE ADVANCEMENT OF SCIENCE

This is a reconstruction of the skull of *Pakicetus*. The pieces that we have are shown here in darker shading. The missing parts are based on the remains of other ancient whales.

2001
Pakicetus Becomes a Land Animal

Eighteen years after Dr. Gingerich found the paltry skull fragments and teeth, four more partial skulls and 150 bones of *Pakicetus* were found, allowing other scientists to construct a nearly complete skeleton of *Pakicetus*.[38] This skeleton (above and below left) was quite different than what Dr. Gingerich had envisioned in 1983. *Pakicetus* changed from an amphibious whale to a *land* mammal capable of running.[34, 35, 38, 39] *Pakicetus* now had a *nose* at the tip of the snout (not a blowhole), *hoofed feet* for running (not paddle feet for swimming), a *long visible neck* (not an absent neck as in whales), and *eyes on the top of the head* (not eyes low on the

side of the skull as in toothed whales). (See arrows.)

Dr. Hans Thewissen, who assembled the full skeleton, said *Pakicetus* was a land mammal and "no more amphibious than a tapir."[38] The whale-like images of *Pakicetus* on the 1983 cover of *Science* (previous page) stand in stark contrast to the painting of *Pakicetus* (below) currently on display at the Smithsonian National Museum of Natural History (2011). Surprisingly, some scientists and museums still use the older whale-like skull of *Pakicetus* instead of the corrected 2001 land animal skull. (See next page.)

Should Scientists Use Misleading Plaster Skulls?

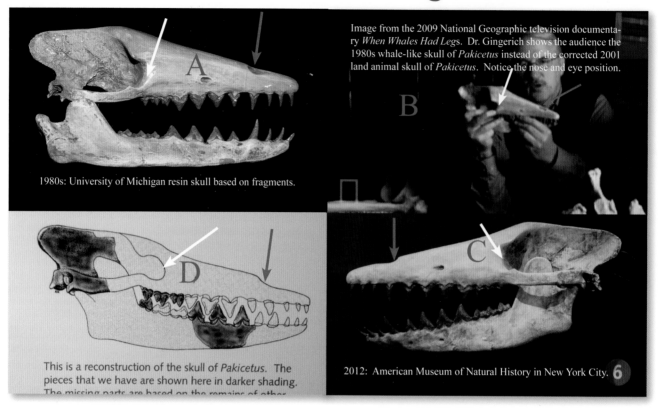

Image from the 2009 National Geographic television documentary *When Whales Had Legs*. Dr. Gingerich shows the audience the 1980s whale-like skull of *Pakicetus* instead of the corrected 2001 land animal skull of *Pakicetus*. Notice the nose and eye position.

1980s: University of Michigan resin skull based on fragments.

This is a reconstruction of the skull of *Pakicetus*. The pieces that we have are shown here in darker shading. The missing parts are based on the remains of other

2012: American Museum of Natural History in New York City. 6

Should *Museums* Display Misleading Skulls?

Clockwise from top left:

A: *This skull from the University of Michigan looks real but was created in the 1980s from a few skull fossil fragments Dr. Gingerich had found. (Oddly, the rest was made up and based on fossils of whales.) This whale-like reconstruction supported the idea that Pakicetus was a whale, a walking whale, and a "perfect missing link between whales and their terrestrial forebears."* [34, 35] *Compare this older skull to the new more complete skull found in 2001 on the previous page. The new skull shows that Pakicetus has a nose (not a blowhole), eyes on the top of the head (not eyes on the side like modern toothed whales), and was a land animal.*

B: *In the 2009 National Geographic television show* **When Whales Had Legs**, *Dr. Gingerich showed the audience the older 1980s whale-like skull of Pakicetus instead of the corrected 2001 land animal skull.* [40] *Notice the blowhole (red arrow) and the eye sockets on the side of the head (white arrow)—both features make Pakicetus look whale-like. Compare the skull that Dr. Gingerich showed the audience in 2009 to the corrected 2001 land animal skull on the previous page.*

C: *In 2012, on a visit to the American Museum of Natural History in New York City, the author noticed the 1980s whale-like skull of Pakicetus was displayed, giving visitors the false impression that Pakicetus looked whale-like.*

D: *Diagram from the University of Michigan shows which fossils were known when scientists created the resin skull of Pakicetus in the 1980s.*

2009

Dr. Gingerich Reveals Why *Pakicetus* Was a Whale

In the 2009 National Geographic television production *When Whales Had Legs*, Dr. Phil Gingerich explained *why Pakicetus* was a whale. [40]

In his examination of the skull, he saw an S-shaped bony process (called a sigmoid process) on the ear bone of *Pakicetus*. Until this discovery, sigmoid processes were only known in the ears of whales! On national television, Dr. Gingerich recounted his historic discovery of a sigmoid process and the conclusions he was forced to make.

Script from 2009 National Geographic TV Program *When Whales Had Legs*

NARRATOR: *But Gingerich still couldn't identify which order of animals it [Pakicetus] belongs to. <u>Then he spots a tiny S-shaped bone in the ear region.</u> He finds out that this bone is known as a <u>sigmoid process and it is unique to one order of animals that today lives in the water.</u> Gingerich finally realized what this creature is.*

DR. GINGERICH: *It's something primitive. It's something transitional but, nonetheless, <u>with a sigmoid process, it's a primitive whale.</u>*

NARRATOR: *This can only mean one thing:* [Music builds] *The modern whale began life as a land animal.*

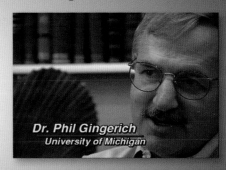

Dr. Phil Gingerich
University of Michigan

A Discrepancy?

In a sense, whale evolution (the best fossil proof for the theory of evolution) boiled down to one scientist, Dr. Phil Gingerich, finding one small bump, a sigmoid process, on the ear bone (auditory bulla) of *Pakicetus*. It allowed Dr. Gingerich to declare that *Pakicetus* was a whale, a walking whale, and a perfect intermediate between land mammals and whales. Had Dr. Gingerich not seen this small bump on the auditory bulla, scientists would simply have called *Pakicetus* an ordinary land mammal. [39]

But there is a problem. Eleven years before the National Geographic show was aired, Dr. Zhe-Xi Luo from the Carnegie Museum determined that *Pakicetus* did *not* have a sigmoid process, but a simple flat plate on the auditory bulla. Simple flat plates are found in some land mammals. [41] (See Dr. Luo's statement below and photos next page.)

In summary, Dr. Gingerich called *Pakicetus* a walking whale and a perfect missing link because it had a sigmoid process but, according to Dr. Luo (and others) *Pakicetus* did not have a sigmoid process. [41, 42] Logically, it would follow that *Pakicetus* was not a whale or a walking whale as Dr. Gingerich reported. [39] Few scientists are aware of this discrepancy.

1998: *"Other diagnostic characters, such as the sigmoid process as discussed below, are now open to question in the wake of the new fossil evidence from Pakicetus...[The] sigmoid process [in Pakicetus] is a simple plate [and is] equivocal, [since it is also] present in the artiodactyl Diacodexis... compromising its utility as a "dead ringer" apomorphy [unique trait] for cetaceans."* [41] [Words in brackets added by author for clarification.]
— Dr. Luo

Dr. Zhe-Xi Luo is a mammal evolution expert. At the time of this statement, he was the curator of vertebrate paleontology at the Carnegie Museum of Natural History in Pittsburgh. He is the author of **Homology and Transformation of Cetacean Ectotympanic Structures.** [41]

Did *Pakicetus* Have a Cetacean (Whale) Sigmoid Process?

Sigmoid process

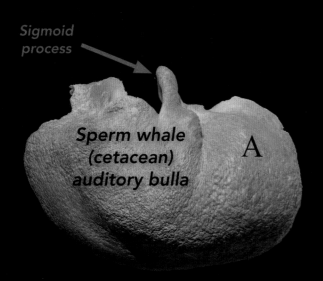

Sperm whale (cetacean) auditory bulla

A

Sigmoid process

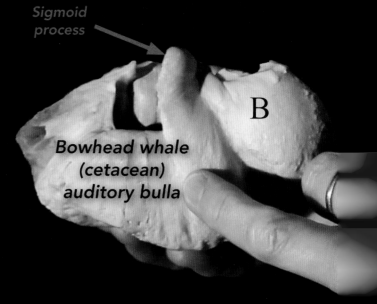

Bowhead whale (cetacean) auditory bulla

B

Clockwise from top left:

A, B, C: The first three photos on this page show the typical sigmoid process on the auditory bulla of three modern cetaceans (two whales and a dolphin). Notice the sigmoid process (red arrow) is curved, three dimensional, thick, and appears similar to a bent finger.

D: Dr. Gingerich called this thin plate on *Pakicetus* a "sigmoid process" and used it to define *Pakicetus* as a whale, a walking whale, and a perfect intermediate. In 1998, Dr. Luo reported that such flat plates occur in land mammals. [41]

Author's Note: The *Pakicetus* ear bulla (D) is oriented in the same manner as the dolphin ear bulla (C) according to Dr. Hans Thewissen.

"Sigmoid process"

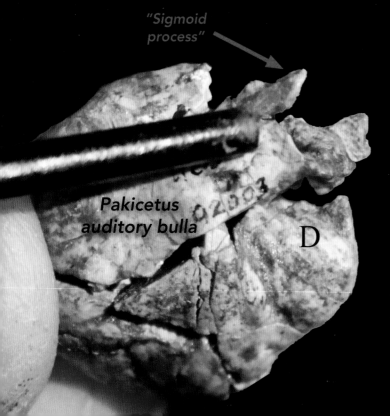

Pakicetus auditory bulla

D

Sigmoid process

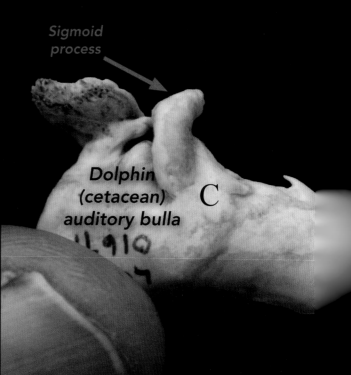

Dolphin (cetacean) auditory bulla

C

Unfortunately, as exemplified in the museum displays below, *Pakicetus* continues to be advertised as a walking whale, even after the 1998 findings of Dr. Luo. Based on the evidence presented, do you believe *Pakicetus* was a walking whale because of its ear bones? In general, do you believe museum displays and television documentaries mislead the public in some ways? In this instance, do you believe museums should update their whale evolution displays based on new discoveries by other scientists?

Should These Museum Displays be Removed?

A

The First Whale
Ear bones from Pakicetus show a feature that is unique to whales, placing it as the earliest known ancestor to modern whales. Although Pakicetus had a land animal's body, its head has the distinctive shape of a whale's.

Clockwise from top left:

A: *Verbiage from Carnegie Museum whale evolution display (2010).* **Author's Note:** *Oddly, the Carnegie Museum requested visitors not to take any photographs of their whale evolution display.)*

B: *Whale evolution display from the Natural History Museum of Los Angeles County (2012).*

C: *Whale evolution museum sign from the Canadian Museum of Nature, Ottawa (2011).*

B

A "transitional" ancestor provides the clues

In the 1970s, parts of jaws and skulls of *Pakicetus* were discovered in lake and stream deposits in Pakistan. Their inner ear bones had some features seen in those of modern whales. In 2001, ankle bones were discovered which indicated that, although *Pakicetus* apparently lived in water, it also walked on land. *Pakicetus* is transitional between ancient land-dwelling, plant-eating mammals and later whales, dolphins, and porpoises.

C

The ear bones of whales are isolated in a special structure that is seperate from the skull. This gives whales good directional hearing under water. Pakicetus has a whale-like ear-bone structure, but it is still attached to the skull. Because of this, Pakicetus would have had less-than-perfect directional hearing under water.

Author's Note: *For more information about the auditory bulla of whales and Pakicetus, go to TheGrandExperiment.com/Pakicetus.*

1994
Dr. Gingerich's Second Missing Link: *Rodhocetus*

On April 28, 1994, Dr. Philip Gingerich reported finding his second walking whale called *Rodhocetus*. This animal had features of both a land animal (it had four legs) and whales (it had a whale's tail and flippers) and was another perfect missing link, halfway evolved between land mammals and whales. [43, 44]

When Dr. Gingerich reported his discovery in the prestigious journal *Nature,* he wrote, "*It retains primitive features seen in land mammals, but also exhibits derived characteristics found only in later cetaceans.... Thus, the morphology of Rodhocetus is intermediate, as might be expected of a transitional form evolving from land to sea.*" [43]

After the original fossils of *Rodhocetus* were cleaned, they were then assembled into a skeleton. Scientific drawings of *Rodhocetus* were commissioned for the whale evolution display at the University of Michigan Natural History Museum where Dr. Gingerich works. Science leaders touted this exhibit as compelling evidence for evolution. [9, 11] At the time, these scientists did not foresee the difficulties that would eventually arise concerning the first three animals in this whale evolution display—*Sinonyx, Ambulocetus, and Rodhocetus* (as seen on the next page).

In August 2001, problems began to emerge for *Rodhocetus* when Dr. Philip Gingerich revealed in an interview for this book that he had added the flippers and whale tail (called a fluke) to *Rodhocetus* based on speculation. He admitted on camera that he did not have the bones of the flippers or the fluke (ball vertebrae) when these museum drawings were created. [45] He retracted both flippers and fluke of *Rodhocetus* and added that more fossils were subsequently found showing this animal had hoofed toes. [45, 46]

There has been little written about *Rodhocetus* since these 2001 disclosures. In fact, the following museums do not even mention *Rodhocetus* in their extensive whale evolution displays: The Carnegie Museum (2011), The Smithsonian Museum (2011), The Canadian Museum of Nature (2011), Los Angeles Natural History Museum (2012), The Melbourne Museum (2013), and the Natural History Museum of London (2013). Seemingly, *Rodhocetus* was a mistake.

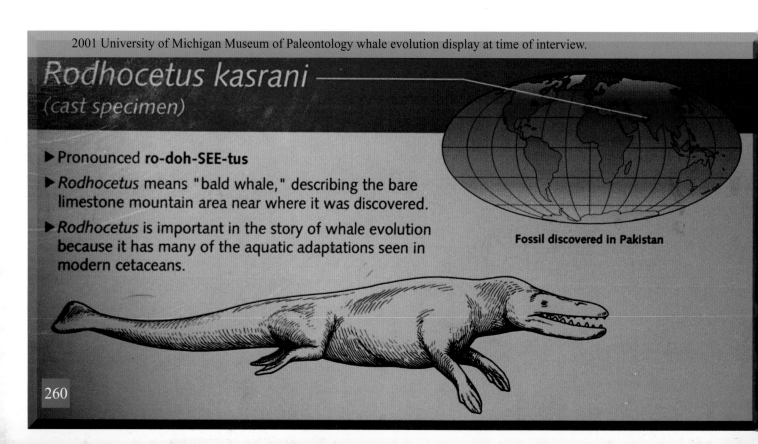

2001 University of Michigan Museum of Paleontology whale evolution display at time of interview.

Rodhocetus kasrani
(cast specimen)

▶ Pronounced **ro-doh-SEE-tus**

▶ *Rodhocetus* means "bald whale," describing the bare limestone mountain area near where it was discovered.

▶ *Rodhocetus* is important in the story of whale evolution because it has many of the aquatic adaptations seen in modern cetaceans.

Fossil discovered in Pakistan

2001 Whale Evolution Display from University of Michigan, Ann Arbor. Author has superimposed the actual fossils of *Rodhocetus* (shown in tan) that were known when this drawing was created. The most spectacular parts of this animal, the flippers and the fluke, were added based on speculation.

These are some of the animals you will meet in this exhibit –

Sinonyx jiashanensis
Lived 56 million years ago
6 feet long

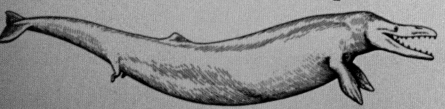

Ambulocetus natans
Lived 49 million years ago
11 feet long

Rodhocetus kasrani
Lived 47 million years ago
15 feet long

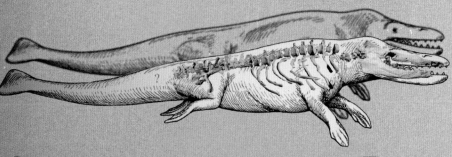

Dorudon atrox
Lived 39 million years ago
20 feet long

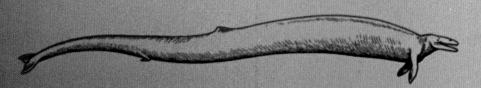

Sinonyx jiashanensis
Lived 56 million years ago
6 feet long

From *Science*, September 21, 2001:

"On land, Rodhocetus walked on a digitigrade hand.... On land, Rodhocetus supported itself on hoofed digits II, III, and IV of the hands and on the plantar surfaces of the feet...." [46]

— **Dr. Gingerich**

What is a digitigrade hand?

Shoulder

Forearm

Upper arm

Wrist

Hand

Finger tips (hooves)

Above: *Fossil pronghorn. Note the hand bones are straight up and down and the animal walks on the tips of the fingers with hooves in a digitigrade fashion. Dr. Gingerich now believes Rodhocetus walked on the tips of the fingers in front and on flat feet with hooves in back.* ***Below:*** *Modern pronghorn.*

1994
A Third Walking Whale: *Ambulocetus*

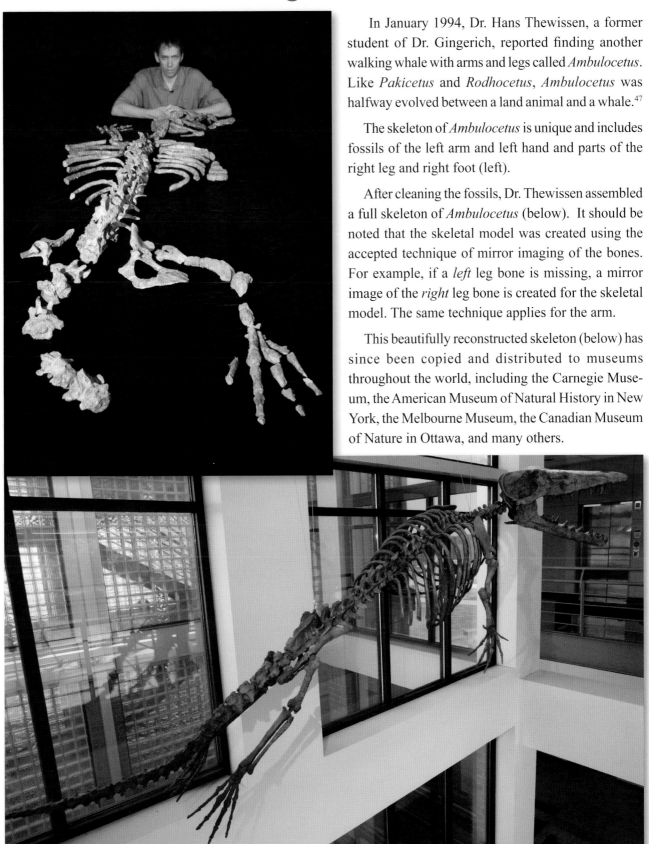

In January 1994, Dr. Hans Thewissen, a former student of Dr. Gingerich, reported finding another walking whale with arms and legs called *Ambulocetus*. Like *Pakicetus* and *Rodhocetus*, *Ambulocetus* was halfway evolved between a land animal and a whale.[47]

The skeleton of *Ambulocetus* is unique and includes fossils of the left arm and left hand and parts of the right leg and right foot (left).

After cleaning the fossils, Dr. Thewissen assembled a full skeleton of *Ambulocetus* (below). It should be noted that the skeletal model was created using the accepted technique of mirror imaging of the bones. For example, if a *left* leg bone is missing, a mirror image of the *right* leg bone is created for the skeletal model. The same technique applies for the arm.

This beautifully reconstructed skeleton (below) has since been copied and distributed to museums throughout the world, including the Carnegie Museum, the American Museum of Natural History in New York, the Melbourne Museum, the Canadian Museum of Nature in Ottawa, and many others.

Ambulocetus
Ears and Blowhole

The reconstructed model of *Ambulocetus* (as seen on the previous page), including this close-up photograph of the snout area (right) looks complete.

What is not apparent is that the original skull fossils (as seen on the top of the next page) are severely damaged and incomplete. The area of the fossil skull where the blowhole would be was never recovered.

When Dr. Thewissen created the full skeletal model, he did not know if this animal had a nose at the tip of the snout (as in land mammals) or a partially evolved blowhole on the top of the snout (as in a theoretical

walking whale). He believed this animal was a walking whale and so he placed a partially evolved blowhole (red arrow) on the recreated skeleton (left).[48] Artists (below) then took this interpretation one step further and drew tiny ears (black arrows) on *Ambulocetus* even though there were no fossils of the external ears. Both of these added features, a blowhole and small external ears, made *Ambulocetus* look more whale-like.

On the following page, the reader will be shown the actual fossils of the skull region that were found.

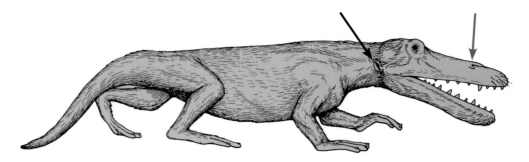

Above: Ambulocetus drawing from the University of Michigan whale evolution display 2001.
Below: Painting of Ambulocetus currently on display at the Smithsonian Museum. Notice both drawings include a partially evolved blowhole and small ears to make this animal look whale-like.

As you can see, the actual fossil skull (above, right) is very fragmented and does not contain the front of the snout where a nose or blowhole would be (red arrow). When these fossils are overlaid on a photo of the skull model (above, left), areas of conjecture are revealed. This is somewhat pertinent since the fossil evidence for the evolution of whales is labeled as the "best fossil proof for evolution." In turn, the evolution of whales essentially rests on the three walking whales *Rodhocetus*, *Pakicetus,* and *Ambulocetus*. We now know there are problems with the fluke and flippers of *Rodhocetus* (which turned out to be conjecture and were retracted) and the sigmoid process of *Pakicetus* (which appears not to be a sigmoid process). Therefore, the interpretation of *Ambulocetus* as a whale requires even closer scrutiny.

Was *Ambulocetus* a Whale?

In his original report, Dr. Thewissen said that *Ambulocetus*, a four-legged mammal, was *"clearly"* a whale based on seven characters of the skull. [47] Dr. Thewisssen wrote, *"Ambulocetus is clearly a cetacean: it has [1] an inflated ectotympanic [auditory bulla] [2] that is poorly attached to the skull and [3] bears a sigmoid process, [4] reduced zygomatic arch, [5] long, narrow muzzle, [6] broad supraorbital process, and [7] teeth that resemble those of other archaeocetes, the paraphyletic stem group of cetaceans."* [47] [For clarification, the author added the numbers and words in brackets.]

At the time Dr. Thewissen wrote about these seven whale characters, he was confident that *Ambulocetus* was a whale, but another whale evolution expert, Dr. Anna Lisa Berta from San Diego State University, was not so sure. She portrayed Dr. Thewissen's seven "whale characters" as *purported* whale characters." [49] In other words, the characters Dr. Thewissen used to define *Ambulocetus* as a whale may or may not be valid. His combination of these particular seven characters had never been used to identify a whale in the past.

This concept—that *Ambulocetus* was a whale—is so critical to the theory of evolution, the reader will be given the opportunity to visually review all seven traits that Dr. Thewissen used to define *Ambulocetus* as a whale. If *Ambulocetus* is *not* a whale (by virtue of these seven "whale characters" of the skull), then it would logically follow that this is a hoofed land mammal—not a "*whale,*" a walking whale, or "a *critical intermediate.*"

"Thewissen et al. use other characters to establish Ambulocetus as a whale, including an inflated ectotympanic [bulla] that is poorly attached to the skull and bears a sigmoid process, reduced zygomatic arch, long narrow muzzle, broad supraorbital process, and teeth that resemble other archaeocetes. Before these purported whale characters can be used in a phylogenetic definition of whales, however, the possibility that some of them may have a broader distribution (for example, in mesonychids) needs to be examined." [49]

— **Dr. Berta**

Dr. Annalisa Berta, Professor at San Diego State University, specializes in aquatic mammal evolution.
Dr. Berta has held the position of president of the prestigious Society of Vertebrate Paleontology.

The Seven Whale Characters of *Ambulocetus*

[1] *Ambulocetus has an inflated ectotympanic* [auditory bulla]. Counterpoint: In whales, the auditory bulla has a concave surface, meaning one side is hollowed out. The auditory bulla of *Ambulocetus* does not have a concave surface. It looks *nothing* like a whale auditory bulla and is not particularly inflated given the large size of this animal. (It is about the size of a golf ball.)

[2] *The auditory bulla of Ambulocetus is poorly attached to the skull.* Counterpoint: When a modern whale or dolphin dies and the flesh decays, the auditory bulla falls off the skull. This is a unique distinguishing trait of whales. *Ambulocetus* was found as a mostly disarticulated specimen, meaning the bones of the body became separated from each other before the animal was fossilized. If *Ambulocetus* were a whale, one would expect the bulla of *Ambulocetus* to have fallen away from the skull since the skeleton was mostly disarticulated.

Although Dr. Thewissen said the bullae of *Ambulocetus* were "poorly attached" to the skull; in reality, they were attached. He reported, "*The skull of Ambulocetus came as one big block that had indeed the skull with both ear bones attached to it. As we took the skull apart to take the rock off of it, the ear bones also came off. So we have them now separate.*" [50]

[3] *The auditory bulla of Ambulocetus bears a sigmoid process.* Counterpoint: All modern whales have a distinct, S-shaped, three-dimensional, finger-like sigmoid process (as seen on the modern whale bulla on this page). The sigmoid process of *Ambulocetus* looks nothing like the sigmoid process of a modern whale. Rather, it is a thin ridge running on the surface of the auditory bulla. (See red arrows.)

In 2013 Dr. Thewissen retreated from his previous position. He now believes the "sigmoid process" of *Ambulocetus* is "*as questionable*" as the "sigmoid process" of *Pakicetus* (which others have rejected outright). [51] He said the "sigmoid process" of *Ambulocetus* may simply be the result of a deformity caused by the jawbone pressing up against the auditory bulla. To demonstrate this, he placed the jawbone next to the "sigmoid process," and they made a perfect match. This suggests to him that this thin bony ridge is not a whale sigmoid process. (See pictures right.) [51, 52]

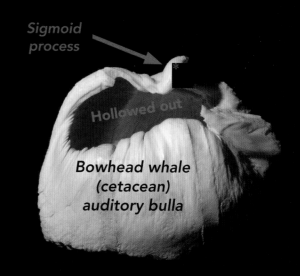

Sigmoid process

Hollowed out

Bowhead whale (cetacean) auditory bulla

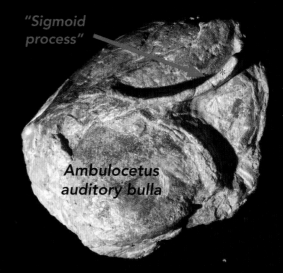

"Sigmoid process"

Ambulocetus auditory bulla

Jaw bone

"Sigmoid process"

Bulla

Ambulocetus auditory bulla

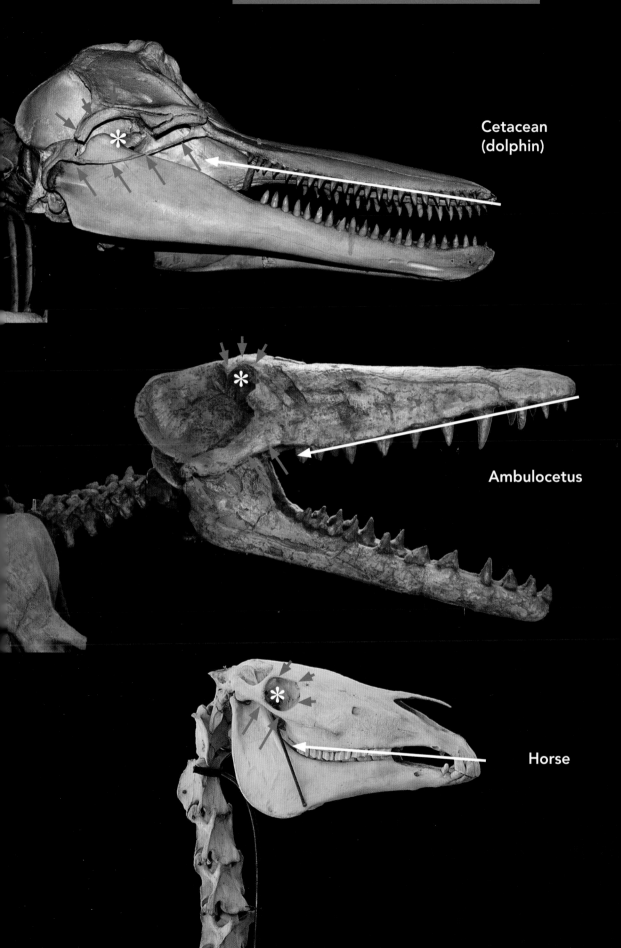

Cetacean
(dolphin)

Ambulocetus

Horse

[4] *Ambulocetus* had a *reduced zygomatic arch.* Counterpoint: Cetaceans (whales and dolphins) have a strikingly thin, almost string-like cheekbone called a zygomatic arch. Dr. Thewissen classified *Ambulocetus* as a "cetacean" because he believed it had a "*reduced zygomatic arch*" like a whale.

Compare the cheekbone of *Ambulocetus* (green arrows) to the cheekbone of a dolphin and a horse (green arrows previous page). Do you agree with Dr. Thewissen's observation that the cheekbone of *Ambulocetus* (green arrows) is "reduced" like a dolphin's cheekbone? Which is more reduced: the cheekbone of a horse or the cheekbone of *Ambulocetus*? If your answer was a horse, does that make a horse more whale-like than *Ambulocetus*?

Author's Note: Dr. Thewissen emphasized the cheekbone but de-emphasized the long neck of *Ambulocetus.* Long necks are a trait of land animals. Absent (short) necks are a trait of whales and dolphins. Compare the short neck of the dolphin (cetacean) to the long neck of *Ambulocetus* and the horse on the previous page. Since *Ambulocetus* had a long neck like a land animal, should that make it *not* a whale?

[5] *Ambulocetus* had *a long, narrow muzzle* like a whale. Counterpoint: Dr. Thewissen reported he had found the entire lower jaw of *Ambulocetus*, allowing him to determine how long the snout was. "*However, we did find the whole lower jaw so we do know how long that snout was.*" [48, 53] But comparing the lower jaw of *Ambulocetus* (on the recreated model) to the fossils actually found, it appears that the lower jaw was *not* complete. (See page 271.) The snout length of *Ambulocetus* may have been overestimated.

It should be noted that a long snout is not a unique characteristic of whales and can be seen in land mammals too. [54]

[6] *Ambulocetus* had whale-like *broad supraorbital processes.* Counterpoint: As can be seen on the previous page, cetacean skulls (whales and dolphins) have broad, thick eyebrow ridges. (See red arrows). Dr. Thewissen classified *Ambulocetus* as a whale because he believed it also had thick eyebrow ridges. Do you agree that *Ambulocetus* had thick eyebrow ridges like a whale?

It should be noted that broad, thick eyebrow ridges are also seen in some land mammals, making this character a poor defining trait when determining if an animal is a whale. (See pronghorn skull on page 268.)

Author's Note: Dr. Thewissen emphasized the eyebrow ridges of *Ambulocetus* but de-emphasized the more important *location* of the eyes in relation to the teeth. As seen in the photograph on the previous page, the eye sockets (white asterisk) of whales and dolphins are nearly in line with the upper teeth (white line). In land mammals, the eye sockets are much higher than the upper teeth. Dr. Gingerich has suggested that the location of the eye sockets of *Ambulocetus* were too high (not in line with the teeth) for this animal to be a direct ancestor of whales. [55] Do you agree?

[7] *Ambulocetus* had teeth that resemble those of other archaeocetes. Counterpoint: In the past, Dr. Thewissen also claimed that mesonychids (such as *Sinonyx, Pachyaena,* and *Mesonyx)* were the ancestors of whales because they have the same shaped teeth as extinct whales. He then later rejected this logic. He said, "*In the past, people thought that whales were derived from a group of carnivorous animals that are now extinct, and they are called mesonychians. And the main reason people thought that was the teeth of these early whales are dead ringers for mesonychid teeth. However if you look at all of the skeleton, all of the features of the fossil whales and compare those to mesonychians, that idea is really discredited now.*" [50] How can teeth be used to define *Ambulocetus* as a whale since mesonychids also have whale-like teeth but are considered unrelated?

Summary: All seven traits used to classify *Ambulocetus* as a whale are questionable, resulting in a less-than-convincing claim that this animal is a whale, a walking whale, or a missing link. Museums and textbooks have not yet made this clear.

1988
Odd-Toed Ungulates In

It would seem to an outside observer that evolution scientists are simply guessing which order of hoofed mammals may have evolved into a whale. In the 1980s and 1990s, as one group of scientists was arguing that the extinct mesonychid hoofed mammals were the land animal ancestor of whales, another group of scientists suggested it was the odd-toed hoofed mammals that evolved into whales. [56, 57, 58, 59] Even so, these scientists were unable to identify which specific odd-toed ungulate (horse, tapir, rhino) was the true ancestor of whales, but that did not lessen their support for this idea.

1999
Cows Out—Hippos In

Since the 1950s, another group of evolution scientists have suggested one of the even-toed hoofed ungulates (mammal order Artiodactyla) was the ancestor of whales. Even so, these scientists also were unable to identify which specific even-toed ungulate living today (cows, hippos, pigs, and deer) was most closely related to whales. Cows? Pigs? Deer? Hippos? This question is characterized in a 2001 science cartoon displayed at the University of Michigan Natural History Museum in which a dolphin is telling a cow that they are cousins (right). The cow answers with a questioning moo.

In 1999, scientists from the Tokyo Institute of Technology reported they had finally identified which hoofed mammal was the closest living relative of whales. Dr. Norihiro Okada, Biologist and Professor at the Tokyo Institute of Technology said, *"I am **one hundred percent confident** with the conclusion that the most closely related species to whales, among extant* [living] *mammals, is the hippo."* [60]

This finding, like so many other "firm," "clear," and "unequivocal" conclusions in the whale evolution debate, was very problematic. [61, 62, 63] It implied there were hippo-like relatives that evolved into whales. If true, there should be *"a fossil lineage linking cetaceans (first known in the early Eocene) to hippos (first known in the middle Miocene)."* [63] This idea was unsupported since paleontologists (scientists who study fossils) contended there are no fossils of hippo-like animals connected to fossil whales. Paleontologists called Dr. Okada's ideas *"nonsense"* and *"an absurdity."* (See interview below.)

"To a paleontologist, this is nonsense because whales have been around in the fossil record about five times as long as hippos have. Hippos were very late on the scene, at which time whales had already been around for tens of millions of years...And to associate those two is really an absurdity to anyone who takes the fossil record seriously." [64]

— Dr. Domning

Dr. Daryl Domning, Paleontologist and Professor of Anatomy, Howard University. Dr. Domning specializes in aquatic mammal evolution.

2007
Hippos Out—Deer In

In 2007, Dr. Thewissen reported he had found the land animal that evolved into whales, a deer-like animal called *Indohyus,* similar in size and shape to the living mouse-deer (right).[65] Since his announcement, the Melbourne Museum erected this display (below).

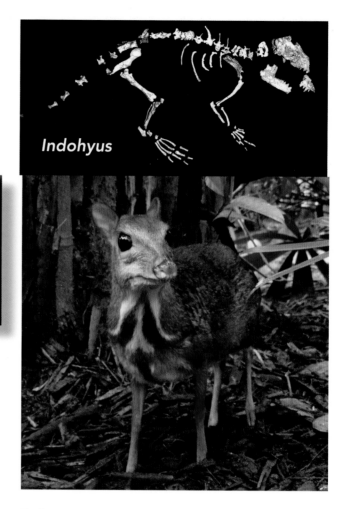

Indohyus

The walking whales

Whales descended from hoofed, deer-like land mammals. These earliest 'walking whales' caught their prey by ambushing them in shallow water.

Melbourne Museum 2013

Dr. Thewissen made his case that *Indohyus* was the ancestor of whales because it had a whale-like auditory bulla. He wrote, "*Most significantly, Indohyus has a thickened medial lip* [inner wall] *of its auditory bulla, the involucrum, a feature previously thought to be present exclusively in cetaceans.*"[65] Since few have ever heard of the involucrum of a whale, this normal part of whale anatomy will now be explained.

In modern cetaceans (whales and dolphins), the inside wall of the auditory bulla is 10x thicker than the outer wall. This thick wall is called the *involucrum* and can be seen (yellow arrows) on the CT scan in the middle of the next page.

In contrast, the inner wall of the auditory bulla in modern land animals is not thicker as compared to the outer wall, as can be seen on the CT scan on the top of the next page (yellow arrows).

Now you will be afforded the opportunity to judge for yourself if the inner wall of the auditory bulla of *Indohyus* is 10x thicker than the outer wall. Only a few scientists in the world have seen the following close-up photograph.

Left: *Dr. Hans Thewissen suggests whales evolved from Indohyus, an extinct deer-like animal similar in appearance to this living mouse-deer.*[65]

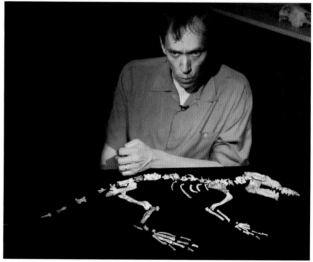

Above: *Dr. Thewissen explains how Indohyus has a whale-like thickened ear bone (called an involucrum).*

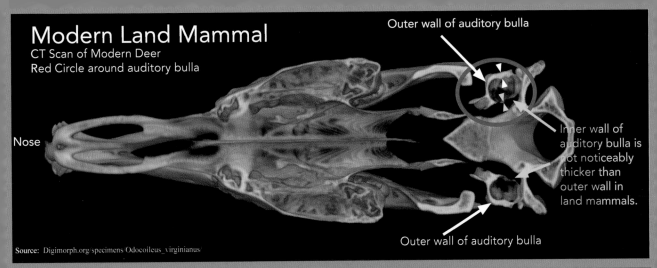

Modern Land Mammal
CT Scan of Modern Deer
Red Circle around auditory bulla

Outer wall of auditory bulla

Nose

Inner wall of auditory bulla is not noticeably thicker than outer wall in land mammals.

Outer wall of auditory bulla

Source: Digimorph.org/specimens/Odocoileus_virginianus/

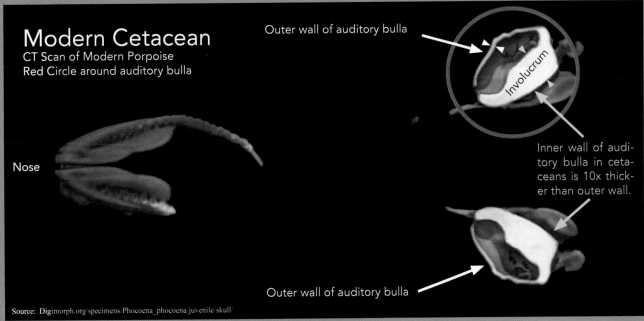

Modern Cetacean
CT Scan of Modern Porpoise
Red Circle around auditory bulla

Outer wall of auditory bulla

Involucrum

Nose

Inner wall of auditory bulla in cetaceans is 10x thicker than outer wall.

Outer wall of auditory bulla

Source: Digimorph.org/specimens/Phocoena_phocoena/juvenile/skull/

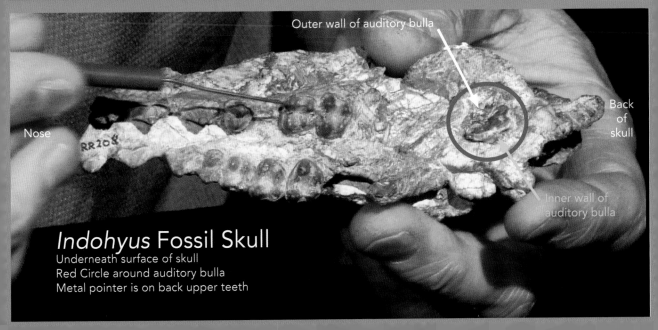

Outer wall of auditory bulla

Nose

RR208

Back of skull

Inner wall of auditory bulla

Indohyus Fossil Skull
Underneath surface of skull
Red Circle around auditory bulla
Metal pointer is on back upper teeth

Outer wall

Inner wall

Indohyus
Close-up of Auditory Bulla

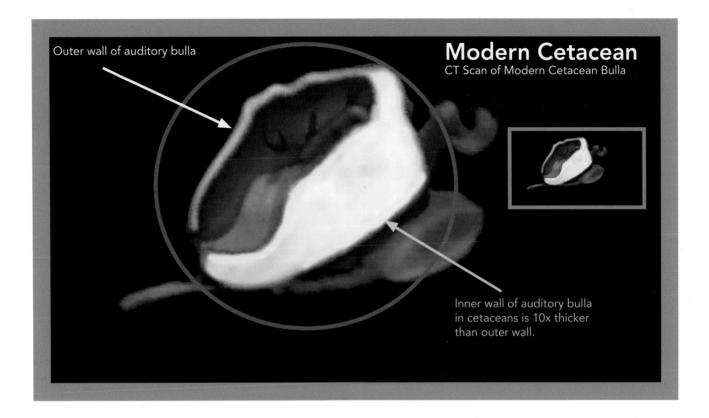

Modern Cetacean
CT Scan of Modern Cetacean Bulla

Outer wall of auditory bulla

Inner wall of auditory bulla in cetaceans is 10x thicker than outer wall.

If you asked ten people to measure the widest part of the inner and outer walls of the auditory bulla of *Indohyus* on the previous page, it may result in wildly different measurements and conclusions. Most would conclude the ***inner*** wall of the auditory bulla of *Indohyus* (yellow arrows) is not significantly thicker than the outer wall (meaning no involucrum)—making *Indohyus* simply a land mammal.

Dr. Thewissen concluded something different—that the inner wall (yellow arrows) of the auditory bulla of *Indohyus* was 10x thicker than the outer wall (meaning it had an involucrum)—making this animal a whale ancestor.

Do you agree with Dr. Thewissen's assessment that the *inner* wall of the auditory bulla of *Indohyus*

(on the previous page) is 10x thicker than the outer wall? Is this evidence clear and convincing or is it simply his interpretation?

Author's Note #1: Dr. Thewissen measured the outer wall only in the area where the white asterisks are.

Author's Note #2: The CT images of the two modern animals are from the University of Texas website. To get a better sense of the variability in the thickness of the walls of the auditory bulla, view the entire CT scan slice movies from this website: Digimorph.org/specimens/Phocoena_phocoena/ juvenile/skull/ and Digimorph.org/specimens/ Odocoileus_virginianus/.

Could *Indohyus* simply have been a land animal?

Evolution Opponents Weigh In

Opponents of evolution have said enough is enough! Since the mid 1990s, whale evolution has been showcased as an extraordinary, unusual, and best example of macroevolution. Yet the evidence for this evolution is unreliable, always changing and unstable.

Since the theory of evolution was offered by Charles Darwin, the land animal thought to have evolved into a whale has changed at least seven times from a bear (1859-Charles Darwin), to the hyena-like *Pachyaena* (1998-California Academy of Sciences Museum of Natural History), to a hippopotamus or a hippopotamus-like animal (1999-Tokyo Institute of Technology and others), to the cat-like *Sinonyx* (2001-University of Michigan), to the wolf-like *Pakicetus* (2011-Carnegie Museum), to the wolf-like *Mesonyx* (2013-Natural History Museum of London), to the lion-like *Andrewsarchus* (2013-American Museum of Natural History), to the deer-like animal *Indohyus* (2013-Melbourne Museum).

Taking this criticism one step further, evolution scientists have expressed their support for four different mammal *orders* as the land animal progenitor of whales: the mammal order which includes bears (Order Carnivora), the extinct mammal order containing the mesonychids (Order Condylartha), the living mammal order containing the odd-toed hoofed mammals (Order Perissodactyla), to the living order containing the even-toed hoofed mammals (Order Artiodactyla).

The evidence offered for the "missing links," animals halfway evolved between land animals and whales, has relied upon missing fossils, as we have seen with *Rodhocetus* (whale tail and flippers), *Ambulocetus* (the blowhole, the lower jaw, and small ears), and *Pakicetus* (flipper-like hands, blowhole, whale-like eye location, and whale-like neck). When more fossils were eventually found, as in the case of *Rodhocetus* and *Pakicetus*, the defining whale-like characters disappeared or were less convincing. In *Ambulocetus*, all seven "whale characters" are highly questionable.

In both the land animals and the "walking whales," there was over reliance on whale-like ear anatomy, which took years for others to overturn. The original interpretations for *Pakicetus* (sigmoid process), *Ambulocetus* (sigmoid process, attached bulla) and *Indohyus* (involucrum) are all questionable.

Scientists who oppose evolution also raise another issue. Two men, Dr. Gingerich and his former student Dr. Thewissen, have been involved in the discovery of nearly all whale ancestors displayed in museums in the Western world in the last 15 years. How is that possible? Tens of thousands of geologists and paleontologists have scoured the earth for fossils since Darwin's time yet just two men have personally been involved in the discovery and/or initial reports of so many purported whale ancestor fossils. These fossils are currently on display in museums including: *Sinonyx,* [24] *Pakicetus,* [34] *Rodhocetus,* [43] *Indohyus,* [65] *Ambulocetus,* [47] and *Kutchicetus.* [66] (*Kutchicetus* and other minor fossils were not covered here because of the author's lack of resources.) Is it possible that these two scientists were simply seeing what they wanted to see (sigmoid processes, involucrums, detached bullae, flippers, fins, blowholes, long snouts, string-like cheekbones)? Could they be victims of their own zeal as they searched for evolutionary ancestors?

Dr. Gould's famous 1977 assessment of the fossil record still resonates, especially in light of the problems with this purported best proof of evolution. Dr. Gould wrote, *"The extreme rarity of transitional forms in the fossil record persists as the trade secret of paleontology. The evolutionary trees that adorn our textbooks have data only at the tips and nodes of their branches; the rest is inference, however reasonable, not the evidence of fossils."* [4]

Which Land Animal Did Whales Evolve From?

Land Mammal	Who Promoted*	Year**	Mammal Order
Bears	Charles Darwin	1859	Carnivora
Carnivorous Ungulates	Dr. William Flowers	1883	Unknown
Even-toed Ungulates	Boyden and Gemeroy	1950	Artiodactyla
Mesonychids	Van Valen	1966	Condylartha
Odd-toed Ungulates	Prothero and Novacek	1988	Perissodactyla
Hyena-like *Pachyaena*	California Academy of Sciences	1998	Condylartha
Hippo or Hippo-like	Tokyo Institute of Sciences	1999	Artiodactyla
Cat/wolf-like *Sinonyx*	University of Michigan, Ann Arbor	2001	Condylartha
Wolf-like *Pakicetus*	Carnegie Museum	2011	"Cetacean"
Wolf-like *Mesonyx*	Natural History Museum London	2013	Condylartha
Deer-like *Indohyus*	Melbourne Museum	2013	Artiodactyla
Lion-like *Andrewsarchus*	American Museum of Natural History [25, 26, 27, 29, 67]	2013	Condylartha
	*Organization/Scientist Promoting	** Year promoted or publicly displayed	

Bird Evolution Update

Modern Birds with Dinosaurs

Since the first edition of this book was printed in 2007, there have been several important developments.

In 2009, as reported in *Living Fossils* (the second volume of this book and video series), many modern types of birds have now been found in Cretaceous dinosaur rock layers. [1,2] Loons, parrots, flamingos, cormorants, sandpipers, owls, penguins, avocets, duck-like waterfowl, and tube-nose albatross-like birds have been found in the same rock layers as *T. rex* and *Triceratops*. [1,2]

One year after *Living Fossils* was released, Dr. Gareth Dyke wrote an article which appeared in *Scientific American* titled *Winged Victory: Modern Birds Now Found to Have Been Contemporaries of Dinosaurs*. Dr. Dyke suggested that modern birds living with dinosaurs is not a new discovery. In this article he states: *"One investigator, Sylvia Hope of the California Academy of Sciences in San Francisco, had been arguing **for years** that bird species she has identified from fossils found in New Jersey and Wyoming that date to between 80 million and 100 million years ago **are modern**."* [3]

Finding modern bird groups in Cretaceous rock layers is a serious contradiction to the evolution time line for bird evolution. [1,2,3] It appears that modern types of birds lived alongside dinosaurs, not millions of years later.

China's Fake Fossil Industry

Another important development is the realization that there is a fake-fossil *industry* in China. It is now apparent that the fossil of a so-called feathered dinosaur called *Archaeoraptor liaoningensis*, discussed in Chapter 15, was not an isolated hoax made by a single Chinese farmer trying to get rich. Rather, the British Broadcasting Company (BBC) has uncovered an entire fossil-faking industry in China, which is churning out many high quality fake fossils that go undetected by even the most qualified experts. [4] These fakes are made by assembling different fossil animals into a single fossil animal, sometimes creating a "missing link."

In the BBC documentary, *The Dinosaur that Fooled the World*, the narrator reported, *"The Liaoning region of China is not just famous for its fabulous fossils. It's also home to a highly developed faking industry. Dr. Zhonge Zhou, a scientist at Beijing's Institute of Palaeontology, has been monitoring it.* DR. ZHONGE ZHOU: *"In one place I saw them putting all the bits from a dinosaur's leg into a box, just like a box of machine spare parts so that they could add them to different fossils."* [4]

Dr. Mark Norrell, from the American Museum of Natural History, Dr. Alan Feduccia, and many other evolution scientists have written about the fossil-faking industry in China. [5] Dr. Feduccia wrote, *"Archaeoraptor is just the tip of the iceberg. There are scores of fake fossils out there, and they have cast a dark shadow over the whole field. When you go to these fossil shows, it's difficult to tell which ones are faked and which ones are not. I have heard that there is a fake-fossil factory in northeastern China, in Liaoning Province, near the deposits where many of these recent alleged feathered dinosaurs were found. Journals like Nature don't require specimens to be authenticated, and the specimens immediately end up back in China, so nobody can examine them. They may be miraculous discoveries, they may be missing links as they are claimed, but there is no way to authenticate any of this stuff."* [5]

Of note, the bulk of fossils labeled "feathered dinosaurs" come from China. All feathered dinosaurs should be considered tentative until they are CT scanned by independent researchers outside of that country. This process may take decades to untangle.

Wrong Layer/Wrong Time

The third problem with the feathered dinosaurs is that the fossils found are in the wrong layers. Dr. Storrs Olson from the Smithsonian National Museum pointed this out in 2001. "All these so-called feathered dinosaurs are younger than the first real known bird." [6] Evolution scientists believe the first flying bird called *Archaeopteryx* lived in the Jurassic period 150 million years ago. Therefore, feathered dinosaurs should be coming from the rock layers below the Jurassic. Instead, all of the "feathered dinosaurs" are found in the Cretaceous rock layers above the Jurassic. If feathered dinosaurs are supposed to be the ancestor of birds, then how can this be?

A

Acquired Characteristics: The disproved idea that changes acquired in the body during life, such as enlarged muscles or a suntan, can be passed on to the next generation.

Amino Acids: Chemical molecules which make up a protein chain. Amino acids are composed of carbon atoms, hydrogen atoms, oxygen atoms, nitrogen atoms, and sometimes sulfur atoms.

Angiosperms: Flowering plants. This group of plants includes roses, tomatoes, rhododendrons, the various grasses, and the flowering trees, such as sassafras, oak, palm, and apple.

Archaeopteryx: This animal, according to some scientists, is the oldest known bird and had both bird-like and dinosaur-like features. Not all scientists agree.

B

Big Bang: The theory that the universe was created by a large explosion in space 10 to 20 billion years ago. The theory is based on the observation of the universe expanding.

C

Chance Mutations: See Mutation.

Cretaceous: The most recent dinosaur fossil layer (also referred to as a geological time zone), the other two being the Triassic and Jurassic. Not all scientists agree on the age of these layers.

D

Darwin, Charles: 1809–1882. A naturalist and evolution theorist. Charles Darwin did not invent the theory of evolution. His grandfather, Erasamus Darwin, and many others, discussed and speculated about various evolutionary ideas. However, Charles Darwin was credited with providing a mechanism for evolution (natural selection), which he articulated in his book *The Origin of Species*. Not all scientists agree that his theory is valid. Darwin lived in England.

DNA (deoxyribonucleic acid): A chemical compound in the cells which gives the commands regarding how to build the cell. DNA is made up of ribose sugar molecules with an oxygen atom *removed*, hence the name deoxyribose nucleic acid (DNA).

E

Echinoderm: An invertebrate animal with five-fold symmetry, meaning an animal without a backbone having five equal body parts. Echinoderms include sea star, brittle stars, sea cucumbers, sea lilies, and sea urchins.

Evolution: A scientific theory regarding how life came about. The theory of evolution suggests that all living plants and animals evolved from one another over long periods of time: Humans evolved from apes, apes evolved from monkeys, monkeys evolved from lemurs, lemurs evolved from non-primate mammals, mammals evolved from reptiles, reptiles evolved from amphibians, amphibians evolved from fish, fish evolved from invertebrates, invertebrates evolved from bacteria, and bacteria evolved from a single-cell organism which formed spontaneously in the ocean.

According to the theory, this process, from a single-cell organism to a human, took 4 billion years. Not all scientists agree that the theory is valid.

F

Fossil Record: The combined worldwide collection of known fossils. This collection tells the story of what kinds of animals and plants lived before the present time. As more fossils are collected, the fossil record becomes more complete. Currently, nearly one billion fossils have been collected by museums. Trillions of additional fossils lie in the field uncollected.

G

Genetic Mistakes: See Mutation.

Germ Cell: An egg (ovum) or sperm cell. These cells pass information to the next generation by the DNA in their nuclei. The DNA from germ cells is the only DNA of an organism passed on to the next generation. (See Somatic Cell.)

I

Invertebrates: Animals without a backbone, such as sea stars, insects, and jellyfish.

J

Jurassic: The middle dinosaur fossil layer (also referred to as a geological time zone), the other two being the Triassic and Cretaceous. Not all scientists agree on the age of these layers.

L

Living Fossil: A fossil plant or animal which looks very similar to a modern organism.[1]

M

Mesozoic Era: The time period of the dinosaurs which includes all three dinosaur fossil layers, including the Cretaceous, Jurassic, and Triassic.

Mutation: A change in the sequence of letters in DNA or RNA which occurs accidently when the DNA or RNA is copied or exposed to radiation or toxic chemicals. The theory of evolution suggests that animals (and plants) changed from one type into another type by a series of accidental letter mutations in the DNA which most often occurred during the process of copying the DNA while producing the reproductive cells of an animal or plant.

N

Natural Selection: One of the suggested mechanisms for *how* evolution works. A large number of plants or animals would naturally display slight variations, such as smaller or larger size, lighter or darker color, etc. Darwin suggested that the most fit of these animals or plants would survive because of their stronger characteristics. The weaker would be killed off by nature, i.e., natural selection. The killing off of weaker varieties is thought to have caused a species to continually improve or evolve.

A criticism of natural selection is that it fails to describe how animals could acquire the information for new body parts such as an eye, a brain or a heart. Natural selection can only account for the removal of certain varieties but cannot, by itself, explain how new body systems came about. Darwin thought new varieties of plants or animals came about by the law of Acquired Characteristics, but this was proven wrong in 1889. New varieties of a species can only come about by accidental mutations. The question then becomes: Can accidental mutations cause a completely new type of animal to evolve, such as a dinosaur accidently mutating into a bird, or an invertebrate into a fish, over millions of years?

Nucleic Acid: DNA or RNA. See DNA and RNA.

O

Organic Chemicals: Chemical compounds which contain the element carbon. All living plants and animals contain organic chemicals.

Origin of Life: The theoretical evolutionary event on earth when the very first form of life, a single-cell organism, formed spontaneously from chemicals.

P

Phylum: The largest grouping of animals with similar traits. Examples include the worms, corals, sponges, arthropods, molluscs, and echinoderms. From largest to smallest, all living organisms can be grouped by kingdom, phylum, class, order, family, genus, and species.

Protein: A chain of amino acids. Proteins have many functions in a cell, such as a catalyzing (speeding up) chemical reactions, copying DNA and forming essential structures in the cell.

Proteinoid: An unnatural organic compound brought about by heating dried, purified amino acids. A proteinoid does not have the normal bonds between amino acids that a protein has and has limited functions. Proteinoids are theorized by some evolution scientists to be the precursors to proteins but proteinoids have never been observed to convert to proteins.

R

RNA (ribonucleic acid): A nucleic acid (similar to DNA) which carries the instructions given by DNA regarding how to build a cell. RNA is made up of ribose sugar molecules, hence the name ribo(se) nucleic acid (RNA).

S

Somatic Cell: Any cell of a plant or animal other than the reproductive cells (egg or sperm). Also called a body cell. Somatic cells and their DNA are not passed to the next generation. (See Germ Cell.)

Spontaneous Generation: The disproved theory that animals came about spontaneously, over short periods of time. This theory suggested that maggots developed out of decaying meat over a period of two weeks and that mice developed out of dirty underwear over a period of three weeks. The last vestiges of this theory were disproved by the work of Louis Pasteur in 1859.

T

Triassic: The oldest, or first, dinosaur fossil layer (also referred to as a geological time zone), the other two being the Jurassic and Cretaceous. Not all scientists agree on the age of these layers.

V

Vertebrates: Animals with a backbone, such as fish, amphibians, reptiles, mammals, and birds.

Glossary

1. Strickberger, M. (1996). *Evolution* (2nd Edition). Boston: Jones and Bartlett Publishers. p. 604. "An existing species whose similarity to ancient ancestral species indicates that very few morphological changes have occurred over a long period of geological time."

Chapter 1: The Origin of Life: Two Opposing Views

1. Long, J. & Schouten, P. (2008). *Feathered Dinosaurs: The Origin of Birds.* New York: Oxford University Press, Inc. p. 2. "The fossil record, as held in all the world's major museums, government organisations, universities and private collections, now tallies close to a billion fossil specimens."

2. Interview with Dr. Duane Gish, Biochemist, Institute for Creation Research, Santee, California, for video series *Evolution: The Grand Experiment*, conducted in February 1998, by author.

3. Interview with Dr. Kevin Padian, Paleontologist, University of California, Berkeley, for video series *Evolution: The Grand Experiment*, conducted in November 1998, by author.

Chapter 2: Evolution's False Start: Spontaneous Generation (322 B.C.– A.D. 1859)

1. Fankhauser, D.B. and Carter, J. Stein (2004). *Spontaneous Generation.* Retrieved August 24, 2006, from University of Cincinnati, Clermont College, http://biology.clc.uc. edu/courses/bio114/carter.htm. "Among these ideas, for centuries, since at least the time of Aristotle [4th Century BC], people [including scientists] believed that simple living organisms could come into being by spontaneous generation. This was the idea that non-living *objects* can give rise to living *organisms*. It was common 'knowledge' that simple organisms like worms, beetles, frogs, and salamanders could come from dust, mud, etc., and food left out, quickly 'swarmed' with life."

2. **Author's Note:** Aristotle died in the year 322 B.C. Pasteur disproved spontaneous generation finally in A.D. 1859.

3. Bastian, H. C. (1870). Facts and reasonings concerning the heterogenous evolution of living things. [Electronic version]. *Nature,* 2, p. 170. Retrieved September 25, 2006, from Origin of Life Studies, In Defence of Spontaneous Generation, http://www.asa3.org/asa/topics/Origin%20 of%20Life/Bastian.html. "In all ages it has been believed by many that living things of various kinds could come into being de novo, and without ordinary parentage. Much difference of opinion has, however, always prevailed as to the kinds of organisms which might so arise. And although

received as an article of faith by many biologists — perhaps by most in the earlier ages, this doctrine or belief has, in more recent times, been rejected by a very large section of them. Definitely to prove or disprove the doctrine in some of its aspects is a matter of the utmost difficulty, and there are reasons enough to account for the wave of skepticism on this subject, which has been so powerful in its influence during the last century."

4. Fankhauser, D.B. and Carter, J. Stein (2004). *Spontaneous Generation.* Retrieved August 24, 2006, from University of Cincinnati, Clermont College, http://biology.clc.uc. edu/courses/bio114/carter.htm. "Jan Baptista van Helmont's recipe for mice: Place a dirty shirt or some rags in an open pot or barrel containing a few grains of wheat or some wheat bran, and in 21 days, mice will appear. There will be adult males and females present, and they will be capable of mating and reproducing more mice."

5. Strickberger, M. (1996). *Evolution* (2nd Edition). Boston: Jones and Bartlett Publishers. p. 13.

6. Levin, R. and Evers, C. (1999). *The Slow Death of Spontaneous Generation (1668–1859).* Retrieved August 24, 2006, from Access Excellence - The National Health Museum, http://www.accessexcellence.org/RC/AB/BC/ Spontaneous_Generation.html. "The first serious attack on the idea of spontaneous generation was made in 1668 by Francesco Redi, an Italian physician and poet. At that time, it was widely held that maggots arose spontaneously in rotting meat. Redi believed that maggots developed from eggs laid by flies. To test his hypothesis, he set out meat in a variety of flasks, some open to the air, some sealed completely, and others covered with gauze. As he had expected, maggots appeared only in the open flasks in which the flies could reach the meat and lay their eggs."

7. *Francesco Redi* (n.d.). Retrieved September 25, 2006, from http://experts.about.com/e/f/fr/Francesco_Redi.htm. "Francesco Redi (February 18/19, 1626 – March 1, 1697) was a physician born in Arezzo, Italy. He is most well-known for his experiment in 1668 which is regarded as one of the first steps in refuting abiogenesis. At the time, prevailing wisdom was that maggots formed naturally from rotting meat. In the experiment, Redi took three jars and put meat in each. He tightly sealed one, left one open, and covered the top of another with gauze. Maggots appeared on the meat in the open jar, but not in the sealed one, and maggots also hatched on the gauze cover of the gauze jar. He continued his experiments, by capturing the maggots and waiting for them to hatch, which they did, becoming common flies. Also, when dead flies or maggots were put in sealed jars with meat, no maggots appeared. But, when the same thing was done with living flies, maggots did

appear. (Experiments on the generation of insects by Francesco Redi, trans. by M. Bigelow, Chicago, 1909)."

8. Levin, R. and Evers, C. (1999). *The Slow Death of Spontaneous Generation (1668–1859)*. Retrieved August 24, 2006, from Access Excellence - The National Health Museum, http://www.accessexcellence.org/RC/AB/BC/Spontaneous_Generation.html. "The theory of spontaneous generation was finally laid to rest in 1859 by the young French chemist, Louis Pasteur. The French Academy of Sciences sponsored a contest for the best experiment either proving or disproving spontaneous generation. Pasteur's winning experiment was a variation of the methods of Needham and Spallanzani. He boiled meat broth in a flask, heated the neck of the flask in a flame until it became pliable, and bent it into the shape of an S. Air could enter the flask, but airborne microorganisms could not — they would settle by gravity in the neck. As Pasteur had expected, no microorganisms grew. When Pasteur tilted the flask so that the broth reached the lowest point in the neck, where any airborne particles would have settled, the broth rapidly became cloudy with life. Pasteur had both refuted the theory of spontaneous generation and convincingly demonstrated that microorganisms are everywhere even in the air."

Chapter 3: Darwin's False Mechanism for Evolution: Acquired Characteristics (Antiquity– A.D. 1889+)

1. Darwin, C. (1859). *On The Origin of Species by Means of Natural Selection, or The Preservation of Favoured Races in the Struggle for Life* (1st Edition Facsimile). Cambridge: Harvard University Press. p. 484. "Analogy would lead me one step further, namely, to the belief that all animals and plants have descended from some one prototype...Therefore I should infer from analogy that probably all the organic beings which have ever lived on this earth have descended from some one primordial form, into which life was first breathed."

2. Ghiselin, M. (1994). *The Imaginary Lamarck: A Look at Bogus "History" in Schoolbooks*. Retrieved August 24, 2006, from The Textbook Letter, http://www.textbook-league.org/54marck.htm. "Lamarck did not originate the idea of organic evolution (a concept that dates from ancient times), did not originate any ideas to explain why evolution happens, and did not originate the doctrine that acquired characteristics could be inherited. That doctrine [acquired characteristics], the one with which Lamarck's name is most famously associated, had been widely accepted since antiquity and was taken for granted by most 19th-century biologists."

3. Darwin, C. (1859). *On The Origin of Species by Means of Natural Selection, or The Preservation of Favoured Races in the Struggle for Life (*1st Edition Facsimile). Cambridge: Harvard University Press. p. 134.

4. Darwin, C. (1875). Darwin wrote his cousin Francis Galton (Letter 271 dated November 7,1875). Retrieved September 25, 2006, from http://galton.org/letters/darwin/correspondence.htm.

5. Ghiselin, M. (1994). *The Imaginary Lamarck: A Look at Bogus "History" in Schoolbooks*. Retrieved August 24, 2006, from The Textbook Letter, http://www.textbook-league.org/54marck.htm.

Chapter 4: Natural Selection and Chance Mutations

1. **Author's Note:** Scientists also use many other mechanisms to explain how DNA could be responsible for new traits. The duplication and mutation of whole sets of genes, small changes in hox genes that control development, transfer of genes between species and other mechanisms have been used to explain the increasingly complex picture of evolutionary theory.

2. Milner, R. (1990). *The Encyclopedia of Evolution: Humanity's Search for Its Origins*. New York: Facts on File Publishers. p. 320.

3. Darwin, C. (1885). *On The Origin of Species by Means of Natural Selection, or The Preservation of Favoured Races in the Struggle for Life* (New Edition from the 6th English Edition). New York: D. Appleton and Company. p. 134.

4. Darwin, C. (1859). *On The Origin of Species by Means of Natural Selection, or The Preservation of Favoured Races in the Struggle for Life* (1st Edition Facsimile). Cambridge: Harvard University Press. p. 82.

5. Milner, R. (1990). *The Encyclopedia of Evolution: Humanity's Search for Its Origins*. New York: Facts on File Publishers. pp. 3–4.

6. Pfeiffer, J.E. (1969). *The Emergence of Man*. New York: Harper and Row Publishers. p. 197.

7. Thomas, H. (1995). *Human Origins: The Search for Our Beginnings*. New York: Harry N. Abrams, Inc.Publishers. p. 65.

8. Pfeiffer, J.E. (1969). *The Emergence of Man*. New York: Harper and Row Publishers. p. 165.

9. Tattersal, I. (1995). *The Fossil Trail: How We Know What We Think We Know About Human Evolution*. New York: Oxford University Press. p. 238.

10. Pilbeam, D. (March 1968). Human Origins. *The Advancement of Science, Volume 24, No. 12*, p. 375.

11. Thomas, H. (1995). *Human Origins: The Search for Our Beginnings*. New York: Harry N. Abrams, Inc. Publishers. p. 37.

12. Sinclair, M., Valdimarsson, G., & Food and Agriculture Organization of the United Nations. (2003). *Responsible Fisheries in the Marine Ecosystem*. Rome, Italy: Food and Agriculture Organization of the United Nations. p. 143. "Eighty-four species of cetaceans (whales, dolphins and porpoises) inhabit the world, of which 79 species live in the sea (13 baleen whales and 71 toothed whales; IWC, 2001)."

13. Brown, L. N. (1997). *A Guide to the Mammals of the Southeastern United States*. Knoxville: University of Tennessee Press. p. 209. "The gigantic blue whale, also called the sulphur-bottomed whale, is the largest animal ever to live (including the dinosaurs), measuring up to 100 feet long and weighing 200 tons."

14. Miller, G. T., & Spoolman, S. (2011). *Living in the Environment: Concepts, Connections, and Solutions. (*17th International Edition). Pacific Grove, CA: Brooks/Cole. p. 255. "The adult has a heart the size of a compact car, some of its arteries are big enough for a child to swim through, and its tongue alone is as heavy as an adult elephant."

15. Fothergill, A. (Producer). (2001). *Ocean world. The blue planet: Seas of life*. [DVD Video]. England: British Broadcasting Corporation. (Available from Warner Home Video, 4000 Warner Boulevard, Burbank, CA 91522.) Regarding the blue whale: "Some of its blood vessels are so wide that you could swim down them."

16. Darwin, C. (1859). *On The Origin of Species by Means of Natural Selection, or The Preservation of Favoured Races in the Struggle for Life* (1st Edition Facsimile). Cambridge: Harvard University Press. p. 184.

17. Milner, R. (1990). *The Encyclopedia of Evolution: Humanity's Search for Its Origins*. New York: Facts on File Publishers. p. 463.

18. Milner, R. (1990). *The Encyclopedia of Evolution: Humanity's Search for Its Origins*. New York: Facts on File Publishers. p. 347.

19. Interview with Dr. William Clemens, Professor of Integrated Biology, Curator of Museum of Paleontology, University of California, Berkeley, for video series *Evolution: The Grand Experiment*, conducted November 9, 1998, by author.

20. The California Academy of Sciences Museum display (December 1998) on whale evolution suggests it was this hyena-like animal called *Pachyaena* that eventually evolved into a whale. The photograph at the bottom of the page is from this display.

21. Monastersky, R. (November 6, 1999). The Whale's Tale: Searching for the landlubbing ancestors of marine mammals. *Science News on Line*. Retrieved September 29, 2006, from http://www.findarticles.com/p/articles/mi_m1200/is_19_156/ai_57828404. On page 3 of the on-line article, Dr. Monastersky quotes Dr. Norihiro Okada, a Biologist and Professor at the Tokyo Institute of Technology: "I am one hundred percent confident with the conclusion that the most closely related species to whales, among extant mammals, is the hippo."

22. Robinson, E., Benjamin-Phariss, B. (Executive Producer and Director of Documentary Productions). WGBH Video (Firm). (2001). Great Transformations: Extinction! Boston, MA: WGBH Boston Video. [Nova DVD Series.] Produced by Clear Blue Sky Productions, (Available from WGBH Boston http://www.pbs.org/wgbh/evolution/). "Narrator: Scientists now think that the earliest ancestor of whales was similar to this 50 million year old wolf-like mammal called *Sinonyx*."

23. See Appendix F: Whale Evolution Update.

24. Marshall, K. (1999). *Blue Whales*. Retrieved August 25, 2006, from http://whale.wheelock.edu/archives/ask99/0387.html. States that a blue whale's heart valves are the size of a hubcap.

25. Menduno, M. (2004, December). Dive! Dive! Dive! *Wired Magazine*, Issue 12.12. Retrieved August 25, 2006, from http://www.wired.com/wired/archive/12.12/dive.html.

26. **Author's Note:** Scientists who oppose evolution would argue that more than 2,700 letters of DNA would be needed based on the following assumptions: Most proteins are between 100 and 1,000 amino acids long. They argue that choosing 100 amino acids for each new protein is too low of an estimate; 300–400 amino acids long would be more accurate. They would also argue that for any one of the changes listed on the previous pages in this chapter, more than *one* simple protein would be needed. For example, a baleen bone is very complicated. It would be hard to imagine that an entire baleen bone could be brought about by one simple protein addition. They would argue that it would take many proteins to make such a change for this or any of the other changes listed on the previous pages in this chapter.

Scientists who support evolution would argue that less than 2,700 letters of DNA would be needed. They would suggest that new proteins are not needed to bring about body changes, rather it would simply be a matter of altering the existing proteins. As an example, it is possible the baleen bone is only a modification of a tooth protein, not the result of an entirely new protein. The same principle would apply for the tail to fluke, the front legs to flippers, air passage to blowhole, etc. If only a few dozen letters of DNA (24) were needed to change in each of the 9 proteins, this would reduce the number to 216 DNA letter changes. This would reduce the odds of this happening to $1/4^{216}$ or $1/1.09^{130}$.

27. *Medical Aspects of Lightning* (n.d.). Retrieved September 28, 2006, from http://www.lightningsafety.noaa.gov/medical.htm.

28. Powerball odds 1/80,089,128 from *Power Ball Details* (n.d.). Retrieved August 15, 2006, from http://www.lotterybuddy.com/powerball/powerodd.htm. **Author's Note:** The odds for winning the national powerball lottery are subject to change. For simplicity, this number was rounded to 1/80,000,000.

Chapter 5: Similarities: A Basic Proof of Evolution?

1. Information on display outside the Red Panda Exhibit (2001) at the St. Louis Zoo in Missouri. "Scientists once believed that the red panda and the giant panda were closely related. Both animals have strong crushing teeth and an extra 'thumb.' Recent genetic studies prove that the giant panda belongs to the bear family, and the red panda is related to raccoons. Their physical similarities are the result of feeding on the same specialized diet, bamboo." **Author's Note:** The above statement is genetically impossible. Eating a particular type of diet (bamboo) does not change the DNA or anatomy of the offspring of an animal.

2. Interview with Dr. Daryl Domning, Paleontologist and Professor of Anatomy, Howard University, for video series *Evolution: The Grand Experiment*, conducted October 8, 1998, by author.

3. Interview with Dr. William Clemens, Professor of Integrated Biology, Curator of Museum of Paleontology, University of California, Berkeley, for video series *Evolution: The Grand Experiment*, conducted November 9, 1998, by author.

4. Dawkins, R. (June 16, 1995). Where d'you get those peepers? *New Statesman & Society, Volume 8*, p. 29. Article retrieved August 28, 2006, from http://www.simonyi.ox.ac.uk/dawkins/WorldOfDawkins-archive/Dawkins/Work/Articles/1995-06-16peepers.shtml. "When one says 'the' eye, by the way, one implicitly means the vertebrate eye, but serviceable image-forming eyes have evolved between 40 and 60 times, independently from scratch, in many different invertebrate groups."

5. Darwin, C. (1885). *On The Origin of Species by Means of Natural Selection, or The Preservation of Favoured Races in the Struggle for Life* (New Edition from the 6th English Edition). New York: D. Appleton and Company. p. 100.

6. Gish, D. (1995). *Evolution: The Fossils Still Say No!* Santee, California: Institute for Creation Research. p. 91.

Chapter 6: The Fossil Record and Darwin's Prediction

1. Darwin, C. (1885). *On The Origin of Species by Means of Natural Selection, or The Preservation of Favoured Races in the Struggle for Life* (New Edition from the 6th English Edition). New York: D. Appleton and Company. pp. 264–265.

2. Interview with Dr. Andrew Knoll, Professor of Biology, Harvard University, for video series *Evolution: The Grand Experiment*, conducted October 13, 1998, by author.

3. See Appendix A: The Number of Fossils.

4. Interview with Dr. John Long, Head of Science at Museum Victoria, Melbourne, Australia, for video series *Evolution: The Grand Experiment,* conducted March 8, 2005, by author.

5. *Invertebrate Paleontology. About the Division* (n.d.). Retrieved August 28, 2006, from the University of Nebraska State Museum, http://www.unl.edu/museum/research/invertpaleo/about.html.

6. *The Collections. Invertebrate Paleontology* (n.d.). Retrieved August 28, 2006, from the Yale Peabody Museum, http://www.peabody.yale.edu/collections/ip/.

7. *Invertebrate Paleontology* (n.d.). Retrieved August 28, 2006, from the University of Michigan Museum of Paleontology, http://www.paleontology.lsa.umich.edu (under Invertebrate Paleontology).

8. *Invertebrate Paleontology Database* (n.d.). Retrieved August 28, 2006, from the Florida Museum of Natural History, http://www.flmnh.ufl.edu/databases/ivp/default.htm.

9. *About the Vertebrate Paleontology Collections at the University of Nebraska State Museum* (2004). Retrieved August 28, 2006, from the University of Nebraska State Museum, http://www.museum.unl.edu/research/vertpaleo/welcome.html.

10. *Vertebrate Paleontology Databases* (n.d.). Retrieved August 28, 2006, from the Florida Museum of Natural History, http://www.flmnh.ufl.edu/databases/vp/intro.htm.

11. *Vertebrate Collection: Holdings and Catalog Information* (n.d.). Retrieved August 28, 2006, from the University of California, Berkeley, Museum of Paleontology, http://www.ucmp.berkeley.edu/collections/vertebrate.html.

12. *Vertebrate Paleontology* (n.d.). Retrieved August 28, 2006, from the University of Michigan Museum of Paleontology, http://paleontology.lsa.umich.edu (under Vertebrate Paleontology).

13. *The Collections. Vertebrate Paleontology* (n.d.). Retrieved August 28, 2006, from the Yale Peabody Museum, http://www.peabody.yale.edu/collections/vp/.

14. *Research and Collections* (n.d.). Retrieved August 28, 2006, from the Raymond M. Alf Museum of Paleontology, http://www.alfmuseum.org/visitorpages_research.html.

15. *Paleobotany and Paleontology at the Florida Museum of Natural History* (2006). Retrieved August 28, 2006, from the Florida Museum of Natural History, http://www.flmnh.ufl.edu/natsci/paleobotany/paleobotany.htm.

16. *The Collections. Paleobotany* (n.d.). Retrieved August 28, 2006, from the Yale Peabody Museum of Paleontology, http://www.peabody.yale.edu/collections/pb/.

17. Levin, H. (1996). *The Earth Through Time* (5th Edition). Fort Worth: Saunders College Publishing. p. 118.

18. Horner, J. (1988). *Digging Dinosaurs*. New York: Harper Collins Publishers. p. 193.

19. Milner, R. (1990). *The Encyclopedia of Evolution: Humanity's Search for Its Origins*. New York: Facts on File Publishers. p. 52.

20. Novacek, M. (1996). *Dinosaurs of the Flaming Cliffs*. New York: Anchor Books, A Division of Doubleday.

21. Horner, J. (1988). *Digging Dinosaurs*. New York: Harper Collins Publishers. p. 99.

22. Long, J., & Schouten, P. (2008). *Feathered Dinosaurs: The Origin of Birds*. New York: Oxford University Press, Inc. p. 2. "The fossil record, as held in all the world's major museums, government organisations, universities and private collections, now tallies close to a billion fossil specimens."

23. Horner, J. (1988). *Digging Dinosaurs*. New York: Harper Collins Publishers. p. 128.

24. Interview with Dr. Lance Grande, Curator, Department of Geology, Chicago Field Museum, for video series *Evolution: The Grand Experiment*, conducted in January 1998, by author.

25. Milner, R. (1990). *The Encyclopedia of Evolution: Humanity's Search for Its Origins*. New York: Facts on File Publishers. p. 330.

26. Willis, D. (1992). *The Leakey Family: Leaders in the Search for Human Origins*. New York: Facts on File Publishers. pp. 41–42.

27. Denton, M. (1985). *Evolution: A Theory in Crisis*. Bethesda, MD: Adler and Adler Publishers (Woodbine House). p. 190.

Chapter 7: The Fossil Record of Invertebrates

1. See Appendix A: The Number of Fossils.

2. E-mail interview with Dr. Jonathan M. Adrain, Professor, Department of Geoscience, University of Iowa, conducted September 10, 2011, by author. Dr. Adrain is the author of *A global species database of Trilobita: progress, results, and revision of the Treatise* (2008). In: Rábano, I., Gozalo, R. & Garcia-Bellido, D. (eds.), *Advances in trilobite research*. Cuadernos del Museo Geominero, 9. Instituto Geologico y Minero de Espana, Madrid, 27–28. Question: "Approximately how many species of trilobites are there?" Dr. Adrain: "Approximately 23,000." Question: "What species of trilobite is the oldest?" Dr. Adrain: "There isn't really an answer to that. Trilobites appear in the fossil record more or less at the same time in Laurentia (present day North America), Siberia, and the big southern supercontinent Gondwanaland (present-day South America, Africa, Australia, India, southwestern Europe, etc.). The first species are assigned to the genus Repinaella, but it's basically impossible to say which individual species is the absolute oldest known. The earliest species date to about 525 million years old." Question: "Approximately how many trilobites have been collected by museums worldwide?" Dr. Adrain: "I don't think there's any way to put a number on that, if you mean individual specimens. Likely hundreds of thousands to millions, but there's no tabulation of the actual number that I know of. If you mean species, then the basic answer is "all of them" as in order to be formally named the fossil material must be deposited in a recognized, usually public, collection so that it is available to future researchers. These collections are mainly housed in museums, but also in universities (often in small university museums) and national geological survey organizations." Question: "Dr. Andrew Knoll (Harvard Biology) did an interview on Ediacaran fauna for our book. He implied that some of these early Cambrian invertebrates, such as the first trilobites, do not have any bona fide uncontested fossil ancestors and attributed this to rapid radiations of some of the invertebrate phyla. Does that sound right to you? I thought that someone had come up with an early pre-trilobite ancestors." Dr. Adrain: "The only significant complex metazoans prior to the Cambrian are the so-called Ediacaran Fauna, which appeared around the world a little bit earlier. There has been considerable debate about the affinities of the Ediacaran animals, with one school of thought considering them related mostly only to each other, and comprising a kind of early failed phylum with no descendents. The other view is that some of the Ediacaran taxa belong to various of the later (and modern) phyla. There has been an argument that some represent arthropods, the phylum to which trilobites belong, but it's awful tenuous. Beyond those (which aren't a whole lot older than the Early Cambrian anyway) there isn't much of anything that has turned up. Trilobites have a trace fossil record in the Early Cambrian prior to their appearance as body fossils, but it doesn't extend their origins all that much. Andy's view reflects what seems to be an emerging consensus, that the "Cambrian Explosion" was a real, and (geologically) sudden

radiation event. So what he apparently said sounds right in terms of what a majority of paleontologists think at this point. The other line of evidence that led to a lot of argument about this came from molecular systematics and "molecular clocks" — as that whole field matured, there were published estimates of the divergence times of the major phyla that were very ancient, pushing the events (and hence the unrecorded presence of the phyla) way back into the pre-Cambrian. That particular debate, though, has also more or less resolved itself, as more sophisticated calibrations for the "clocks" have tended to support much younger divergences, such that the molecular and paleontological data sets are now basically reconciled, and in agreement on a massive and rapid evolutionary radiation near the start of the Cambrian."

3. Quote from display at the Smithsonian National Museum of Natural History, Washington D.C. (July 2011). "Trilobites are among the most diverse groups of extinct organisms. More than 15,000 species evolved during their 300 million year history."

4. Hartmann, A. (2007). *Rapid evolution in early trilobites fueled by high variation.* Retrieved July 14, 2013, from *Geotimes,* http://www.geotimes.org/july07/articlehtml?id=WebExtra072707.html. "Webster compiled morphological data for nearly 1,000 of the 17,000 different species of trilobites, a class of marine arthropods that died out by 250 million years ago, from 49 previously published sources."

5. Interview with Dr. Andrew Knoll, Professor of Biology, Harvard University, for video series *Evolution: The Grand Experiment,* conducted October 13, 1998, by author. "What bothered Darwin about the fossil record more than anything else was the pattern of paleontology that we've been talking about...the oldest fossils you see are both diverse and complex, [such as] fabulously complicated things like trilobites." "Despite 30 years of research on Ediacaran fossils, there are very few, if any, unambiguous ancestors of things that appear in the Cambrian."

6. Interview with Dr. James Valentine, Professor Emeritus, University of California, Berkeley, Department of Integrated Biology, for video series *Evolution: The Grand Experiment,* conducted April 22, 1998, by author. At the "beginning of the Cambrian Explosion proper...one finds brachiopods [shellfish] and gastropods [shellfish]...We also see trilobites for the first time."

Chapter 8: The Fossil Record of Fish

1. See Appendix A: The Number of Fossils.

2. Interview with Dr. Duane Gish, Biochemist, Institute for Creation Research, Santee, California, for video series *Evolution: The Grand Experiment,* conducted in February 1998, by author.

3. Interview with Dr. John Long, Head of Science at Museum Victoria, Melbourne, Australia, for video series *Evolution: The Grand Experiment,* conducted March 8, 2005, by author.

4. Long, J. (1995). *The Rise of Fishes: 500 Million Years of Evolution.* Baltimore: Johns Hopkins University Press. p. 30.

5. Long, J. (1995). *The Rise of Fishes: 500 Million Years of Evolution.* Baltimore: Johns Hopkins University Press. p. 66.

6. Long, J. (1995). *The Rise of Fishes: 500 Million Years of Evolution.* Baltimore: Johns Hopkins University Press. p. 69.

7. Long, J. (1995). *The Rise of Fishes: 500 Million Years of Evolution.* Baltimore: Johns Hopkins University Press. p. 91.

Chapter 9: The Fossil Record of Bats

1. See Appendix A: The Number of Fossils.

2. **Author's Note:** The phrase "millions of other fossils have been collected" was based on two pieces of information: Namely, the proposed or theoretical time period during which bats evolved and the number of fossils that have been collected from that time period.

Some evolution scientists suggest that bats evolved from a land mammal between 66 million years ago (lowest Tertiary) and 52 million years ago. In an interview with Dr. Gunter Viohl, Curator of the Jura Museum in Eichstaat, Germany, Dr. Viohl suggested that the evolution of bats "must have happened in the lowest Tertiary [66 million years ago]. But we have no evidence for this evolution. Also, the bats appear perfectly developed in the Eocene [52 million years ago]."

This 14-million-year period (66 million years minus 52 million years) represents 2.2 percent of the 630 million years from the Ediacaran Period, when multicellular organisms appear. If nearly one billion fossils have been collected during this 630-million-year period, then 2.2 percent of the one billion fossils collected equals 22 million fossils. In other words, museums have collected approximately 22 million fossils from the 14 million year time period when bats were supposed to have evolved. Furthermore, the estimate of 22 million fossils is actually a conservative estimate due to the following issues.

First, in the history of life, it has been observed that many animals lived for tens of millions of years, relatively unchanged, with examples being the garfish, the *Nautilus,* the *Coelacanth*, the dragonfly, the guitarfish, and the sea star. Animals that evolved from the ground mammal into the bat would have lived not only during these 14 million years, but also past the 52-million-year-old mark. As the life span of these intermediates increases, the opportunities for possible fossilization increases, and so do the expectations of finding these intermediate forms.

Second, the above discussion assumes that the evolution of bats started 66 million years ago. Other scientists believe bat evolution started much earlier than this. If true, the number of fossils from the time period of bat evolution again increases, which further exacerbates the problem of a lack of ancestral intermediates. See Chapter 6 — The Fossil Record and Darwin's Prediction.

3. Interview with Dr. Gary Morgan, Assistant Curator of Paleontology, New Mexico Museum of Natural History and Science, for video series *Evolution: The Grand Experiment*, conducted March 19, 2002, by author.

4. Interview with Dr. Gunter Viohl, Curator of the Jura Museum in Eichstatt, Germany, for video series *Evolution: The Grand Experiment*, conducted August 17, 2000, by author.

5. Interview with Dr. Nicholas Czeplewski, Staff Curator of Paleontology, Sam Noble Oklahoma Museum of Science and Natural History, for video series *Evolution: The Grand Experiment*, conducted April 1, 2002, by author.

6. Interview with Dr. Joerg Habersetzer, Senckenberg Museum of Natural History, Frankfurt, Germany, for the video series *Evolution: The Grand Experiment*, conducted in August 2000, by author. "We have no fossil records of bats during the Cretaceous period. And this means that we are only depending on speculation when it started and what happened in that time. Of course, when we have the oldest bats, like *Icaronycteris*, they were completely developed in their morphology and their flight apparatus, and also the Messel bats were completely developed. So we can only speculate."

Chapter 10: The Fossil Record of Pinnipeds: Seals and Sea Lions

1. *Mammals: Sea Lion* (n.d.). Retrieved August 29, 2006, from San Diego Zoo, http://www.sandiegozoo.org/animalbytes/t-sea_lion.html.

2. *California Sea Lion* (n.d.). Retrieved August 29, 2006, from http://www.bcadventure.com/adventure/wilderness/animals/sealion.htm.

3. *PIER 39's Fascinating Facts about the Sea Lions* (n.d.). Retrieved August 29, 2006, from the Marine Mammal Center, http://www.tmmc.org/learning/education/pier39/facts.asp.

4. Interview with Dr. Irina Koretsky, Paleontologist and Research Associate, Smithsonian Museum of Natural History, and Assistant Professor of Anatomy, Howard University, for video series *Evolution: The Grand Experiment*, conducted on October 9, 1998, by author.

5. Interview with Dr. Annalisa Berta, Professor at San Diego State University, for video series *Evolution: The Grand Experiment*, conducted February 16, 1998, by author.

6. See Appendix A: The Number of Fossils.

7. Interview with Dr. Annalisa Berta, Professor at San Diego State University, for video series *Evolution: The Grand Experiment*, conducted February 16, 1998, by author. "*Pinnipeds first appear in the fossil record about twenty-seven--**twenty-nine million years ago**. The earliest known pinniped is a specimen that's known as Enaliarctos. It consists of five different species.*"

"*Enaliarctos when it first appears between twenty-five and **twenty-nine million years** is the earliest record. And, as I said, it's from the North Pacific, from localities in Washington, Oregon, and California.*"

8. E-mail interview with Dr. Clayton Ray, Curator at the Smithsonian National Museum of Natural History from 1963 to 1994, and subsequently Curator Emeritus at the Smithsonian, conducted December 12, 2005, by author.

9. *Video Footage Reveals Secret to Marine Mammal Diving* (2000). Retrieved August 29, 2006, from the British Sub-Aqua Club, http://www.bsac.org/news/mammal040500.htm. "Elephant seals are the most remarkable divers. One has been recorded diving nearly a mile deep and remaining submerged for nearly two hours."

10. *Los Angeles class submarine* (n.d.). Retrieved August 29, 2006, from http://www.answers.com/topic/los-angeles-class-submarine.

11. Koretsky, I. A. & Sanders, A. E. (2002). Paleontology of the late Oligocene Ashley and Chandler Bridge Formations of South Carolina, 1: Paleogene Pinniped Remains; The Oldest Known Seal (Carnivora, Phocidae). *Smithsonian Contributions to Paleobiology, No 93*, 179. "The proximal halves of two femora from the Chandler Bridge and Ashley Formations (early Chattian, late Oligocene) near Charleston, South Carolina, provide the earliest evidence to date of true seals." **Author's Note:** Chattian is 28 to 23 MYA and Early Chattian is 28 to 25 MYA.

Chapter 11: The Fossil Record of Flying Reptiles

1. See Appendix A: The Number of Fossils.

2. From museum display (May 2005) at the Nebraska State Museum in Lincoln, Nebraska. "More than a 100 species of pterosaurs have been found worldwide. They range in size from tiny sparrow-size flyers to giants with 40-foot wingspans." (Source: AVC CD Image 6363.)

3. Bergmans, W. (2006). *Fighter Planes*. Retrieved August 30, 2006, from www.fighter-planes.com (under 1960–1970). Gives wingspan of F-4E Phantom II fighter jet as 11.71 meters (38 feet).

4. Interview with Dr. Peter Wellnhofer, Curator Emeritus of the Bavarian State Collection of Paleontology in Munich, Germany, and author of the book *The Illustrated Encyclopedia of Prehistoric Flying Reptiles*, for video series *Evolution: The Grand Experiment*, conducted August 17, 2000, by author.

5. Interview with Dr. Gunter Viohl, Curator of the Jura Museum in Eichstaat, Germany, for video series *Evolution: The Grand Experiment*, conducted August 17, 2000, by author.

Chapter 12: The Fossil Record of Dinosaurs

1. Lessem, D. and Glut, D. (1993). *Dinosaur Encyclopedia*. New York: Random House. p. 497.

2. Lindsay, W. and Norell, M. (1992). *Tyrannosaurus*. New York: Dorling Kindersley Publishers. p. 26.

3. Lindsay, W. and Norell, M. (1992). *Tyrannosaurus*. New York: Dorling Kindersley Publishers. p. 8.

4. Interview with Dr. Paul Sereno, Paleontologist and Professor at the University of Chicago, for video series *Evolution: The Grand Experiment*, conducted February 24, 1999, by author.

5. Lessem, D. and Glut, D. (1993). *Dinosaur Encyclopedia*. New York: Random House. p. 486.

6. Interview with Dr. David Weishampel, Anatomist and Paleontologist, Johns Hopkins University and Lead Editor of the encyclopedic reference book *The Dinosauria*, for video series *Evolution: The Grand Experiment*, conducted November 16, 1998, by author.

7. Interview with Dr. Angela Milner, Paleontologist and Head of Vertebrate Paleontology, Natural History Museum of London, for video series *Evolution: The Grand Experiment*, conducted August 24, 2000, by author.

8. Lessem, D. and Glut, D. (1993). *Dinosaur Encyclopedia*. New York: Random House. p. 38.

9. E-mail interview (for clarification purposes) with Dr. David Weishampel, Anatomist and Paleontologist, Johns Hopkins University and Lead Editor of the encyclopedic

reference book *The Dinosauria*, conducted December 6, 2005, by author.

10. See Appendix B: Dinosaur Evolution Chart.

Chapter 13: The Fossil Record of Whales

1. Sinclair, M., Valdimarsson, G., & Food and Agriculture Organization of the United Nations. (2003). *Responsible Fisheries in the Marine Ecosystem*. Rome, Italy: Food and Agriculture Organization of the United Nations. p. 143. "Eighty-four species of cetaceans (whales, dolphins and porpoises) inhabit the world, of which 79 species live in the sea (13 baleen whales and 71 toothed whales; IWC, 2001)."

2. E-mail interview with Dr. Clayton Ray, Curator at the Smithsonian National Museum of Natural History from 1963 to 1994, and subsequently Curator Emeritus at the Smithsonian, conducted December 12, 2005, by author.

3. Interview with Dr. Kevin Padian, Paleontologist, University of California, Berkeley, for video series *Evolution: The Grand Experiment*, conducted in November 1998, by author.

4. Interview with Dr. Annalisa Berta, Professor at San Diego State University, for video series *Evolution: The Grand Experiment*, conducted February 16, 1998, by author.

5. Interview with Dr. Duane Gish, author of the book *Evolution: The Fossils Still Say No!* (published by the Institute for Creation Research, 1995), for video series *Evolution: The Grand Experiment*, conducted in February 1998, by author.

6. The California Academy of Sciences Museum display (December 1998) on whale evolution reads "Pachyaena This extinct, wolf-like mammal is closely related to modern whales. Pachyaena had hoofed feet, and its teeth were modified for shearing and holding meat." (Source AVC Tape 41).

7. Exhibit Museum of Natural History, University of Michigan, Ann Arbor, display on whale evolution (August 2001) suggests the common ancestor to whales was the cougar-like mesonychid called *Sinonyx*. The museum sign reads "*Sinonyx* is important in the story of whale evolution because it is an example of the kind of land-dwelling mesonychid from which cetaceans evolved and it comes from Asia where we think this change happened." (Source AVC CD 117 Image 36)

8. Monastersky, R. (November 6, 1999). The Whale's Tale: Searching for the landlubbing ancestors of marine mammals. *Science News on Line*. Retrieved September 29, 2006, from http://www.findarticles.com/p/articles/mi_m1200/is_19_156/ai_57828404. On page 3 of the on-line article, Dr. Monaster-

sky quotes Dr. Norihiro Okada, a Biologist and Professor at the Tokyo Institute of Technology: "I am one hundred percent confident with the conclusion that the most closely related species to whales, among extant mammals, is the hippo."

9. Interview with Dr. Phil Gingerich, Paleontologist, University of Michigan, for video series *Evolution: The Grand Experiment*, conducted on August 28, 2001, by author.

10. Interview with Dr. Daryl Domning, Paleontologist and Professor of Anatomy, Howard University, for video series *Evolution: The Grand Experiment*, conducted October 8, 1998, by author.

11. Berta, A. (January 14, 1994). What is a whale? *Science*, Volume 263, pp. 180–181.

12. Interview with Dr. Phil Gingerich, Paleontologist, University of Michigan, for video series *Evolution: The Grand Experiment*, conducted on August 28, 2001, by author. Dr. Gingerich: "If you have a whale tail, very heavy bones, very muscular, really powerful things for swimming, the vertebrae are blocky, and they come down, down, down, until you get to the one we call the ball vertebrae. And we call it a ball because it is equally long, equally high and equally wide. And behind that, the vertebrae, even the bony vertebrae, flatten out a little bit and that is what is normally enclosed in connective tissue that makes the fluke that powers the swimming. So if you have a tail that's coming down narrow, get a ball vertebrae and then broadens out, you can even see the fluke in the bones. So we would dearly love a tail of *Rodhocetus*."

13. Interview with Dr. Taseer Hussain, Paleontologist and Professor of Anatomy, Howard University, and Research Associate, Smithsonian National Museum of Natural History, for video series *Evolution: The Grand Experiment*, conducted October 9, 1998, by author.

14. E-mail interview with Lawrence G. Barnes, Curator of Vertebrate Paleontology at the Natural History Museum of Los Angeles County, California, conducted on December 21, 2005, by author. Dr. Barnes was asked if *Basilosaurus* was an ancestor to modern whales. In this interview, Dr. Barnes indicated that *Basilosaurus* was *not* on the line to modern whales. Question: "In your opinion, was *Basilosaurus* on the line to modern whales? Why or why not?" Dr. Barnes: "*Basilosaurus* was, for its time, a relatively highly modified early whale (gigantic body size, incredibly elongated vertebrae, loss of the last molar in each cheek tooth row). These features are not present in the earliest of the mysticetes (the group of baleen whales), nor of the odontocetes (the group of echolocating toothed whales). Following the principle of parsimony, it is more likely that the modern mysticetes and odontocetes were derived from more conservative archaeocetes than the basilosaurines, and

such candidates are known to us, and they have smaller body size, shorter vertebrae, and they retained the last molar in each cheek tooth row. Also, *Basilosaurus* existed at a time when baleen-bearing mysticetes are known to have existed, and echolocating odontocetes are presumed to have existed."

15. See Appendix A: The Number of Fossils.

Chapter 14: The Fossil Record of Birds — Part 1: *Archaeopteryx*

1. Interview with Dr. Gunter Viohl, Curator of the Jura Museum in Eichstaat, Germany, for video series *Evolution: The Grand Experiment*, conducted August 17, 2000, by author.

2. Interview with Dr. Peter Wellnhofer, Curator Emeritus of the Bavarian State Collection of Paleontology, Munich, Germany, for video series *Evolution: The Grand Experiment*, conducted August 17, 2000, by author.

3. *Bird Extremes!* (n.d.). Retrieved October 18, 2006, from http://www.enchantedlearning.com/subjects/birds/Birdextremes.shtml. "Birds With Wing Claws. The Hoatzin has small claws on the first and second wing digits when it is young (it uses the claws to climb trees). The African touraco also has wing claws when it is young. The ostrich has three claws on each wing."

4. Interview with Dr. Timothy Rowe, Professor of Biology and Geology at the University of Texas and Director of the Vertebrate Paleontology Laboratory of the Texas Memorial Museum, for video series *Evolution: The Grand Experiment*, conducted in March 2003, by author. Dr. Rowe: "And, the biggest difference between them is [that] in *Tyrannosaurus rex*, the teeth are serrated like a steak knife, front and back, and it was really for ripping flesh. Whereas in *Archaeopteryx*, the teeth are pretty smooth on either edge; and if they have any serrations at all, they're very, very, very faint serrations."

5. Chicago Field Museum display on evolution (January 1998). In this display, there is an overlay of the bones of the upper extremities of *Archaeopteryx* and the bones of the upper extremities of *Deinonychus*. It gives the impression that these two animals are closely related based on the shape of the bones.

6. See Appendix A: The Number of Fossils.

7. Interview with Dr. Duane Gish, author of the book *Evolution: The Fossils Still Say No!* (published by the Institute for Creation Research, 1995), for video series *Evolution: The Grand Experiment*, conducted in February 1998, by author.

Chapter 15: The Fossil Record of Birds — Part 2: Feathered Dinosaurs

1. Interview with Dr. Peter Wellnhofer, Curator Emeritus of the Bavarian State Collection of Paleontology, Munich, Germany, for video series *Evolution: The Grand Experiment*, conducted August 17, 2000, by author.

2. Interview with Dr. Gunter Viohl, Curator of the Jura Museum in Eichstaat, Germany, for video series *Evolution: The Grand Experiment*, conducted August 17, 2000, by author.

3. Interview with Dr. Timothy Rowe, Professor of Biology and Geology at the University of Texas and Director of the Vertebrate Paleontology Laboratory of the Texas Memorial Museum, for video series *Evolution: The Grand Experiment*, conducted in March 2003, by author.

4. Sloan, Christopher P. (1999, November). Feathered dinosaurs. *National Geographic, Volume 196, No. 5,* pp. 98–107.

5. Feathers for *T. rex* [on second page of *Forum* section] (2000, March). *National Geographic, Volume 197,* No. 3.

Chapter 16: The Fossil Record of Flowering Plants

1. *More Letters of Charles Darwin, Volume 2* (2006). The Echo Library, Middlesex, England. p. 378. Letter 395. To J.D. Hooker. Down, July 22, 1879. "The rapid development as far as we can judge of all the higher plants within recent geological times is an abominable mystery."

2. Arnold, C. (1947). *An Introduction to Paleobotany.* New York: McGraw-Hill Publishing Company. p. 7.

3. Milner, R. (1990). The Encyclopedia of Evolution: Humanity's Search for Its Origins. New York: Facts on File Publishers. p. 14

4. Interview with Dr. Peter Crane, Director of the Royal Botanic Gardens in London, England, for video series *Evolution: The Grand Experiment*, conducted August 26, 2002, by author. Professor Sir Peter Crane is one of the world's leading experts in plant evolution. Dr. Crane holds academic appointments in the Department of Botany at the University of Reading and the Department of Geology at the Royal Holloway College.

Chapter 17: The Origin of Life — Part 1: The Formation of DNA

1. Druyan, A. (Executive Producer), and Gibson, K. (Producer) (2000). *Cosmos. Carl Sagan. Episode III: The harmony of the worlds* (DVD Video - 7 Disc Collector's Edition). (Available from Cosmos Studios, Inc., 11440 Ventura Boulevard, Suite 200, Studio City, CA 91604-3145) In this episode, Carl Sagan states that life began 4 billion years ago.

2. Darwin, C. (1859). *On The Origin of Species by Means of Natural Selection, or The Preservation of Favoured Races in the Struggle for Life* (1st Edition Facsimile). Cambridge: Harvard University Press. p. 484. "Analogy would lead me one step further, namely, to the belief that all animals and plants have descended from some one prototype...Therefore I should infer from analogy that probably all the organic beings which have ever lived on this earth have descended from some one primordial form, into which life was first breathed."

3. Strickberger, M. (1996). *Evolution* (2nd Edition). Boston: Jones and Bartlett Publishers. p. 117. "These observations strongly indicate that the laboratory experiments probably reflect actual chemical processes that also occurred in the synthesis of prebiotic organic compounds."

4. E-mail interview with Dr. Georgia Purdom, Ph.d., Molecular Genetics, Researcher and Speaker for Answers in Genesis, Petersburg, Kentucky, for this book *Evolution: The Grand Experiment*, conducted April 30, 2007, by author.

5. Thaxton, C., Bradley, W., Olsen, R. (1984). *The Mystery of Life's Origin: Reassessing Current Theories.* Dallas: Lewis and Stanley Publishers. p. 163. "To date, researchers have only succeeded in making oligonucleotides, or relatively short chains of nucleotides, with neither consistent 3'-5' links nor specific base sequencing."

6. Thaxton, C., Bradley, W., Olsen, R. (1984). *The Mystery of Life's Origin: Reassessing Current Theories.* Dallas: Lewis and Stanley Publishers. p. 164. "As we stated before, a minimum of 20–40 proteins as well as DNA and RNA are required to make even a simple replicating system."

7. *Medical Aspects of Lightning* (n.d.). Retrieved September 28, 2006, from http://www.lightningsafety.noaa.gov/medical.htm.

8. Powerball odds 1/80,089,128 from *Power Ball Details* (n.d.). Retrieved August 15, 2006, from http://www.lotterybuddy.com/powerball/powerodd.htm. **Author's Note:** The odds for winning the national powerball lottery are subject to change. For simplicity, this number was rounded to 1/80,000,000.

9. **Author's Note:** The calculation for winning the national Powerball Lottery every day for 365 days is 80,000,000^{365} which is equal to 1/4,244 followed by 2,881 zeros.

Chapter 18: The Origin of Life — Part 2: The Formation of Proteins

1. Interview with Dr. Duane Gish, Biochemist, Institute for Creation Research, Santee, California, for video series *Evolution: The Grand Experiment*, conducted in February 1998, by author.

2. Strickberger, M. (1996). *Evolution* (2nd Edition). Boston: Jones and Bartlett Publishers. p. 125. "Surfaces near some volcanic regions may have maintained appropriate temperatures for the condensation of amino acids, and cooling rains may have dispersed such thermally produced proteinoids to places where further interactions could take place."

3. Thaxton, C., Bradley, W., Olsen, R. (1984). *The Mystery of Life's Origin: Reassessing Current Theories.* Dallas: Lewis and Stanley Publishers. p. 156. On this page, Thaxton is quoting from page 87 of C. E. Folsom's book, *The Origin of Life* (published by W.H. Freeman, Publishers, San Francisco, 1979). "The central question...is where did all those pure, dry, concentrated, and optically active amino acids come from in the real, abiological world?"

4. Strickberger, M. (1996). *Evolution* (2nd Edition). Boston: Jones and Bartlett Publishers. p. 125.

5. Strickberger, M. (1996). *Evolution* (2nd Edition). Boston: Jones and Bartlett Publishers. p. 124.

6. Strickberger, M. (1996). *Evolution* (2nd Edition). Boston: Jones and Bartlett Publishers. p. 115.

7. Strickberger, M. (1996). *Evolution* (2nd Edition). Boston: Jones and Bartlett Publishers. p. 125. "Fox and Dose have suggested that some of these reactions, combined into a particular sequence, may have served as the beginnings of later metabolic systems."

8. Thaxton, C., Bradley, W., Olsen, R. (1984). *The Mystery of Life's Origin: Reassessing Current Theories.* Dallas: Lewis and Stanley Publishers. p. 99. "We provide this to point out the need for a criterion for the acceptable role of the investigator in prebiotic simulation experiments."

9. Thaxton, C., Bradley, W., Olsen, R. (1984). *The Mystery of Life's Origin: Reassessing Current Theories.* Dallas: Lewis and Stanley Publishers. pp. 155–156. Here Thaxton is quoting P.A. Temussi *et al* from J. Mol. Evol. (1976) 7, 105.

10. Thaxton, C., Bradley, W., Olsen, R. (1984). *The Mystery of Life's Origin: Reassessing Current Theories.* Dallas: Lewis and Stanley Publishers. p. 156. "Second, thermal proteinoids are composed of approximately equal numbers of L- and D-amino acids in contrast to viable proteins with all L-amino acids."

Chapter 19: The Origin of Life — Part 3: The Formation of Amino Acids

1. Strickberger, M. (1996). *Evolution* (2nd Edition). Boston: Jones and Bartlett Publishers. p. 117. "These observations strongly indicate that the laboratory experiments probably reflect actual chemical processes that also occurred in the synthesis of prebiotic organic compounds."

2. Thaxton, C., Bradley, W., Olsen, R. (1984). *The Mystery of Life's Origin: Reassessing Current Theories.* Dallas: Lewis and Stanley Publishers. p. 99. "We provide this to point out the need for a criterion for the acceptable role of the investigator in prebiotic simulation experiments."

3. Thaxton, C., Bradley, W., Olsen, R. (1984). *The Mystery of Life's Origin: Reassessing Current Theories.* Dallas: Lewis and Stanley Publishers. pp. 76–77. "That point, central to the theory of chemical evolution, is that the primitive atmosphere could not contain any but the smallest amount of free (molecular) oxygen (O_2). It is necessary to exclude oxygen for two reasons. First, all organic compounds (such as the essential precursor chemicals or basic building blocks that must have accumulated for chemical evolution to proceed) are decomposed rather quickly in the presence of oxygen. Second, if even trace quantities of molecular oxygen were present, organic molecules could not be formed at all. In the words of Shklovskii and Sagan, 'As soon as the net (laboratory) conditions become oxidizing, the organic syntheses effectively turn off.'"

4. Thaxton, C., Bradley, W., Olsen, R. (1984). *The Mystery of Life's Origin: Reassessing Current Theories.* Dallas: Lewis and Stanley Publishers. p. 91. "Walker disagrees, however, stating, 'The presence of banded iron formation in the Isua rocks of West Greenland therefore implies that oxygen-evolving photosynthesis appeared on earth prior to 3.8 billion years ago.'"

5. Thaxton, C., Bradley, W., Olsen, R. (1984). *The Mystery of Life's Origin: Reassessing Current Theories.* Dallas: Lewis and Stanley Publishers. p. 81.

6. Thaxton, C., Bradley, W., Olsen, R. (1984). *The Mystery of Life's Origin: Reassessing Current Theories.* Dallas: Lewis and Stanley Publishers. p. 52. "In addition, the amino acids produced in these experiments form a racemic mixture-an equal amount of both D- and L-amino acids... Protein not only requires exclusive use of L-amino acids, but also the use of a particular subset of only 20 amino acids."

7. Strickberger, M. (1996). *Evolution* (2nd Edition). Boston: Jones and Bartlett Publishers. p. 114. "In contrast, the amino acids of living forms generally show optical activity of only one type, levorotary."

8. Powerball odds 1/80,089,128 from *Power Ball Details* (n.d.). Retrieved August 15, 2006, from http://www.lotterybuddy.com/powerball/powerodd.htm. **Author's Note:** The odds for winning the national powerball lottery are subject to change. For simplicity, this number was rounded to 1/80,000,000. The calculation for winning the national Powerball Lottery every day for 365 days is $80{,}000{,}000^{365}$ which is equal to 1/4,244 followed by 2,881 zeros.

Chapter 20: Conclusions — Evolution: Points of Controversy

1. **Author's Note:** The expected number of fossil ancestors was calculated using two assumptions. The first assumption is there would be, on average, one new species of animal arising on the evolutionary line every one million years. The author derived this estimate based on general patterns of evolution as seen in various animals, the frequency of genetic mutations causing new species to arise, the calculated numbers of mutations necessary for new species traits, and the number of trait differences between two evolutionary successive animals. This is an estimation and could range from less than 100,000 years to more than tens of millions of years. Also of note, this estimate would not be the length of time a species existed but would simply be the frequency by which new species occurred. The second assumption used in these calculations is that the fossil record is fairly uniform and representative of the past.

Apatosaurus: If the dinosaur *Apatosaurus* lived 150 million years ago (mya) and evolved from the common ancestor of all dinosaurs (which theoretically lived 220 mya), there would be 70 million years of evolution from the dinosaur common ancestor to *Apatosaurus*, resulting in 70 intermediate ancestor species. Assuming the fossil record is uniform and representative of the past, then 1,750 direct ancestors of *Apatosaurus* would be expected to have been discovered by now. (25 *Apatosaurus* skeletons have been found suggesting that *approximately* 25 of each of the 70 intermediates should also have been found by now, or 25 x 70 =1,750 expected fossil finds.) These numbers are, of course, gross estimates. Variations in fossil preservation could result in more than or less than 25 fossil finds of each of these theoretical dinosaur precursors of *Apatosaurus.*

T. rex: This dinosaur appears in the fossil record fully developed at 70 mya. Thirty-two of these dinosaurs have been found. If the common ancestor to all dinosaurs lived 220 mya, we would expect to find 4,800 ancestors of *T. rex.* That is to say 150 million years of evolution = 150 different species of direct ancestors of *T. rex* x 32 expected finds for each of these species = 4,800 predicted direct ancestors.

Pterosaur: Pterosaurs appear fully developed in the Triassic around 228 mya and, according to Dr. Peter Wellnhofer, pterosaurs evolved *"from small, land-bound reptiles... about 250 million years ago..."* (Wellnhofer, P. (1996) in *The Illustrated Encyclopedia of Prehistoric Flying Reptiles.* p. 44.) Approximately 1,000 pterosaurs have been found so far. If the common ancestor to all pterosaurs lived 250 mya (age for land-based reptile), we would expect to find 22,000 ancestors of pterosaurs. That is to say 22 million years of evolution = 22 different species of direct ancestors of pterosaurs x 1,000 expected finds for each of these species = 22,000 predicted direct ancestors.

Bat: If bat evolution began 66 mya, and bats appear in the fossil record 52 mya, then there would be 14 million years of bat evolution. If one new species appeared every million years, this evolutionary process should have produced 14 species of the direct ancestors of bats. Since there are over 1,000 known fully developed fossil bats, then 14 species of bat intermediates x 1,000 expected fossil finds for each of these species = 14,000 predicted direct ancestors.

Appendix A: The Number of Fossils

1. Long, J. & Schouten, P. (2008). *Feathered Dinosaurs: The Origin of Birds.* New York: Oxford University Press, Inc. p. 2. "The fossil record, as held in all the world's major museums, government organisations, universities and private collections, now tallies close to a billion fossil specimens."

2. Interview with Dr. Angela Milner, Paleontologist and Head of Vertebrate Paleontology, Natural History Museum of London, for video series *Evolution: The Grand Experiment*, conducted August 24, 2000, by author. "Well, the Natural History Museum is one of the largest of its kind in the world. We house something like sixty-eight million specimens from all around the world and, of those, there are about nine million fossils in the collections. And the whole of the building, from one end to other, is about a quarter of a mile long."

3. *Invertebrate Paleontology. About the Division* (n.d.). Retrieved August 28, 2006, from the University of Nebraska State Museum, http://www.unl.edu/museum/research/invertpaleo/about.html.

4. *Paleontology* (n.d.). Retrieved November 6, 2006, from the American Museum of Natural History, http://www.amnh.org/science/divisions/paleo/.

5. Interview with Dr. John Long, Head of Science at Museum Victoria, Melbourne, Australia, for video series *Evolution: The Grand Experiment,* conducted March 8, 2005, by author.

6. *Invertebrate Paleontology* (n.d.). Retrieved August 28, 2006, from the University of Michigan Museum of Paleontology, http://www.paleontology.lsa.umich.edu (under Invertebrate Paleontology).

7. *Invertebrate Paleontology Database* (n.d.). Retrieved August 28, 2006, from the Florida Museum of Natural History, http://www.flmnh.ufl.edu/databases/ivp/default.htm.

8. *About the Vertebrate Paleontology Collections at the University of Nebraska State Museum* (2004). Retrieved August 28, 2006, from the University of Nebraska State Museum, http://www.museum.unl.edu/research/vertpaleo/welcome.html.

9. Interview with Dr. Lance Grande, Curator, Department of Geology, Chicago Field Museum, for video series *Evolution: The Grand Experiment*, conducted in January 1998, by author.

10. E-mail interview with Dr. Peter Dodson, Editor of *The Dinosauria*, author of *The Horned Dinosaurs*, and Professor of Anatomy, University of Pennsylvania School of Veterinary Medicine, conducted November 1, 2006, by author. Question: "How many dinosaurs are in museum collections worldwide now?" Dr. Dodson: "By the reckoning Steve Wang and I did, based on the 2004 *Dinosauria*, the number of skeletons in museum collections worldwide is now just over 3,000 (ca. 3,050)." Question: "I have one question for clarification. You said the number of skeletons in museum collections is 3,050. By this, I assume you mean articulated specimens? If so, using a more liberal definition of dinosaur counts in museums, how many fossil dinosaurs do museums have in their collections? For example, if the Carnegie Museum had just a single femur bone from a *T. rex* and they counted this as one dinosaur, or if another museum had a single forearm bone from a *Coelophysis* and they counted this as one dinosaur in their collection, how many dinosaurs (counting both articulated dinosaur skeletons and unarticulated bones of dinosaurs) are in museum collections worldwide?" Dr. Dodson: "I was afraid you would ask that question, and I suspect nobody really knows the answer...I myself have collected well over 6,000 dinosaur teeth in a massive paleoecological study I did 20 years ago in Alberta. So we are looking at order-of-magnitude estimates. I would guess the total number of specimens is between 10 and 100 times that estimate of 3,000 — so between 30,000 and 300,000 — more reasonably perhaps around 100,000. That is my best shot."

11. Horner, J. (1988). *Digging Dinosaurs*. New York: Harper Collins Publishers. pp. 128, 193. "In a total area of a few square miles, we have so far found two large bone beds of ceratopsian dinosaurs and three large bone beds of hadrosaurs and lambeosaurs...We had one huge bed of maiasaur bones — and nothing but maiasaur bones — stretching a mile and a quarter east to west and a quarter-mile north to south. Judging from the concentration of bones in various pits, there were up to 30 million fossil fragments in that area. At a conservative estimate, we had discovered the tomb of 10,000 dinosaurs."

12. Interview with Dr. Phillip Currie, Site Paleontologist, Dinosaur Provincial Park and Curator of Royal Tyrell Museum, Alberta Canada, for video series *Evolution: The Grand Experiment*, conducted July 28, 1997, by author. Dr. Currie: "The *Centrosaurus* [dinosaur] bone beds we find in Dinosaur Park are very, very numerous to say the least... *Centrosaurus* bone beds that are spread over a distance of about five miles in Dinosaur Provincial Park. The concentration of bones in any one of these *Centrosaurus* bone beds can reach anywhere from 60 to 100 bones per square yard... That meant that in that one small area, we had at least 300 or 400 animals represented. Now you spread that out over a five-mile distance, and we're talking about thousands and thousands and thousands of animals. In fact, there has been some attempt in recent years to calculate how many individuals we're looking at in each one of these bone beds, and it does exceed thousands of animals. We may be looking at herds of as many as ten thousand animals. It's not unreasonable anymore given the number of bones we are finding at these levels."

13. Psihoyos, L. (1994). *Hunting Dinosaurs*. New York: Random House. p. 25. "They were vindicated to a degree in 1947 when paleontologist Ned Colbert of the Amercian Museum of Natural History found a mass grave of some one thousand predatory dinosaurs called *Coelophysis*."

14. Interview with Dr. David Weishampel, Anatomist and Paleontologist, Johns Hopkins University and Lead Editor of the encyclopedic reference book *The Dinosauria*, for video series *Evolution: The Grand Experiment*, conducted November 16, 1998, by author. "I suspect we probably know a hundred or hundreds of *Triceratops* from their skulls."

15. West, L. and Chure, D. (1994). *Dinosaur: The Dinosaur National Monument Quarry*. Vernal, Utah: Dinosaur Nature Association. p. 22. "But their world it was, for more dinosaur remains have been found in the Morrison Formation than anywhere else. Ten major quarries have produced tens of thousands of bones from hundreds of individual animals — a priceless record of the past."

16. West, L. and Chure, D. (1994). *Dinosaur: The Dinosaur National Monument Quarry*. Vernal, Utah: Dinosaur Nature Association. p. 35. "Although the quarry has produced no new species of dinosaurs, it has yielded a greater variety of species and a larger number of individual animals than any other single dinosaur site. Counting what was excavated and what remains in the rock, roughly 85

individuals, in varying degrees of completeness and representing eleven different species, have been found."

17. Stokes, Wm. (1985). *The Cleveland-Lloyd Dinosaur Quarry: Window to the Past.* Washington, D.C.: U.S. Government Printing Office. p. 24. "Organized professional excavation [of the Cleveland-Lloyd Quarry] yielded about 10,000 individual bones. From these bones, more than 70 individual animals representing at least 14 species have been identified."

18. Informal interview conducted by author for this book with Ty Naus, Geologist, Thermopolis Dinosaur Center, Thermopolis, Wyoming, in July 1997. Ty Naus estimated that there were 250,000 dinosaur bones buried at the Thermopolis Wyoming Dinosaur Center site.

19. Taken from pamphlet at the Wyoming Dinosaur Center, Thermopolis, Wyoming, entitled *"The Wyoming Dinosaur Center: Unique Experience Waiting to be Discovered,"* undated. "Wyoming Dinosaur Center geologists estimate 38 sites exist on Warm Springs Ranch, which may contain 100,000 to 300,0000 bones."

20. Weishampel, D., Dodson, P., and Osmolska, H. (1990). *The Dinosauria.* Berkeley: University of California Press. **Author's Note:** The number of 2,610 individual dinosaurs was obtained by adding the number of individual dinosaurs listed in this book.

21. Willis, D. (1992). *The Leakey Family, Leaders in the Search for Human Origins.* New York: Facts on File Publishers. pp. 41–42. "...Mary Leakey and her team excavated 55,000 square feet [at Olduvai site in Africa]. A total of 37,127 artifacts and 32,378 fossils were recorded — that second figure does not include over 14,000 rodent fossils, plus fragmentary finds of birds and frogs!"

22. Quote from display at the Harvard Museum of Paleontology (October 1998) over fossil bone bed reconstruction. "In western Nebraska, near Agate Springs, one of the most remarkable fossil beds ever [is] found. It extends over several acres maintaining a thickness of somewhat over a foot... Furthermore, the vast majority of the bones represent but a single species, the small rhinoceros *Diceratherium cooki*..." **Author's Note:** Author interpreted the above information to represent at least hundreds of rhinos in this particular bone bed.

23. E-mail interview with Dr. Lawrence Barnes, Curator of Vertebrate Paleontology at the Natural History Museum of Los Angeles County in California, on December 21, 2005, by author.

24. Interview with Dr. Phil Gingerich, Paleontologist, University of Michigan, for video series *Evolution: The Grand Experiment,* conducted August 28, 2001, by author. Question: How many fossil whales have been discovered — not individual bones but individual whales? Dr. Gingerich: "If you asked me about archaic whales, I can tell you thousands. I mean, when I say there are three hundred *Basilosaurus,* I'm talking about pretty good skeletons. When I say there's one or that there are half a dozen *Rodhocetus,* I'm talking about pretty good skeletons. I've got thousands of bones here in the lab that are whales, archaic whales, they're just not complete enough to be able to tell what they are...Like I was saying for *Dorudon,* we have about a hundred and fifty skeletons, of which we've collected probably six. So, there are six in museums, and there are a hundred and forty-four lying in the field and about three hundred and some *Basilosaurus* skeletons lying in the field. There's a good skeleton in Germany. There's a good one at the Smithsonian. There's a good part of one in Louisiana at the Natural History Museum there. And mostly, they're lying in the field because they're too big." Question: How many fossil whales have been found that are not archaeocetes — more modern types? Dr. Gingerich: "Oh, there must be thousands, thousands. Of good skeletons there must be hundreds, I would think. I mean, there are places in California — there's a place called Sharktooth Hill that has many skeletons coming out of it. In New Zealand, there are many. There are places in the world — in Holland there are many. There are places in the world where these are common." **Author's Note:** The number 4,000 was derived from "thousands of archaeocetes" plus "thousands" of whales other than the archaeocetes.

25. E-mail interview with Dr. Annalisa Berta, Professor and Associate Chair, Department of Evolutionary Biology, San Diego State University, conducted December 31, 2005, by author.

26. E-mail interview with Dr. Larry Martin, Professor and Senior Curator at the University of Kansas, conducted December 3, 2005, by author.

27. E-mail interview with Dr. Storrs Olson, Senior Zoologist, Division of Birds, Smithsonian Institution, on October 24, 2006, by author.

28. *Australia's Lost Kingdoms* (2004). Retrieved September 6, 2006, from http://www.lostkingdoms.com/facts/factsheet28.htm. "Hundreds of fossils of the Riversleigh Leaf-nosed Bat have been collected from Riversleigh in northwestern Queensland." **Author's Note:** Age 16–24 million years ago (late Oligocene–early Miocene).

29. Interview with Dr. Nicholas Czeplewski, Staff Curator of Paleontology, Sam Noble Oklahoma Museum of Science and Natural History, for video series *Evolution: The Grand Experiment,* conducted April 1, 2002, by author. "...They get large numbers of bats and a lot of other kinds of animals that were going into these paleo-caves. And so the numbers of fossils from Riversleigh, I suspect, must be in the hundreds or thousands, but I couldn't give you a count."

30. Interview with Joerg Habersetzer from the Senckenberg Museum of Natural History in Frankfurt, Germany, for

video series: *Evolution: The Grand Experiment*, conducted August 17, 2000, by author. Dr Habersetzer studies bat evolution in Germany. "We have found more than 650–670 specimens so far [at this one location alone in Germany]."

31. Interview with Dr. Gary Morgan, Assistant Curator of Paleontology, New Mexico Museum of Natural History and Science, for video series *Evolution: The Grand Experiment*, conducted March 19, 2002, by author. "Yeah, I would guess that the entire Florida sample of bats, numbering in the several thousands [fossil bones], would amount to no more than a hundred individuals, representing ten to twelve different species."

32. Interview with Dr. Peter Wellnhofer, Curator Emeritus of the Bavarian State Collection of Paleontology, Munich, Germany, for video series *Evolution: The Grand Experiment*, conducted August 17, 2000, by author.

33. E-mail interview with Dr. James Parham, Postdoctoral Associate, University of California, Berkeley, Museum of Paleontology, conducted November 13, 2006, by author.

34. E-mail interview with Dr. Eugene S. Gaffney, Department of Vertebrate Paleontology, American Museum of Natural History, New York, conducted November 6, 2006, by author.

35. E-mail interview with Dr. Conrad C. Labandeira, Curator of Paleoentomology, Smithsonian National Museum of Natural History, on November 8, 2006, by author.

Appendix B: Dinosaur Evolution Chart

1. Weishampel, D., Dodson, P., and Osmolska, H. (Editors) (1990). *The Dinosauria.* Berkeley: University of California Press.

2. Preiss, B. and Silverberg, R. (1992). *The Ultimate Dinosaur.* New York: Bantam Books.

3. E-mail interview (for clarification purposes) with Dr. David Weishampel, Anatomist and Paleontologist, Johns Hopkins University and Lead Editor of the encyclopedic reference book *The Dinosauria*, conducted December 6, 2005, by author.

4. Interview with Dr. Paul Sereno, Paleontologist and Professor at the University of Chicago, for video series *Evolution: The Grand Experiment*, conducted February 24, 1999, by author.

5. Psihoyos, L. (1994). *Hunting Dinosaurs.* New York: Random House. p. 25. "They were vindicated to a degree in 1947 when paleontologist Ned Colbert of the American Museum of Natural History found a mass grave of some one thousand predatory dinosaurs called *Coelophysis*."

6. Weishampel, D., Dodson, P., and Osmolska, H. (Editors) (1990). *The Dinosauria.* Berkeley: University of California Press. p. 269. **Author's Note:** This chapter of *The Dinosauria* was written by Dr. John Ostrom.

7. Weishampel, D., Dodson, P., and Osmolska, H. (Editors) (1990). *The Dinosauria.* Berkeley: University of California Press. p. 189. **Author's Note:** This chapter of *The Dinosauria* was written by Drs. Ralph Molnar, Sergei Kurzanov, and Dong Zhiming.

8. Weishampel, D., Dodson, P., and Osmolska, H. (Editors) (1990). *The Dinosauria.* Berkeley: University of California Press. p. 578. **Author's Note:** This chapter of *The Dinosauria* was written by Dr. Peter Dodson, Associate Professor, University of Pennsylvania, School of Veterinary Medicine.

9. Interview with Dr. Phillip Currie, Site Paleontologist, Dinosaur Provincial Park and Curator of Royal Tyrell Museum, Alberta Canada, for video series *Evolution: The Grand Experiment,* conducted July 28, 1997, by author. Dr. Currie: "The *Centrosaurus* [dinosaur] bone beds we find in Dinosaur Park are very, very numerous to say the least...*Centrosaurus* bone beds that are spread over a distance of about five miles in Dinosaur Provincial Park. The concentration of bones in any one of these *Centrosaurus* bone beds can reach anywhere from 60 to 100 bones per square yard...That meant that in that one small area, we had at least 300 or 400 animals represented. Now you spread that out over a five-mile distance, and we're talking about thousands and thousands and thousands of animals. In fact, there has been some attempt in recent years to calculate how many individuals we're looking at in each one of these bone beds, and it does exceed thousands of animals. We may be looking at herds of as many as ten thousand animals. It's not unreasonable anymore given the number of bones we are finding at these levels."

10. Interview with Dr. David Weishampel, Anatomist and Paleontologist, Johns Hopkins University and Lead Editor of the encyclopedic reference book *The Dinosauria*, for video series *Evolution: The Grand Experiment*, conducted November 16, 1998, by author. "I suspect we probably know a hundred or hundreds of *Triceratops* from their skulls."

11. Horner, J. (1988). *Digging Dinosaurs.* New York: Harper Collins Publishers. p. 128.

12. Interview with Dr. Angela Milner, Paleontologist and Head of Vertebrate Paleontology, Natural History Museum of London, for video series *Evolution: The Grand Experiment*, conducted August 24, 2000, by author.

13. Interview with Dr. David Weishampel, Anatomist and Paleontologist, Johns Hopkins University and Lead Editor of the encyclopedic reference book *The Dinosauria*, for

video series *Evolution: The Grand Experiment*, conducted November 16, 1998, by author.

14. Preiss, B. and Silverberg, R. (1992). *The Ultimate Dinosaur.* New York: Bantam Books. pp. 321–324.

15. Interview with Dr. Phillip Currie, Site Paleontologist, Dinosaur Provincial Park and Curator of Royal Tyrell Museum, Alberta Canada, for video series *Evolution: The Grand Experiment*, conducted July 28, 1997, by author.

16. Weishampel, D., Dodson, P., and Osmolska, H. (Editors) (1990). *The Dinosauria.* Berkeley: University of California Press. **Author's Note:** Information for this reference was taken from p. 27, chapter written by Dr. Michael Benton, and p. 529, chapter written by Drs. David B. Norman and David Weishampel, Anatomist and Paleontologist, Johns Hopkins University.

Appendix C: Fish Evolution Chart

1. Long, J. (1995). *The Rise of Fishes: 500 Million Years of Evolution.* Baltimore: Johns Hopkins University Press.

2. Dixon, D., Cox, B., Savage, R., and Gardiner, B. (1988). *The Macmillan Illustrated Encyclopedia of Dinosaurs and Prehistoric Animals.* New York: Macmillan Publishers. p. 18.

3. Interview with Dr. John Long, Head of Science at Museum Victoria, Melbourne, Australia, for video series *Evolution: The Grand Experiment*, conducted March 8, 2005, by author.

Appendix D: Bat Evolution Update

1. Simmons, N., Seymour, K. L., Habersetzer, J., & Gunnell, G. (February 14, 2008). Primitive early Eocene bat from Wyoming and the evolution of flight and echolocation. *Nature, Vol 451*, p. 818.

Author's Note: To see the *Nature* cover, google the words "*Onychonycteris finneyi* in *Nature* Journal" using Google Images.

 2. See Appendix A: The Number of Fossils.

Appendix E: Pinniped Evolution Update

1. Rybczynski, N., Dawson, M. R., & Tedford, R. H. (April 23, 2009). A semi-aquatic Arctic mammalian carnivore from the Miocene epoch and origin of Pinnipedia. *Nature*, Vol. 458, pp. 1021–1024.

2. Display at the American Museum of Natural History, New York (July 2011). "*Enaliarctos mealsi.* This partially disarticulated skeleton is the oldest pinniped now known.

Enaliarctos was fully aquatic and had most of the skeletal adaptations of modern sea lions. Miocene 23 million years ago."

3. *Puijila, A Prehistoric Walking Seal* (Updated June 7, 2011). Retrieved July 19, 2011, from the Canadian Museum of Nature, http://nature.ca/puijila/fb_e.cfm, under The Fossil & The Breakthrough, A Missing Link. "The fossil mammal *Puijila darwini* is a 'missing link' in the evolution of a prehistoric land mammal into modern, marine ones—specifically seals and their relatives."

4. Press Release (April 11, 2009). Retrieved July 28, 2011, from the Carnegie Museum of Natural History, http://www.carnegiemnh.org/press/09-apr-jun/042309puijila-images.htm. "The new taxon, *Puijila*, is a freshwater semi-aquatic pinniped found in the High Arctic."

5. Northover, J., Rybczynski, N., & Schroder-Adams, C. (September 2009). Pectoral Girdle and Forelimb of Puijila Darwini, A Fossil Pinniped from the Haughton Crater Formation, Devon Island, Nunavut. *Journal of Vertebrate Paleontology, Vol 29, Supplement to Number 3*, p. 156A. "Although *Puijila is a pinniped*, its limb proportions and long tail are reminiscent of modern otters (Lutrinae), particularly *Lontra canadensis*."

6. Dawkins, R. (2009). *The Greatest Show on Earth: The Evidence for Evolution.* New York: Free Press. p. 173.

7. Rybczynski, N., Dawson, M. R., & Tedford, R. H. (April 23, 2009). A semi-aquatic Arctic mammalian carnivore from the Miocene epoch and origin of Pinnipedia. *Nature*, Vol. 458, p. 1021. "The previously reported vertebrate fauna from the lake deposits includes at least two taxa of freshwater teleost fishes, one bird and four mammalian taxa (shrew, rabbit, rhinoceros and small artiodactyl)."

8. *Puijila, A Prehistoric Walking Seal* (Updated June 7, 2011). Retrieved July 19, 2011, from the Canadian Museum of Nature, http://nature.ca/puijila/fb_so_e.cfm, under About the Animal. "This powerful predator hunted on land and in the water, eating terrestrial and freshwater animals. What appears to be stomach contents were found with the skeleton of *Puijila*. An initial inspection suggests the contents may include a small rodent and a duck. Further study is underway."

9. Interview with Dr. Annalisa Berta, Professor at San Diego State University, for video series *Evolution: The Grand Experiment*, conducted February 16, 1998, by author. "Pinnipeds first appear in the fossil record about twenty-seven, twenty-nine million years ago. The earliest known pinniped is a specimen that's known as *Enaliarctos*. It consists of five different species." "...Enaliarctos, when it first appears, between twenty-five and twenty-nine million years [ago], is the earliest record. And, as I said, it's from

the North Pacific, from localities in Washington, Oregon, and California."

10. Koretsky, I. A. & Sanders, A. E. (2002). Paleontology of the late Oligocene Ashley and Chandler Bridge Formations of South Carolina, 1: Paleogene Pinniped Remains; The Oldest Known Seal (Carnivora, Phocidae). *Smithsonian Contributions to Paleobiology, No 93,* 179. "The proximal halves of two femora from the Chandler Bridge and Ashley Formations (early Chattian, late Oligocene) near Charleston, South Carolina, provide the earliest evidence to date of true seals." **Author's Note:** Chattian is 28 to 23 MYA and Early Chattian is 28 to 25 MYA.

11. Berta, A., Sumich, J. L., & Kovacs, K. M. (2006). *Marine Mammals: Evolutionary Biology* (2nd Edition). Boston: Elsevier/Academic Press. p. 29: "Digit I and V on the foot emphasized. Pinnipeds have elongated side toes (digit I and V equivalent to the big toe and little toe) of the foot, whereas in other carnivores the central digits are the most strongly developed."

12. Berta, A., Sumich, J. L., & Kovacs, K. M. (2006). *Marine Mammals: Evolutionary Biology* (2nd Edition). Boston: Elsevier/Academic Press. p. 29: "Digit I on the hand emphasized. In the hand of pinnipeds the first digit (thumb equivalent) is elongated, whereas in other carnivores the central digits are the most strongly developed."

13. *River Otter, Lontra canadensis* (n.d.) Retrieved June 14, 2011, from the Defenders of Wildlife web site, http://www. defenders.org/wildlife_and_habitat/wildlife/river_otter.php. **Author's Note:** This site reports male river otters are generally 3.7 feet long (112 cm).

14. **Author's Note:** In the *Nature* article cited in Footnote 1 above, the scientists reported that the tail of *Puijila* was slightly "shorter and more gracile" than a river otter. This is speculative since some of the bones of the tail of *Puijila* were never found. The reader can form his own opinion by comparing the photographs on page 246.

15. **Author's Note:** In Dr. Rybczynski's article, referenced in Footnote 1 above, the scientists describing *Puijila* reported the total number of upper incisors as unknown, possibly four. The dental formula of *Puijila* was stated as "Dentition: 2?/2, 1/1, 4/4/ 2/2."

Subsequent to the *Nature* article, the Canadian Museum of Nature web site shows *six* upper incisor teeth on *Puijila,* the same number of upper incisors as the North American River Otter. Reference http://nature.ca/puijila/fb_so_e.cfm, under The Fossil & The Breakthrough, More Seal Than Otter, Infraorbital Foramen (March 25, 2010).

16. E-mail interview with Dr. Natalia Rybczynski, Paleobiologist and Professor, Canadian Museum of Nature, for *Evolution: The Grand Experiment*, conducted September

17, 2011, by author. **Question:** *"We noticed that the dental formula that Dr. Dawson, Dr. Tedford and you reported in Nature was still up in the air as of April 2009: 2?/2,1/1, 4/4, 2/2. When we went to the Canadian Museum of Nature web site we saw a flash video showing Puijila having a total of 6 upper incisors. I am aware that there was a second season of collecting fossil remains and that the dental formula may have been sorted out since the original article. Has this been sorted out? Do you have an updated dental formula that we should use?"* **Dr. Rybczynski:** *"We have not published an amendment to the 2?/2,1/1, 4/4, 2/2. Specifically we have evidence for at least two incisors, but there could be three. (Three is primitive for the group, so it would not be surprising at all to find that there are three.)"*

17. Mr. Eric Ekdale, 2006, "Lontra canadensis" (On-line), Digital Morphology. Accessed July 24, 2013 at http:// digimorph.org/specimens/Lontra_canadensis/female/. "The dental formula of Lontra canadensis is 3/3, 1/1, 4/3, 1/2."

18. *Order Carnivora, Family Mustelidae, Weasel Family* (n.d.). Retrieved 21 July, 2011, from the University of Edinburgh, United Kingdom, http://www.nhc.ed.ac.uk/ index.php?page=493.172.292. "Most members of the subfamily Mustelinae have a dental formula of I3/3, I 1/1, PM3/3, M1/2 = 34 with prominent, sharp canines and cutting carnassials. The dentition of members of other subfamilies differs slightly from this arrangement."

19. Rybczynski, N., Dawson, M. R., & Tedford, R. H. (April 23, 2009). A semi-aquatic Arctic mammalian carnivore from the Miocene epoch and origin of Pinnipedia. *Nature,* Vol. 458, p. 1022. **Author's Note:** These scientists report *Puijila* had four lower incisors, but I was not able to visually confirm this. As discussed in Footnote 15 above, the number of lower incisors of *Puijila* may change as well.

20. Nowak, R. M. & Wilson, D. E. (1991). *Walker's Mammals of the World (Volume II).* Baltimore: Johns Hopkins University Press, p. 705. "Enhydra is the only genus with two lower incisors." **Author's Note:** Enhydra is the genus for sea otters. Nowak quotes two lower incisors for each half of the lower jaw meaning, four lower incisors total for sea otters.

21. Estes, James, *Enhydra lutris, Mammalian Species, No. 133,* April 15, 1980, Published by the American Society of Mammalogists, http://www.science.smith.edu/msi/pdf/ i0076-3519-133-01-0001.pdf. Accessed July 24, 2013. "Adult dental formula is i 3/2, c 1/1, p 3/3, m 1/2, total 32."

22. Berta, A., Sumich, J. L., & Kovacs, K. M. (2006). *Marine Mammals: Evolutionary Biology* (2nd Edition). Boston: Elsevier/Academic Press. p. 316: "Among phocids, [earless seals or true seals] the phocines have incisors 3/2 (except the hooded seal, which has 2/1) and

the monachines [subfamily of earless seals] have incisors 2/2 (except for the elephant seal which has 2/1)."

23. *Puijila, A Prehistoric Walking Seal* (Updated June 7, 2011). Retrieved September 9, 2011, from the Canadian Museum of Nature, http://nature.ca/puijila/aa_e.cfm, under About The Animal. "At about 110 cm long, *Puijila darwini* was a medium-sized, semi-aquatic carnivore with a long, slender tail. It lived 24 to 20 million years ago, in what is now Canada's High Arctic. One can loosely describe *Puijila* as having the head of a seal and the body of an otter."

24. *Puijila, A Prehistoric Walking Seal* (Updated March 25, 2010). Retrieved July 29, 2011, from the Canadian Museum of Nature, http://nature.ca/puijila/fb_e.cfm, under The Fossils & The Breakthrough, More Seal Than Otter. Pinniped Characters. "4. Eyes. Seals have large eyes, which are useful for seeing prey under water. Puijila was not a deep diver, but its large eyes would have been useful for hunting in water, especially during dark Arctic winter months."

25. Rybczynski, N., Dawson, M. R., & Tedford, R. H. (April 23, 2009). A semi-aquatic Arctic mammalian carnivore from the Miocene epoch and origin of Pinnipedia. *Nature*, Vol. 458, p. 1022. "Diagnosis. Arctoid mammal. Skull having short, high rostrum; large infraorbital foramen; large orbit; and zygomatic bones strongly arched dorsally...."

26. Berta, A., Sumich, J. L., & Kovacs, K. M. (2006). *Marine Mammals: Evolutionary Biology* (2nd Edition). Boston: Elsevier/Academic Press. p. 28. "Large infraorbital foramen. The infraorbital foramen, as the name indicates, is located below the eye orbit and allows passage of blood vessels and nerves. It is large in pinnipeds in contrast to its small size in most terrestrial carnivores."

27. *Puijila, A Prehistoric Walking Seal* (Updated March 25, 2010). Retrieved July 29, 2011, from the Canadian Museum of Nature, http://nature.ca/puijila/fb_e.cfm, under The Fossils & The Breakthrough, More Seal Than Otter. Pinniped Characters. "3. Infraorbital foramen. The infraorbital foramen is an opening in the skull below the eye socket. The opening allows nerves and blood vessels to reach from the back of the head to the front of the snout, including the whiskers. The opening tends to be larger if these snout structures are large or specialized. This is true of modern seals, whose whiskers are very well developed (in some seals the whiskers can sense water-borne vibrations from the movement of prey). The large infraorbital foramen in *Puijila* may correspond to the presence of well-developed whiskers, suggesting

enhanced sensitivity of the snout. Not an otter: Although some of these characters are seen in other carnivores, it is only in pinnipeds that they all appear together. Otters, for example, have a large infraorbital foramen, just as pinnipeds do. Otters, however, also have relatively small eyes, and they don't have the pinniped tooth characters."

28. *Puijila, A Prehistoric Walking Seal* (Updated March 25, 2010). Retrieved July 29, 2011, from the Canadian Museum of Nature, http://nature.ca/puijila/fb_e.cfm, under The Fossils & The Breakthrough, More Seal Than Otter. Pinniped Characters. 2. Upper Molars.

29. Berta, A., Sumich, J. L., & Kovacs, K. M. (2006). *Marine Mammals: Evolutionary Biology* (2nd Edition). Boston: Elsevier/Academic Press. p. 314. "Premolars and molars are typically similar in size and shape and are often collectively called post-canines."

Appendix F: Whale Evolution Update

1. Long, J. & Schouten, P. (2008). *Feathered Dinosaurs: The Origin of Birds.* New York: Oxford University Press, Inc. p. 2. "The fossil record, as held in all the world's major museums, government organisations, universities and private collections, now tallies close to a billion fossil specimens."

2. Darwin, C. (1859). *On The Origin of Species by Means of Natural Selection, or The Preservation of Favoured Races in the Struggle for Life* (1st Edition Facsimile). Cambridge: Harvard University Press. p. 484. "Analogy would lead me one step further, namely, to the belief that all animals and plants have descended from some one prototype...Therefore I should infer from analogy that probably all the organic beings which have ever lived on this earth have descended from some one primordial form, into which life was first breathed."

3. Poiani, A. (Editor) (2012). *Pragmatic Evolution: Applications of Evolutionary Theory.* Cambridge: Cambridge University Press. Chapter 1: "Evolution, missing links and climate change: recent advances in understanding transformational macroevolution." Long, J., p. 24. "...Bearing all these considerations in mind, the modern paleontologist knows well that the likelihood of ever finding a finely graded series of transitional forms between one species and another is mathematically close to impossible. Although such cases might be extremely rare in higher animals, they do exist amongst similar organisms, particularly in the continuous marine microfossil record of foraminiferans, such as *Globigerina* species transition in the Miocene marine record."

4. See Cambrian Explosion in Chapter 7, The Fossil Record

of Invertebrates; Chapter 8, The Fossil Record of Fish; Chapter 9, The Fossil Record of Bats; Chapter 11, The Fossil Record of Flying Reptiles; and Chapter 12, The Fossil Record of Dinosaurs.

5. Gould, S. J., McGarr, P., & Rose, S. P. R. (2006). *The Richness of life: The Essential Stephen Jay Gould.* New York: Norton. p. 263–264. "The extreme rarity of transitional forms in the fossil record persists as the trade secret of paleontology. The evolutionary trees that adorn our textbooks have data only at the tips and nodes of their branches; the rest is inference, however reasonable, not the evidence of fossils." **Author's Note:** Dr. Gould died in 2002. A footnote at the bottom of page 264 says he wrote this essay entitled "The Episodic Nature of Evolutionary Change" in 1977.

6. Thewissen, J. G. M. and Williams, E. M. (November 2002). The early radiations of Cetacea (Mammalia): Evolutionary pattern and developmental correlations. *Annual Review of Ecology and Systematics, Vol 33,* pp. 73–90. Published by: Annual Reviews Stable URL: http://www.jstor.org/stable/3069257 "The origin and early evolution of Cetacea (whales, dolphins, and porpoises) is one of the best examples of macroevolution as documented by fossils."

7. E-mail interview with Dr. Clayton Ray, Curator at the Smithsonian National Museum of Natural History from 1963 to 1994, and subsequently Curator Emeritus at the Smithsonian, conducted December 12, 2005, by author. "Fifteen years ago, the origin and early evolution of whales was even more hopeless than that of pinnipeds [seals and sea lions] and gave the creationists much to crow about. Now, suddenly, the paleontology of early whales is one of our most widely and justly trumpeted success stories."

8. Interview with Dr. Annalisa Berta, Professor at San Diego State University, for video series *Evolution: The Grand Experiment*, conducted February 16, 1998, by author. "What is good to show about these particular fossil whale specimens is that they do show us intermediates in the evolution of whales. We don't often get fossil intermediates so we can actually trace the development of characters, say, for example, the evolution of swimming in whales. We don't often have that opportunity."

9. Interview with Dr. Kevin Padian, Paleontologist, University of California, Berkeley, for video series *Evolution: The Grand Experiment*, conducted in November 1998, by author. "We now have whales with legs, whales with reduced legs, whales with little tiny legs, whales with no legs at all, and their heads are getting bigger and their teeth are getting stranger...They have a big exhibit on it out in Michigan, in Ann Arbor. Yeah, I was just there. They have all these things just sitting out there. They're all there.

I mean, you really have to be blind or three days dead not to see the transition among these. You know, you have to not want to see it. And, a big part of the question, why doesn't everybody agree on these things, is that it comes down to what you bring to the questions to begin with. If you don't want to see things, you're not going to see them. And we are all guilty of not wanting to see certain things."

10. Foreword: Evolution in the Century of Biology. Thomas R. Meagher and Douglas J. Futuyma. (October 2001). *The American Naturalist, Vol 158, No. S4*, pp. S1-S46, Executive Document: Evolution Science and Society. Published by the University of Chicago Press for the American Society of Naturalists. Stable URL: http://www.jstor.org/stable/10.1086/509090. Accessed: August 31, 2013. Transitions in the Fossil Record: Whales from Ungulates, J. John Sepkoski, Jr., University of Chicago. Excerpt from Appendix II, paragraph 1, p. S43. "At the invitation of their respective society presidents, representatives* from the American Society of Naturalists (ASN), the Society for the Study of Evolution (SSE), the Society for Molecular Biology and Evolution (SMBE), the Ecological Society of America (ESA), the Society of Systematic Biologists (SSB), the Genetics Society of America (GSA), the Animal Behavior Society (ABS), and the Paleontological Society (PS) met in Indianapolis, Indiana, on April 22–23, 1995, to discuss the need for preparation of a report defining the challenges and opportunities facing the science of evolution." p. S22: "It is now known, through a seamless series of transitions found in the fossil record, that cetaceans evolved during the Early Eocene from a primitive group of carnivorous ungulates (hoofed mammals) called mesonychids."

11. Robinson, E., Benjamin-Phariss, B. (Executive Producer and Director of Documentary Productions). WGBH Video (Firm). (2001). Great Transformations: Extinction! Boston, MA: WGBH Boston Video. [Nova DVD Series.] Produced by Clear Blue Sky Productions, (Available from WGBH Boston http://www.pbs.org/wgbh/evolution/). "Narrator: Scientists now think that the earliest ancestor of whales was similar to this 50 million year old wolf-like mammal called *Sinonyx*."

12. Darwin, C. (1859). *On The Origin of Species by Means of Natural Selection, or The Preservation of Favoured Races in the Struggle for Life* (1st Edition Facsimile). Cambridge: Harvard University Press. p. 184. "In North America the black bear was seen by Hearne swimming for hours with widely open mouth, thus catching, like a whale, insects in the water. Even in so extreme a case as this, if the supply of insects were constant, and if better adapted competitors did not already exist in the country, I can see no difficulty in a race of bears being rendered, by natural selection, more and more aquatic in their structure and habits, with larger

and larger mouths, till a creature was produced as monstrous as a whale."

13. Milner, R. (1990). *The Encyclopedia of Evolution: Humanity's Search for Its Origins.* New York: Facts on File Publishers. p. 463. "'Preposterous!' snorted zoologists. Such an example, they thought, sounded so wild and far-fetched it would brand Darwin as a teller of tall tales. Professor Richard Owen of the British Museum prevailed on Darwin to leave out the 'whale-bear story' or at least tone it down. Darwin cut it from later editions, but privately regretted giving in to his critics, as he saw 'no special difficulty in a bear's mouth being enlarged to any degree useful to its changing habits.' Years later he still thought the example 'quite reasonable.' "

14. Monastersky, R. (November 06, 1999). The Whale's Tale: Searching for the landlubbing ancestors of marine mammals. *Science News Washington*, 156, 19, 296–298. "In 1883, Flower offered an idea that on the face of it-seemed positively daft. The legless leviathans, he suggested, had evolved from mammals known as ungulates, a group whose best-known characteristic is a set of hoofed feet. In other words, dolphins, porpoises, humpbacks, orcas, and all other whales are close kin of cows, horses, pigs, and related barn-yard stock."

15. Flower, W. H., (August 1, 1883). On the arrangement of the orders of existing mammalia. *Proceedings of the Zoological Society of London*, p. 178–186. "There is nothing known at present to connect the Ceatacea with any other order of mammals; but it is quite as likely that they are offsets of a primitive ungulate as of a Carnivorous type."

16. Van Valen, L., (May 9, 1966). Deltatheridia, a new order of mammals. *Bulletin of the American Museum of Natural History, Vol 132,* p. 90. "Only two known families need be considered seriously as possibly ancestral to the archaeocetes and therefore to recent whales. These are the Mesonychidae and Hyaenodontidae (or just possibly some hyaenodontid-like palaeoryctid)."

17. Interview with Dr. Hans Thewissen, Northeast Ohio Medical University, for upcoming video tentatively titled The Emergence of Eocene Whales, conducted in August 2013, by author. "In the past, people thought that whales were derived from a group of carnivorous animals that are now extinct, and they are called mesonychians. And the main reason people though that was the teeth of these early whales are dead ringers for mesonychid teeth. However, if you look at all of the skeleton, all of the features of the fossil whales and compare those to mesonychians, that idea is really discredited now."

18. Gingerich, P. D., Raza, S.M., Arif, M., Anwar, M. and Zhou, X. (April 28, 1994). New whale from the Eocene of Pakistan and the origin of cetacean swimming. *Nature,*

Vol 368, pp. 844-847. "Modern whales (order Cetacea) are marine mammals that evolved from a land-mammal ancestor, probably a cursorial Palaeocene-Eocene mesony-chid."

19. O'Leary, M. A. and Geisler, J.H. (September 1999). The position of Cetacea within mammalia: phylogenetic analysis of morphological data from extinct and extant taxa. *Systematic Biology, Vol 48(3)*, pp. 455-490. "Morphologists argue that cetaceans are most closely related to mesonychians, an extinct group of terrestrial ungulates."

20. O'Leary, M. A., & Uhen, M. D. (October 01, 1999). The Time of Origin of Whales and the Role of Behavioral Changes in the Terrestrial-Aquatic Transition. *Paleobiology, Vol 25(4)*, p. 535. "This analysis subsumed two earlier phylogenetic analyses of the position of cetaceans among ungulates: one based exclusively on dental characters (O'Leary 1998) in which evidence emerged for a monophyletic Mesonychia (Hapalodectidae + Mesonychidae, excluding *Andrewsarchus*) as the sister taxon of Cetacea, and another based on a larger variety of morphological evidence (Geisler and Luo 1998) that supported a monophyletic Mesonychidae as the sister taxon of Cetacea."

21. Thewissen, J. G. and Hussain, S. T. (February 4, 1993). Origin of underwater hearing in whales. *Nature, Vol 361*, p. 444. "Cetaceans probably originated from extinct mesonychid condylarths."

22. Boisserie, J.R., Lihoreau, F., Brunet, M., (February 1, 2005). The position of Hippopotamidae within Cetartiodactyla. *Proceedings of the National Academy of Sciences (USA). Vol 102(5),* pp. 1537–1541. "On the contrary, most previous morphology-based studies designated a non-artiodactyl stem group for cetaceans: the Paleogene paraxonian mesonychians."

23. **Author's note:** Dr. Phillip Gingerich promoted *Sinonyx* as the ancestor of whales in the PBS documentary Great Transformations. He and his colleague from the University of Michigan, Dr. Xiaoyuan Zhou, were involved in the description, analysis, and promotion of this animal when they wrote their original scientific article "Skull of a New Mesonychid (Mammalia, Mesonychia) from the Late Paleocene of China in 1995."

24. Zhou, X., Zhai, R., Gingerich, P. D., & Chen, L. (June 13, 1995). Skull of a New Mesonychid (Mammalia, Mesonychia) from the Late Paleocene of China. *Journal of Vertebrate Paleontology, Vol 15(2)* p. 387–400.

25. **Author's note:** The American Museum of Natural History (AMNH) promotes two mesonychids (*Mesonyx* and *Andrewsarchus*) as the true ancestor of whales. *Mesonyx* was found by the past president of the American Museum, Dr. Henry Fairfield Osborn. *Andrewsarchus* was found

by a member of the AMNH Central Asiatic Expedition and was named after Roy Chapman Andrews, who led the expedition. Oddly, since artiodactyls have replaced mesonychids as the ancestor of whales, the museum now suggests that *Andrewsarchus* is now an Artiodactyl and no longer a mesonychid, thus maintaining *Andrewsarchus'* status as an important ancestor of whales. A 2013 public display on whale evolution at the American Museum of Natural History in New York reads, "This ancient creature likely evolved on the same branch of the mammal family tree as whales and hippos. It belongs to the group Artiodactyla, along with hoofed mammals such as deer, pigs and camels."

26. American Museum of Natural History press release, March 2013, titled Paleontology at the American Museum of Natural History. "Early expeditions carried out by Museum scientists include Roy Chapman Andrews' Central Asiatic Expeditions (1922–1930), which uncovered a treasure trove of fossils in the Gobi Desert of Mongolia, including the massive skull of the land-dwelling relative of whales and hippos *Andrewsarchus* mongoliensis (on view in Whales: Giants of the Deep)."

27. American Museum of Natural History press release, March 2013, titled Whales: Giants of the Deep on View at American Museum of Natural History from March 23, 2013 to January 5, 2014. New Exhibition Highlights Whale Evolution, Biology and Importance to Human Cultures. "In *Whales*, visitors will explore this evolutionary tree and meet a number of whale cousins, including *Andrewsarchus mongoliensis*, which, weighing about 1 ton, was the largest meat-eating land mammal that ever lived. Like many ancient whale relatives, *Andrewsarchus*, which lived about 45 million years ago, walked on all fours and likely had hooves."

28. American Museum of Natural History whale evolution display June 29, 2011. Display title: "Evolutionary Tree for Cetaceans. Whales, Dolphins and Relatives." "*Mesonyx*, an extinct relative of cetaceans. Before evolutionary change relatively short body with limbs having feet for walking." Image shows arrow from *Mesonyx* pointing to *Basilosaurus* with this caption: "*Basilosaurus*, an extinct early whale skeleton. After evolutionary change long body with front limbs developed as paddles and hind limbs reduced."

29. Osborn, H. F., (Nov. 11, 1924). *Andrewsarchus*, Giant Mesonychid of Mongolia, *American Museum Novitiates*, No. 146. Article accessed October 1, 2014 at http://digitallibrary.amnh.org/dspace/bitstream/handle/2246/3226/N0146.pdf;jsessionid=94D934158C548423CA37BB3357D21DB5?sequence=1 "When the specimen reached the laboratory, it was compared with the giant *Mesonyx* (Harpagolestes) uintensis of the Upper Eocene of Wyoming

(Osborn, 1895.98, p. 79, Fig. 4)."

30. Gingerich, P. D., Haq, M., Zalmout, I.S., Khan, I. H. and Malkani, M. S. (September 21, 2001). Origin of whales from early artiodactyls: hands and feet of Eocene Protocetidae from Pakistan. *Science, Vol 293 (5538)*, pp. 2239–2242. "Although there is a general resemblance of the teeth of archaeocetes to those of mesonychids, such resemblance is sometimes overstated and evidently represents evolutionary convergence." "...Cetacea evolved from early Artiodactyla rather than Mesonychia...."

31. Evolution, About the Project, Evolution Project Overview. (2001) http://www.pbs.org/wgbh/evolution/about/overview_project.html. Article accessed October 1, 2013. "Evolution, which premiered on PBS September 24–27, 2001...."

32. Whitfield, J. (September 20, 2001). Almost like a whale. *News@nature*. http://www.nature.com/news/2001/010920/full/news010920-11.html. Accessed October 1, 2013. "Earlier fossil studies related them to the mesonychians, an extinct group of meat eaters. The new discoveries send this idea "out the window", says Thewwissen."

33. Carley, W., (January 01, 2002). One for the faithful: A review of the television series *Evolution. Bioscience, Vol 52(4)*, pp. 383-385. http://www.bioone.org/doi/pdf/10.1641/0006-3568(2002)052%5B0385%3ADST%5D2.0.CO%3B2. Accessed October 1, 2013.

34. Gingerich, P. D., Wells, N.A., Russell, D.E, and Shah, S. M. I. (April 22, 1983). Origin of whales in epicontinental remnant seas: new evidence from the early Eocene of Pakistan. *Science, Vol 220, Issue 4595*, p. 405, "Evidence suggests that *Pakicetus* and other early Eocene cetaceans represent an amphibious stage in the gradual evolutionary transition of primitive whales from land to sea." "*Pakicetus inachus* from the early Eocene of Pakistan is the oldest and most primitive cetacean known." "The basicranium of *Pakicetus* is unequivocally that of a primitive cetacean."

35. When whales abandoned the land. (April 23, 1983). (Author not clearly listed.) *Science News, Vol. 123, Issue 17*. "*Pakicetus* is the 'perfect missing link' between whales and their terrestrial forebears, Gingerich says." "It had the ear structure of an ordinary land mammal."

36. (April 22, 1983). *Science, Vol 220, Issue 4595*, p. 353 "Cover Description: Artist's reconstruction of the oldest and most primitive whale (*Pakicetus inachus*) entering an early Eocene epicontinental sea to feed on abundant herrings and other fishes. The skull of *Pakicetus*, recently discovered in Pakistan, is little modified for hearing under water, and all remains found to date are in fluvial red beds

associated with land mammals. *Pakicetus* provides the first direct evidence of an amphibious stage in the evolutionary transition of whales from land to sea. See page 403: Watercolor by Karen Klitz, University of Michigan; reconstruction of postcranial skeleton is entirely hypothetical."

37. Gingerich, P., *Research on the Origin and Early Evolution of Whales (Cetacea).* Accessed July 29, 2013. Page updated 12/27/10. http://www-personal.umich. edu/~gingeric/PDGwhales/Whales.htm. "The *Pakicetus* cover was painted by Karen Klitz of the University of Michigan Museum of Paleontology (now at U. C. Berkeley), and the *Rodhocetus* cover was drawn by John Klausmeyer of the University of Michigan Exhibit Museum."

38. Thewissen, J. G., Williams, E. M., Roe, L. J. & Hussain, S. T. (September 20, 2001). Skeletons of terrestrial cetaceans and the relationships of whales to artiodactyls. *Nature, Vol 413*, pp. 277–281. "We excavated four partial skulls, two of which retain the orbital region, several snout fragments, and approximately 150 isolated postcranial bones of pakicetids from multiple individuals." "Pakicetids were terrestrial mammals, no more amphibious than a tapir."

39. de Muizon, C. (September 20, 2001). Walking with whales. *Nature, Vol 413 (6853),* pp. 259–60. "The newly found fossils include several skulls and postcranial bones from two early pakicetid species — which, it seems, had the head of a primitive cetacean (as indicated by the ear region) and the body of an artiodactyl. All the postcranial bones indicate that pakicetids were land mammals, and it is likely that they would have been thought of as some primitive terrestrial artiodactyl if they had been found without their skulls." "Many of the fossils' features — including the length of the cervical vertebrae, the relatively rigid articulations of the lumbar vertebrae, and the long, slender limb bones — indicate that the animals were runners, moving with only their digits touching the ground."

40. http://www.imdb.com/title/tt1383652/ Morphed: When Whales Had Legs, released 8 Feb. 2009. http://channel. nationalgeographic.com/wild/episodes/when-whales-had-legs/. **Author's Note:** This show was also released under the title Evolutions: The Walking Whale Season 5 Episode 16.

41. Luo, Z.X., (1998). Homology and Transformation of the cetacean ectotympanic structures in The Emergence of Whales: Evolutionary Patterns in the Origin of Cetacea (J. G. M. Thewissen, ed.). Plenum Press, New York. p. 274. Table II. "Sigmoid process is a simple plate (equivocal, present in the Artiodactyl Diacodexis)." p. 283. "Other diagnostic characters, such as the sigmoid process, as discussed below, are now open to question in the wake of the new fossil evidence from *Pakicetus* and *Ichthyolestes...* In view of the new evidence from *Ichthyolestes* and *Pakicetus* (that the sigmoid is a simple plate, not S-shaped, and lacking the involuted margins) and its development from the anterior crus of the ectotympanic ring, the sigmoid process should be redefined as a systematic character, and its value as a cetacean synapomorphy should be reconsidered." p. 284. "No matter how the distribution of the sigmoid process is optimized among the artiodactyl *Diacodexis*, mesonychids and cetaceans, it is clear that this character (i.e., an independent and enlarged projection derived form the embryonic anterior crus) has some degree of homoplasy, compromising its utility as a "dead ringer" apomorphy for cetaceans."

42. Interview with Dr. Hans Thewissen, Northeast Ohio Medical University, for upcoming video tentatively titled *The Emergence of Eocene Whales*, conducted in August 2013, by author. **Question:** "Now is that sigmoid process [of *Ambulocetus*] unquestionable because I know that on *Pakicetus* there were some questions about that one. It was more like a plate or something." **Answer:** "No this one [the sigmoid process of *Ambulocetus*] is as questionable [as the sigmoid process of *Pakicetus*]." Words in bracket added by author for clarification.

43. Gingerich, P. D., Raza, S.M., Arif, M., Anwar, M. and Zhou, X. (April 28, 1994). New whale from the Eocene of Pakistan and the origin of cetacean swimming. *Nature, Vol 368*, pp. 844–847. "*Rodhocetus* could support its body weight on land." "These are primitive characteristics of mammals that support their weight on land, and both suggest that *Rodhocetus* or an immediate predecessor was still partly terrestrial." "Thus the morphology of *Rodhocetus* is intermediate, as might be expected of a transitional form evolving from land to sea." "Terminal caudates are lacking in the type specimen *Rodhocetus* and we cannot assess the possible presence of a caudal fluke, but it is reasonable to expect development of a fluke to coincide with shortening of the neck, flexibility of the sacrum and reduction of hind limbs first observed in *Rodhocetus*. This idea can be tested when a more complete tail of *Rodhocetus* is found." "It retains primitive features seen in land mammals, but also exhibits derived characteristics found only in later cetaceans."

44. Heyning, J. E. (February 12, 1999). Whale origins— conquering the seas. *Science, Vol 283 (5404)*, p. 943. "*Rodhocetus* and its kin were probably swimming with tail flukes, while feeding and drinking exclusively in the marine realm."

45. Interview conducted with Dr. Phil Gingerich, Paleontologist, University of Michigan, for Episode 1,

Evolution: The Grand Experiment, conducted August 28, 2001, by author. "I speculated it might have had a fluke. Now since then, we have found the forelimbs, the hands and the front arms of *Rodhocetus* and we understand that it doesn't have the kind of arms that can be spread out like flippers are on a whale...And if you don't have flippers, I don't think you can have a fluked tail and really powered swimming. I now doubt that *Rodhocetus* would have had a fluked tail." "Okay, first of all, they have a long upper arm bone. The middle segment, or the lower arm is relatively short. And then they have a compact wrist and four main bones in the hand with a strong thumb yet. And then the second, third, and fourth toes, fingers, end in a little hoof. The first and the fifth don't. They're very thin bones, the first and the fifth digits, and I think they probably only carried a webbing that was useful in swimming, but not supporting the body. But the three central fingers in *Rodhocetus* are capable of supporting the body."

46. Gingerich, P. D., Haq, M, Zalmout, I.S., Khan, I. H. and Malkani, M. S. (September 21, 2001). Origin of whales from early artiodactyls: hands and feet of Eocene Protocetidae from Pakistan. *Science, Vol 293 (5538),* pp. 2239–2242. "On land, *Rodhocetus* walked on a digitigrade hand, with the central digits II through IV bearing weight." "Proximal phalanges of digits II through IV were constrained to be habitually slightly extended by flat articular surfaces and large sesamoids on metacarpals II through IV. These are the digits with relatively short, broad, hoof-bearing distal phalanges (preserved in II and IV)." "On land, *Rodhocetus* supported itself on hoofed digits II, III, and IV of the hands and on the plantar surfaces of the feet, and probably progressed somewhat like a modern eared seal or sea lion." "The forelimbs and hands could not be extended as broad pectoral flippers, which would be required to control recoil from undulation or oscillation of a caudal fluke; hence, it is doubtful that *Rodhocetus* had such a fluke."

47. Thewissen, J. G. M., Hussain, S. T. and Arif, M. (January 14, 1994). Fossil evidence for the origin of aquatic locomotion in archaeocete whales. *Science Vol 263,* p. 210–212. "*Ambulocetus* represents a critical intermediate between land mammals and marine cetaceans."

48. Interview with Dr. Hans Thewissen, Northeast Ohio Medical University, for upcoming video tentatively titled The Emergence of Eocene Whales, conducted in August 2013, by author. **Question:** "I was surprised that the skull [of *Ambulocetus*] was not more complete. I thought you had this full skull because I have always seen the models in the museums of the full skull. How did you figure out what the shape of the skull was? Was it based on these bones or did you have other fossils to go from?" **Answer:** "So the shape of the skull is based on the fossils that we

have. So we have the parts that have the eye and the braincase and the back of the snout. We don't have the tip of the snout, which is unfortunate because we don't know where the nasal opening was therefore. However, we did find the whole lower jaw so we do know how long that snout was. We don't have a sense for its exact shape. So that's based on related animals. Those related animals all have the nasal opening way in the front. So those related animals would be *Kutchicetus* and *Pakicetus*. They have their nasal opening way in the front. So it's likely that *Ambulocetus* had that too, but we don't know that."

49. Berta, A., (January 14, 1994). What Is a Whale? *Science, Vol 263, 5144,* pp. 180-181.

50. Interview with Dr. Hans Thewissen, Northeast Ohio Medical University, for upcoming video tentatively titled The Emergence of Eocene Whales, conducted in August 2013, by author.

51. Interview with Dr. Hans Thewissen, Northeast Ohio Medical University, for upcoming video tentatively titled *The Emergence of Eocene Whales*, conducted in August 2013, by author. **Question:** "Now is that sigmoid process [of *Ambulocetus*] unquestionable because I know that on *Pakicetus* there were some questions about that one. It was more like a plate or something." **Answer:** "No this one [the sigmoid process of *Ambulocetus*] is as questionable [as the sigmoid process of *Pakicetus*]. And, frankly I think that there is something else going on that we have never published. I think that the lower jaw contacts this, so they actually have a different sound transmission mechanism which occurs in some animals, not whales, not modern whales but for instance in mole rats which live underground and they have sound transmission through their lower jaw. And I think that could be a precursor of what modern whales have which is where they hear through their lower jaw and there is a fat pad connecting the lower jaw to the ear, and I can show you that in a modern skull."

52. Interview with Dr. Hans Thewissen, Northeast Ohio Medical University, for upcoming video tentatively titled *The Emergence of Eocene Whales*, conducted in August 2013, by author. **Question:** "So this shows that the sigmoid is not a process but more like a plate?" **Answer:** "Yea, I worry that this is actually somewhat crushed too. But what is cool, the lower jaw thing that I was saying. This was actually found like this. This is the joint of the lower jaw. That's like actually attaching that has an impression in the ear. That's what makes me think that it is involved in sound transmission. Like I said, that is what mole rats have. But no other whale has it, not fossil, nor recent. So this is not quite enough, strong enough argument to make that on so that is why I have actually never published this." "This particular shape is because this jaw

was pushed back and forth into it. It's possible. I can't exclude that so I don't want—I need to find another one that—well that's just not going to happen."

53. Thewissen, J. G. M., Hussain, S. T. and Arif, M. (January 14, 1994). Fossil evidence for the origin of aquatic locomotion in archaeocete whales. *Science Vol 263*, p. 211. **Author's Note:** In Figure 2, the lower mandible is shown to be complete (as indicated by stippling on the diagram) except for the very end of the mandible.

54. Verbiage from whale evolution display at the American Museum of Natural History, 2011: "Whales leaving the land. Early relatives of whales, such as *Pakicetus* had a long snout and meat slicing teeth similar to some land dwelling carnivorous mammals like *Andrewsarchus* and *Harpagolestes*."

55. Interview with Dr. Phil Gingerich, Paleontologist, University of Michigan, for video series *Evolution: The Grand Experiment*, conducted on August 28, 2001, by author. "*Ambulocetus* has its eyes raised up on top of its head in a very strange way, and it is unusually large for an early whale... maybe it's not on the main line [in whale evolution]."

56. Thewissen, J. G. M. (1998). The Emergence of Whales: Evolutionary Patterns in the Origin of Cetacea. New York: Plenum Press. This quote is from Chapter 3, Molecular Evidence for the Phylogenetic Affinities of Cetacea by John Gatesy, p. 63 "Among extant ungulates, the cladistic analysis of Prothero et al. (1988) and Novacek (1989) position Cetacean closer to Perissodactyla and Paenungulata (Sirenia + Hyracoidea + Proboscidea) than to Artiodactyla (Fig 1B).

57. Thewissen, J. G. M. (1998). The Emergence of Whales: Evolutionary Patterns in the Origin of Cetacea. New York: Plenum Press. This quote is from Chapter 5, Phylogenetic and Morphometric Reassessment of the Dental Evidence for a Mesonychian and Cetacean Clade by Maureen O'Leary, p. 133. "The living sister taxon of Cetacea has been shown by some studies to be Perissodactyla (Novacek and Wyss, 1986; Prothero et al., 1988; Novacek, 1989; Thewissen, 1994).

58. Heyning, J. E. (February 12, 1999). Whale origins—conquering the seas. *Science, Vol 283 (5404)*, p. 943. "Contradicting morphology-based phylogenies, some analyses of molecular data, including two in this volume, suggest that cetaceans actually arose from within the order Artiodactyl (cows, pigs, camels) and that hippos are the living sister taxa to cetaceans."

59. O'Leary, M. A. and Geisler, J.H. (September 1999). The position of Cetacea within mammalia: phylogenetic analysis of morphological data from extinct and extant taxa. Systematic Biology, Vol 48(3), pp. 455–490. "Morphologists argue that cetaceans are most closely related

to mesonychians, an extinct group of terrestrial ungulates. They have disagreed, however, as to whether Perissodactyla (odd-toed ungulates) or Artiodactyla (even-toed ungualtes) is the extant clade most closely related to Cetacea, and have long maintained that each of these orders is monophyletic."

60. Monastersky, R. (November 6, 1999). The Whale's Tale: Searching for the landlubbing ancestors of marine mammals. *Science News, Vol 156, No. 19*, pp. 296–298. Monastersky quotes Dr. Norihiro Okada, a Biologist and Professor at the Tokyo Institute of Technology: "I am one hundred percent confident with the conclusion that the most closely related species to whales, among extant mammals, is the hippo."

61. Interview conducted with Dr. Phil Gingerich, Paleontologist, University of Michigan, for video series *Evolution: The Grand Experiment*, conducted August 28, 2001, by author. "Well, molecular biologists are always very confident, more so than paleontologists. And so, it isn't surprising to us that they have been very confident in recent years about whales evolving from hippos."

62. Gingerich, P. D., Haq, M., Zalmout, I.S., Khan, I. H. and Malkani, M. S. (September 21, 2001). Origin of whales from early artiodactyls: hands and feet of Eocene Protocetidae from Pakistan. *Science, Vol 293 (5538)*, pp. 2239–2242. "The new skeletons are important in augmenting the diversity of early Protocetidae, clarifying that Cetacea evolved from early Artiodactyla rather than Mesonychia and showing how early protocetids swam." "Most morphologists and paleontologists have favored a mesonychid origin of whales, but further immunological, DNA hybridization, and molecular sequencing studies support close relationship of Cetacea to artiodactyls and more specifically to hippopotami within Artiodactyla. Here we provide paleontological evidence showing that whales evolved from early artiodactyls rather than mesonychid condylarths."

63. Boisserie, J.R., Lihoreau, F., Brunet, M., (February 1, 2005). The position of Hippopotamidae within Cetartiodactyla. *Proceedings of the National Academy of Sciences (USA) Vol* 102(5), pp. 1537–1541. "Molecular comparisons indicate that Cetacea should be the modern sister group of hippos. This finding implies the existence of a fossil lineage linking cetaceans (first known in the early Eocene) to hippos (first known in the middle Miocene). The relationships of hippos within Artiodactyla are challenging, and the immediate affinities of Hippopotamidae have been studied by biologists for almost two centuries without resolution." "On the contrary, most previous morphology-based studies designated a non-artiodactyl stem group for cetaceans: the Paleogene paraxonian mesonychians."

64. Interview with Dr. Daryl Domning, Paleontologist and Professor of Anatomy, Howard University, for video series *Evolution: The Grand Experiment*, conducted October 8, 1998, by author.

65. Thewissen, J. G., Cooper, L. N., Clementz, M. T., Bajpai, S., & Tiwari, B. N. (January 1, 2007). Whales originated from aquatic artiodactyls in the Eocene epoch of India. *Nature, Vol 450 (7173)*, p. 1193. "Cetaceans originated from an *Indohyus*-like ancestor and switched to a diet of aquatic prey." "The modern artiodactyl morphologically most similar to *Indohyus* is probably the African mouse-deer *Hyemoschus aquaticus*." "Until now, the involucrum was the only character occurring in all fossil and recent cetaceans but in no other mammals. Identification of the involucrum in *Indohyus* calls into question what it is to be a cetacean: it requires either that the concept of Cetacea be expanded to include *Indohyus* or that the involucrum cease to characterize cetaceans."

66. Bajpai, S., Thewissen, J.G.M. (November 25, 2000). A new, diminutive Eocene whale from Kachchh (Gujarat, India) and its implications for the locomotor evolution of cetaceans. *Current Science Vol 79(10)*, pp. 1478–1482.

67. Whale evolution display at the American Museum of Natural History (2013). "By comparing features of the skull displayed in this case with those of other animals, researchers have linked *Andrewsarchus* with its closest relatives. This ancient creature likely evolved on the same branch of the mammal family tree as whales and hippos. It belongs to the group Artiodactyla, along with familiar hoofed mammals such as deer, pigs and camels."

Appendix G: Bird Evolution Update

1. Werner, C. (2009) *Evolution: The Grand Experiment: Volume II, Living Fossils* (First Edition). Arkansas: New Leaf Press. p. 163–168.

2. Werner, C. (2012). *Evolution: The Grand Experiment: Volume II, Living Fossils* (Second Edition eBook). Arkansas: New Leaf Press. Kindle location 1468–1483.

3. Dyke, G. (July 2010). Winged Victory: Modern Birds Now Found to Have Been Contemporaries of Dinosaurs. *Scientific American*. 303 (1): 70–75. "It is funny to think of a robin perched on the back of a *Velociraptor* or a duck paddling alongside a *Spinosaurus*. But the molecular evidence for the contemporaneity of modern birds and dinosaurs was so compelling that even the paleontologists— who have typically viewed with skepticism those DNA findings that conflict with the fossil record — began to embrace it. Still, those of us who study ancient skeletons urgently wanted fossil confirmation of this new view of bird evolution.... Yet our comparisons in the museum that cold winter in 2001 demonstrated conclusively that the wing — with its straight carpometacarpus (the bone formed by the fusion of the hand bones) and details of canals, ridges and muscle scars — did indeed belong to a presbyornithid, which, moreover, was the oldest unequivocal representative of any neornithine group. Our finding fit the predictions of the molecular biologists perfectly. In a 2002 paper that formally described the animal, we gave it the name Teviornis.... One investigator, Sylvia Hope of the California Academy of Sciences in San Francisco, had been arguing for years that bird species she has identified from fossils found in New Jersey and Wyoming that date to between 80 million and 100 million years ago are modern."

4. *The Dinosaur That Fooled the World*. Broadcast as part of a British Broadcasting Company (BBC) Horizon series February 21, 2002.

5. Norrell, M. and Xu, X. (2005). Feathered Dinosaurs. *Annual Review of Earth and Planetary Sciences*. Vol. 33:277–99. "There is also a substantial amount of chicanery involved related to the "improvement" or faking of specimens. Sometimes, even parts of multiple specimens have been cobbled together into chimaeras (Chiappe et al. 2001, Hwang et al. 2004). This was most apparent with the case of *Archaeoraptor*, which was pitched as a definitive feathered missing link between dinosaurs and birds (Sloan 1999). After a great deal of embarrassment to those involved, this specimen was shown conclusively to be a chimera (Xu 2000). Some of these fakes and doctored specimens have been used to discredit the validity of actual feathered dinosaurs by both scientists (Feduccia 2002) and antiscience creationists (a simple online search shows just how damaging this affair was)."

6. Wang, L. (March 10, 2001). Dinosaur fossil yields feathery structures. *Science News*. Washington. Vol. 159, No. 10. p. 149. "Some researchers aren't convinced. All these so-called feathered dinosaurs are younger than the first real known birds," points out Storrs L. Olson, an ornithologist at the National Museum of Natural History in Washington, D.C.

Front Cover: Fossil fish, Wyoming Dinosaur Center, Thermopolis; Fossil angiosperm leaf and dinosaur skull, Sam Noble Oklahoma Museum of Science and Natural History, Oklahoma; Trilobite, California Academy of Sciences, San Francisco; Gastropod shellfish, Museum Victoria, Melbourne, Australia; Fossil dragonfly, Pink Palace Museum, Memphis, Tennessee.

Introduction: Dinosaur picture, Lost World Studios/Missouri Botanical Gardens.

Chapter 1: Title page photo, St. Louis New Cathedral, Missouri.

Chapter 4: Some hyena photos, St. Louis Zoo, Missouri.

Chapter 5: Dinosaur arm and bird wing photos, Chicago Field Museum, Illinois; Whale's fin, Exhibit Museum of Natural History, University of Michigan, Ann Arbor; Chimpanzee skeleton, Pink Palace Museum, Memphis, Tennessee; Photo of Dr. Daryl Domning, courtesy of Dr. Domning, Howard University; Hyrax, Mesker Park Zoo and Botanical Gardens, Evansville, Indiana; Manatee photo, courtesy of U.S. Geological Survey, Sirenia Project, Gainesville, Florida; Ichthyosaur painting, Wyoming Dinosaur Center, Thermopolis; Live Nautilus, California Academy of Sciences, San Francisco; Duck-billed platypus, Milwaukee Public Museum, Wisconsin; Duck-billed dinosaur and *Oviraptor*, Lost/World Studios/Missouri Botanical Gardens; Cassowary, Parndana Wildlife Park, Kangaroo Island, South Australia; Juliana's Golden Mole, Tim Jackson/Oxford Scientific/Photolibrary.

Chapter 6: James Kirkland at Mygatt Moore Quarry courtesy of the Bureau of Land Management, Grand Junction, Colorado.

Chapter 7: Trilobite sheet and various trilobites, University of Nebraska State Museum, Lincoln; Other trilobites, Museum Victoria, Melbourne, Australia, South Australian Museum, Adelaide, University of Wisconsin, Madison, Geological Museum, and Sam Noble Oklahoma Museum of Science and Natural History, Oklahoma; Living brachiopod shellfish, photo by Dr. Svetlana Belorustseva, Moscow State University; Live gastropod shellfish, photo by Corel stock images © 2007 AVC Inc.; Fossil shellfish, University of Nebraska State Museum, Lincoln; Live sea pen, photo by Ian Skipworth © Ianskipworth. com.

Chapter 9: Live bat, Milwaukee County Zoo, Wisconsin; Fossil bat, Fossil Butte National Monument, Wyoming; *Onychonycteris finneyi*, cast of second specimen, used with permission from the Royal Ontario Museum © ROM; Museum drawing of the oldest fossil bat in the world, *Icaronycteris index* from the Smithsonian National Museum of Natural History; Ghost bat photo taken at Museum Victoria, Melbourne, Australia.

Chapter 10: Bear and river otter photos, St. Louis Zoo, Missouri; Fossil seal skull, Exhibit Museum of Natural History, University of Michigan, Ann Arbor; Australian sea lion skeleton, South Australian Museum, Adelaide; Modern fur seal skull, San Diego State University, California; Harbor seal skull, Alaska Sea Life Center, Seward; Clayton Ray photo by Leah Ray.

Chapter 12: *T. rex* full skeleton reconstructions University of California, Berkeley, Museum of Paleontology. *Triceratops* skull, sauropod skeleton and *Dryosaurus* skeleton, Carnegie Museum of Natural History, Pittsburgh, Pennsylvania; *Triceratops* model skull and *Edmontosaurus* skeleton, University of Wisconsin, Madison, Geological Museum; *Coelophysis* skeleton, Milwaukee Public Museum, Wisconsin; *Dromaeosaur* skeleton, Mesalands Community College's Dinosaur Museum, Tucumcari, New Mexico.

Chapter 13: Cat, Taronga Zoo, Sydney, Australia; Hippo teeth/mouth Milwaukee County Zoo, Wisconsin; *Rodhocetus* jaw,

Sinonyx skull and dolphin tail (skeleton), Exhibit Museum of Natural History, University of Michigan, Ann Arbor; Pakistan dig site, photo courtesy of Dr. Taseer Hussain, Howard University.

Chapter 14: *Archaeopteryx* model photo, Milwaukee Public Museum, Wisconsin; Fossil shore bird photo used with permission of Florissant Fossil Quarry, photo by Arnim Walter; Pterosaur model Jura Museum, Germany; Live bat photo, South Australian Museum, Adelaide; Live bird photo page: *Archaeopteryx* painting courtesy of Sam Noble Oklahoma Museum of Science and Natural History, Oklahoma; Two-page spread of modern bird skeleton photos: A, B, D, F, G, I, J, L, and N, Museum Victoria, Melbourne, Australia; Modern bird skeleton photos: C, H, K, M, O, University of Nebraska State Museum, Lincoln; Modern bird skeleton photo: E, Pink Palace Museum, Memphis, Tennessee; Modern bird skeleton photo: P, Sam Noble Oklahoma Museum of Science and Natural History, Oklahoma; Live sea star and live horseshoe crab, St. Louis Children's Aquarium, Missouri.

Chapter 15: Emu feather, South Australian Museum, Adelaide. Painting of *Caudipteryx zoui* by Denis Finnin, courtesy of the American Museum of Natural History Library.

Chapter 20: Polar bear, hyena, and pterosaur model, St. Louis Zoo, Missouri; Marsupial pouched mouse, South Australian Museum, Adelaide; *Apatosaurus* model, Pink Palace Museum, Memphis, Tennessee; *T. rex* skeleton, University of California, Berkeley; Live bat, Mesker Park Zoo & Botanical Gardens, Evansville, Indiana; Whale evolution diagram (modified from original), Exhibit Museum of Natural History, University of Michigan, Ann Arbor; Feathered dinosaur model, Museum Victoria, Melbourne Australia; CT scan diagram and chart, courtesy of the University of Texas CT Scan Lab, Austin.

Appendix B: Dinosaur evolution chart (modified from original), Chicago Field Museum, Illinois.

Appendix D: Greater mouse-tail bat photo by Eyal Bartov, EyalBartov.com. *Nature* cover, Wikimedia Commons.

Appendix E: Enaliarctos illustration by Michael Long, used with permission from the Natural History Museum, London; Modern Australian Sea Lion Skeleton, South Australian Museum, Adelaide; Fossil bones of *Enaliarctos mealsi* and *Acrophoca longirostris*, Smithsonian National Museum of Natural History, Washington D.C.; All *Puijila darwini* photographs reproduced with permission from the Canadian Museum of Nature, Ottawa, Canada. The following photos were by Martin Lipman: Preparing the fossil, bottom of skull, front foot, and rear foot. All *Puijila darwini* 3-D model photographs (full skeleton and skull) reproduced with permission from the Canadian Museum of Nature, Ottawa, Canada by Alex Tirabasso. Painting of recreated model of *Puijila darwini* by Nobu Tamura, Wikimedia Commons.

Appendix F: NHM London photo by David Iliff, License: CC-BY-SA 3.0; Lesser mouse-deer photo (Tragulus kanchil) by Bjørn Christian Tørrissen, CC-BYSA 3.0 Wikimedia Commons, http://bjornfree.com/galleries.html; Whale and deer CT slice courtesy of Digimorph.com, University of Texas, Austin; Walking whale sign Melbourne Museum by Peter Newland.

Other Photos: Photos of Charles Darwin, courtesy of Down House, England; Some space photos, courtesy of National Aeronautic Space Administration, Washington D.C.; Some whale photos, courtesy of National Oceanic and Atmospheric Administration, Washington D.C.; Other photos © 2007 Jupiterimages Corporation, © 2007 iStockphoto or © 2007 Audio Visual Consultants, Inc. Unless stated otherwise, all photos with © 2007 Audio Visual Consultants, Inc. were taken by Debbie Werner.

EVOLUTION: THE GRAND EXPERIMENT

Evolution: The Grand Experiment teacher's manual, book, and video series are designed to teach a critical examination of the theory of evolution to students of public, private and home schools from grades 8–14.

As one of the most controversial topics of our day, it behooves all of us to review the current evidence both for and against the theory of evolution. The material presented in this course contains interviews with over 60 expert scientists from some of the most highly acclaimed scientific institutions, universities, and museums of the world.

This Teacher's Manual contains all of the tools needed to assist a teacher including:

• Purpose of Chapter – To summarize the purpose of each chapter.

• Class Discussion Questions – To stimulate student interest in the chapter material.

• Objectives of Chapter for Students – To assist students in preparing for examinations.

• Chapter Examinations – To assess if students adequately understand the materials.

• Sectional Examinations – To prepare students for the comprehensive final examination.

• Comprehensive Final Examination – To assure students retain the information.

The entire teaching program is a turnkey system and does not require scientific expertise to teach the course. The Presentation CD (an optional product) allows the teacher to show full color pages from the book using the teacher's laptop computer and a TV or video projector. The teacher may use the Presentation CD to prepare a lecture for the students or have the students create a power point presentation for the class for extra credit.

LIVING FOSSILS!

Did dinosaurs live with modern plants (apple trees, sassafras trees, roses, and rhododendrons) and modern animals (ducks, dogs, possums, and humans) thousands of years ago, as the story of creation suggests? Or did dinosaurs live at a remote time, millions of years ago, with other extinct, strange, and unusual animals, as the theory of evolution suggests?

Dr. Carl Werner traveled 160,000 miles to find the answer, visiting 10 dinosaur dig sites and 60 natural history museums. To his surprise, he found examples of all of the major plant divisions and all of the major animal phyla groups living today, fossilized alongside the dinosaurs.

The biggest discovery Dr. Werner made was that some of the most important fossils were not displayed in any of the museums he visited. Have natural history museums withheld these critical fossils from their public displays, fossils that would place the theory of evolution in jeopardy?

In this book, Dr. Werner invites you to be a part of his grand experiment and his thoughts as he travels to museums and dig sites studying evolution and all the types of animal and plant fossils.

A Teacher's Manual and Presentation CD are available for school use in this four semester curriculum addressing the evolution versus creation controversy.

The accompanying DVD has the feel of a PBS documentary, with British narrator Andres Williams, and contains spectacular underwater footage of Dr. Werner diving at the Great Barrier Reef in Australia and the coral reefs in the Caribbean Sea, plus footage from dinosaur dig sites in Europe and North America. Filmed over 13 years on three continents and eight countries including many active dinosaur dig sites, museums and universities.

For more information visit www.TheGrandExperiment.com and www.youtube.com/user/EvolutionVsCreation.

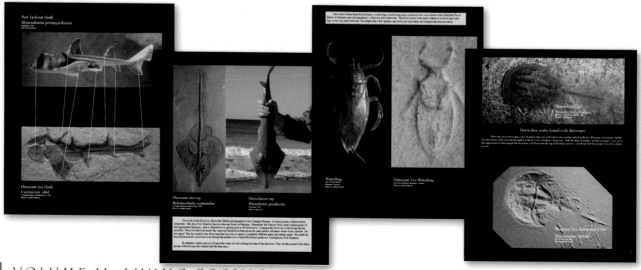

HUMAN EVOLUTION

In the third volume of this series, Dr. Carl Werner dissects the complex theory of human evolution in a simple, straightforward style. He accomplishes this using graphs, photos, charts, and interviews with scientists personally involved in the discoveries of *Australopithecus*, Neanderthal, *Homo Erectus* and many more. Dr. Werner, in his 30-year effort to get to the bottom of the theory of evolution, asks if human evolution is real.

In Volume III, *Human Evolution*, students can learn the answers to these important questions:

•Which Princeton University trained evolutionary anthropologist abandoned the idea that humans evolved from apes?

•Which large metropolitan museum displays the skeleton of an ape man, which was significantly altered by the scientist who discovered the fossil?

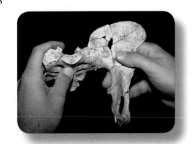

•Which natural history museum staff misidentified 300 random rocks and random fossil bones as "advanced tools"?

•Which museum curator planted fossils at a dig site for other scientists to find, and why?

•Which natural history museum director misidentified the leg bone of a Procyonid (raccoon family) as the leg of an upright walking ape man?

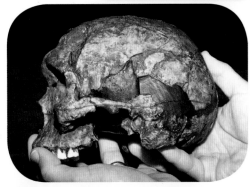

•Which natural history museum currently displays a fossil zebra skull fragment and interprets it as an "ape man" skull?

The accompanying DVD, to be released in 2015, has the feel of a Discovery Channel documentary. Dr. Werner and his wife, Debbie, filmed interviews on location in four continents with such notables as Dr. Donald Johanson, the discoverer of Lucy; the late Dr. F. Clark Howell, leader of the international expedition to southern Ethiopia; Dr. Charles Oxnard, recipient of the Charles Darwin Lifetime Achievement Award; Dr. Gert Wenegert, curator of the Neanderthal Museum in Germany; Dr. Ralf Schmitz, archaeologist of the Rhine State Department of Archeology; Dr. Angela Milner, Natural History Museum, London; Dr. Daniel Lieberman, professor of biological anthropology at Harvard University; Dr. Taseer Hussain, professor of human anatomy, Howard University; and Dr. Daniel Gasman, professor of history at John J. College of Criminal Justice.

For more information and updates visit www.TheGrandExperiment.com.

VOLUME IV, *GEOLOGY*

- All new information!
- A fresh, new approach.
- The most spectacular volume in the series!
- Filmed on five continents.

FUTURE RELEASE!

Easy-to-use one-year curriculum packages
for high school students that powerfully display
the fallacy of evolutionary beliefs!

NATURAL SCIENCE: THE STORY OF ORIGINS

1 year
10th – 12th grade
½ Credit

Package Includes: *Evolution: the Grand Experiment; Evolution: the Grand Experiment Teacher's Guide, Evolution: the Grand Experiment DVD; Parent Lesson Planner*

3 Book, 1 DVD Package
978-0-89051-762-8   *$71.99*

FREE DOWNLOAD
at: www.nlpg.com

Concerned about science and a biblical worldview? Now enjoy a science exploration that presents both evolution and creation, allowing students to get answers to common questions and discover why the biblical account of the world's creation fits the evidence we see in the geologic and fossil records. Break down core theories of evolution and equip students with truth with this ½ credit course!

PALEONTOLOGY: LIVING FOSSILS

1 year
10th – 12th grade
½ Credit

Package Includes: *Living Fossils, Living Fossils Teacher Guide, Living Fossils DVD; Parent Lesson Planner*

3 Book, 1 DVD Package
978-0-89051-763-5   *$66.99*

FREE DOWNLOAD
at: www.nlpg.com

When it comes to evolution, living fossils prove this the theory is flawed. Despite claims of millions of years to "evolve" to what we see today, see photos and examples of living fossils that disprove Darwin's theory. Why they exist, what it means in terms of scientific timelines, and how this alters your own understanding are revealed in this unique ½ credit course.

Both titles include: Weekly lesson schedules, alternate sectional and final exams, and alternate exam answer keys.